The Quarter Running Horse

The Quarter Running Horse

America's Oldest Breed

Robert Moorman Denhardt

University of Oklahoma Press   Norman

By Robert Moorman Denhardt

The Quarter Horse (3 volumes, Amarillo, 1941–50)

The Horse of the Americas (Norman, 1947, 1975)

Horses of the Conquest (editor), by R. B. Cunninghame Graham (Norman, 1949)

Quarter Horses: A Story of Two Centuries (Norman, 1967)

The King Ranch Quarter Horses: And Something of the Ranch and the Men That Bred Them (Norman, 1970)

Foundation Sires of the American Quarter Horse (Norman, 1976)

The Quarter Running Horse: America's Oldest Breed (Norman, 1979)

Denhardt, Robert Moorman, 1912–
    The quarter running horse.

    Bibliography: p. 291
    Includes index.
    1.   Quarter horse—History.   2.   Quarter racing—
United States—History.   3.   Horse breeding—United
States—History.   4.   Race horses—United States—
History.   I.   Title.
SF293.Q3D43   636.1'3   78–21381

Contents

v

Illustrations

Preface

A COMPLETE HISTORY of the quarter running horse should have several objectives. First, it should give to this distinctive American breed a legitimacy it has lacked in the past. This can be done only by statements backed by chapter and verse of authorities too numerous and respected to be ignored. Second, it should render the frequently made observation of many long horse men that the Quarter Horse is only a second-rate Thoroughbred to be a misstatement of fact, if not an admission of ignorance. Last, such a book should trace the lineage of the Quarter Horse, showing his parentage to be as long and honorable as that of the American Thoroughbred—no more so, but certainly no less so. Both have ancestors that cannot be traced; both have ancestors that go directly to the original eastern foundation stallions.

The Quarter Horse has always been more specifically native American than has the Thoroughbred. Instead of consciously emulating the racing customs of England, the short horse man charted a new course. He felt no obligation to English racing procedures or to English racing bloodlines. Certain individuals, certain bloodlines produced sprinters, and it was to those stallions that he took his mares. The American short horse man cared little what Weatherby, Skinner, Edgar, or Bruce might say about the sire of his choice. He just wanted to breed to blazing speed—and did.

The paragraph above should not be construed to indicate that I am against registration and all that it can accomplish. Without the early efforts of the studbook compilers, this book would have been much more difficult to write. What is important to remember is that it was "early speed" that was the objective of the breeder of the quarter running horse. That is precisely why some of the great foundation sires, such as Printer (1800), Cherokee (1847), and Traveler (1900), with no known pedigree can still be listed as among the greatest. That the sires and dams of these three stallions were unknown bothered the short horse breeder not at all.

It would be equally absurd to ignore a Quarter Horse sire because he was a Thoroughbred. If one arbitrarily eliminated registered horses who were great producers of early speed, such as Sir Archy (1805), *Bonnie Scotland (1853), or Uncle Jimmy Gray (1906), part of the history of the quarter running horse would be missing. These three Thoroughbred stallions are no less important than their unpedigreed contemporaries Printer, Cherokee, and Traveler. If the reader will not spend time trying to classify sprinters into Thoroughbreds and Quarter Horses, he will get a good over-all view of the history of a unique equine type, the only American contribution to the running horses of the world.

The information on horse breeding and racing in the 1600's is admittedly cursory. Although short races were common before the middle of the eighteenth century, I do not consider the quarter running horse a distinct type until the importation of *Janus, whose influence was, and to some extent still is paramount.

One does not have to look far to find the reason why short racing was popular in the colonies. Think how much easier it was to find a short, level, straight stretch on which to match a race and how difficult it would have been to build a smooth, oval surface large enough for horse racing. The early straightaway races seldom even reached a quarter of a mile. After all everyone wanted to see the races from start to finish. So the early races in the colonies were short, and generally only two horses raced at a time. This style of racing followed the frontier as it moved across the continent to the Pacific Ocean.

Much of the popularity of horse racing lies in the thrilling stretch run for the finish. Even among the long horse devotees, who think a race should be a mile or more, it is not until the horses near the wire that they jump to their feet and roar for their favorites. The early jockeying for position is interesting to the knowledgeable horse-man, but the final stretch run is the thriller. Quarter racing has distilled the essence of racing and bottled it all to explode in about twenty seconds of ecstatic emotion.

Sprinting has always been a "traveling" sport, and the best quarter running horses were always on the move, looking for new competition and new money. Owners, trainers, jockeys, and horses traveled the country over looking for just the right race. In constrast, most of the better Thoroughbred stallions ran for a few years at the established race tracks and then retired to stud. The good mares were taken to them, so most of their offspring could be found in a fairly concentrated area. The quarter running stallions, on the other hand, traveled far and wide, campaigning and breeding for ten or twelve years until their speed diminished. That explains why the blood of the better sprinters was widely dispersed.

All histories must end someplace. The closer the story comes to modern times, the greater the chance of distortion. It seems impossible that a person can live through any period without allowing certain aspects to assume an importance out of propor-tion, probably just because he was there. That is why, with very few exceptions, I have ended the narrative of this book at the 1930's, with a short look at racing today in the Epilogue. Those of you who have run across my earlier writings may find that parts of this book do not jibe with them. I trust that the you will not let this bother you any more than it does me. As you dig, you learn that some earlier beliefs you held were wrong and that even authorities you respect can err.

During the years we spent collecting the information found in this book, my wife and I found ourselves traveling in states as widely separated as Virginia and California, Illinois and Texas, with stops in almost all the states in between. We enjoyed every minute of the time.

The material for the period before the Civil War was dug out of books, magazines, newspapers, court records, and any other records we could find that contained information on the short horse. For the period after 1860, reminiscences of old-timers could be added to the above. I was fortunate in knowing and talking to a half dozen or more race horse men who were active during the second half of the nineteenth century. One other good source, especially for the personal history of the men, were the various local historical societies.

In Virginia we got our biggest help from Alexander Mackay-Smith, knowledgeable director of the National Sporting Library of Middleburg. Lynne Doyle, the fine librarian, also spared no effort to help us uncover pertinent details. In Kentucky we used Keeneland Library, in Lexington, more than any other resource facility. I question if there are any better libraries for early American racing resource materials than those at Middleburg and Keeneland. At Keeneland we were very appreciative of the help given us by charming Amelia Buckley and her capable assistant, Janet Marshall. Both did everything in their power to assist us in our research, and we called upon them several times after we left for additional materials.

While we were in Illinois, which had more than its share of top quarter race horse men, we encountered several individuals who deserve special mention. For example, Gene Boeker, of Oakford, has made a study of the Watkins family and their horses. Joe Johnson and Jim Lawton, of Plymouth, are good sources for information on Grant Rea or Robert Wade. Charles Shinn, of Smithville, has information on Bill Owen, one of Missouri's top breeders; and Bill Robinson of Berlin, Illinois, helped us with information on James Owen, who was one of his father's good friends. Again in Missouri, Frances Stockton Brown, whose work with the Dade County Historical Society is deeply appreciated, helped us obtain information on her relative, Bill Stockton, of the Stockton racing family.

In Kansas, trying to learn something about Mike Smiley, we found Harvey Nelson. He was a friend of Mike's son and had a fund of stories about Mike, many more than I could include in this book. Charley Walker and Coke Roberds, both of whom have now passed on, knew just about everything that happened to the short horses in Colorado; and Coke Blake, Ronald Mason, and Jim Minnick had similar information about Oklahoma. When we lived in Texas some forty years ago, we had an opportunity to know some of the old-time breeders—so many that I hesitate to single out particular ones. They all were willing to sit by the hour and talk horse.

In New Mexico, there were Ed Springer, John Zurick, and Warren Shoemaker; in

Arizona, W. D. Wears, the Parkers, and Ernest Browning; and so it goes on and on, state after state. It is no exaggeration to say that hundreds of people gave us information for this book.

Portions of the book have appeared in the *Speedhorse*, the *Quarter Horse Journal*, and *Western Horseman*.

Joe Mazzini, of Arbuckle, California, typed the final draft of the manuscript of this book and picked up errors in form, style, and grammar. All of the early correcting and typing were done by my wife, Sarah. I will accept the blame for what is wrong; they deserve much credit for what is good. May the grass always be green and the water fresh wherever they travel.

Lander, Wyoming   ROBERT MOORMAN DENHARDT

PART I
THE COLONIAL PERIOD
1607–1780

It is the most ridiculous amusement imaginable. If you happen to be looking the other way, the race is terminated before you can turn your head, not withstanding which, very considerable sums are betted.

—Thomas Anbury, *Travels Through the Interior Parts of North America*, (London, 1789).

QUARTER RUNNING HORSE SIRES

1607–1780

(J) indicates horse sired by *Janus.
Superior horses in capital letters.

Aeolus (J)	Fox	Randle
Augustus (J)	Garrick	Randolph (J)
Ariel	Janus (J)	Ranger (J)
*Babraham	Jim Rover	Rochester
BABRAM (Goode's) (J)	*Jolly Roger (Jones)	Saint Tammany
BACCHUS	JUPITER (J)	Sampson
BALL (BANDY) (J)	King Tammany	Scott (J)
Blue Boar (J)	Kouilikhan	SHAD (J)
Bowlaway	MARK ANTHONY	Sorrel (J)
BRIMMER (Goode's)	Moggy (J)	SPADILLE (J)
Budd	Moggy-chickey	Spider (J)
BUIE (J)	Monarch	Statley
Camden (J)	Nabob (J)	Statesman (J)
Camillus (J)	Nonpareil	Sweet Briar
CELER (J)	One Eye (J)	Sweet Larry
Cloudius (J)	PADDY WHACK	Syphax
Clubfoot (J)	PARTNER	*Traveler (Morton's)
Comet	PEACOCK (Brinkley's) (J)	Twickham (J)
Cripple (J)	Phoenix (J)	TWIGG (J)
Darius	PILGARLICK (J)	*Wildair
Dreadnot	Purse Full (J)	Wilkes (J)
Fabricus (J)	Quicksilver	WOODPECKER
Fleetwood (J)		

CHAPTER ONE

Origin of the Sprinters

EASTERN BLOOD

THOROUGHBREDS are sometimes called hot bloods, which is to say that they trace back to Oriental or Eastern blood. They are not, however, the only breed that has Oriental or Eastern blood. It is found in all of the better saddle horses. The term *hot blood* is used to differentiate the horse with Oriental blood from the *cold blood*, or draft animal. *Cold blood* is used here not in a derogatory sense but only to indicate the absence of Oriental or Eastern blood. Today many Thoroughbred breeders and owners use *hot blood* in place of Thoroughbred, meaning a horse that is registered in the Jockey Club.

The draft horse originated in northern Europe, especially in the Flanders region. He is the horse of the forest and the wet lowlands. The Arab horse, the original hot blood, had his beginnings on the dry, hot desert lands of western Asia and North Africa. Since most running quarter horses are not registered Thoroughbreds, one occasionally hears uninformed horsemen referring to them as cold bloods. Their line of thought is that, since short horses are not registered Thoroughbreds, they must be cold-blooded. There are more ways to identify a hot blood than just registration in the Jockey Club. All hot bloods have a common ancestry, distinctive body conformation, characteristic dispositions, and a desire for physical activity.

One of the best ways to gain a clear picture of a hot blood is to compare him with his opposite number, the cold blood, or draft horse. All the great breeds of draft horses belong to the non-Oriental group of cold bloods: the Belgians, Shires, Percherons, Clydesdales, and so on. This is not to say that somewhere back in their pedigree there may not be a saddle animal of Eastern blood—only that draft blood is primary. The horse of northern Europe came into his own during medieval days, when fighting demanded heavy armor on both man and horse. It was then that these massive chargers proved their worth. They could carry the weight of armor and men without becoming overtired. The characteristics of cold-blooded horses made them ideal as medieval chargers. Henry William Herbert described them as follows:

> . . . vast ponderous animals . . . huge quadrupeds . . . that vary from sixteen to nine-

3

teen hands and are distinguished by their broad chests, short backs, round barrels, their immense volume of mane, resembling that of a lion, their heavy tails, great hairy fetlocks, and immense well formed feet.[1]

Because of their large size they needed considerable encouragement to go any faster than a walk or a lumbering trot.

The Oriental horses, on the other hand, whether Arab, Barb, or Turk, were small horses. They averaged thirteen to fifteen hands high and generally weighed less than a thousand pounds. Besides their characteristic small size, the hot bloods had other features in common, such as short hair, clean legs, smart heads, slender necks, and small hoofs. In sharp contrast to the draft animals, they seemed to thrive on activity. They more often had to be held up than urged to move out.

The hot bloods, called Arabs, Barbs, or Turks, depending on their country of origin, came into Europe by many different routes. Two of the better-known entries occurred when they were brought in by the returning Crusaders and by the invading Moslems. The Moors entered Spain in the year A.D. 711, and the Crusades were in progress between the eleventh and fourteenth centuries. The Oriental blood brought into Europe proved to be the foundation of all the modern breeds of saddle horses. Their descendants today are the ones classified as hot bloods, to distinguish them from their larger and coarser northern European cousins. With the possible exception of the Arab, all have some minor outcrosses. Care, adequate feed, and judicious breeding over the centuries have also increased the size of the modern horse. But they are still hot bloods. Their enthusiastic desire to perform physically, their affectionate disposition, and their physical refinement are always evident.

CHICKASAW AND CHEROKEE

Oriental hot blood was brought to America by the early explorers and settlers. Cortés was responsible for the arrival of the first European horses in the New World. He brought them to Veracruz, Mexico, in 1519. No doubt the first short race in America occurred soon afterward—probably during a lull in the conquest of Mexico, when some of his men disagreed about who had the fastest horse.

We do not have a record of the first short race held in what is now the United States. Almost certainly it was run in Spanish Florida. Admiral Pedro Menéndez de Avilés brought one hundred head of horses with him when he established the first settlement, Saint Augustine, in 1565. By the middle 1600s the Spanish provinces in the Southeast had seventy-two missions, eight fair-sized towns, and two royal ranches where horses and cattle were raised. It was from these settlements and ranches that the Indians of the Southeast obtained their first horses. The two tribes bordering the

Spanish settlements were the Chickasaw and the Cherokee. Both of these tribes were ideally suited to raising horses. Both were inclined to permanent settlements and pursued agriculture to a certain extent, and both had developed a rather advanced society. They soon gained fame for their horse breeding. A horse originating in one of these tribes could command a premium price in the English colonies.

John B. Irving said, in speaking of the southern colonies, that before 1754 the most highly regarded saddle animals were the Chickasaws' horses, whose ancestors had been introduced by the Spaniards.[2] He described them as small, around thirteen to fourteen hands high, but remarkable for their muscular development. When crossed with horses imported from England, they produced offspring of great beauty and speed.

J. F. D. Smyth, who traveled extensively through the southern colonies late in the eighteenth century, wrote in his book that the Chickasaw Indians "have a beautiful breed of horses amongst them, which they carefully preserve unmixed."[3] David Ramsay said that the Chickasaw horses were introduced into Florida by the Spaniards and from there passed to the Cherokees and Chickasaws. He adds that when the mares were crossed with English blooded horses they produced beautiful colts.[4]

Francis Haines spent much time investigating the origin and spread of the Spanish horse among the Indians of North America. In a letter to Thornton Chard, who was studying the Chickasaw horse, Haines wrote:

> It is well to keep in mind that the woods Indians along the [Mississippi] river did not use horses, and the Chickasaws would have had to travel a hundred miles west of the river to buy their animals. Although I have no proof (written contemporary records) I doubt that this traffic developed before 1750, because of the danger from hostile tribes, the difficult natural barriers of timber, swamp and river to be crossed, and the difficulty of ferrying [horses] in Indian canoes. Until 1800 the chief source of supply of horses to the Indians east of the Mississippi was, most probably, the Spanish Missions in Northern Florida and Southern Georgia.[5]

Clark Wissler wrote that the Indians in the Southeast got their horses from Spanish settlements on the Gulf and even from tribes west of the Mississippi.[6] David Ramsay in his history of South Carolina also credits the Spanish settlements in the Southeast as the source of Chickasaw horses, as did Francis Culver in his scholarly work on the blood horse of colonial days.[7]

Still another early reference to the excellence of the Chickasaw horse is found in the December 3, 1763, issue of the *South Carolina Gazette*. The quotation has to do with a horse race won by a Chickasaw mare:

> Last Thursday, a great sweepstakes was run for, round the course at Edmonsburg, Ashepoo, the best of three heats, by horses, etc., which came in as follows:

5

Mr. Edmund Bellinger Jr.'s Chicasah mare Bonnie Jane, rising 5 year old. 1, 2, 1.
Mr. Gibbs' Buzzard (quarter part English blood) 2, 1, 2.
Capt. Smith's English horse dis.[qualified]
Mr. Cochran's Chicasah h. Childers d.
Mr. Coachman's grey gelding d.
The last heat afforded excellent sport, as the jockeys whipped from start to ending post.

Since these Chickasaw horses are in the background of the quarter running horse, it is helpful to know something about the breeding of the horses the Spaniards brought to America.[8] Some facts are known. It is generally conceded that they were of Oriental origin. At that time Spanish horses were commonly referred to as Barbs—sometimes as Arabs. The Moslem invaders who conquered Spain in the eighth century came from the Barbary States of North Africa. Contemporary writers refer to their horses as being of African, Moorish, Barbary, or Tlemcen stock. The horses are seldom referred to as Arabs, and they were somewhat different in conformation. The Arab horse of the eastern Mediterranean had a more refined and dished-faced head and a shorter back than his descendants in North Africa that were taken into Spain. The first Spanish horses that came to the New World can be grouped under the general name Barb.

ENGLISH CONTRIBUTIONS

Quarter racing as a recognized sport grew and blossomed in the New World, and yet it would be a mistake to think that it was in colonial America that the first short races were held. Although records are scarce, short races were run in the ancient world as well as in the medieval. Short races, especially those featuring two horses, were not common in England, but they were not unknown. P. R. Saward wrote about a quarter race that was held in August, 1782. This particular meet was held at Up Park, near Chichester, Sussex County. It consisted of a two-day program of four matches and a sweepstakes for the winners. A horse named Rockingham, owned by Sir Henry Fetherston, was the winner.[9] So it is possible that some of the imported English running horses did have at least a passing acquaintance with a short race, especially those brought over before the Thoroughbred and long racing became established in England.

Few details are available about these very first imported animals, just simple statements in shipping manifests. For example, in 1609, English ships coming to supply the new colony of Jamestown, in Virginia, brought six mares and a stallion. A few years later one Francis Higginson, of Leicestershire County, brought a good supply of mares and stallions to Massachusetts. Horses arrived in New York in 1625. They were brought over from Holland by the Dutch West India Company. They were not described, but one would suspect that they were very likely Flemish (draft) horses. They may have been the basis of the later Conestoga horse of Pennsylvania.

The first important supply of racehorses came into Virginia in 1620, shipped by the firm of Wood, Sandys, and Gookin. Sir Francis Nicholson, governor of the Virginia colony, 1698–1705, liked racing, and soon healthy purses were being offered the winner, often in hogheads of tobacco. The absence of formal tracks proved no hindrance at all; any flat commons or village green provided a track sufficient for the occasion.

Most of the early light horses imported into the colonies were Hobbies and Galloways. The part the sturdy little Galloways—the fourteen-hand iron horses of Solway Firth — played in the foundation of the Thoroughbred has never been examined fully.

William Youatt, writing his book on the horse in London in 1883, said that the pure Galloway was about fourteen hands high—sometimes more—a bright bay or brown, with black legs, a small head, a short neck, and very clean legs. He said that its outstanding qualities included speed, stoutness, and surefootedness. These were also to be common characteristics of the short running horse.

In the southern colonies horse racing was popular from the start. It is to be expected that the settlers would continue their normal recreational pursuits in their new homeland. In the 1640's, when Charles I lost his long fight with Parliament (and his head), many of his loyal followers escaped to the New World. They brought with them, and later had sent over, some of their good horses. In fact, Virginia prospered during England's "kingless period." In 1649 the colony contained about fifteen thousand people; in 1666 the population had jumped to around forty thousand. This migration was not limited to the supporters of Charles I, but they were the ones who had the money and the desire to import English racehorses.

The Thoroughbred was not in existence at this time, although an English running horse type was being created. *Tamerlane, imported into Pennsylvania by William Penn in 1699, is said to be the first English blood horse in America. Unlike that of *Bulle Rock, (a later arrival), however, *Tamerlane's blood was lost. The development of the racehorse in England got a big boost with the importation of the Godolphin Barb in 1728. The first studbook for the Thoroughbred was not published until 1808, and so one can only loosely call the English running horse a blood horse before 1800. This does not mean that the cavaliers and other colonial importers brought in inferior horses. The horses were well bred, just not "thoroughly bred." They were predominantly Eastern blood crosses on native English mares. When these English imports were bred to colonial running mares, the Celebrated American Quarter Running Horse was on his way. While some of the better breeders tried to use only pure English running blood in their sprinters, the average man did not have that option. He took his best common (Chickasaw) mare to the best English running horse that was available to him. There are many existing records of these crossbred sprinters. They were a vigorous outcross on the English running horse. A small number of breeders along the Atlantic coast were able to concentrate pure English blood in their short horses; more about them later. Although the number of horses they bred were relatively few, they were most influential.

THE LONG AND THE SHORT

The colonial races were short in the early days. Henry Herbert said that there was little beyond quarter racing.[10] Quarter racing as an organized sport began almost simultaneously in Virginia and Maryland. Regular meets that were held each year at designated spots can be called organized, in contrast to spur-of-the-moment matches. Long races got a boost in Maryland with the importation of *Selima, a daughter of the Godolphin Barb, in 1750. In one of the first celebrated long races in the colonies she defeated Tryall in a match race for five hundred *pistoles* (a Spanish gold coin in use in the colonies). *Selima was owned by Colonel Tasker, and Tryall by Colonel Byrd. The race was run at Gloucester, Virginia, in December, 1752. It was not until later that long races were commonly held. More about *Selima's race will be found below.

Speed trials, generally for short horses, were held during the 1700s at New Market, near Petersburg, Virginia, and at the Washington tracks near Charleston, South Carolina. Races were also held at Richmond, Virginia, and even in New York in Queens and Suffolk counties. In 1804 the New Market race paths (near the center of Suffolk County,) were remodeled for long horses, and a club was established to promote the breeding of better horses. After that regular races of two-and three-mile heats were conducted.

The early short race horses, as mentioned above, were generally crosses of imported English blood horses on native mares. Certain imported blood horses seemed to nick well on the colonial mares. When this occurred, the stallions became famous, like the renowned sire *Janus. More will appear on *Janus in a later chapter. Patrick Nisbett Edgar classified many of the horses he registered as Celebrated American Quarter Running Horses or Mares. Today some could not be enrolled in the English studbook because of the Jersey Act, which requires that both sides of a horse's pedigree trace to an animal already registered in the *General Stud Book* of England. Nevertheless they were sprinters and in great demand in the colonies. Exactly the same can be said about some of the American Thoroughbreds. On occasion the same blood was responsible for creating the short horse and the long horse.

By the 1800's the philosophy or objectives of the breeders of long horses and short horses had changed enough to be distinctively different. In early colonial days almost without exception the production of horses had had a utilitarian motive. Racing these utility horses was generally secondary and just for sport. Beginning in the late 1700s and early 1800s, however, the Virginia and North Carolina breeders, most of whom were wealthy and so not overly concerned with the utilitarian factor, began raising horses for their own pleasure. For them racing and breeding became a way of life and occupied most of their time. In an attempt to "improve the breed," they endeavored to raise horses that could run faster than those raised by their friends and rivals in the adjoining county or on the neighboring plantation. Some specialized in stayers, others in sprinters. Newcomers brought English blood horses to America with them and imported more after they arrived. Their sons were sent back to England to complete their schooling, and they too brought new blood home.

Frontiersmen and pioneers did not live in luxury on large plantations with all the physical labor done by someone else. They lacked both the land and the time to care for many mares and stallions. The few horses they could raise had to be utility animals, able to be ridden, driven, or worked. However, these men too enjoyed recreation, which included racing and gambling, as much as their more wealthy cousins on the tidewater plantations. It was just that they were in no position to spend many dollars "improving the breed." They kept a few mares, and would take any that showed speed to some well-known short horse stallion, such as a descendant of *Janus. The offspring they would race, drive, work, or ride as the circumstances required. The horses were not coddled or pampered, and a sturdy breed thus evolved.

For both the horse breeder on the plantation and the horse breeder on the frontier racing was not just a way to make money. They both raced with pride—to beat their friends—and the wager was the icing on the cake. The professional racehorse men, on the other hand, whether they used long horses, short horses, or both, raced solely for money. They bought their horses and seldom bred their own.

The cleavage between the breeder of the sprinter and the breeder of the stayer was bound to come. Edgar, in the Introduction to his *General Stud Book*, wrote "In the ancient days, quarter racing was much in fashion, and generally kept up, in Virginia, until the importation of *Fearnought, after that distance racers were sought after."[11]

Frontiersmen, small farmers, and stockmen did not care if their using horses could not run three 4-mile heats in one day. The work they had laid out for their horses was of somewhat different nature. Their run was for fun, with a using horse. It was not a race designed to improve the breed. Their sprinters were far from common, and they had their own Godolphin Barb in an imported horse named *Janus.

The quarter running horse was carefully bred, but records were minimal. The

French and Indian War and the American Revolution did not help any, for many records were destroyed during the fighting. Nevertheless colonial writers called them a breed, meaning a definite type, and described them minutely. They were short, stocky, and deep-chested. They had short, broad heads with little ears and prominent jaws. They had short cannons and pasterns and were clean-legged. One outstanding feature was their heavily muscled rear quarters, joined to a short back. They often stood higher at the hips than at the withers. When a very fast short horse appeared, he gained popularity and so became useful in improving the breed. He was the one who attracted the most mares.

All in all, the separation of the long horse and the short horse that began in colonial days created a rivalry that continues to this day. Both have stamina and endurance. While the sprinter may not be able to run as far as fast as the Thoroughbred, he has proved to be faster in a short distance and is considered a better all-around utility animal.

CHAPTER TWO

Colonial Sprinters

BACKGROUND

TO REVIEW BRIEFLY: the best quarter running horses before the Revolutionary War were crosses of imported English running horses on mares already in the colonies. These colonial mares had come from two sources, and had been interbred. Some had been brought to the colonies by the English, while others had filtered north and east from Spanish colonies and either were captured running wild or were acquired from the Indians. Generally the horses were obtained from the Chickasaw, Cherokee, Choctaw, Creek, or Seminole tribes, all of whom had contact with the Spanish settlers in Georgia and Florida. Perhaps some of the horses came from west of the Mississippi, although that seems unlikely during the early period.

The horses that were not obtained from the Indians were corralled, trapped, or otherwise captured, in the borderlands of the South. Capturing these semiferal horses (and cattle) was one way for a poor boy to get started in the livestock business. A famous revolutionary war battle, the Battle of Cowpens, occurred at one such trapping location, on the frontier of South Carolina. In Beverly's *History of Virginia*, published in London in 1705, reference is made to hunting wild horses. As far north as Rhode Island, Governor Robinson, had one of these semiferal horses, named Old Snip. He was captured running wild on Point Judith.

Because the southern colonies generally and Virginia and North Carolina particularly were the home of the American short horses, most space will be given to them in these pages. This does not mean, however, that the northern colonies were without horses or lacked the natural urge for competition. For example, in 1665, one year after New Netherlands was seized by the authority of the Duke of York (later James II) and divided into two American colonies, New York and New Jersey, the new English governor of New York, Richard Nicolls, supported a race program at Hempstead Plains. The track was called New Market, after the well-known English race course. Governor Nicolls' successor continued the program, and in time two regular meets were held, one in the spring and one in the autumn. Races were run at all the popular distances.

There is a contemporary description of the land on which this first track was laid out. It says that

> toward the middle of Long Island lyeth a plain sixteen miles long and four broad, upon which grows very fine grass, that makes exceedingly good Hay, and is very good pasture for sheep and other Cattel; where you shall find neither stick nor stone to hinder the Horse heels, or endanger them in their Races, and once a year the best Horses in the Island are brought hither to try their swiftness, and the swiftest rewarded with a silver cup, two being annually procured for that purpose.[1]

Among the earliest importations that helped New York and the northern colonies was *Wildair, a bay horse bred by a man named Swinburne and imported into New York in 1763 by Colonel James Delancy, of Kings Bridge. *Wildair had been foaled in 1753 and was by Cade by the Godolphin Arabian and out of a mare by Steady who was by Flying Childers. After remaining in America for a few years, *Wildair was sold and shipped back to England, where he was at stud for forty guineas, a large sum for those days.

Delancy also imported one of the most valuable mares ever to come to the northern colonies, the Cub Mare. She was foaled in 1762 and bred by a Mr. Leedes. She was by Cub and out of Aramanthus. *Slovern, a black stallion, was also imported into New York in 1764, and Delancy imported *Lath, a bay stallion, in 1768.

Short racing was popular because almost anyone could condition and race a quarter horse. Money, time, and equipment were at a minimum. The purses offered in these races were called "subscription purses." This racing continued until the Revolution with only minor changes. In 1751, at the insistence of the short horse men, the following condition was put in the rules: "Free to any horse, mare, or gelding bred in America."[2]

THE IMPORTANCE OF VIRGINIA

J. F. D. Smyth, the Englishman who traveled through the southern colonies, was surprised that quarter racing was so popular. He was also astounded that they had developed a "breed" for these match races. To quote him, these short races were "always a match between two horses to run a quarter of a mile straight out."[3] He continued that, particularly in Virginia and the Carolinas, the horses were so swift that he doubted that any other horses in England or the world could beat them at their distance.

The early short horses referred to by Smyth, bred in the southern colonies, were well suited for their place and time. In other colonies they were often referred to simply as "Virginia horses." A Virginia horse was a horse of great stamina, short,

12

rather heavyset, and with a quick burst of speed. In short, a "Virginia horse" was one of superior quality and all-around ability. Such horses were considered tops for turf, field, road, wagon, coach, or saddle. Their ability to run quarter races was universally acknowledged.

Virginia was without doubt the horse capital of the colonies. Under the circumstances it seems only right that they should have been the first to import horses, such as the seventeen horses brought in by Sir Thomas Dale in 1611 and the twenty mares sent over by the Virginia Company in 1620.

The Virginians were so successful with their horses because they had the time to devote to breeding and racing. They raised a crop that was in demand in England, and for which they could get cash. Their labor supply was such that the necessity for personal involvement was limited primarily to planning and selling, leaving them the bulk of their time free for other pursuits. Tobacco made many a plantation owner wealthy, and it was augmented by other cash crops. Another factor, which could easily be overemphasized, was that many of the Virginians were cavaliers, who belonged to the Anglican church, whose doctrine was a far cry from that of the Puritans. The Catholic and the Anglican churches looked on horse racing with a lenient eye. The Protestants, Puritans, Quakers, and Baptists did not. Most Virginians could indulge in recreation with a clear conscience. The absence of Indian troubles was one more reason why they could give time to horse racing.

As soon as the Virginia planter had a good credit balance in London from his plantation sales, he would order his agent to send him over a stallion and a mare or two. When they arrived in America, his neighbors would be envious. They could see that they would suffer in upcoming race meets if they did not possess equally good racing stock. This urge to import started in the 1700s, and some of the best blood known to America entered the southern colonies around this time, starting with *Bulle Rock and culminating with *Janus. The Reverend Andrew Burnaby, in his *Travels Through the Middle Settlements of North America in 1759 and 1760*, remarked that Virginia horses were swift and beautiful and that the Virginia gentlemen spared no expense to import and raise the very best.

So it is easy to see why the gentlemen along the James and Rappahannock rivers had the means and the desire to race and to breed horses. They improved their horses by importing. Some of the early imported horses were *Bulle Rock in 1730, *Dabster in 1742, *Monkey in 1737, *Jolly Roger in 1751, Morton's *Traveler in 1748,[4] *Silver Eye and *Childers in 1756, and, the greatest of them all, *Janus in 1752.

Like their neighbors in Virginia the Carolinians also began importing some horses, beginning about 1754. Up to that time their best horses were basically of Chickasaw blood. While the Chickasaw horse was comparatively small, he was active and vigorous, and when "crossed on the English stock produced animals of great beauty, strength, and speed.''[5] The Carolinians' best horses were Babraham, Borrock Billy, Bosphorus, Cade, Centinel, Flag of Truce, Follower, Flimnap, Fire, Lofty, Matchless, Nonpareil, Oroonoko, Prince, Slim, Snipe, and Sprightly. One of the most valuable early horses in North Carolina was Toby (also called Sporting Toby). He was a sorrel stallion standing fourteen hands, three inches and owned by Colonel William Alston, a well-known racing figure. Toby was by *Janus, and his dam was by Fox.

The Carolinians obtained their best blood from Virginia. John B. Irving wrote: ''In the infancy of our turf, when George the Third was king, South Carolina purchased and transferred to her borders many Virginia brood mares, got by the noted horses Fearnought, Shadow, Lofty, and Sentinel. This was the foundation of our racing stock, whence spring the Bertrand families.''[6]

Participation in short races in the southern colonies were not limited to the wealthy plantation owners, although they had some very obvious advantages. As John H. Wallace wrote in his book *The Horse of America*, the craze for racing was not local or restricted. The people in every county had their annual and semiannual meets, which everyone attended. Hugh Jones, in his book about Virginia published in London in 1724, said that the ''saddle horses, though not very large, are hardy, strong and fleet.''[7] Even the Galloways were included in the races. Weights were assigned according to size. The larger horses carried 140 pounds and smaller ones, such as Galloways and Indian ponies, were assigned weights by inches. Wallace said that this showed that ''the tribe of little Scotch pacers were still to the fore on this side of the water, that they were just as fleet as the larger horses, provided the weight was graduated to the inches.''[8] There were long races as well as short races at these meetings. Before the American Revolution most of the races held in Virginia and the Carolinas were short; afterward many were run longer distances, up to four miles.

COURT CASES

In 1689 a most interesting court case was recorded in Henrico County, Virginia. It seems that on August 1, 1689, William Randolph, who was aged thirty-eight, went to court and told the following story. He said that two weeks earlier he had been to a match race at Malvern Hills race paths and that at that race two men, William Epes and Stephen Cocke, came to him and asked him to be the judge, to see that all the conditions of the race were met, and to start the race. The match was for ten shillings a side, and each horse was to stay in his own pathway. They were not to cross, unless Cocke's horse could get the path of the other within two or three jumps of the start. They must not bump. Randolph started the horses in good shape, but then the trouble started, as Randolph wrote in his deposition. Cocke's horse crowded over onto Epes's pathway, ''but to ye best of this deponent's judgment he did not get it at two or three jumps nor many more, upon which they josseled upon Mr. Epes' horses' path all most part of the race. And further saith not."[9]

Another court case resulting from a quarter horse race was held in Virginia in 1698, and is also recorded in the Henrico County records. It is particularly interesting because one of the horses belonged to the grandfather of President Thomas Jefferson.

The court, convening at Varina on April 1, 1698, to hear a complaint filed against John Stewart, Jr., by Richard Ward. The case went to a jury, and the plaintiff was awarded five pounds sterling. The case was decided on the basis of the conditions set up for the match race. Since they are interesting, the agreement is quoted in full:

At a Court held at Varina, Ap'l 1st, 1698, Richard Ward complains against John Steward, Jun'r, in a plea of debt for that, that is to say, the s'd plaintiff & defendant did on the 12th day of June Last, covenant and agree in the following words:

It is Convenanted and agreed this 12th day of June, 1697, Between Mr. Richard Ward of the one part, in Hen'co Co'ty, & John Steward, Jun'r, of ye other part in ye same Co'ty: Witnesseth, that the aforesaid Mr. Richard Ward doth hereby covenant, promise & agree to run a mare named Bonny, be-longing to Thomas Jefferson, ag'st a horse now belonging to Mr. John Hardiman, named Watt, the said horse & mare to run at the raceplace commonly called ye Ware, to run one quarter of a mile. And ye said John Steward, Jun'r doth hereby coven't & agree to Run a horse now belonging to Mr. Jno. Hardiman, of Cha. 'City Co'ty, the said horse named Watt to run ag'st a mare belonging to Thomas Jefferson, Jun'r, named Bonny. The s'd horse to give the s'd mare five horse Lengths, vizt: that is to say ten yards. And it is further agreed upon by the parties above s'd, that the s'd horse & mare are to Run on the first day of July next Ensuing the date hereof. And it is further agreed upon by the parties above s'd that if the s'd mare doth come within five Lengths of the fores'd Horse, the fores'd John Steward to pay unto Mr. Rich'd Ward the sum of five pounds, Sterling on Demand. & the s'd Richard Ward doth oblige himself that if the afores'd horse doth come before s'd mare five Lengths, then to pay unto the afres'd John Steward, Jun'r. the sum of six pounds Sterling on Demand. It is further agreed by the p'ties aforesaid, that there by fair Rideing & the Riders to weigh about one hundred & thirty Weight. To the true p'formance of all & singular the p'misses, the p'ties above s'd have hereunto set their hands the day and year above written.

And the plaintiff in fact saith, that pursuant to the afores'd agreement, the s'd horse & mare, to-wit: The horse named Watt, belonging to Mr. John Hardiman, & the mare named Bonny, belonging to Mr. Tho. Jefferson, Jun'r, were by the s'd pl't'f & Def'd't brought upon the afores'd Ground to Run upon the first day of July, and the word being given by the person who was appointed to start the s'd horse & mare, the afors'd mare, with her Rider who weighted about one hundred and thirty weight, did Leap off, and out-running the afores'd horse came in first between the poles which were placed at the comeing in of the s'd Race ground, commonly called the Ware, one quarter of a mile distance from the starting place appointed; and was by the s'd mare, with her Rider of about one hund'd & thirty weight as afores'd, fairly Run. Wherefore the afores'd pl't'f saith that the afores'd Mare, Bonny, with fair Running & Rideing, according to agreement, Did beat the s'd horse Watt, and that according to the true meaning of the s'd agreem't he, the s'd plaintiff, hath Won the wager, to-wit: the sum of five pounds sterling of the afores'd John Steward, And thereupon he brings suit ag'st the afores'd John Steward, Jun'r, & demands Judgem't for the afores'd sum of five p'ds Sterl., with Co'ts & co.

To which the Defend't, by Mr. Bartholomew Fowler, his attorney, appears and upon oyer *of the* plaintiff declaracon pleads that he oweth nothing by the covenants, & C., and thereof puts himself upon ye country & ye pl't'f likewise.

Whereupon, it is ordered that a Jury be impanelled & sworn to try the issue, To-wit: Thomas Edwards, Wm Ballard, Phill Childers, John Watson, Edward Bowman, Will Hatcher, Amos Ladd, John Wilson, Phill, Jones, Edw'd Good, John Bowman.

Who Returned this Verdict: We find for the plaintiff. Upon the motion of the plaintiff's attorney the s'd Verdict is Recorded, & Judgment is awarded the s'd pl't'f against the Def'd't for the sum of five pounds Sterling, to be p'd with Costs, als Ex'n.[10]

LIKE AN ARROW FROM A BOW

As Wallace pointed out, the people of Virginia had a strain of horses they bred and raced for a hundred years before the Revolutionary War. They could, and did, race four miles or a quarter of a mile, sometimes the same horse, occasionally on the same day. One could not call these short horses a breed—nor the long horses, for that matter, for neither had a registry. Breeding for speed for a hundred years had certainly tended to establish the type. The sprinting type is still evident in the modern quarter running horse, although good feed and care has increased his size by a full hand.

Let us let Wallace tell what happened in Virginia at the close of the eighteenth century:

> We have a stock of horses that the people of Virginia have bred and ridden and raced for a hundred years, and we know practically nothing about them. . . . they could run four miles, or they could run a quarter of a mile, like an arrow from a bow. They were not a breed, although selecting and crossing and interbreeding for a hundred years would make them quite homogeneous.
>
> By the middle of the eighteenth century all the successive idols of the race loving people are about to be dethroned by their own act, and their homage transferred to a stranger—a larger and finer animal and faster over a distance of ground. Whatever of glory and honor, to say nothing of money, that was to be achieved from this time forward, was to be ascribed to the newly arrived English race horse. But the truth should not be concealed that this old stock furnished half the foundation, in a vast majority of cases, for the triumphs of future generations of the Virginia race horse.[11]

The early Virginia sprinters, or quarter running horses, were very much like our modern short horses. The stallions ranged from thirteen hands, two inches, to fifteen hands high, with most closer to fourteen than fifteen hands. For example, Gimcrack was thirteen hands, three inches; *Janus, fourteen hands, three quarters inch; Twigg, fourteen hands, one inch; and *Flimnap, fourteen hands, one inch. This may seem pony-sized today, but one authority places the average height of the English racer in 1700 as thirteen hands, three inches.

Another interesting facet of the story is that in early colonial racing, when it was common to run two or more elimination four-mile heats and one final heat, sometimes all in a day, the long horses often resembled the modern-day short horses. In other words, these four-mile horses, according to the many descriptions we have of them, more closely resembled the quarter running horse than the Thoroughbred. When you run twelve or fourteen miles, pure blazing speed around a mile oval is of less importance than the ability to stay in there and keep knocking. In addition, one must remember that they were carrying in the neighborhood of 140 pounds. Perhaps the compact musculature and the shorter legs of the quarter horse stood up better under the heavy weight. Soundness was doubly important in these grueling races.

The change in conformation did not really begin until 1809, when the Jockey Club reset its standards for "improving the breed." Many of the better imported English racehorses were unaccustomed to such long races with such heavy weights. The logical action, as they saw it, was to make some adjustments. Multimile races and ability to carry heavy weight suddenly seemed less important for "the improvement of the breed." In the future the blood horse was to run much shorter and carry a lot less weight. Today there are three or four races at less than a mile for every race that is run at a mile or more. Any weight over 115 pounds is on the heavy side. To illustrate, let us take a typical day of races at Bay Meadows. There are 124 horses listed as starters in nine races. Of these only 5 carry as much as 120 pounds, and 72 carry 115 pounds or less. 44 carry 116 to 119 pounds. Compare this with the colonial racer running twelve miles carrying as much as 168 pounds. That's some difference.

The severe requirements made of the running horse before the 1800s placed a premium on stoutness, stamina, and soundness. These same characteristics made him a useful all-round horse for the colonial settlers. They are also the features of the quarter horse today.

When the new regulations were issued by the English Jockey Club in 1809, a new era for Thoroughbreds began, and the final separation of the quarter horse and the Thoroughbred was sealed. As one of the founders of the American Quarter Horse Association, James Goodman Hall, said:

> The single quality of given speed possessed by our modern racers is not a substitute for the union of speed, stoutness and structural power possessed by the old horses and which is absolutely necessary in the quarter horse.[12]

These lines were written not to criticize the modern Thoroughbred but to explain his transition after the American Revolution. It is intended to point out how both the short and the long horse were rather similar in the colonial days but gradually grew apart as new rules were made and oval racing increased in the populated centers. On the frontier, where all-around utility was still a factor to be considered in breeding programs, the old-style heavier-built, shorter-legged sprinter retained his popularity. He is still popular today as the American Quarter Horse. Many of those who do not race their Quarter Horses fear that the modern breeders are taking almost the same steps today that the Thoroughbred breeders did in the early 1800s and that the Quarter Horse will gradually become more of a Thoroughbred type. Only time will tell how this present use of Thoroughbred blood, lighter weight, and longer races will affect the American Quarter Horse.

IMPORTS

Patrick Nisbett Edgar, compiler of the first studbook for the American Thoroughbred, listed the early blood horses imported into America in four classes. First he listed those imported from England and Ireland. Then he listed the Arabs imported from countries other than England or Ireland. He followed with a list of Barb horses, and last he named Spanish horses that were imported into the new United States, all listed in the first seventy-five pages of the book.

Later compilers of pedigrees and registries have been critical of Edgar's work. True, he made mistakes, as his critics point out, but then they themselves are criticized today for similar errors. It's a never-ending chain and just shows that all books (including this one) err, the only variation being in degree.

This author often uses Edgar's information, although he has checked with the other compilers, such as J. S. Skinner, J. H. Wallace, W. H. Herbert, and S. D. Bruce.[13] Some of the inconsistencies found among the early compilers can be shown by using *Badger as an example. He was listed by all five compilers. Note the variations in dates, locations, and so on:

BADGER, a grey horse imported by the late Governor Eden, of Maryland, previous to the Revolutionary War—got by Lord Chedworth's Bosphorun—Black and All Black— Devonshire, or Flying Childers. Maryland 1779 [Edgar, 1833]

BADGER, (Imp's) gr. h. Bozphorus, (a son of Babraham) dam by Black and All Black—Flying Childers, etc. N. Carolina, 1777 Governor Eden. [Skinner, 1854]

Badger—Said to be by Bosphorus, dam by Black and All Black, grand dam Flying Childers. Imported into Maryland about 1770. Governor Eden [Herbert, 1857]

BADGER, imp., gr. (Edens) Foaled 1761: got by Lord Chedworth's Bosphorus, dam by

Black and All Black; g. d. by Flying Childers. Imported into Md. by Gov. Eden about 1770. Not to be traced in the British Stud Book. [Wallace, 1867]

BADGER, g.h., imported by Governor Eden, of Maryland, previous to the Revolutionary War; by Lord Chedworth's Bosphorus. We can not find this horse. 1st dam by Black and All Black (Othello). 2nd dam by Devonshire of Flying Childers. [Bruce, 1868]

The variations in the entries should not lead one to suspect that *Badger did not exist. There are other instances of flat contradictions, and each compiler included some horses omitted by the others. The variations in the studbooks that followed Edgar are not of monumental concern at this date, but they do point out the difficulties faced by the modern author and indicate the ease with which someone can say he is wrong and then quote a different authority as proof. There are known errors in all the five basic sources.[14] In fact, subsequent newspaper research, begun by that grand old man John L. O'Connor, has shown all the early studbooks to have errors. Nevertheless, since Edgar was the earliest of the compilers (his book was published twenty-one years before the next studbook appeared), since he was able to talk to many of the horsemen active during the 1700s, and since he had a soft spot in his heart for the Southside quarter horses of the olden times, I will ride along with Edgar in most cases.

Edgar could not find any imported horses of running blood before *Bulle Rock in 1730, probably for the very good reason that there were few if any. If some blood did arrive earlier, it was not capable of reproducing its excellence and so was promptly forgotten. There were four or five in the 1740s and twice as many in the fifties. *Janus was the greatest of all quarter running horse sires.

Among the earliest importations that are of particular interest to short horse breeders are the following stallions. For the most part they are arranged chronologically by their foaling date. Here is Edgar's entry for *Bulle Rock:

BULLE-ROCK, Imported into Virginia before the Revolution in 1730, and foaled about the year 1718—got by the Darley Arabian—Byerly Turk—Lyster Turk, out of a natural Arabian mare.[15]

Skinner does not list *Bulle Rock at all. Wallace does, as follows:

BULLE ROCK, imp., Foaled about 1718; got by Darley Arabian; dam by Byerly Turk; g. d. by Lysters Turk, out of a natural Barb mare. This horse is not found in Weatherby. He is said to have been imported into Va., 1730.[16]

Apparently a horse named *Shock was imported; he is shown in both Edgar and Skinner. They conflict over pedigree and dates. Skinner says that *Shock was foaled in 1729. Both Edgar and Skinner show a *Porto. Edgar gives no date, but Skinner says that he was foaled in 1731. They also both list *Buzzard, Edgar saying that he was imported in 1804 and Skinner saying 1737. Edgar's entry for *Crab reads:

> CRAB, bred by Mr. Routh, foaled in 1736 and imported into America about the year 1746. Got by Old Crab—Donsellor—Coneyskin—Huttons Arabian. He died in Virginia in 1750.[17]

Skinner lists *Crab as sired by Old Fox and out of a Galloway mare, and says that he was foaled in 1739. Herbert says that *Crab was one of the oldest and finest of English Thoroughbreds and that he had many descendants in the colonies.

Edgar and Skinner list *Bajazett, Edgar spelling it Bajazette. Wallace uses only one *t* in the name, the form I have used in this book. Edgar shows his sire as Lord March's Old Crab, Skinner says it was the Godolphin Arabian, and Herbert gives the nod to Lord March's Bajazet, adding that the horse cannot be traced in the English studbook. *Bajazet was imported in or around 1740.

> JOLLY ROGER, (Alias Roger of the Vale) a chestnut horse, bred by Mr. Craddock; foaled in 1741—got by Roundhead—his dam by Crofts Pardner—Woodcock—Croft's Bay Barb—Makeless—Brimmer—Dickey Pearson (son of Old Dodsworth)—Burton Barb Mare. Jolly Roger died at the stable of Mr. James Belford, in Grenville Co., Va., in 1772, age 31 years. He produced most excellent bottomed stock in Virginia.[18]

Skinner generally agreed with Edgar on *Jolly Roger and adds that he was imported in 1748. Skinner also gives a variation in the pedigree, saying that he was a son of Flying Childers. Herbert and Wallace agree with Edgar's pedigree. Both Wallace and Herbert add that he was one of the greatest, Wallace saying that he was second only to *Fearnought.

> BUFFCOAT, a dun horse, foaled in 1742—got by Godolphin Arabian—Silver Locks, by the Bold Galloway—Araster Turk—Leedes—Spanker. He died in Virginia in 1757.[19]

The next imported horse to be listed is *Janus. He deserves a section by himself, for he is the original, and the only true, foundation sire of the quarter running horse.

*JANUS

*Janus was the first great progenitor of the sprinting quarter horse. There are very few references to quarter horses or sprinting families before *Janus arrived in America during the 1750s. On the other hand, the special type of sprinter that he created is still popular. The type that he did so much to establish is today the largest horse-breed registry in the world. *Janus had a unique conformation, and that conformation can be recognized today just as easily as it was in colonial days.

No doubt the consistent inbreeding that took place in the colonies helped set his characteristics. They became a trademark recognized by all horsemen. It was a common practice for the Virginians of the Southside, where *Janus stood for over half of his American life, to breed his daughters and granddaughters back to him. Three crosses were common, seven not unheard of. John Hervey says that it is almost impossible to expect posterity to believe seven crosses of *Janus on *Janus. John L. O'Connor, in his rare book *Notes on the Thoroughbred from Kentucky Newspapers*, listed just such a stallion, named Terror. He found him advertised at stud in the *Kentucky Gazette*, where he was stated to be 13/16 *Janus. The stallion had recently been brought from South Carolina to Virginia and was to stand the season seven miles south of Lexington on the Boonesville road. Terror was a mahogany bay, 14 hands, 2 inches high, and was said to possess more than just ordinary beauty, strength, and action. The advertisement was dated March 20, 1826, and signed B. R. Jenkins.

*Janus was never as popular in the Tidewater region as he was in the southside of Virginia. He left the Tidewater when the colts were still young, in the winter of 1760, and never returned. One reason why he never went back is that the East Coast was then becoming more interested in long races and long horses. It was only when one crossed the James River going south and west and reached the Roanoke that he was in quarter running horse country. There a match race was as easy to get up as a sweat. Just over the southern border of Virginia in North Carolina was a neighboring group of horsemen equally dedicated to quarter racing. *Janus produced just the kind of colt that the horsemen of Virginia and North Carolina wanted, and so they never let him leave.

It is from Edgar's studbook that we get much of our information about *Janus and his offspring. Edgar lists over sixty horses as quarter running horses, most of them foaled before the end of the Revolutionary War. Of this group only four had no *Janus blood. A horseman of Virginia or North Carolina who possessed a son or daughter of the old horse was more likely to tell a listener the pedigree of the animal than its name. This is why there are so many Januses, little Januses, Young Januses, Janus Juniors, and so on, and any number of mares referred to only as Janus mares. That *Janus was in their pedigree was all that really mattered.

*Janus is mentioned in all the early studbooks, and because he is an important figure for the quarter horse, each entry is to be examined below, in chronological order beginning with the latest entry, in Bruce's *American Stud Book*:

JANUS ch. c., foaled in 1746, by Old Janus (son of the Godolphin Arabian out of the

Little Hartley Mare) bred by Mr. Swymmer, imported into Virginia, about the year 1752. He was the property of John Goode, Sr., of Mecklenburg County, Va. who agreed to give Ł 150, Virginia currency, for him, provided he was safely delivered to his stable, in the winter of 1779 or 1780, being in the 34th year of his age. Janus started for the stable of Mr. Goode, as aforesaid, and progressed as far as the stable of Col. Haynes, where he died in 1780. This colt is not laid down in the Stud Book or Racing Calendar. He was foaled before the issue of either. No doubt a correct pedigree. 1st dam by Fox, 2nd dam by Bald Galloway.[20]

Wallace's American Stud-Book, compiled by John H. Wallace, appeared one year before Bruce's studbook. His entry for *Janus was as follows:

JANUS, imp., ch., Foaled 1746; got by Janus, son of Godolphin Arabian; dam by Fox; g.d. by Bald Galloway.

He is not to be found in the British Stud Book, but is no doubt genuine. He was imported into Virginia in 1752, and lived till 1779. He stood on the Roanoke in North Carolina and Virginia, and left a very numerous progeny of fast short-distance racers. He was highly prized in his day, and remote cross from him is still desireable.[21]

A few years before Wallace, in 1857, Henry William Herbert made a list of imported stallions to include in his *Frank Forester's Horse and Horsemanship of the United States*. He also noted *Janus' reputation for siring sprinters:

JANUS—Foaled in 1746. Imported into Va., about 1752. Said to be by Old Janus, son of the Godolphin Arab out of the Little Hartley Mare, dam by Fox, g. dam by Galloway. Not in the Stud Book, but probably genuine. He is said to have been the sire of an immense quantity of speedy, short-distance racers. His immediate descendants could not stay a distance, but his remote posterity are said to have had great muscle and bottom, and his blood still holds in excellent repute.

Celer was justly considered the best son of old Janus, as he propagated a stock equal in every quality to those of the stock begotten by his sire. He was bred by Mr. Mead of Virginia, and foaled in 1774, died in 1802, aged 28 years.[22]

Three years before Wallace's book appeared, Skinner listed six horses under the name *Janus. Two were imports, three were native, and one was a mare. It seems that the first and second listings, the imports, are the same horse—both *Janus—but Skinner has them somewhat confused. Below are his entries for the first two *Januses:

JANUS, (imp'd) bl. h. fifteen hands one inch high, by Old Stirling—Old Crab Monkey—Basto, etc. Foaled 1744.

———, (imp'd) ch. by Janus, dam by Fox—Bald Galloway, etc. Died 1779-80, aged 34. Gloucester Cy, Va. Mordecai Booth.[23]

The Quarter Horse. From Richard Mason, *The Gentleman's New Pocket Farrier*. 1833.

The second of these two listings is the more nearly correct.

This brings us to the earliest and best entry for *Janus, in Edgar's studbook. Edgar, active some thirty-five years before Bruce, would seem to have had the best opportunity to get the correct information. Edgar was able to talk to many horsemen who had known *Janus personally, and from them he gathered his entry:

JANUS   A chestnut horse, "sui generis," of low stature, about 14 hands ¾ of an inch high, bred by Mr. Swymmer, imported into Virginia about the year 1752; foaled in 1746—"The stock of Old Janus in Virginia and the Southern States has been distinctly marked for the last fifty years, as if he had been of a different species. For power, swiftness and durability they have been equaled by no other breed of horses.

Janus had great bone and muscle, round, very compact, large quarters, and very swift; all of which desirable qualities he imparted so perfectly to his progeny, that many of them remain in the stock at this remote period, and great speed and muscular form are still found

23

in many horses whose pedigrees reach him, if accurately traced through different branches, or when, as it is sometimes called, there is a "doubt Janus cross." Nearly all his immediate descendents were "swift Quarter nags"; they never could run far.

He was the sire of an immense number of short distance racers, broodmares and stallions. Indeed, a remote cross of him in the most superior race horses of the present day, is generally sought after, as an example from a letter, lately received, will show:

"A remote cross of Janus is indispensably necessary, at this day, in a distance race horse; indeed, there is no other at this time which can be said to be more desirable, as to use the slang of a jockey, "Speed always will help out bottom."

He was the property of the late Mr. John Goode, Sen. of Mecklenburgh County, Virginia, who agreed to give Ł 150, Virginia currency for him, provided he was safely delivered at his stable in the winter of 1779 or 1780, being in the 34th year of his age. Janus started for the stable of his new proprietor, Mr. Goode, as aforesaid, and progressed as far as the stable of Col. Haynes, where he died in 1780.—

He was got by Old Janus (son of the Godolphin Arabian, out of the little Hartley Mare)—his dam by Fox—his grand dam by the Bald Galloway.

Va.   1757. MORDECAI BOOTH,
       1780. JOHN GOODE, Sen.
       1781. JOHN BIBBO,
       1782. ALLAN YOUNG,
             SAMUEL YOUNG,
       1783. SAMUEL GOODE.[24]

The *American Turf Register and Sporting Magazine*, a racehorse newspaper founded in 1829 by John Stuart Skinner, contains an interesting letter concerning Janus. It appeared in an 1836 issue, fifty-six years after *Janus' death.

A little before the war of the Revolution, old Janus stood on the northern border of North Carolina, and at that time short races were fashionable, and large sums staked on quarter mile races. In these the colts of Janus were always victors. Some gentlemen then thought that if a single cross was good, a double cross must be better; not so, however. The finest Janus mares, and those most successful in matches, were bred to their sire, and in no single instance, did they produce a single nag capable of running a single quarter of a mile. Many of them, it is true, had great speed; but they were not able to continue their rate beyond 300 yards—many not even that distance!

These facts I had from many gentlemen along the Roanoke, who had themselves bred fast horses; and they invariably concurred in the statement, that the colts of Janus, from even scrub mares, though inferior in finish and general symmetry to the double Janus stock, always beat them when they ran a full quarter of a mile, when there was in the commencement of the race an evident superiority in the double cross.[25]

In 1830, six years before the letter above was printed, John Randolph of Roanoke stated, also in *American Turf Register*, that almost the opposite was the case. In addition to being one of America's statesmen Randolph was also a horseman. As a gentleman plantation owner, he frequented Newmarket and Epsom. On one of his visits to England he went to see the Houghton portrait of the grandsire of *Janus, the immortal Godolphin Arabian. He was an admirer of *Janus and knew personally much about the stallion.

Of the many false charges about *Janus, Randolph said, the worst was that his stock had no bottom and could not go the distance.[26] He blamed this misconception, which arose in later years, on the fact that *Janus produced so many fast quarter horses out of ordinary mares. Many of these mares, having come from the Cherokees and the Chickasaws, had little or no English racing blood. They were not distance horses. Randolph pointed out that *Janus easily defeated Colonel Byrd's famous Valiant in a four-mile match race. When *Janus was bred to a clean-bred mare, he got as many stayers as any other stallion. Randolph felt that, because there was so much interest in short racing during *Janus day, especially in the region where he stood, his success in breeding sprinters received the most publicity.

Imported *Janus was sired by Old Janus, who is sometimes referred to as B. Rogers' Janus. Old Janus was bred and raised by Lord Godolphin, and his sire was Lord Godolphin's famous Arabian stallion. There is no good description of Old Janus. There was no Thoroughbred studbook at the time, just racing notices and calendars. One of these mentions him as being a coming seven-year-old chestnut colt, free from all blemishes.

The young *Janus ran his first race in England as a four-year-old in 1750. He was entered in the race program as Anthony L. Swymmer's chestnut colt Stiff Dick. He got the name because a tendon in his right rear leg had been strained and left him with a stiff leg—until he warmed up. After the first race, which he won, he was called Little Janus. There are records of six more races *Janus entered before he was shipped to America. He won two, placed in three, and showed once. Thereafter *Janus was used as a stallion until he was sent to America. He was purchased by an agent for Mordecai Booth, of Gloucester, Virginia. In colonial America there were no widely printed and distributed racing calendars, and information about *Janus is difficult to come by. Fortunately, he was almost a public figure in Virginia and North Carolina, and so we do have some reports about him, as well as some newspaper advertisements.

There are a few further references to Swymmer and Booth. Swymmer, *Janus' English owner, was a member of Parliament from Southhampton. Swymmer had many influential relatives, not the least of whom was his wife, who was a sister of the Countess Tankerville. He was wealthy and a successful racehorse breeder. He had extensive commercial holdings in Jamaica, eventually moved there, and stayed until his death.

Mordecai Booth was a wealthy Virginia planter who lived near Gloucester and had business connections in Yorktown. His father lived in England and had wide shipping interests in the Americas. When Booth was in England, he visited the stud at Grisewood, and the horse made a big impression on him. When *Janus arrived in America, Booth put him in service on his plantation and also raced him some.

When Booth died, *Janus was sold to the father of John Willis, who farmed in Brunswick County, Virginia. There Willis used him both as a stallion and as a racehorse, just as Booth had. He was later sold and stood at Cumberland, Powhatan, Amelia, and again in Brunswick County. He then was in North Carolina until 1774, when he was sold to John Goode, of Chesterfield County, Virginia, who bred him for two years. There is a mix-up in dates here, for Edgar has Twigg, Paddy Whack, and Brimmer foaled at Goode's plantation in 1778. *Janus was probably sold in 1777, or else Goode took mares to *Janus. When Goode sold *Janus to W. Barnes, of Halifax County, North Carolina, Twigg and Babram were just foals. As they were growing up, he saw that he had sold a stallion he should have kept. He began bargaining with Barnes to get *Janus back. In 1780, after many negotiations, Goode succeeded in buying *Janus. He had to pay 150 pounds sterling for the thirty-four-year-old stallion. Unfortunately, *Janus died on the way back to Virginia, while resting at Colonel Haynes's farm.

*Janus was quite a horse. Despite a tendon—referred to in the old records as a "foul sinew,"—that bothered him all his life, he had success on the race course and was phenomenal as a sire. He had one of the best hind legs ever seen on a horse in America. He was an Oriental hot blood, carrying a strong infusion of the blood of the Godolphin Arabian. He was an unusual four-mile horse—unusual because he had a lot of early foot. It was his ability to transmit this early speed that made him such a great quarter horse sire.

*Janus satisfied the horsemen of the South who wanted sprinters. As a result he, his sons, and their blood were eagerly sought. *Janus' blood went west as new states and territories were formed, Kentucky, Illinois, Missouri, and Tennessee. *Janus' blood was taken there by his sons and their get. Particularly influential were Babram, Blue Boar, Celer, Jupiter, Peacock, Printer, Switch, and Twigg. For seventy-five years *Janus' blood was popular with breeders who wanted a quarter horse.

Many horses sired by *Janus can be found in the appendix of The American Stud Book. Bruce listed some that Edgar does not have. Examples are Buie, which should have been spelled Bowie; Clodius, a full brother of Celer;[27] and Syphax, sometimes spelled Cyphax or Cyphase. The American Stud Book also lists Printer,[28] but since he died in 1828, it is unlikely that he was by *Janus. *Janus had eight sons called Janus, and Printer's sire could easily have been one of them.

Another interesting variation between Bruce's studbook and Edgar's involves a Janus offspring called Sportly. Bruce says that Sportly was sired by Janus out of a Spanish mare.[29] Bruce adds that she produced a filly called Tristram Shandy. Edgar says that Sportly was a stallion, bred by Nelson, with the same sire and dam. To add to the confusion, Bruce[30] in another place says that Sportly was a stallion. It could be that a full brother and sister had the same name. About thirty mares are listed as by *Janus, and well over one hundred have dams listed simply as by *Janus but with no names of their own.

Even without the advent of *Janus in America, there would have been quarter racing, but it is doubtful that the breed would have had such a distinct and uniform conformation. The ideal quarter running horse today still fills the description of the colonial *Janus family. They are as distinct from the Thoroughbred in conformation as the Arab is from the Tennessee Walking Horse.

Imported *Janus lived in America for twenty-eight years. He was somewhat of a freak as far as his conformation went because he possessed the same bloodlines as the other English stallions imported at the time. He did not, however, look like them; he had more muscle and was compact in conformation. His remarkable prepotency—his ability to pass on to his descendants his early speed and unique conformation— enabled him to establish almost singlehandedly the sprinting quarter horse in America.

*Janus
Owners, Addresses, and Dates

Owner	Location	Date
A. L. Swymmer	Morton (near Oxford), England	1750–55
(Purchased by Booth and sent to America, 1756)		
Mordecai Booth	Gloucester, Va.	1757–60
John Willis	Brunswick County, Va.	1761–66
R. James	Cumberland County, Va.	1767–68
J. Harris	Powhatan County, Va.	1769
C. Haskins	Amelia County, Va.	1770
T. Persons	Brunswick County, Va.	1771
J. Atherton	Northampton County, N.C.	1772–74
John Goode	Chesterfield County, Va.	1775–76
W. Barnes	Halifax County, N.C.	1780
(Sold back to John Goode, died enroute, 1780)		

Source: From Fairfax Harrison, *Early American Turf Stock, 1730–1830*

Only two good English-bred mares were bred to *Janus. One was *Selima, by the Godolphin Arabian. She was imported by Benjamin Tasker, Jr., of Belair, Maryland. In 1761 she was bred to *Janus, and the foal was Spadille, the great quarter horse stallion who was owned by Wyllie Jones, of Halifax County, North Carolina. The other imported mare was *Mary Grey by Roundhead. She was imported in 1748 by Ralph Wormeley, of Middlesex County, Virginia. Her descendants include Blue Boar by *Janus, Club Foot by *Janus, Poll Smiling by *Janus, Polly Williams by Lee's Mark Anthony, and Red Bacchus by a son of *Janus. Brimmer's dam, Poll Flaxen, was out of *Mary Grey. All of the above had blazing short speed.

Advertisements concerning *Janus appeared in several issues of the *Virginia Gazette*, such as the following:

April 9, 1767:

The subscriber takes this method to acquaint those persons who put their mares to Janus (late the property of Col. John Willis, deceased) by the season, and have not had them got with foal, that he is able to stand the present season at Richard James in Cumberland County. . . .

Signed Mildred Willis

March 3, 1768:

Janus stands this season at my stable for covering mares at four lbs. a season. . . . Cumberland County, March 1, 1768   Richard James

May 24, 1770:

The noted English Horse stands at my stable in order to cover mares at 4 lbs a season. . . .
Amelia County, April 25, 1770

Christopher Haskins

May 9, 1771:

The noted English horse Janus stands at my stable this season in order to cover mares, four lbs a season.
Brunswich County   March 15, 1771   Thomas Person

March 18, 1773:

Old Janus is now very fat and active as a lamb, and stands at Northampton Court House, North Carolina, in order to cover mares at four lbs a season.   J. Atherton

March 10, 1775:

The noted English horse Janus is in great perfection. He stands at my house and covers at five lbs the season.   Goodes Bridge,
Chesterfield   March 8, 1775   John Goode

March 25, 1775:

Whereas Mr. Goode has advertised my horse Janus for the season, contrary to his agreement with me in this respect, I do hereby give notice to those who put mares to him, the season is to expire August 15.

Jeph. Atherton

These ads are interesting. The stallion starts out as just plain *Janus and ends up as the "noted English Horse." His fee also increased to five pounds. It also shows how he progressed from owner to owner, each of whom made a profit as his popularity increased. J. Harris apparently did not see the need to advertise *Janus, nor did Barnes, who lived in North Carolina. Atherton, however, who also lived in North Carolina, did advertise in the *Virginia Gazette*. The last ad shows a disagreement between John Goode and Joseph Atherton. Apparently the latter thought Goode would not advertise during the 1775 season.

A good description of *Janus, which the ads do not supply, is found in the *American Turf Register*, by Allan Jonès Davie, of Halifax County, North Carolina. Davie was a nephew of Wyllie Jones and a well-known short horse man of the period. He used *Janus blood extensively in his racing and breeding programs. Davie probably knew *Janus personally. In any case, that he once owned Sir Archy speaks well for his ability to recognize good horseflesh.

Allan Davie described *Janus as a small but beautiful horse, with uncommon muscular development. He said that he was a dark sorrel with speckles on his rump, which became more distinct as he grew older, a white blaze, and one white hind foot. Davie described his legs and feet as "as fine as those of a deer."[31]

In 1830 there was considerable discussion in the sporting journals regarding *Janus and his progeny, and John Randolph was right in the middle of it, for he knew the value of *Janus stock. Randolph had been only seven years old when *Janus died, but his father and their horse-raising friends all knew, and used, *Janus and his blood. Randolph wrote, "No stock of horses I ever knew possessed the stamina or vigor possessed by Janus, or had such good feet." He also claimed that, although *Janus was primarily used to breed sprinters, when blooded mares were taken to him, he got foals that could run on out.

*Janus, himself, was a better than average four-mile horse, winning more races than he lost. In May, 1757, after he came to America, *Janus won a four-mile race against *Valiant, who belonged to William Byrd III, of Westover. Byrd was the son of the wealthy Virginia aristocrat of the same name who had built up his land holdings from 26,000 acres to 180,000 acres. *Valiant was supposed to be one of the best horses in Virginia; he was by Dormouse, his dam by Crab. When the race took place, *Janus was eleven years old, past his prime. *Janus won the match with no great trouble. It is a fact that *Janus and other early quarter horses did run—and win—four-mile heats on occasion. Some of those races are described later in this book.

During some of the time he stood in America, *Janus was available to English-bred mares, particularly when he stood in Gloucester, on the James River, and on the Appomattox. When he was in North Carolina, he stood in Halifax County and so was not accessible to long mares, although he was in the center of the quarter racing region. Of the roughly thirty stallions and thirty-seven mares listed in Bruce as quarter racers, almost all originated in the six counties adjoining the Virginia–North Carolina border. As might be expected, most came from Roanoke Valley.[32]

In the short horse region of Virginia and North Carolina there were good mares, even if they were not "of concentrated oriental hot blood." Here were found the best of the Cherokee and Chickasaw horses, obtained by the settlers and used by them because they had proved to be good all-round utility horses. They were sometimes referred to as "common mares," but you can bet that their owners were not riding and racing them, or leading them long distances to pay a four-pound stud fee because they considered them common. *Janus took them as they came and produced speedy quarter racers from them.

Fairfax Harrison made an interesting observation. He said that the very fact that the mares were "common" was the reason so many of their fillies were returned to *Janus. He said the "very multiplication of his crosses is perhaps an indication of the mares to which *Janus had access."[33] There is another much more logical reason why they were returned to *Janus. The short horse breeder would return *Janus fillies to the old horse, even if they were more "thoroughly bred," in order to set the sprinting and utility characteristics he liked. It was in this fashion that Bob Kleberg, of the King Ranch, established his strain of sorrel quarter horses—by taking Old Sorrel fillies back to their sire.

Fairfax Harrison brought up an interesting point concerning the date *Janus was imported into the colonies. He quoted early records and a letter dated May 13, 1757, to prove that *Janus was not imported until 1756. In a letter from Mrs. William Byrd III to her husband, who was commanding the Second Virginia Regiment in the French and Indian War, she wrote that their horse *Valiant had lost a race to Mordacai Booth. Booth's horse was *Janus. In Randolph's "Register," appearing in *Turf, Field, and Farm* in 1886, among other statements concerning *Janus it says that he was publicly advertised at stud in England during the 1753 to 1755 seasons. These facts would seem to make it clear that he came to America in 1756.

After the Revolution, *Janus blood spread west and north into the territories and new states, especially into Kentucky and Tennessee. The pioneers took along their horses with their cows, pigs, and chickens. Those who were racing took *Janus blood with them, sons and daughters, grandsons and granddaughters. The first two sprinters known to stand in Kentucky were Darius and Pilgarlick, both sons of *Janus. Tennessee had Jupiter, Lewis' Comet, and Bowie's horse, the last of whom took his owner's name, though it was spelled Buie. Buie was bred by Dr. Bowie, of Virginia, by *Janus and out of an imported mare. Will Williams says his get in Tennessee were unequaled as quarter horses.[34] Buie stood in Jefferson City, owned in 1787 by John Park and David Berclay. A Buie mare produced Procter Knott and Advanced Guard.

There are two other brief notices about *Janus in the *American Turf Register*:

Mr. Editor:

I have heard a revolutionary officer say, the imported chestnut Janus had a blaze in his face, and both hinder legs half up white; that he was about fifteen hands high, of singular strength and roundness of form; and that he died in Northhampton county, N.C. about 1779-80 about thirty-three or thirty-four years old.[35]

In the 1832 issue of the *American Turf Register* are the following words about *Janus:

THE RACE HORSE IN AMERICA

. . . . The Janus Horse, bred in and in, or crossed on any of the others had heels and were run short distances, with or without preparation. When prepared with the skill of Col. Bynum, or Stud Harry Hunter, their celerity was astonishing. The "Universal tool" speed, is therefore at the foundation of the Roanoke race horse. Contemporaneously with Hunter and Bynum, flourished Austin Curtis, a man of color indeed, but one of judgement, skill and courteous manners. He knew how to "get the length into them," or to bring out their game. Under his auspices the fame of Collector grew and the powers of Snap Dragon were developed. Mr. Wilkes in succession, displayed the energies of Surprise, Wonder, Potomac, & O.

*Janus, on the common stock of the country, it is said, produced some good runners, which shews the common stock were not "cold blooded."[36]

A good way to end the discussion of *Janus is to repeat the flamboyant praise heaped on the great stallion by John Hervey. Hervey said that *Janus was a phenomenal pony, that, "like the God from which he was named, was double faced, begetting speed so terrific, that it expended itself in a moment, yet so flamingly alive, it is still unquenched."[37]

LATER IMPORTS

*Janus, although the greatest, was not the first imported racehorse to influence the quarter running horse, nor was he to be the last. Breeders brought in many animals. A large portion of the imports of the 1700s were brought in by a relatively few individuals, most of whom resided in Virginia. Colonel John Hoomes, of that state, imported over twenty stallions, and General John Tayloe imported more than that many mares (each, of course, bought and imported horses of both sexes). The more thoroughly bred the imported horses were the better their records were in the colonies. The top breeders of sprinters in Virginia include the following family names: Goode, Hoomes, Tayloe, and Morton. Occasionally one finds Morton's name spelled Moreton, especially in references to Morton's horse *Traveler. Perhaps Edgar first made the mistake and then was copied verbatim by Herbert and Bruce. Wallace and Skinner properly spelled it Morton. The reference is to Joseph Morton, of Leedstown, Virginia, who was the primary owner of *Traveler. Maryland was another state that imported good horses; the families involved were Tasker, Sharpe, Ogle, and Carroll. Jones and Davie in North Carolina should also be mentioned. All these breeders made valuable contributions to the sprinting horses of the colonies, although none were more successful than John C. Goode, of Mecklenburg County, Virginia. Actually three Goodes were involved in breeding and running short horses: Thomas, Samuel, and John. The family tradition of raising racehorses was started by Thomas, and it was he who imported most of the basic blood. The Goodes are discussed further in a later chapter.

One top import owned by the Goodes was *Selim. He was brought over to the colonies in 1752 in his dam's belly, as Edgar put it. Perhaps the year was actually in 1760, depending on which authority you choose to accept. Edgar claimed that *Selim was a capital racer. His dam was called *Selim by Edgar and *Selima by most other authorities. *Selim, the stallion who got free passage across the Atlantic, was sired by Bajazet. He had been bred by the Duke of Cumberland. *Selim, though foaled in America, is properly considered imported.

The Tayloes, father and son, of Virginia, raised some of the greatest short horses of the day, and some long ones too. During their active years the Tayloes imported the following horses: *Adeline, br. m. 1806; *Avelina, m. 1799; *Britannia, m. 1800; *Brilliant, h. 1791; *Castianira m. 1796; *Chance, h. 1797; *Dungannon h. 1793; *Flying Childers h. 1751; *Lady Northumberland; *Lucy Gwynn; *Madcap, m.

1794; *Mol-in-the-Wad, m. 1803; *Mufti, h. 1775; *Peggy, m. 1788; *Trumpetta, m. 1797. The list is undoubtedly incomplete and varies from one early studbook to the other. The dates given above, taken from the studbooks, are sometimes foaling dates, sometimes importing dates, and sometimes just dates given without explanation. In any case, these imports are a good indication of why the Tayloes were so successful.

Morton's *Traveler, a bay horse, was foaled in 1748, and bred by a man named Crofts, of Raby, in Yorkshire. He was sired by a stallion owned by Croft known as Partner and was out of the well-known mare Bloody Buttocks. *Traveler was imported by Morton in about 1750. There have been many arguments over his pedigree, but there can be none about his influence on the colonial quarter running horse. *Traveler sired Tryall and Yorick when bred to *Blazella. (Bruce called her *Betty Blazella). More about her later. In addition to Tryall and Yorick, *Traveler also got Burwell's Traveler and Tristram Shandy out of *Janus mares, Ariel and Partner out of Tasker's *Selima, and Lloyd's Traveler out of *Jenny Cameron. In 1748, *Regulus was imported. He was a grandson of the Godolphin Arabian, just as *Janus was (it is surprising how many short horses trace to the Godolphin). Other importations included *Sober John and *Brutis, *Sober John going to Virginia and *Brutis to South Carolina. *Brutis was a roan sired by Regulus in England.

Another interesting import was *Othello, also known as *Black-and-All-Black, foaled in 1743. Governor Sharpe of Maryland imported him from Ireland, where he was bred and raised. One of his better-known sons was the American Black-and-All-Black, of Revolutionary War fame.

Another import of note was *Childers, who was brought into Virginia by John Tayloe II in 1751. He was a grandson of Flying Childers, and his dam was by Bald Galloway. *Babraham was another popular name among the short horse fraternity. Bruce lists three imported horses with the name. The other two were a bay by *Wildair, foaled in 1775, and one listed as by Babraham (by *Fearnought), foaled after 1760 and taken into South Carolina. The first two went to Virginia. Skinner lists only one, by Jupiter and out of *Selima.

In 1764, *Fearnought came to America. Edgar wrote that *Fearnought did ''more to improve the breed of thoroughly bred race horses than any other stallion in the United States of his day.''[38] He was a large, good-looking bay stallion, foaled in 1755, by Regulus and out of Silvertail. His great-grandsire was the Godolphin Arabian. He was imported by Colonel John Baylor, of Virginia, who paid 289 pounds, five shillings, nine pence sterling for him. Baylor used him for a while and then, when the horse was twenty-one, sold him to William Edwards, of Greenville County, Virginia.

Despite Edgar's statement about *Fearnought, echoed by later writers, short racing did not falter with the introduction of *Fearnought, nor did long racing start at

*Babraham, a bay colt foaled in 1738 and imported in 1775. He was sired by the Godolphin Arabian. He was a brother of *Selima, the dam of Spadille, and Jupiter's Babraham. From Fairfax Harrison, *Early American Turf Stock*. 1934–35.

that point. Long races had been held for many years. Maryland's Governor Ogle held long races at Annapolis in 1745, and the Maryland Jockey Club, which regularly held long races, was organized about the same time. Obviously many examples could be cited of short races held after the introduction of *Fearnought. What Edgar and the other writers were allowing to show by such statements was provincialism. To them everything of importance happened in the East; what was being done west of them was of little import. Since long racing had become popular in the Tidewater, where they lived and wrote, that to them was the racing world.

Long races got a good start with the importation of *Jolly Roger, foaled in England in 1741. *Jolly Roger died in the ownership of James Belford, of Greenville County, Virginia, in 1772 at the age of thirty-one. He produced some of the best long horses of his day. They all had bottom. In 1752 four-mile races were common, and there was interstate competition between Maryland and Virginia. That was before the days of *Regulus and *Fearnought. Some of the greatest quarter racers came along after the importation of *Fearnought. Both Twigg and Paddy Whack ran their justly famous match races after *Fearnought's time. In fact, probably the second-greatest sire of sprinters, *Bonnie Scotland, did not even arrive in America until 1857, about one hundred years later.

A stallion always gets more attention than a mare because his influence is spread among many more individuals. That does not make the contribution of the dam any less important. Many colonial quarter horse breeders liked to use a few English mares as a safety factor. Most were inbreeding to outstanding sires like *Janus, and an occasional indirect outcross to the right type of English mare helped eliminate recessive defects. Another reason for using imported English mares was that many of the native mares, with close up Indian ancestors, while sturdy and swift, lacked quality. The English outcross added refinement to the offspring.

Tasker's *Selima was one of the best of the imported mares. According to Bruce, *Selima was bred by Lord Craven, foaled in 1746, and imported by Colonel Tasker. She was by the Godolphin Arabian and was a full sister of a Babraham, according to Bruce. *Selima was a great producing mare, and she was used by Tasker, Goode, and finally Tayloe. She foaled Spadille when bred to *Janus; Black Selima when bred to *Fearnought; and a horse called Babraham when bred to Jupiter. She was bred to Morton's *Traveler three times and produced Bellair, Partner, and Ariel. Herbert said that she "was one of the most distinguished mares that ever ran in America, and progenitrix of half of the best and most fashionable blood in America."[39]

Another great imported mare was *Jenny Cameron. She was imported by John Tayloe before the Revolution. Bruce said that he had a certificate from Colonel Tayloe, dated 1773, that said she was by Cuddly, a son of Fox, and out of Witty's famous mare Cabbagewise.[40] Bruce added that none of her pedigree could be verified in *The General Stud Book*. Regardless of her breeding, her produce was the best. While in England she was bred to Blaze and foaled *Betty Blazella, about whom more will be said later. In America she produced Silver Legs and Lloyd's Traveler when bred to Morton's *Traveler; Smiling Tom when bred to Tom Jones; Little David when bred to *Childers; and several fillies.

*Blazella, or *Betty Blazella, as she was called by Bruce, was imported by Colonel Tayloe with her dam, *Jenny Cameron. In December, 1752, *Jenny Cameron and her contemporary *Selima competed in a sweepstakes. This time it was Colonel Tasker's turn to win, and *Selima defeated *Jenny, as well as one of Jenny's descendants, Tryall, owned by Colonel Byrd. Both *Jenny Cameron and *Selima were run before and after foaling.

Another outstanding mare was *Kitty Fisher, a gray imported in 1759 by Carter Braxton, of Virginia. She was sired by Cade, and her dam by Cullen Arabian. She was bred by the Marquis of Granby and arrived in New Market in the spring of 1759. When she was bred to *Fearnought, she foaled King Herold, Young Kitty Fisher, and Crippled Fearnought. When bred to Partner, she produced Virginia Cade. She was bred twice to Americus and produced Forest Garrick and then Gallatin. Finally she was bred to Quicksilver and brought forth Pilot.

One of the greatest of all imported mares was *Castianira. She was a strikingly beautiful brown mare bred by Popham and foaled in 1796. She was imported by John Tayloe, the master of Mount Airy on the Rappahannock. She had been sired by Rockingham and was out of Tabitha by Trentham. Her first American foal was a black filly by *Mufti. In 1805 she produced one of the few truly great sires of all time, Sir Archy. He was sired by *Diomed. When rebred to *Diomed, she produced a bay filly named Highland Mary. She then was bred to four other stallions and produced winners by all of them. They were Hephestion by *Buzzard, Castania by Archduke, Birgo by Sir Peter Teagle, and Noli-Me-Tangere by Top Gallant. Had she produced only Sir Archy, her fame would have been secure. Although primarily famous as a producer of long horses, Sir Archy's blood was influential in the short horse. Perhaps only *Janus and *Bonnie Scotland were better.

Another import was *Bonny Lass. She was a mature mare when she arrived in America in the early 1700s. She had been sired by Bay Bolton and was out of a mare by the Darley Arabian. Her granddam was by the Byerly Turk. In America she produced Merry Andrew by Fox, a bay colt by Pardner, a filly that produced Spectator, and also got Paragon, who was the dam of Mystery. Another imported mare was *Lady Bull, a bay mare foaled in 1796. She was sired by John Bull, and her dam was Pumpkin. Her granddam was by Fleacatcher. Colonel John Hoomes brought her to Virginia. She was a great race mare with blazing short speed.

RANGER, AN INTERESTING IMPORT

One of the most unusual stories ever to excite the interest of horsemen occurred at the time of the Revolutionary War. It concerns one of the forerunners of the American Thoroughbred and of the American Quarter Horse—*Ranger, later known as the *Lindsay Arabian. According to W. R. Brown, George Washington was painted mounted on a son of *Ranger.[41] Washington received the horse as a gift from General Light-Horse Harry Lee, and he liked the horse so well that he secured more offspring of *Ranger to pull Martha's coach.

*Ranger is of importance because he had as much influence as any other Oriental imported up to the time of the Revolution. Edgar listed a few other Arabs imported before *Ranger, but most were imported later.[42] Bruce, Wallace, and Skinner also provided information about *Ranger.[43] Skinner said that the stallion was presented by the emperor of Morocco to the captain of an English vessel and was taken to the West Indies, where he broke three legs. He was given to a Connecticut man, who took him home and called him *Ranger. Skinner added that a Captain Lindsay was sent by General Lee to purchase the horse in 1777 or 1778 and that Lindsay took the stallion to Virginia. Skinner gave the *American Farmer* as his reference.[44]

The *American Farmer* evidently got some of its information from Edgar, who told the story of the stallion in his studbook. As far as I can determine, Edgar's account, written before 1883, was the first to appear in print. It may have been embroidered some, but it is worth repeating.

In 1776 or 1777, right after the outbreak of the Revolution, General Light-Horse Harry Lee, the father of Robert E. Lee, had his attention drawn to a group of fine horses. According to Edgar, the horses were uncommonly good Eastern horses employed in the public service. Their attractive appearance and superior form caused Lee to inquire about their origin, and he sent Captain Lyndsay (Edgar's spelling) to examine the stallion who had sired them and buy him if possible.

Captain Lindsay succeeded in buying *Ranger and took him to Virginia, where he stood to the public. He commanded a high fee and covered many mares. Edgar said that the *Lindsay Arabian was old and feeble when he first saw him. Edgar had ridden thirty miles expressly to see the horse and found him to be a "white horse of the most perfect form and symmetry." Edgar then proceeded to tell the story as told to him by "highly respectable persons" from Connecticut:

In return for an important service rendered by the commander of a British frigate to the son of the emperor of Morocco, the commander was presented with the most valuable horse in the royal stud. The commander was very pleased, expecting to sell the horse for a high price when he arrived in England. For some reason the frigate first had to go to one of the islands of the West Indies. Believing that the stallion needed exercise after being cooped up aboard the vessel, the commander landed the horse so that he could have some exercise. The horse was turned loose in the only enclosed place where he could be left, a large lumberyard. The stallion was delighted to be free to run, but freedom proved to be his undoing. He climbed upon a stack of lumber, which tumbled down, breaking three of his legs. On the island was an old friend of the commander, a captain from the colonies. The commander offered the friend the stallion, saying that he would be extremely valuable if he could be saved. The Yankee captain gladly accepted the horse. He took him aboard his vessel, put him in a sling, and carefully set and bound his legs. The captain was in port some time before he disposed of all of his cargo, and during that time the stallion had a chance to heal before they set sail. The stallion was put ashore in Connecticut in 1766. He was then four years old. His stock proved valuable, and many capital racehorses and brood mares descended from him. In Connecticut he was known as *Ranger; later, when Lindsay took him to Virginia, he became known as *Lindsay's Arabian.

John Wallace questioned the truthfulness of the story in *The Horse of America.* He wrote, "The whole story about Ranger was fabricated in Maryland and the Connecticut horsemen never heard of it."[45] Perhaps Wallace is right, but where there is so much smoke there could be some fire. Bruce was an equally respected historian of horse pedigrees and origins. In his *American Stud Book* he repeated the story. Wallace admitted that the stallion may have been imported from England but added that, to judge from public advertisements, his owners knew nothing of his blood. Of course, neither Edgar nor Bruce mentioned any of the Arabian's ancestors, saying only that he came from Morocco.

Since Wallace's account is different in many respects, it is worth reviewing.

Wallace pointed out that until the middle of the 1800's very few Arabians were imported into the United States, probably fewer than thirty. Some were called Arabians, some Barbs, and some Arab Barbs. Wallace says that most of them were fakes, although they were generally accepted as genuine at the time. Only five or six were *real* Arabs, Wallace claimed, and most of them were brought in by one man, Keene Richards, of Kentucky. Of the thirty-odd so-called Arabians, the Lindsay Arabian was the only one Wallace gave any credit to as a sire. In his version of the story Wallace said that *Ranger was a Barb and was given to the commander of a British man-o-war by the ruler of one of the Barbary States. The commander had saved the life of the ruler's son. The captain accepted the gift of the colt and sailed for South America. In port he put his colt ashore for exercise in a lumberyard. The colt began playing, and a pile of lumber fell on him, breaking three legs. The British officer was about to knock the colt on the head when the skipper of a Yankee trading vessel said that he could save him.

The British captain told the American skipper the story of the colt and gave him to the American. Soon the Yankee skipper had the colt aboard his vessel, hung up in a hammock with his legs set and bound. In time the American vessel arrived in New London, and the colt was taken to the vicinity of Hartford, where he came into the possession of a Colonel Wyllis, and was advertised as standing at stud by Wyllis under the name *Ranger. In the advertisement *Ranger was described as a "fine English stallion of the Barbary Breed, bred in England."[46]

Wallace said that this advertisement indicates that nothing was known of his history. Perhaps what Wallace failed to perceive was that Wyllis felt he could get more business for his stallion if he advertised him as an English horse rather than take a chance that the public would accept his bizarre history.

In any case, as Wallace continued the story, General George Washington happened to notice the excellence of the horses in a troop of Connecticut cavalry. His interest aroused, he asked Captain Lindsay to investigate and, upon learning that they were all sired by *Ranger, suggested that Lindsay buy the stallion. Lindsay followed Washington's advise and took *Ranger to Maryland, where he became known as *Lindsay's Arabian. For a time he stood for James Howard, of Windham, Connecticut, who advertised him as an imported Arabian horse.

At this late date it is difficult to determine which story is correct. The facts that seem beyond question are that a horse known as both *Ranger and *Lindsay's Arabian was imported into Connecticut in 1766 as a four-year-old and that the first owner of record was a Colonel Wyllis, of Hartford, who advertised him at stud in the *Connecticut Courant* in 1777. We also know that John Howard had him in Windham in 1778 and stood him during that season. It also seems probable that, through his produce, he came to the attention of Captain Lindsay. We can say for certain that Lindsay bought the horse and took him to Virginia. It is also accepted by all the authorities that he was a great sire and must rank along with other early great imported stallions. His name is found in the pedigrees of many of the most respectable short and long running horse families.

EARLY SIRES OF SPRINTERS

There were many native-born quarter running horses before the Revolutionary War. *Janus was responsible for more than his share, but other stallions, such as *Monkey, *Crab, Morton's *Traveler, Sober John, Mead's Celer, and Babram also sired their share of speedy short horses. In all there were about twenty-five superior sires of speed merchants in America during the colonial era.

One of the earliest quarter horses to attract the attention of the colonial race fans was Shad. Not much is known about him except that he was able to defeat almost every horse against whom he was matched. He was bred and raced by John Haskins, and most of our knowledge about Shad comes from Haskins' son, Thomas. Shad is listed in Edgar as a Famous American Quarter Running Horse. A dark chestnut, he was foaled on Haskins' farm in Brunswick County, Virginia, in 1761. His sire was *Janus, and his dam was an imported mare.

Some of Shad's greatest rivals were also sired by *Janus. Three horses sired by *Janus were called Peacock: a dark brown, foaled in 1772; a dark chestnut, foaled in 1762; and the most famous, Alston's pale sorrel, foaled in 1760. Shad never ran against the brown called Roland's Peacock, for he had passed his prime before the brown gained any fame. The chestnut Peacock was no match for Shad, but Old Peacock, as Alston's Peacock was generally called, furnished plenty of competition for Shad. John Alston raised another Celebrated American Quarter Running Horse named Spider, a full brother of Old Peacock. Old Peacock could defeat Shad most of the time; Spider never did.

Old Peacock was also designated a Famous American Quarter Running Horse by Edgar. Edgar describes him as

> a pale sorrel horse, elegantly but very lightly formed, possessing great power and strength for a horse of his make, fifteen hands fully high. [He was] got by I.H. Old Janus—his dam was an imported mare, brought from Old Spain. N.B. This Horse was foaled the property of Joseph John Alston, Esq. of Halifax County, N.C. in 1760 and transferred to the late Mr. Brinkley of that County and State, and afterwards was called "Brinkley's Peacock." He died in the state of South Carolina, aged 26 years. He was one of the swiftest quarter of a mile racers in America of his day, and won upwards of $40,000.[47]

Just a word more about the other two Peacocks. The brown horse was foaled in 1772, and, as has been noted, was sired by *Janus. His dam was by Lee's Mark Anthony, and in later years he was generally known as Roland's Peacock. The dark-chestnut Peacock, also known as Williamson's Peacock, was a typical *Janus, heavily made but only fourteen hands high. His dam was sired by Brinkley's Peacock.

One other *Janus horse was running during those years. On occasion he could run as fast as any horse, but he was erratic. His name was Moggy. He was bred by Batts Peter Stewart, a black freedman who lived for many years in Greensville County, Virginia. Moggy was a somewhat leggy gray horse, one of the few *Janus colts that did not have his sire's compact conformation. His dam's dam was probably a light draft horse. Moggy made a name for himself by beating Shad early in his career, but he was wisely not rematched. His best-known son was called Chickey Moggy, and he inherited much from his sire. Chickey was a brown stallion of poor conformation, loosely coupled, and over fifteen hands high. His dam was by Lee's Old Mark Anthony.

Two other Celebrated Quarter Running Horses of the 1760s are worth a word or two. They were Babram, occasionally referred to as Babraham, and Spadille. Both became more famous than Shad, Spider, or Old Peacock. Both Spadille and Babram were born in 1766, Spadille in Halifax County, North Carolina, and Babram in Virginia. I could not find out whether they were ever matched against each other, although each owner claimed that his was the fastest sprinter in America.

Spadille, a Celebrated American Quarter Running Horse, was owned by Wyllie Jones, of Halifax County, North Carolina. He was by *Janus, and his dam was *Selima by the Godolphin Arabian. Spadille had two sons, both known as Little Spadille, who were also noted short racehorses. Wallace said that *Selima never had a foal by *Janus, but both Edgar and Bruce show Spadille as out of *Selima.

Babram, bred by John Goode, of Mecklenburgh County, Virginia, has been called Babraham by some chroniclers; moreover, there have been several Babrahams and Babrams. The one most important for the history of the running quarter horse is Goode's Babram, (also called Old Babram) who was foaled around 1766. Both his sire and his dam were by *Janus. His second dam was by *Jolly Roger. Bruce commented in small print at the end of the entry, "He was the best and fastest quarter-horse in his day."[48]

Babram ended his racing career as perhaps all good Quarter Horses may wish to, while winning a race. He had been matched against Old Jupiter, a Virginia horse probably raised by John Goode in the late 1760s or early 1770s. He was by *Janus, and his dam was also by *Janus; his second dam, by Lee's Mark Anthony. The race was held in Virginia at the Lewis paths and run for five hundred pounds, Virginia currency, a side. Babram and Jupiter broke even, but then Babram pulled ahead. At the four-hundred-yard mark Babram had daylight on Jupiter, when he crossed his legs and fell, breaking his neck. Babram had been used for covering mares and racing from his second year on, and he sired some of the best quarter horses in the colonies. The only better contemporary sire of speed bred in America was Celer.

While there were other quarter running horses, these were among the best running before 1770. A little later, during the Revolutionary War period, a large number of excellent quarter running horses appeared. Outstanding during this period were Bacchus, 1774; Jupiter, 1774; Celer, 1776; Brimmer, 1776; Paddy Whack, 1778; and Twigg, 1778. Paddy Whack and Twigg will be discussed in Part II.

Old Bacchus, foaled in 1774, was the oldest horse on the list. He was a son of the Celebrated American Quarter Running Horse Old Babram. Old Bacchus was so termed because he had so many sons named after him. He was a blood bay, beautifully made and very heavy for his height. He stood only fourteen hands. His physical description makes him seem similar to Ott Adams' famous Joe Moore of the 1930s. Old Bacchus was bred by John Potter, of Granville County, North Carolina. Potter gained respect for Babram when he attended a match race and lost money on him. As a result he took his best *Janus mare to Goode's, and the resulting colt he named Bacchus. Like his sire, Bacchus became a Famous American Quarter Running Horse. Old Bacchus was run and bred until his death in 1789. Had it not been for the war, which made racing next to impossible and prevented mares from coming to him, he would have no doubt made an even greater record.

There were three Jupiters sired by *Janus—a black and two sorrels. One had Lee's Mark Anthony as the sire of his dam, and one had *Jolly Roger. Only one, however, was able to establish himself as a Celebrated American Quarter Running Horse. This Jupiter was a sorrel with two crosses of *Janus, plus Mark Anthony and *Jolly Roger. He was bred by Augustine Willis and was considered one of the fastest sprinters ever produced in Virginia.

Brimmer is one of many great quarter horse sires who are difficult to pin down. There were just too many Brimmers—not just sons of the old horse but some that were not even related. Edgar listed eight foaled around the time of the Revolution. Three, a gray, a black, and a bay, were by Harris' Eclipse. A sorrel and a dun were sired by Old Valiant, a bay by Herod, a sorrel by *St. George, and a gray by *Janus. Bruce also listed eight Brimmers: six like Edgar's plus one by Blue Beard and one by Eben Bess' Brimmer. Bruce does not show a Brimmer foaled by *Janus. In the early 1790s the *Knoxville Register and State Gazette* advertised still another Brimmer at stud. He was by Old Clubfoot by *Janus and out of Doll Pearson. John Goode had three (Bruce said two), and these are the ones we might look to as being important to the quarter horse breeder, for Goode specialized in sprinters.

The Brimmer that Goode considered one of his best horses was bought from Captain T. Turpin, of Powhatan County, Virginia. Although bred and raised by Turpin, he became known as Goode's Brimmer. He was sired by Harris' Eclipse, by Bright's Pardner. Harris' Eclipse died in 1771, so he must have been foaled in 1772 at the latest. Bruce has him foaled in 1766 or 1767. Brimmer's dam was extremely well bred. She was Poll Flaxen by *Jolly Roger and out of *Mary Grey. More will be found on Poll Flaxen later in the book. Another Brimmer owned by Goode was by *St. George and out of a *Janus mare. He was foaled about 1800. The third Brimmer owned by John Goode was by *Diomed, and his dam was *Robin Red Breast.

Another good word picture of Goode's Brimmer is found in the *American Turf Register*:

Near Carterville, VA
Aug. 8, 1830

Mr. Editor.
    Never having seen any notice of Brimmer in your interesting register, I have obtained from M.I.G. a short memoir of that celebrated Horse which I send now below.

Brimmer was foaled in the county of Powhatan in the year of 1776 or 7, the property of Captain Thomas Turpin, who also raised Leviathan. He was a blood bay with a white streak in his face, his hind feet white above the fetlocks, barely 15 hands high. My informant states that he was a horse of fine form and great muscular power. Brimmer was got by Col. John Harris Eclipse, his dam Polly Flaxen by Jolly Roger and out of Carter Baxtons imported mare, Mary Grey. The only certain recollection Mr. G. has of his performance was a race that he ran at Hobbs Hale, in four mile heats. The first heat he lost as a consequence of one of his plates springing. He ran with 140 pounds against some of the best horses in Virginia. The first heat he ran in 8:04 and the second he ran in 8:08, and the third in 8:12. No horse being able to put him to the top of his speed. My informant adds that he ran many races and was rarely if ever beaten. If you think this imperfect account of that fine animal worth a place in your register, you are at liberty to publish it.[49]

Another Brimmer listed by Edgar and by Battell shows both his sire and his dam's sire to be by *Janus.[50] This one was an iron-gray horse. It is not said who raised him, only that he was formerly the property of a man named Walker, of Virginia.

An additional comment on the Goode's Brimmer is found in *The Horse of America*, where Herbert reprinted a letter from Will Williams:

As to Brimmer, my father bought Eclipse about the close of the Revolution, of Colonel Harris, and he stated that Eclipse was the sire of Col. Goode's Brimmer, confirmed by a circumstantial statement in one volume of the *American Turf Register*.

Will Williams
Popular Grove, Near
Nashville
March 25, 1856[51]

Mead's Celer was one of the greatest sires of sprinting horses of his day. Many considered him second only to *Janus. Celer lived during the Revolutionary War era. He was bred by General Everard Mead, who lived on a Southside plantation in Virginia. Mead loved horses and had a good eye for them. Certainly one of the best purchases he ever made was the great mare Brandon, who was to become Celer's dam. Brandon had been sired by *Aristotle, and her dam was by the imported *Whittington. Her first foal, dropped in 1774, was Pilgrim, by *Fearnought. Then came Mead's Celer, followed by Clodius, Buckskin, Tippoo Saib, Chevalier, Quicksilver, and Fitz Partner. The Brandon mare had been bred by Benjamin Harrison, the father of the ninth president. Mead bred the mare to the very best stallions available, once to *Fearnought, Twice to *Janus, and once each to Mark Anthony, Lath, Celer, Mercury, and Partner. All these matings resulted in colts. Brandon's only filly was sired by Pilgrim, foaled in 1784. The filly was her last foal, for she died the next year. Mead sold these eight colts for about fourteen thousand pounds, which made him a wealthy man.

The American Stud Book says that Celer was a full brother of Clodius, although two years older. Celer was foaled in 1776, Clodius in 1778. Edgar quoted Theophilus Feild as saying that Clodius "was for a long time assigned to *Janus, but the fact is positively asserted upon the most undoubted authority, that Gen. Mead was imposed upon, and that Apollo, was really his sire."[52] Apollo was by Morton's *Traveler, so if that is true, Clodius had a first-rate pedigree either way.

Mead's Celer was the first of many horses to be known by that name. The word is Latin for "fast," an excellent name for a sprinter or a sire of sprinters.

Celer's dam was by imported *Aristotle, an excellently bred brown stallion, foaled in 1755. He was brought into Virginia from England in 1764, where he had been a well-known racehorse. *Aristotle was used for breeding only in America. He was sired by the Cullen Arabian, and his dam was by Old Crab. He died in 1776 at twenty-one.

William Henry Herbert claimed that Celer was the best son *Janus produced. However, there were so many *Janus colts and so many Celer colts that the claim would be difficult to prove. Herbert said that Celer propagated a stock equal in every quality to the stock got by his sire. Will Williams, who actually knew Celer, said: "I frequently saw Celer, by Janus, dam Mead's Aristotle mare. He was highly finished, and gave both speed and bottom.[53] That was true of many of the early quarter running sires, and their offspring ran long or short, depending upon what type of mare they were bred to or how they were trained.

Celer spent much of his life in the Tidewater area of Virginia. His popularity there was amazing, and he became responsible for a brand-new line of sprinters. He eventually was taken to North Carolina and stood for a number of years at Colonel Eaton's establishment in Granville.

An interesting side note on Celer is found in Bruce's *American Stud Book*.[54] He pointed out that one of Celer's sons sired a mare that became the dam of the two famous quarter-mile sprinting brothers Copperhead and Cock Robin. Edgar claims that Hendrick's Celer, by Mead's Celer and out of a mare by Cooper's Janus, was the swiftest quarter race horse in the United States in his day. Cooper's Janus had eight crosses of *Janus in his pedigree. Jordan's Celer was another fast son of Mead's Celer. Mead's Celer lived a full life, dying in 1802 at twenty-six years.

Twigg was still another great individual. He was one of the last crop of foals that John Goode got out of *Janus. His dam was a top mare named Switch. She had had a great racing career before being placed in the brood-mare band. She was a beautiful chestnut standing just fourteen hands. She had been bred by Shippey Allen Pucket, of North Carolina, and foaled on or about the year 1765. She, like Twigg, had been sired by *Janus. Her dam was also by *Janus, as was her granddam (in fact, one has to go back four generations to find the first top line that did not trace to *Janus, and it went to *Jolly Roger). In her fairly brief racing career Switch won thousands of dollars.

Twigg matured into a beautifully formed horse, a picture quarter horse like his sire, *Janus. He was a bright bay, with a smooth, heavily muscled body. A rather large blaze ran down his face, and he had two white feet. He stood fourteen hands, one inch. A contemporary observer of Twigg said that he was very compact and highly formed and possessed great muscular power, symmetry, action, and strength.

Twigg was also a good sire. One of his better colts was Budd, foaled in 1789. He also sired Jacob Bugg's Drednot and Betsy Dancey. Betsy was a famous short mare, foaled in 1795 on the farm of William Moody in North Carolina. Her dam was by Spadille.

Paddy Whack was a rival of Twigg's on the race paths. Paddy Whack's sire and dam, according to Edgar and Bruce, were imported from England. Fairfax Harrison, however, contended that Paddy was by *Janus and that John Goode was his breeder. This may well be so, but according to the studbooks he was by *Jolly Roger, who was by Roundhead and out of a mare by *Shock. *Jolly Roger was registered in the English studbook as Roger of the Vale. He had been bred in England by a Mr. Craddock and foaled in 1741. *Jolly Roger was a good sire in England and a great sire in America. For the most part he produced horses with bottom, although some of his colts, like Paddy Whack, could run short. Paddy Whack's dam was by *Shock, an English horse, imported by Colonel Tayloe, of Virginia. He was a grandson of Croft's Partner. Paddy Whack's second dam was by *Sober John, who also was imported into Virginia by Tayloe.

Paddy Whack was a bay with a little white on his face. He was several inches taller than Twigg but, because he was of a more slender build, looked smaller. When the two stallions were not seen together, they were occasionally mistaken for each other. In fact, Paddy Whack was sometimes known as Little Twigg.

Another great sprinter, named Blue Boar, was foaled in 1774. He was a blue-gray horse, well formed, and he stood fourteen hands, two inches. He was bred by Wyllie Jones, of Halifax, North Carolina. He too was sired by *Janus, although his dam was by *Fearnought. During his racing days he was considered the fastest horse in North Carolina, and they had some good ones in that state.

In 1775, Statesman was foaled. He was a son of *Janus, and his dam was by Old *Fearnought. His second dam was by *Jolly Rogers. Edgar says simply that he was "a capital race horse."[55]

One of *Janus' better colts was born a cripple, with a club left forefoot. However, foreshadowing the great mare Queenie, who was Champion Quarter Mare in 1945, he did not let his foot slow him down. His deformity led to his name, Clubfoot. He was bred by Colonel Thomas Eaton, of Halifax County, North Carolina, and foaled in 1778. His dam was by *Fearnought. He was a dark sorrel, fifteen hands tall, and very sturdily built. He was an excellent quarter mile racer. Edgar said that he was a horse of prodigious powers.

Old Bacchus, mentioned above, sired a host of fleet-footed sons. Two stand out: both foaled in 1778 during the Revolutionary War. Both were also called Bacchus. One was differentiated by being referred to as Little Bacchus. He had to stand on his bedding to reach fourteen hands. The other was identified by his color. He was called Red Bacchus because he was a bright-red bay. He was so red that he looked like a sorrel with a black mane and tail. Both became Celebrated American Quarter Running Horses.

Little Bacchus, a bay, was bred by William Mills, of Granville County, North Carolina. Once his speed became apparent, he was purchased by a neighbor, the well-known runner of short horses John Dickinson. Dickinson was a close relative of the statesman of the same name. He had been trying to raise a fast horse from Old Bacchus and had in fact a couple of years before taken a mare sired by Morton's *Traveler to Old Bacchus, hoping to get a sprinter. He got a good horse by this cross, whom he called Little Bacchus, but he was just fast enough to lose money. When he heard that his neighbor, Mills, had a full sister of Dickinson's Apollo, who had been bred to Bacchus, he went over and bought the foal. He also called the Mills-bred colt Little Bacchus, and he turned out to be the racehorse he had been looking for.

The other Bacchus colt, Red Bacchus, stood fourteen hands, two inches; most of *Janus' descendants were small horses. He also was raised by Dickinson, but was out of a mare by Babram. Little Bacchus was best at the shorter distances, and Dickinson seldom matched him over 300 or 350 yards. Red Bacchus, on the other hand, could run up to a full quarter, and on occasion ran farther.

About fifty miles east of John Dickinson's home and horse-breeding establishment was the farm of John Whitaker, of Halifax County, North Carolina. One of the best matches in North Carolina occurred when Little Bacchus nosed out Sir Walter Raleigh, who was bred and raced by his owner, Whitaker. Sir Walter Raleigh was a top sprinter, but Whittaker matched him a little short when he ran Little Bacchus. Sir Walter was a dark bay horse, and, while rather compact, as were most Mark Anthony colts, he stood a good fifteen hands high. He sired many good quarter racers. He was Old Mark Anthony's last foal. His dam was a half sister of Little Bacchus, both mares being by Spotswood's Apollo.

CHAPTER THREE

The Horses and the People

RACING, AND HOW

ONE of the very first accounts of a race in Virginia is contained in the court records of York County, dated September 10, 1674. The following was quoted by John Hervey in his excellent book *Racing in America, 1665–1865*:

> James Bullock, a tailor, having made a race for his mare to run with a horse belonging to Mr. Matthew Slader, for two thousand lbs. of Tobacco and caske, it be contrary to law for a laborer to make a race, being a sport only for gentlemen, is fined for the same, 100 lbs. of Tobacco and caske. Whereas Mr. Matthew Slader and James Bullock are conditioned under the hand and seal of the said Slader, that his horse should run out of the way that Bullocks mare might win, which is an apparent cheat, is ordered to be put in stocks, and there sit a space of one hour.

The commoner, Bullock, had matched a race with a gentleman named Slader. One of the conditions was that the race must be run in such a manner as to allow Bullock's mare to win. Since a commoner's horse was not supposed to beat a gentleman's, judicious betting would allow both Bullock and Slader to clean up. Word got out, however, and it went to court, with the judge equalizing everything by fining Bullock for presuming to race against a gentleman and having the so-called gentleman who agreed to throw the race confined to the stocks.

One of the first statutes passed in Jamestown was one that forbade racing in the streets. This indicates that the Virginians liked to match horse races, even in the early 1600s. Jamestown was not exactly an ideal spot for a colony, let alone an important capital. It was not long until the colonists began moving upriver to higher and drier sites. When Jamestown was destroyed during Bacon's Rebellion in 1676, it never again regained its importance. Williamsburg took its place and became the capital in 1699. Richmond, the next important city in Virginia, was settled in 1637, incorporated in 1782, and became the capital in 1779. By the early 1700s Richmond and Henrico County had become the center of quarter racing. Fortunately for a researcher, many arguments arose over match races, and when they ended up in the courts, the records were preserved.

Across the river from Richmond was another settlement known as Bermuda Hundred. A horse race was held there in the summer of 1677. The men matching the race were Abraham Womock and Richard Ligon. They selected as a starter (which has always been a problem in a match race when no gates are used) one Abraham Childers and as a finish judge Captain Thomas Chamberlain. The purse was three hundred pounds of tobacco. Thomas Chamberlain furnished the jockey for Womock's horse, and Thomas Cocke rode for Ligon. The argument began and waxed vigorously when Ligon's jockey got such a poor start that he pulled up his horse and refused to run. It seemed obvious to him that the starter was favoring his opponent. The opponent completed the course and claimed the purse. The resulting lawsuits took years to resolve.

Some five or six years later Ligon's name again appeared in a lawsuit over a horse race. In October, 1683, two individuals, just for the fun of it, decided to match a race in which they themselves would be the jockeys. Their names were Edward Hatcher and Andrew Martin. Since they were short of cash, the winner was to get the other's horse. When the day came and everyone was at the starting point, who should turn up but Richard Ligon. He said that Hatcher didn't own the horse—he did—and that the race could not be held. Nevertheless, Andrew Martin ran over the course and claimed Hatcher's horse. You can see why the lawyers loved that match.

For a hundred years, more or less, before the first English Thoroughbred was imported, there were quarter races in the colonies. John H. Wallace summed up the Virginia races as follows:

> The Virginians were a horse-racing people from the start, and it is impossible to tell how long before racing first commenced, but probably just as soon as any two neighbors met, each owning a horse. A few hundred pounds of tobacco were put up the next day, to make it interesting, in determining which was the faster. This racing feeling was not confined to neighbors, or to neighborhoods, but it pervaded the whole colony, and the people of every county had their annual and semi-annual meetings, which everybody attended.[1]

Other colonies, notably Maryland and the Carolinas, also had short races. Every convenient public place and town had its track, some long, but most running from three hundred yards up to a half mile. John Thomas Scharf, in his *History of Maryland*, wrote: "So common in fact were scrub and quarter races at every gathering of people, on Sundays, on Saturday afternoons and at Quaker Meetings. that they had to be prohibited by special acts of legislature."[2]

Francis Barnum Culver mentioned several racing associations that were formed in Virginia before the Revolution, listing Petersburg, Portsmouth, Dumfries, and Warwick. He too pointed out that Williamsburg was a great sporting center. Williamsburg had a one-mile track, but races both shorter and longer were run on the course.[3]

There is little doubt that the Old Dominion was the first home of the quarter racing horse, where he was enthusiastically accepted by rich and poor alike. The yen to run horses seems to be a human trait. Pedigrees were of secondary importance. If a colonist had a running mare, he bred her to the closest fast stallion. It was that simple. There were no registries, and pedigrees were just remembered ones. The few that were written appeared in stud advertisements and in an occasional letter. While undoubtedly some horses were falsely attributed to *Janus or *Jolly Roger, there is no reason to question every pedigree. Breeders, for the first two or three hundred years felt that eight generations without an unknown ancestor was sufficient to make an animal clean-bred.

Hervey, in the book mentioned above, gave a good description of colonial quarter racing, and pointed out the interesting singularity of this type of racing: it was almost without exception a match race set up by the owners of each horse. This is not to say that more than two horses might not be run in a given race, but the various preset conditions of multihorse racing were absent. Weights, length of run, method of starting, and many other important features of a race were agreed to by the interested parties, and not by a racing secretary at an organized track. All of this gave the quarter horse unlimited freedom to run where and when he wanted without having to meet some third party's regulations and conditions. That is why so many early matches could be spur-of-the-moment races, run down the main street of a town or up a country lane, from as far as you could chuck a rock to a bend in the road half a mile away.

As populations increased, opposition to main-street racing developed, and most matches were held on country roads or on some hastily constructed paths on the village commons or a willing farmer's land. When races were held with some regularity, these locations became popular, and many people would come on weekends or holidays to see, or to match, a race.

In the beginning match races were run on two paths, three to five feet wide (each horse had his own path to run on). For the occasional three-horse race the paths were broadened, though they were seldom more than fifteen feet wide. Depending on the terrain, the length of the course, would be anywhere from two hundred to six hundred yards, with a modest bit of ground to pull up on. Fortunately, the quarter horses did not need much starting space; they could whirl and be at full speed in two jumps.

There is a good description of the colonial race paths in the *Colonial Virginians at Play*, by Jane Carson. The following description is based on her book and on Hervey's books mentioned above.

To begin with, they were called paths and not tracks because that is what they were—just two narrow paths that led straight away for at least two hundred yards. A little hump or a grade up or down was not considered a great handicap, as long as it was the same for both horses. There was always a starting space of about fifty feet so that the horses could turn to start or walk up to the start. There were no starting gates so some room was necessary. At the opposite end of the track some clear land had to be available to pull up the horses. Little else was necessary. Poles or stakes were used to mark the start and the finish lines, and only the starting poles were permanent. The judges would line up the poles to judge the start and finish.

One can picture the crowds that lined both sides of the track, just as many of us watched match races in the Southwest during the 1930s and 1940s. Heads would bob up and down to get a glimpse of the horses coming down the lanes. When someone threw an item on the track in front of the horses, the loser had good reason to protest, and undoubtedly many an argument ensued.

The starts were made by the jockeys asking and answering or by a starting judge, who tapped them off if they were closely lapped when they got to the starting line. The tap could be a beat on a drum, a trumpet blast, or a pistol fired into the air. Noise was needed so that the finish judges would be ready, for it was only a matter of a few seconds until the race was over.

Each jockey, of course, tried for the advantage on the start. This was called "jockeying," and the word is widely used today to signify a maneuver for an advantage. A skillful jockey often contributed over half the race, since there was little time to make up for a mistake, especially if the horses were evenly matched. More often than not the horse in the lead at the start maintained his position. Feet, elbows, knees, and the bat or whip were also used to gain the advantage. Jostling and bumping were too often part of the game. Daring and skillful riding as well as a fast horse combined to make the outcome a gamble. A match between two well-known rivals was a picturesque event, and the large crowd that witnessed such a match would talk about it for years.

Occasionally a free spirit would try to run a race a little differently. Perhaps he would want to start the two horses from different ends of the track, with the first to cross the finish line at the middle of the track the winner. Such races were generally started by a pistol shot fired from the finish line. One can suppose that the person who suggested such a race had been outmaneuvered in his last outing or that his horse became nervous and fractious when he knew a race was about to be run. Another version of the match race was to run, say, two hundred yards up the track, turn around, and race back to the start.

Travelers in the southern colonies almost always mentioned the short races. J. F. D. Smyth doubted that any horses in England could run as fast. Thomas Anbury grumbled that if you happened to glance the wrong way you missed the race. A young actor by the name of John Bernard toured the American colonies during the 1700s. He

The ask-and-answer start. As the two horses approached the starting poles, one jockey asked the other if he was ready. If the answer was yes, the race was on. If not, they tried again, each rider seeking the advantage. Print by D'upes Vernet from the Quarter Racing World (now Speed Horse) Museum.

was awed by the quarter racing, vowing that it was the most animated sport he had ever seen. The first one he saw was held in an open field near a tavern. He noted the motley crew that lined the paths; there were Negroes, Dutchmen, Yankee peddlers, farmers, and backwoodsmen. Then the horses arrived, shaggy but frisky as lambs, and were ridden through the crowd.

Mrs. Ann Riston, the English-born wife of a Norfolk merchant, was also impressed by quarter racing. She wrote a rather long poem about the curious ways of the southern colonials, noting that all business came to a standstill when a match race was imminent. There was also Durandoff Dauphine, a Frenchman, who, after seeing a short race, wrote that he doubted that there were better horses in the world than the Virginia sprinters or that any were worse treated. What had aroused his ire was that after a race all that the owner did was unsaddle the horse, give him a little corn (his word for grain), and turn him out.

The more popular race paths were at a crossing of two major roads, or near an important river ford, or just outside a fair-sized town. A tavern was about the first building constructed near a race path—or the track was built near a tavern to start with. Match races were the one sport all pioneers seemed to enjoy, and they could bet and get as excited over a race between two plow horses as they could over one matching two celebrated American racehorses.

Sunday and holiday quarter races were such picturesque affairs that they were written up by many foreign travelers who happened to attend them. John Hervey's descriptions of such races are so good that I have paraphrased them below.

When two well-known quarter horses, each a champion in his own area, were to race, they attracted large crowds. Spectators came from miles around as news of the match reached the outlying districts. The early settlers led a hard and drab life. After several months of clearing, plowing, and planting, they were ready for company and excitement. A big match race was a time for merrymaking, revelry, companionship, and, if the right nag won, wild celebration. If it was rowdy and riotous, so were the times.

Stakes were whatever one person had that seemed of value to another. When money was scarce, produce such as rice, wheat, tobacco, or corn was always acceptable. So were wagons, horses, plows, saddles, bridles, and even the old homestead itself.

At the start and at the finish hawkers set up their booths and sold sundry items, and if no "ordinary," or tavern, was present, a tent bar soon appeared and was, except only for the finish line, the most popular place to be. Itinerant healers and magicians climbed on boxes or wagon beds and called to all to come and watch their feats. Fortune-tellers told, and freaks exhibited their deformities, all trying to make a few pennies off the jovial crowd.

52

The people themselves were colorful, as they packed each side of the track and crowded around the booths and vendors. There would be a group of aristocratic cavaliers, mounted on their blooded horses and accompanied by their richly dressed ladies. Here and there a sporting person might be encountered, no doubt coming back from a fox hunt. Buckskin-clad frontiersmen with their long Kentucky rifles and coonskin caps rubbed elbows with the newly arrived Cockney indentured servant. Maids from a neighboring plantation made eyes at sailors ashore from some brig or merchantman anchored on the James River. Traders from New Amsterdam, militia from Richmond, Cherokees and Choctaws from Carolina or Georgia all mingled in a jigsaw puzzle of colors and noise.

The start of a race often took time. It was supposed to be a simple start, with each horse standing on the line waiting for the word to go. However, the horses, well aware that they were to run and nervous from the crowd and the excitement, reared and plunged more than they stood still. Each jockey also kept his horse out of position until the advantage was in his favor, making the start even more difficult. Generally the horses were faced away from the finish line to keep them quiet, and then at "Go!" wheeled about and took off flying. Sometimes they were both ridden to the start slowly, and if they were closely lapped, neither having too great an advantage, they were "tapped" off, and the race was on. Many other ways of starting were tried, but none were too successful, because each owner and jockey wanted a little advantage. With closely matched horses that little advantage could win the race.

While all of this may seem untidy today, when horses are held in a starting gate, nevertheless, the very uncertainty of the start, with its jockeying for position, added to the excitement of the race. The race itself was over in a few glorious seconds. In a good match the horses ran side by side all the way, jostling, whipping, crowding, and bumping, giving the owners and bettors a chance to rejoice, complain, fight, sue, or just plain go home feeling elated or cheated, depending on whose horse had won.

The starter and the finish judge had to be big, strong, two-fisted and courageous. When the word "Go!" was heard or the drum tapped off the horses, or a pistol shot exploded, it would not be long until the starter and the finish judges found out from the losers what a poor job they had done.

Many times the very conditions of the race made the judges' problems more difficult. Perhaps bets were to be placed at 200, 300, and 400 yards. This meant just that many more judges to argue with. Who would weigh the jockeys if a weight to be carried was specified? If the race was to be run only on a dry track, who would decide whether the track was dry?

And then there were always tricks to watch for—in those days often called "endeavors." An "endeavor" was an attempt to match a fast horse against a horse he could beat easily. Obviously it could not be done if the owner of the slower horse knew whom he was going to be racing against. So any means, fair or foul, were tried to arrange this kind of cinch race—matching sight unseen, camouflaging or changing the looks of a fast horse, or making the last-minute substitution of a fast horse for the one that was originally matched for the race. In match racing one needed to be shrewd to avoid such chicanery. Tales of the various plots, dodges, and subterfuges used in matching a race for the advantage of one side have given to the history of quarter racing a stockpile of legends as absorbing as any in the annals of turf history. Several classical examples of such "endeavors" will be found in the following chapter.[4]

From the 1600s only a few names of quarter race horses have come down to us. One was named Young Fire. He was a gray owned by John Gardner, of Westmoreland, Virginia. In 1693, Gardner offered to race him against the world, the race to be held at Willoughby's Old Field for one thousand pounds of tobacco and twenty shillings in coin. Before long he was challenged by David Sullivant, who borrowed a bay racehorse from one John Baker. Sullivant lost the race, according to the judge, and he was so unhappy with the decision that he sued Gardner in court. But for the suit we would probably have heard nothing about the race. Smoker was another well-known quarter racing horse. He belonged to Joseph Humphries, who loaned him to Captain Rodman Kenner. A race was matched by Kenner against a mare named Folly, owned by Peter Contancean. Smoker was pulled by his jockey and kept from winning, and a great fracas arose. Humphries went to court, and the case was finally carried to the highest court in the colony. While the litigation was going on, Smoker was matched again against a fast horse named Cambell. The race was to be run at Yeocomico for 577 pounds of tobacco a side. Again a donnybrook occurred when the horses approached the finish and Rodham Kenner's brother jumped out on the track toward Cambell, waving his arms and shouting. Cambell shyed, broke stride, and lost the race. Another lawsuit resulted. One more mention of Smoker is found. He won a race in 1695 at Coan, where he defeated John Haines's Prince, and Kenner got a purse of four thousand pounds of tobacco and forty shillings without contest. In yet another court case in the 1600s a jockey was charged with throwing a race because of "too copious indulgence in spiritous liquors" before the start.

FAMOUS "ENDEAVORS"

One of the most famous quarter running mares of the early 1700s was Polly Williams, sired by Mark Anthony. She was a bright sorrel, beautifully formed in front but having a high goose rump and ragged hips.[5] All four legs showed white, and she had a large blaze. She was bred by Peter Williams, of Dinwiddie County, Virginia, out of one of his *Janus mares.

Polly was owned and raced by Randall Davis, who bought her from Peter

Williams as a yearling. She was so successful that soon he was unable to match her, so he took her out of training and used her as a riding horse. Occasionally he lent her to a relative. Once, while on loan, she came into the hands of that shrewd quarter running horseman Henry Delony. As soon as Delony had the horse in his possession, he hurried to Davis and told him that he had a mare that could beat any horse he had or could get, for five hundred pounds of the finest tobacco. Davis immediately took the bait and put up forfeit. The date and place for the race were set, and both men returned home to prepare for it. Davis sent for Polly Williams, and when she did not arrive, went to get her. To his surprise he learned that the man to whom he loaned her no longer had her but had leased her to Henry Delony.

Meanwhile Delony was carefully preparing Polly for the race, for he knew that Davis would have to find another good horse. He guarded her carefully during the day and watered her only at dusk. One night as she put her head down to drink, a rifle shot sounded, and she dropped dead with a ball through her head. Most people believed that the mare had been shot by a Negro slave named Ned owned by Davis. In any event, Delony got his comeuppance, because Davis claimed the forfeit and got it.

Another "endeavor" occurred with a little *Janus colt called Trickem. Trickem was owned by Wyllie Jones, of Quankey Creek, North Carolina. Trickem, a sorrel, weighed 890 pounds in running shape and stood thirteen hands, three and three-quarters inch high. He was best at 200 or 300 yards, although he also won at a full 440 yards. At first Jones ran the colt under his own name, but when he won race after race, matching him became difficult.

Finally a race was agreed to under the following conditions: Jones agreed to run a horse against a well-known racehorse from Virginia named Mud Colt, carrying 165 pounds. Wyllie Jones promised only to produce a horse not over fourteen hands in height, carrying 130 pounds. The match was five hundred pounds sterling a side, and the race was to be run at Tucker's Paths on the second Thursday in May, 1772. The start was to be a "turn and lock," in which the horses would face away from the finish and at the signal turn and start. If they were locked (no daylight showing), the race was on.

On the day of the race Wyllie showed up with a rather small but good-looking horse. Mud Colt, who was larger and more powerful, had the most backers. As the time for the race approached, the judge was called to measure Wyllie's horse to be sure he was fourteen hands or under, according to the race agreement. He was found to be three-fourths of an inch over fourteen hands. Jones ordered the grooms to pare away his hoofs to bring him down to proper height. After they pared away as much as seemed safe, the horse was again measured but still found to be too tall. Jones now appeared to lose his temper at bringing a horse too high, and ordered him pared some more. When blood began to show, a delay occurred. News of the disaster moved

Two sprinters preparing for a match race as in colonial days. In the background can be seen the two paths with poles marking distances and, farther back, the tents erected to sell refreshments and other items to the expected crowd. Steel engraving of Eclipse and Shakespeare, Courtesy of Keeneland Library, Lexington.

swiftly down the track, and everyone dug deeper for money to bet on Mud Colt. The stakes became larger and Mud Colt seemed to have all the advantage.

When the betting eased down, Wyllie Jones asked his trainer if the little horse the groom drove to the baggage wagon might not have tolerable speed. The groom said that he could sure run faster than a horse with no feet. So Jones ordered him unharnessed, and the judges placed him under the standard and pronounced him below the fourteen-hand limit. Once again the betting started on Mud Colt, as word got up the track that Jones would have to run his cart horse.

Because both jockeys felt confident, they started on the first turn and sped up the track. To the dismay of Mud Colt's owners and backers, the cart horse led from the start and won by twenty-seven feet. Under the trace marks and the uncurried coat of the little cart horse was the great Trickem.[6]

Another interesting "endeavor" that involved Trickem is found in the *American*

Turf Register.[7] In the year 1770 a large family named Sharrard lived in Dobbs County, North Carolina. They were industrious and managed to accumulate some property and, with it, influence over their less-wealthy neighbors. They were very fond of horse races and had enough money to buy good horses. They were successful in matches against their neighbors, and began to have confidence in their skill and in their horses. They had great success with their best stallion, Blue Boar (sometimes called Blue Buck). He won so many races in the county that the Sharrards and their neighbors began to think of him as invincible. He had been bred by Wyllie Jones and was by *Janus and out of a mare by *Fearnought.

About this time a new man arrived in town, a gentleman by the name of Henry, of Scots descent. He established a store in Dobbs and was immediately popular. He had a small, handsome saddle horse of *Janus stock, of which he was very proud, and he boasted of his speed. Sharrard thought the Scot an inexperienced young man and figured that he might wind up with the store if he could match a race. He went up to Henry one day riding Blue Boar and began running down Henry's little horse, boasting how easily his horse could outrun the pony. When Henry seemed reluctant, he offered to carry 160 pounds on Blue Boar and to let Henry carry as light a jockey as he could find. On these terms the race was matched. Henry sent for a trainer, who arrived in a few days. Before long the bets were being made, and everything, including the store, was wagered. The day before the race a group of horsemen, friends of Wyllie Jones, came down from Halifax.

To quote directly from the *American Turf Register*:

> On the day of the race all of Dobbs seemed to collect at the paths, confident in the speed of, and willing to back, their favorite, and after their money was exhausted, Negroes, horses and oxen were staked on the race, the gentlemen from Halifax taking all bets offered against the little horse.[8]

Little wonder they were taking all bets. Wyllie Jones had bred both horses and knew their speed. Once the race started, it was soon over, and the little horse won in a manner that made impossible any argument about the finish. The Halifax men loaded their wagons with the goods from the store and with their winnings (and Henry) started back for Halifax. The purpose for which the store had been established was now clear. Henry's little saddle horse was really Wyllie Jones's Trickem.

According to the *American Turf Register*, all the main participants of that "endeavor" had died by 1832 except for Trickem's rider. He was then an old man, but when the race was run, he was so small that he only weighed fifty pounds.

With these words began the story of the celebrated race between Bynum's Big Filly and Paoli:

Some years previous to the War of the Revolution quarter mile racing was the fashionable amusement in the State of North Carolina and the southern part of Virginia. Old Janus stood many years on the Roanoke, propagating a beautiful, hardy, and speedy race of horses; and, as the gentlemen of fortune, in those days, were breeders of fine horses, they encouraged that kind of racing to which their stock was best adapted.[9]

This "endeavor" brought together two of the colonies' best-known quarter horsemen, Henry Delony and Wyllie Jones.

The race was run at Brunswick, Virginia, near the North Carolina border. Colonel Delony met Wyllie Jones one day, apparently by accident, and proposed that they have a match race that the people would remember and a purse to match the importance of the event. Wyllie was agreeable, and they soon came to terms on the conditions. They would run in three months for a minimum of one hundred hogsheads of Petersburg-inspected tobacco. Each horse was to carry 160 pounds, but each man had the privilege of running any horse he wished. Such a match was called a "shake bag," from a cockfighting term meaning the privilege of fighting any fowl, without reference to size.

Wyllie Jones sent his trainer and his horse, Paoli, to the track several days before the race was scheduled, but he did not arrive until the morning of the race. When he got there, his trainer told him that Henry Delony had Bynum's Big Filly there to run. Jones was more than a little upset. He had had an understanding with Big Filly's owner, Jeptha Atherton (who was Turner Bynum's father-in-law), that she would not be used in this race. She had a reputation for being almost unbeatable.

When it came time to get the horses on the track, the trainer and the jockey led out Paoli and walked him up and down the track. Sure enough, Delony's trainer, Old Ned, led out Bynum's Big Filly.

Paoli was a full-bred *Janus and had been bred and raised by Captain Eaton Haynes, of Northhampton, North Carolina. He was tall for a *Janus, a little over fifteen hands, and of uncommon beauty. He had a fine forehand, a round barrel—perhaps a little light overall for a quarter horse—finely developed, and with beautiful, spirited action.

Big Filly was about the same height but much heavier in all her parts, an asset when a heavy weight was to be carried. She was sired by *Janus, and her dam was by *Jolly Roger. She had a wide reputation; some claimed that she had never lost a race. She was bred and owned by Turner Bynum, of Northampton County, North Carolina.

According to the author of the account, Wyllie Jones was a man of high and honorable feelings, and as soon as he recognized Bynum's Big Filly he rode up and down the track looking for her owner. When he found Atherton, he asked why he had let Delony have the filly when they had an agreement that he would not. The owner replied that he had made a previous promise to Delony that he forgot about when he talked to Jones. Also, he explained he had had no chance to inform Jones since Delony had asked for the filly. Jones returned to talk to his trainer and the jockey. His friend Captain Haynes, of North Hampton, Paoli's breeder, agreed to stay at the starting line and keep an eye on the horse and jockey while Jones rode up to the finish line, 440 yards away, to see that all was to his liking at that point. Everything appeared all right to him.

An immense crowd had jammed each side of the track. The fame of the two horses and the reputation of the two gentlemen involved, neither of whom would ever match a race they expected to lose, made it more than just a run-of-the-mill race. That Jones was from North Carolina and Delony from Virginia added to the interest, as did the size of the wager, which now stood at 147,000 pounds of tobacco.

The start was the most critical point of the race. Both sides knew they could not win if they got a bad start. The riders turned once and came to the line, but were not lapped. Again they jockeyed for position and turned at the line, and again they did not start. On the third turn they were off. The narrator says they passed the poles (two stakes on each side of the starting line where they had to be lapped) with the velocity of lightning. He continued: "All was silence; not a man drew his breath; nothing was heard but the hooves of the horses. They passed with the speed of a tempest. It was so close that only those at the finish line had the slightest idea how it came out."[10]

As they passed the finish line, Wyllie Jones saw that his rider had lost a stirrup. He rode down to meet Paoli and his jockey and find out exactly what had happened. The jockey told Jones that his foot was out of the stirrup on purpose. To quote the original teller of the tale: "We made two turns and could not start. I could see that Old Ned did not mean to start fair. The Big Filly was as cool as a cucumber. Paoli was beginning to fret. You know, sir, we had nothing to spare, so I drew one foot, to induce Ned to think I was off guard."[11] By doing this the jockey got about a half a length head at the start. The other jockey thought he was not ready to run because his foot was not in the stirrup.

The judges met, compared notes, and decided that Paoli had won by twenty-three inches.

TWIGG AND PADDY WHACK

The famous series of races between Twigg and Paddy Whack, which began in the 1780s, may well have been the greatest match-up in quarter racing history. Both horses were foaled during the Revolutionary War, when there was very little horse racing, and so both ran as mature horses.

Twigg was bred by John Goode, of Mecklenburg County, Virginia. Goode was never satisfied in just raising racehorses; he wanted to raise the fastest. He also enjoyed racing the horses he raised with his friends and neighboring plantation

59

owners. For this reason he always kept the fastest. One of his friends he especially liked to defeat in a horse race was Henry Delony. It was this rivalry that resulted in the match races between Twigg and Paddy Whack.

Since Delony was more interested in racing than in breeding, he had already campaigned Paddy Whack throughout the South and West, matching all the willing local champions. Paddy was rarely defeated and, when rematched, showed superiority by defeating his rival the second time around. He became so well known that his identity was concealed as much as possible in order to get races. Paddy showed that he was unbeatable any distance from 400 yards to a mile. He could also win as short as 330 yards with most sprinters. John Goode ran Twigg, but almost always on his home track, Nicholson's Race Paths.

It is interesting to read what some of the horsemen living at the time wrote about these two great sprinting champions. Here is what some of those who favored Paddy Whack said:

Jacob Bugg, writing in 1785, said that Paddy Whack was the best racehorse of his day in all Virginia, that he could and did give other horses one hundred feet in a quarter of a mile, and win.

Randall Davis, in 1786, who also watched Paddy run, claimed that he was a superb racer who won large sums of money and beat all the best horses of his day. Patrick N. Edgar quoted Edward Davis as saying in 1790:

> Paddy Whack was a capital racer in Mecklenburg, and adjacent counties in Virginia, also in the states of North and South Carolina, to which places he was frequently carried for express purposes of racing. He was a race horse of the very first class for quarter of a mile, half mile, and mile races. He won immense sums of money, beating all of the best race horses of his day—so that frequently, when taken to strange places, his appearance was altered, in order to procure races to be made upon him, as he was always feared by his competitors, wherever he went or was known.[12]

Followers of Twigg were no less complimentary about their favorite. A doctor named Samuel Hopkins, who lived in Aesculapia, in Mecklenburg County (a settlement which has long since disappeared), wrote about Twigg on June 8, 1788:

> I do hereby certify that Goode's Twigg was one of the swiftest horses, for three hundred yards, in the world. He beat all of the racers this distance, in Virginia and among them the celebrated race horse Paddy Whack. . .and the unconquered mare Polly Williams. . . .[13]

Another observer, writing on May 4, 1791, said that old Twigg was the fastest horse in the world and also the best formed and a capital foal getter. Both Paddy Whack's and Twigg's supporters were legion and vocal.

60

Randall Davis also had certain observations to make about Twigg. He said he was very well acquainted with the horse, which might suggest that he had not only seen the racehorse but also laid a wager on one of his races. Davis claimed that Twigg was a racer of the very first class for three hundred yards to a quarter of a mile but that he could not go a distance. He said that Twigg met every challenger and defeated them all, unless run beyond his regular distance or carrying excessive weight. He put it rather colorfully when he said that Twigg was the fastest nag in the world for three hundred yards, carrying a feather.

Delony finally broached the subject of a match to his friend Goode, probably over a mint julep on the veranda of Goode's lovely plantation home. It was not a question of money or lack of confidence in their horse that made long discussions necessary. It was the conditions of the race that were troublesome, problems of when, where, how far, how much weight, track condition, who would start, who would judge the finish, and so on. Several months passed before the match was set and Goode had his way: catch weights, three hundred yards. In the matter of the wager to be put up by each horseman, cold cash was a scarce item in the newly formed state, but both had a good crop of tobacco, so the race was to be run for 30,000 pounds of prime Virginia tobacco.

Twigg won by a nose. Delony was not satisfied, so they matched two more races, one for the same distance, one for about one hundred yards farther. Twigg won both of these races and 60,000 pounds of tobacco, plus some cash side bets. There is no way to determine how much money and tobacco changed hands among the throng of people who came to the Nicholson Race Paths to see the races, but certainly it was a bundle.

Delony took Paddy Whack home after those losses to brood and nurse his pride. He was still not a believer, and he had won so many races with his horse that he felt there must be a reason for his losses. He and his trainer talked it over. They could probably think of many reasons for each loss, such as the jockey not following instructions, the track being cupped badly, Paddy not working well the day before the race, and so on.

Edgar said that Twigg's real speed was unknown to his competitors. This probably means that the horse only ran fast enough to win, and the jockey did not try to open up daylight. John Goode was sure that for three or four hundred yards Twigg was the strongest and swiftest horse in the world. This probably points up the difference in the two owners. Delony felt that he had the fastest quarter horse in the world. Goode knew that he had the fastest quarter horse in the world for three or four hundred yards. Quarter horse races are commonly run from two hundred to six hundred yards, sometimes a little more, sometimes a little less. Goode would not match his horse over a quarter. Delony and Paddy Whack had had success at all distances, but then they had not tied into Twigg before.

It was now well into the 1780s, and races for both Twigg and Paddy Whack were few and far between. In fact, since 1783, only two horses had dared challenge Goode and Twigg. One was Paddy Whack, and the other was Polly Williams. This Polly Williams, listed by Bruce,[14] is not the same Polly Williams that was borrowed by Henry Delony and discussed at the beginning of the chapter.

Polly had slowly built up her reputation as the fastest mare in the new states. Some believed that there never had been a faster mare. She was foaled in 1780 and had been sired by Flag of Truce by Gold Finder. Gold Finder's dam was by that great sire of quarter horses Spadille. Polly's dam had been sired by no other than Twigg himself, so she was raced against her grandsire. Polly ran at Twigg nine times and only beat him once. Her owner lost 200,000 pounds of tobacco in the races he ran against Twigg.

Several of Delony's friends still believed that Paddy was faster than Twigg and offered to put up the money to run him again. A rematch was arranged to be run in 1786 at Nicholson's Race Paths. Not all of the conditions have come down to us, but the race was to be run for four hundred yards carrying 108 pounds, each side putting up 40,000 pounds of tobacco, winner take all, the race to be run rain or shine.

Twigg won this race by ten feet.

What happened next just goes to show that, if you can't win under one set of conditions, change the conditions to your liking. Goode by this time had won a fabulous amount of money running against Paddy Whack, and he agreed to conditions that he must have known did not favor his horse. Whether he did not mind losing or whether he thought Twigg could win anyway we do not know. We do know that the last race was matched for a full quarter of a mile, Twigg to carry 128 pounds and Paddy Whack 118. When the horses were tapped off, Twigg was in the lead, and he kept his distance for the first 350 yards. At the 375-yard marker, Paddy Whack began to pull up on Twigg. Carrying 20 pounds of lead was just too much, and the distance was too great. Twigg lost by eighteen inches. However, he had defeated Paddy Whack every time but once and then lost only because he was matched too far and asked to carry extra weight.[15]

Strangely, not much was wagered on this last race. Those in the crowd who favored Paddy Whack had gained respect for the great horse Twigg.

SPRINTERS OF THE REVOLUTIONARY PERIOD

The advent of the Revolutionary War pretty well put a stop to horse breeding and to horse racing for the duration. This was especially true along the East Coast and in the other areas that heard the march of soldiers. Unfortunately the better breeding areas seemed to be those most exposed to the effects of the war. Many records were destroyed during the war years; others simply were not kept up during that time.

Besides its effect on records, the war caused the loss of some of the better racing stock. A few examples are of interest.

Romulus, by *Silver-Eye, was an outstanding colt, foaled a year or two before the war. He was owned by two men, named Williams and Darden, both of whom lived in Mecklenburg County, Virginia. The army requisitioned many horses, and he was one of the first taken. He died during the war and so contributed nothing to his breed.[16]

Fitz Eclipse is another example of the war's effect on breeding stallions. The pedigree of his dam, Logania, could never be proved because of the war. It seems that her dam was sent to be bred to Hart's Old Medley, but the war broke out before she could be returned home, and in the confusion her connection with Medley could not be verified. Logania was later owned by John Randolf of Roanoke. The old mare died foaling Logani, who was then raised by hand.[17]

Sweeping Tail was another victim of the war. During her racing career she had the reputation of being the swiftest mare in the world. She had been bred by Joseph John Alston at his great breeding establishment in Halifax County, North Carolina. She was a full sister of Broomtail. Both were by *Janus and out of Poll Pitcher, who was also by *Janus.

Sweeping Tail was captured during the war, at the Battle of Briery Creek, in Georgia. Her owner, who was captured with her, decided that he must somehow save the mare. He offered some gold hidden in his saddlebags to anyone who would take her out of the British camp. A man volunteered and rode her unscathed through the lines, although many shots were fired. Unfortunately the man did not know the country and got lost in a swamp, where he was recaptured by the British and brought back to camp. Lord Cornwallis himself then used the mare as his personal mount. After her recapture she was triumphantly paraded through the town of Halifax, North Carolina, with a band marching and playing to honor her capture.[18]

Some horses were deliberately drowned by the British. That was the fate of two of the better quarter running stallions and of the Celebrated and Famous American Quarter Running Mare Nancy Wake, of Wake County, North Carolina. Sired by John Goode's Babram, who was by *Janus, she had a wide reputation as a mare almost impossible to beat in a match race. The stallions drowned were Little Bacchus and Red Bacchus, both of whom were by Old Bacchus by Babram by *Janus. They were owned by Colonel John Dickinson, who was actively engaged in the rebellion during the prewar years and fought in the Revolution. All three horses were taken from Dickinson and drowned in the York River in Virginia.

Black-and-All-Black (Skipwith's) had a most interesting wartime history. His story was told to Edgar by Levi Rochelle, who said, "I am very well acquainted with every circumstance relative thereto." His statement was written in Southhampton County, Virginia, in August, 1821.[19] It seems that Sir Peyton Skipwith, Baronet, of

Prestwood, Mecklenburg, Virginia, raised Black-and-All-Black and sold him to Tucker and Burge for 500,000 pounds of tobacco. The price would indicate that he had more than average speed. He had been sired by *Othello, and his dam was by *Regulus.[20] During the war the horse was taken by the British army under the command of Colonel Tarlton, only to be captured by the French army under the command of Lafayette. He was then, through some chicanery, taken from Lafayette by William Jones, of Prince George County, Virginia, who took him back to his former owner. They started out for South Carolina but tied him carelessly. The knot slipped, and he pulled back and choked to death.

Many horses were taken to safer quarters for protection during the war years. For example in 1779, John Tayloe III sent *Selim, then nineteen years old, to stay with David Jones, of Amelia, in a remote section of the Southside, to get him out of the path of the Revolution.

*Flimnap was another stallion who was moved about by the war. He was owned by several breeders, and in 1780 he was in the possession of a Mr. Fenwick, who had him at John's Island. That year he was sold to Isaac Harleston, of Silk Hope, not far from Charleston. As the war came closer, Harleston decided that he should do something with his valuable stallion. He was a well-known Patriot and could expect little sympathy if the British took over his plantation. Harleston also had reason to believe that the British officer Tarleton had decided to try to capture the stallion, because several times British raiding parties had come to the plantation. Each time the faithful Negro slaves had led *Flimnap into the nearby swamps to hide him. On one raid a stable boy was offered a large sum of money if he would tell *Flimnap's whereabouts, but he refused. He was then told that he would be hanged if he did not tell, but again he refused. Seeing that they were not getting anywhere with the servant, they took him out and hanged him to a nearby tree. After they rode off, the boy was immediately cut down and recovered.

With all of this going on, Major Harleston decided that he had better move *Flimnap. He had him led to the Quankey Creek plantation of his friend Wyllie Jones, of Halifax County, North Carolina. Jones was happy to have the stallion and bred some of his mares to him. Young Flimnap and Betsy Baker were two of the offspring produced while *Flimnap was with Jones. When the war ended, *Flimnap returned to Harleston's, where he lived out his life, dying in 1794 at the age of twenty-six.

CHAPTER FOUR

Colonial Breeders

JOHN C. GOODE

THERE WERE MANY fine quarter horse breeders before, during, and right after the Revolutionary War who were influential in the development of the quarter horse. Some raised both long and short horses. Few would argue with the statement that John C. Goode was the greatest of the early breeders of the quarter running horse. A prosperous, sports-loving Southside planter, Goode found his greatest happiness in his family and in his quarter horses; little else seemed important to him. He was born in 1725 and died in 1783. He spent most of his life on his farm at Cox's Creek, in Mecklenburg County, Virginia. He was the grandsom of an immigrant from Barbados, one of the first settlers near the falls of the James River, which marked the limit at which ocean sailing ships could go upriver. John was a rather large slaveholder and enjoyed the best that wealth could bring.

He had already built a reputation as a breeder of quarter running horses by the time the country entered the Revolutionary War. In addition to breeding Twigg, who was foaled in 1778, and standing *Janus, whom he bought in 1774, he was the owner and breeder of Babram, Ariel, Brimmer, Dreadnot, Wilkes, perhaps Paddy Whack, Puckett's Switch, the Pumpkin Filly, Sweet Mary, Smiling Poll, and Poll Smiling, to name just a few. He also used and stood St. George for John Hoomes and *Precipitate for William Lightfoot.

There is an interesting story about why the Goodes did not stand *Precipitate very long. *Precipitate was a large, well-formed chestnut who had been bred by Lord Egremont in England. He had been foaled in 1787 and soon thereafter sold to William Lightfoot and brought over from England. He traced to King Herod and to Matchem. The *General Stud Book of England* stated that *Precipitate died before reaching America. This statement confused many racehorse breeders who had his blood in their animals. However, careful search of contemporary newspapers showed that he did stand in America for three years beginning in 1804. This brings us up to Edgar's explanation of his death. He wrote that ''*Precipitate covered a mare, got her with foal, and dropped off from her dead, at the residence of Capt. John C. Goode, of Mecklenburg Co., Va.''[1]

*Precipitate, foaled in 1778 and imported in 1804. The Goodes stood him for William Lightfoot. Many early-day quarter running horses carried his blood. From Fairfax Harrison, *Early American Turf Stock*.

John Goode's oldest son, John Goode II, was also interested in horses and imported many from England. While John, Sr., raced most of his quarter horses himself, he would on occasion let friends have some of his horses to run. As mentioned earlier, two of his best friends, and greatest competitors on the quarter paths, were Wyllie Jones and Henry Delony.[2]

WYLLIE JONES

Wyllie Jones was famous in more areas than quarter racing. He was one of the leading revolutionary leaders from the South. His great-grandfather, Robin Jones, Sr., immigrated to Virginia from Wales in the middle of the seventeenth century. His father, Robin Jones III, went to North Carolina as an attorney and agent for Lord Granville.

Wyllie's mother, Sarah, was the daughter of Robert Cobb of Virginia, a member of another well-known family. Wyllie went to England to complete his studies at Eton. After college he toured Europe, returning to the colonies in the early 1760s.

Wyllie Jones had enormous energies and greatly enjoyed social life, hunting, racing, card playing, cock fighitng, and the other activities of the time. His father left him a large estate, and money was never a problem. He built one of the finest mansions in Halifax, known as "the Grove." There he and his wife entertained lavishly, and his close friend Thomas Jefferson was often present. Allen Jones Davie was his nephew, and it is in Davie's letters to Skinner, editor of *American Turf Register*, that we find the best accounts of Wyllie Jones's racing activities.[3]

It was at Jones's plantation on Quankey Creek that Jones bred Spadille, who was foaled in 1762. Spadille was the son of two of the most famous horses of that day, *Janus and *Selima. Jones also bred Blue Boar by *Janus, who was foaled in 1774. Other well-known running horses that Jones owned or bred were *Jolly Roger, Sweeping Tail, Trickem, Matchless, and Poll Smiling. He also stood *Flimnap for a while.

Wyllie Jones was more than a horse breeder. He was a well-known Patriot, a gentleman planter, a large landholder, and a member of the Royal Heart Masonic Lodge of Halifax, and he was respected throughout the state. He was a benefactor of the needy. One day when Wyllie was in Halifax, he observed a young man who appeared to be lonely and despondent, aimlessly walking around town. Jones is quoted as inquiring:[4]

> "What is your name?"
> "I have none."
> "Where is your home?"
> "I have none."

The young man, whose Christian names were John Paul, was an officer aboard the good ship *Betsy*. He had killed a mutinous sailor in self-defense in Tabago, and serious problems arose for him. Wyllie Jones took John Paul home with him, and he lived with the Jones family for over a year. On leaving he asked to be allowed to add Jones to his name. He said that he would wear it with honor, which he did, as Captain John Paul Jones.

J. J. ALSTON

A good friend of Goode and Jones was Joseph John Alston. He also lived in Halifax County, North Carolina. The Alstons were early settlers in America, and by the time of the Revolution the family fairly bristled with statesmen and military figures. The first John Alston, an immigrant, spelled his name with one *l*. He prospered in the New World, raised a family, and acquired large holdings in Virginia, and the Carolinas. The Alstons were planters. By the end of the third generation they were spelling their name with two ls: *Allston*. Late in the eighteenth century one branch, reverting to the earlier spelling, started a second branch of the family.

Joseph Alston was born in the 1770s, and died fairly young, in 1816. He was a lawyer, planter, and horseman, the son of Colonel William Alston (1756–1839) and Mary Ash Alston. Joseph's best horses were sired by *Janus. Two of his outstanding stallions were Brinkley's Peacock and Spider, full brothers, both sired by *Janus. He also bred the great Nancy Willis. She too, was by *Janus and was out of a mare by Morton's* Traveler. Another famous mare he bred was Poll Pitcher, by *Janus. He bred her back to *Janus twice and got Broomtail and then Sweeping Tail. All the above were outstanding sprinters.

Another member of the family was Gideon Allston, also of North Carolina. He was active during the late 1700s, when he bred Budd, a bay stallion foaled in 1789, and Woodpecker, foaled in 1796. Woodpecker was by Ashe's Roebuck, and Budd was by Twigg.

THE TAYLOES

William Tayloe settled on the north shore of the Rappahannock River in northern Virginia, and there his son, John Tayloe was born in 1687. John was a hard worker and increased the size of the family's holdings as well as its wealth. He died in 1747, and by that time the fame of Mount Airy, his plantation, was widespread. His son, John Tayloe II, was born in 1721 and died in 1779. He is considered by many to be the outstanding racehorse breeder before the Revolution, just as his son, John Tayloe III (1771–1828), became afterward. John Goode was their only equal.

John Tayloe II was educated in England and never knew anything but wealth. When his father died, he became the sole owner of Mount Airy, when he was twenty-six. One of his first moves was to erect a magnificent mansion in the style of the English homes he had known while in college. It still stands today, its three large homes grouped around a court, connected by a curved, covered walkway. At the rear of the house the slope was terraced five times and beautifully manicured with shrubs and flowers, enhancing the scene in the valley below, including the Rappahannock River and the little town of Tappahannock (known in the early days as Hobbs-His-Hole). There a racetrack and clubhouse had been in existence for many years.

The house at Mount Airy was built of Virginia sandstone with walls three feet thick. In the 1840s a fire swept through the home and destroyed much of the

John Tayloe II, who, with his friends the Hoomeses and the Goodes, were primarily responsible for the early development of the quarter running horse. From Fairfax Harrison, *The Background of the American Stud Book*, 1933.

Mount Airy, the home of John Tayloe II. Built in the English manner, it consisted of three large houses connected by curved covered walkways. At the rear the land was terraced, overlooking the Rappahannock River valley and the little town then known as Hobbs-His-Hole. The walls of the buildings were made of Virginia sandstone and were three feet thick. From William H. Robertson, *The History of Thoroughbred Racing in America*, 1964.

woodwork but did no damage to the walls. It was restored, and, since most of the furnishings (draperies, pictures, furniture, bric-a-brac, crystal, and silver) were saved, it was possible to rebuild almost the identical home. Mount Airy is one of the few colonial estates of the Tidewater region that remains in the family that built it.

The Tayloes also kept a home in Washington, D.C. When the British burned all the public buildings and the White House during the War of 1812, the President and Dolly Madison moved into the Tayloe's famous octagonal mansion and were surrounded by more luxury than the White House could provide.

John Tayloe II married Rebecca, the daughter of the Honorable George Plater and the sister of Governor Plater of Maryland. Nothing was too luxurious for him and his bride. John maintained his own musicians and had his own private deer park full of stags and does, in imitation of his friends in England. John Tayloe II was also deeply interested in all things connected with racing, and he spent much of his time in England at racetracks and with racing families. After his father's death he began building his own stable.

He bred and raised his main stallion, Yorick, a rich sorrel, fifteen hands, two inches high, who was sired by Morton's *Traveler and out of *Betty Blazella. Yorick must have been a full brother of Colonel Byrd's Tryall.[5] *Betty Blazella was sired by *Blaze and out of *Jenny Cameron. Yorick swept all races through 1764 and 1765. In 1766 he was put to stud. When he received a challenge to a race in Maryland, Tayloe sent Yorick. *Selim had challenged the world, and Tayloe thought that was taking in too much territory. Yorick lost, but since he had not been in training, the loss might have been expected. When John Tayloe II died during the Revolutionary War, Yorick was nineteen.

John Tayloe III was almost as well known a breeder as his father. Like his father, he was educated at Eton and Cambridge, and he began serious horse breeding on his return to America. From that time until his retirement in 1816 he kept records and was considered one of the nation's top breeders. In 1828, two years after his death, his son, Benjamin Ogle Tayloe (1796–1868), published in the March, 1830, issue of the *American Turf Register* his father's breeding records.

The records made clear why John Tayloe III was so successful. He bred on a large scale because he wanted to win with his own horses. He bought many horses whose possibilities impressed him. He was also willing to sell anything in his stable, if he got the right price. His two greatest racers were Bellair and the chestnut gelding Nantoaka. Bellaire had been bred by his father, by Medley out of a Yorick mare. John Tayloe III's daughter married one of the Lloyds of Maryland. As a wedding gift the proud father gave his new son-in-law a fine young colt out of *Jenny Cameron and sired by his favorite stallion Morton's *Traveler. Later this colt became known as Lloyd's Traveler.

JOHN HOOMES

It is difficult to talk about the Tayloes without mentioning John Hoomes. As Hervey said, until the death of Colonel Hoomes in 1805, John Tayloe III was his partner in many breeding and racing ventures, and it seems possible that Tayloe's retirement in 1816 came as a result of the death of his partner. Hoomes's racing was never as successful as Tayloe's, but he was probably the better horseman of the two. They lived during the transition period, when the new nation's horse people along the Atlantic were turning from quarter horses to long horses. At the time both sprinters and stayers were considered clean-bred. The Tayloes' influence was more on the modern Thoroughbred, while Goode's was more on the short horse. Had Hoomes imported

71

only *Diomed and Tayloe only *Castianira, they would have gained immortality in the horse world by making Sir Archy possible. Another of their mutual horse friends was Colonel Archibald Randolph, who, with John Tayloe, jointly owned Sir Archy.

Hoomes imported many fine horses. Between 1792 and 1805 he selected some thirty stallions and mares to import into America. Tayloe, in about the same period, imported seven stallions and eight mares. Both men died rather prematurely, Hoomes at fifty and Tayloe at fifty-four. Tayloe's son Benjamin raced and bred horses, but never with the success of his father and grandfather. His writings give us the best picture of his father and Hoomes as men and breeders.

John Hoomes was born in 1755 and died in 1805. His family had moved to the Tidewater region in the 1600s. They settled and built up their holdings on the upper waters of the Marraponi, a northern branch of the York River, while the region was still a frontier. Their homestead was built on land patented in 1670, along the main trail between the falls of the Rappahannock and the James rivers, called Bowling Green. The trail was to become, in later years, the main-traveled road between Richmond and Fredricksburg, and the Court House of Carolina was eventually located near the family estate. Hoomes's father, George, was an important man in that area and served the government in several capacities. He died in 1764. John was an assemblyman from his district from 1791 until 1803. He also had the stage contract from 1784 until his death, running coaches on the busy road between Alexandria and Richmond.

Hoomes's first important contact with Tayloe came when he bought the filly Sally Wright from Tayloe some years before the Revolution. Sally was sired by Yorick and became the mainstay of his stud. Hoomes was only twenty when he began to breed commercially. Among his outstanding horses were *Messenger and the important mare Miss Woodford, by Bolton.

There seems to be some confusion over *Messenger. Probably he was a gray horse, foaled in 1780 and imported into the United States in 1788.[6] Of real interest to the quarter horse breeder is a description of *Messenger found in Herbert. The description is given by David W. Jones in a letter dated 1856:

> He not only produced race-horses of the first order, both long and short distances, but as roadsters his get were unequaled. Well do I remember him standing at the stable of Townsend Cock, in this country. His large bony head, rather short straight neck, with windpipe and nostrils nearly twice as large as ordinary, with his low withers, and shoulders somewhat upright, but deep, close, and strong. But behind these lay the perfection and power of the machine. His barrel, loin, hips, and quarters were incomparably superior to all others. His hocks and knees were unusually large, below them his limbs were of medium size.[7]

*Messenger sounds more like a short horse than a long horse.

*Messenger, who produced racehorses of the first order that were able to run both short and long distances. He was imported for and owned by John Hoomes.

When racing was started again after the Revolution, Hoomes had horses ready, and he became an acknowledged leader. He arranged a business contact with James Westerby, of London, and over a span of thirty years, he imported nineteen stallions and thirteen mares. He both bred and sold the imports. Unlike Tayloe, he needed to show a profit in his horse activities. He died the same year his last import, the well-known stallion *Buzzard, arrived.

Colonel Hoomes organized the Virginia Jockey Club in 1788 and kept it humming while he was alive. Passing Bowling Green today, one would hardly guess that it was once a busy breeding and racing center. Hoomes's old home is still standing, set in a terraced garden enclosing a circular drive, beautifully landscaped with bushes and trees.

One of the highlights of Hoomes's life came when he imported *Diomed into Virginia. Hervey said that, after seeing *Diomed, Hoomes wrote his friend and partner John Tayloe III, saying that he wished Tayloe could see *Diomed, for he was the finest horse he had ever seen, as handsome as Cormorant, if not more so, and a great deal larger. Other horsemen must have agreed, because mares came to *Diomed in great numbers. His first stud advertisment appeared in the *Virginia Herald* of Fredricksburg on June 16, 1800. The card, signed by both Hoomes and Tayloe, and dated June 6 at Bowling Green, said that, owing to an injury to Cormorant, *Diomed would fill out that horse's season.

There is a very interesting story about Hoomes's death that has become almost a legend in the family. The racetrack at Bowling Green was near his home. He could, in fact, sit on his porch or in his dining room and look out over the course. While eating one day, with the family around him, he said that he had heard the thunder of hoofs on the racetrack each time a member of the family died. According to the legend, the day he died he was seated at the dining-room table when he thought he heard the sudden drum of hoofbeats on the track. He jumped up and went to the window, but no horses were out on the track; it was deserted. "Another death," he said aloud. Before the sun rose the next day, he, himself, was dead.

SAMUEL OGLE

Perhaps a word or two about Samuel Ogle is in order, since it was from his family that Benjamin Ogle Tayloe was named. Ogle was the foremost Maryland racehorse breeder, and though he was primarily interested in long races, he was not above matching a short one now and then. He was born in Northumberland, England, in 1694 and died in Annapolis, Maryland, in 1752. His family had been prominent in England since the twelfth century. He was appointed governor of Maryland by Lord Baltimore in 1731, and remained in office for a little over ten years. He came to America as a bachelor of thirty-seven and did not marry for ten more years. He selected one of the most beautiful young ladies in the colonies to be his wife, the eighteen-year-old Ann Tasker, the daughter of Benjamin Tasker, a prominent horseman and country gentleman.

Ogle went to England in 1742 and stayed for five years. When he was reappointed governor, he returned to the colonies in March, 1747. He brought with him two horses, a stallion named *Spark and a filly named *Queen Mab. *Spark had been given to Ogle by Lord Baltimore, who had received him as a present from Frederick, Prince of Wales. Both became foundation animals for the Maryland racehorse.

While in England, Ogle had asked his father-in-law, Benjamin Tasker, Sr., to build him a suitable home on his estate, Bellair, where he and his wife would live when they returned from England. The estate was fifteen miles west of Annapolis on the Bladensburg road, and consisted of 2,177 acres. The Georgian-style brick mansion

Benjamin Ogle Tayloe (1796–1868), the son of John Tayloe III. It is through his writings that we have learned much about the horse-breeding operations of the Tayloes and the Hoomeses. From Harrison, *The Background of the American Stud Book*.

had two stories, plus attic. It is still an imposing structure, perfectly preserved today, inside and out.

While Ogle was primarily a long horse breeder, his contacts with Tasker, Hoomes, and Tayloe were influential, and appreciated by them. Colonel Tayloe III named one of his greatest horses, Bellair, after Ogle's home, and his favorite son, Benjamin Ogle Tayloe, after his friend.

PART II
FORKS IN THE ROAD
1780–1830

There is a district in East Tennessee, in which when a man breeds a good colt, the way he is inclined to "roll and rumble" is excruciating. It is rather cautionary too, to hear a Hinds County Mississippian "cavort" when he gets hold of a "singed cat" in the shape of a quarter horse, but to see a race of tackies "rise and shine" in all this glory, you must just drop into Arkansas. He can beat "anything alive and above ground" between June and Jericho, any how you can fix it.
—*American Turf Register and Sporting Magazine*, January–February, 1839.

QUARTER RUNNING HORSE SIRES

1780–1830

Superior horses in capital letters.

Alasco
BERTRAND
Black Snake
Black Whip
BOANERGES
Buck Sorrel
Budd
BUZZARD
CELER
CHEROKEE
Contention
Dappled John
Driver
General Jackson
Gohanna
Jackson
KENTUCKY WHIP
King Tammany
KOSCIUSKO
Lamplighter

Larry O'Gaff
Liberty
Lightfoot
Lighthouse
LIGHTNING
Limber John
Linwood
Long Measure
Long Waist
Lord Canning
Matchless
MEDOC
Morocco
MUCKLE JOHN
PACOLET
PRINTER
Printer Tom
QUICKSILVER
RATTLER

Red, Little
Rifleman
Roanoke
Rob Roy
Silver Heels
SIR ARCHY
Sir Solomon
STOCKHOLDER
Superior
Telegraph
Tennessee Oscar
TIGER
TIMOLEON
Treasurer
Truxton
Veto
Van Tromp
Virginian
WHIP

CHAPTER FIVE

New Paths, New States

THE COMING of the nineteenth century saw great changes both in the life patterns of the people of the United States and in their horses. The sprinters and the stayers, like the Americans and the English, began to follow separate paths, although these paths would often cross.

The independence of the two horse types began before the Revolutionary War, but it became much more pronounced afterward. It was hurried by the westward migration through the Appalachian Mountains. No doubt the absence of fresh English blood farther west increased the division between the quarter running horse and the distance horse, because breeding on the frontier and in the newly formed territories or states was much more informal than that practiced in the Tidewater region. The founding fathers of the breed, the country gentlemen exemplified by the Goodes, the Tayloes, Jones, and Hoomes, were fading away as the major source of sprinters. Too many great stallions like Sir Archy, Whip, Printer, and Cherokee were getting the job done, and their offspring, such as Bertrand, Timoleon, Lightning and Tiger, were moving west and spreading their prepotent seed in the new territories. The old-line breeders no longer had a monopoly on the best producing blood. The families moving west needed a utility horse, one that could be ridden, driven, and worked, but was still good enough for a race or two on the weekend. The running quarter horse fulfilled this need.

The movement of peoples west (and north and south) began in the earliest days, but the time we are interested in begins in 1780, with the first movement south from Virginia into North Carolina. Soon stallions such as Bacchus, Blue Boar, *Jolly Roger, and *Ranger were helping upgrade the local horses in the Carolinas. One of the premier breeders was the Alston family, with the Eatons coming in a close second. Before many years had passed, North Carolina replaced Virginia as the most prolific source of sprinting blood. Many of the best breeding stallions were based in that state. South Carolina then became interested in short racing, and by the 1830's the state had Kosciusko, Andrew Jackson and Haywards Cherokee, all truly superior sires of sprinters.

Kentucky and Tennessee were the next to find themselves among the leaders in the production of sprinting quarter horses. Most of their animals came from North

Carolina, although some came directly from Virginia. Outstanding stallions in early-day Kentucky were Medoc, Van Tromp, Tiger, and Little Quicksilver. In Tennessee's Sullivan County, bordering Virginia, some short horse blood arrived as early as the late 1700s. Examples were Brilliant by Peacock, Brimmer by Clubfoot, Leadall by Celer, and Buie by *Janus. At one time a person could obtain Brilliant's service for thirty shillings and a bushel of oats. Brimmer stood at William Cocke's for six dollars the leap. Leadall was available at William Sheldons on German Creek for the same figure. Lewis' Comet, by Old *Janus, stood near Nashville in 1792, and Cross's Jupiter was also near Nashville at the same time. Later stallions of the caliber of Rifleman, Tom Fletcher, Gray Rebel, Pacolet, Timoleon, Rattler, and Stockholder were available to the quarter horse breeder of that state.

Kentucky had some race meets as early as 1788, and no doubt many match races were run over impromptu paths before then. Both Kentucky and Tennessee had Chickasaw and Cherokee Indian pony blood in their mares. Kentucky breeders, such as Patrick Henry, got some Spanish blood from across the Mississippi, but not much, for there were wide forests and a broad river to cross to reach the prairie Indians. The breeding centers that developed around Nashville and Lexington remained the source of the best blood for many decades. It was primarily the stock from these centers that provided the foundation for the horse industry of the new western states. While a few horses arrived earlier, most of the sprinters moved into Kentucky and Tennessee during the decade just before the Revolutionary War.

There was little hard money (or paper money for that matter) in those early times. As a result almost anything was taken in way of trade for a stallion's service. An excellent example is found in the advertisement, offering the service of Young McKinney Roan, the grandson of Celer. He was standing for service at the Tennessee farm of William Roberts in 1807. The stallion's fee was payable in produce with the following specific suggestions: cotton, pork, rye, wheat, oats, whisky, or brandy.

As the horses moved west with their owners, perhaps the very best running stallions and mares were led, but most immigrants rode, and their goods were packed on the backs of their quarter horses. These horses were, for lack of a better term, grade quarter horses. Many had well-known sires, but most of the dams were local mares. The better ones often carried Indian pony blood. When the mares and their offspring were bred, they went to the best available stallions and produced many a top-flight sprinter, such as the Iowa Cherokee, foaled in 1847. The various Printers, Tigers, and Brimmers in Illinois, Ohio, Missouri, and Arkansas, are examples of these grade mares' offspring crossed on good sires. More often than not the resulting colts were named after their sires. That explains why there were so many Brimmers, Printers, Whips, and Tigers.

A rather good description of how a stallion was advertised, and the conditions attending his services in the new western states, appeared in the *Kentucky Gazette* of February 2, 1804:

Bacchus

Will stand the ensuing season at my stable in Burbon County, within one mile of Paris and will cover mares on the following terms, towit, $6 cash for the season, payable on the 15th day of December next, or it may be discharged by paying $5 when the mare is covered, $5 ½ any time of March and end of the 15th of July, when the season will be discharged by paying of $8 in pork, if paid between the 10th and 15th of October next on foot, hogs must be large and in good order. $8 in beef cattle, whiskey, salt, iron, country made linen or linsey, payable on the 15th of December next at the current selling price. $3 cash when the mare is covered by a single leap. $12 cash, or $16 in the above trade to insure a mare in foal. Also the trade is to be delivered at my house. A promissory note will be required at the same. Any gentleman putting 4 mares will have a reduction made of ¼. I have excellent pasture gratis for mares from a distance, and if required, will be grain fed for 3 shillings per week, all possible care and attention will be paid, but will not be responsible for accidents.

Bacchus was got by the noted Old'Celer, his dam was got by Col. Paul Carrington's Bacchus, a noted running horse. His Bacchus was got by Old Apollo, who came out of Huntleys double Janus mare, called Huntley's race mare, and came out of the Thoroughbred mare now in the possession of Benjamine Bedford, who raised Bacchus, and is so well known that I think it is needless to say any more. Bacchus has proved himself to be an extraordinary refined foal getter, to which the annexed certificates will abundantly testify.

The certificates mentioned in the advertisements were statements of eight or nine prominent horsemen of the area confirming that they knew the horse Bacchus and that his colts were excellent.

Will Williams, of Poplar Grove, Tennessee, in a letter to William Henry Herbert dated March 20, 1856, said:

The first settlers brought here some of their best stock from Virginia and the Carolinas; and McClin had, as I am informed, some Mexican mares, of the Spanish or Barb breed.

The early stallions, here, of the Janus family, were—Jupiter, said to be a son,—Cross's; Comet, Lewis's, son of Harry Hill's Jolly Roger cross; Sterne, Blakemore's; and Bowie's horse, who took his owner's name pronounced Biu-ey. His colts are said to have been unequalled as quarter horses.[1]

In another letter dated March 25, Williams listed the obituaries of some of the better stallions in North Carolina, Kentucky, and Tennessee: Celer, 1802 (North Carolina); Mark Anthony, 1793 (North Carolina); Gray Diomed, 1906 (North Carolina); Sir Archy, 1832 (North Carolina); Spread Eagle, 1805 (Kentucky); Eagle,

1827 (Kentucky); *Buzzard, 1811 (Kentucky); Dragon, 1812 (Tennessee); Pacolet, 1825 (Tennessee); and Constitution, 1827 (Tennessee).

By the close of the 1830s the dominance of the eastern breeders had been broken, and different sires were creating whole new families of sprinters—families that owed their excellence to a large extent to the get of two stallions: Sir Archy and Kentucky Whip, both foaled in the state of Virginia.

Other sires came close to the brilliance of these two, but they were not the equals of Sir Archy or Kentucky Whip in the prepotency of their offspring. The sons of these two, such as Bertrand, Timoleon, Cherokee, Sir Solomon, Contention, Copperbottom, Short Whip, Tiger, Paragon, and Whipstar, cannot be matched by any other two sprinting sires of the period. It is not particularly surprising to find that Sir Archy and Kentucky Whip were related, granted a bit remotely. The English stallion King Herod was Sir Archy's great grandsire and Whip's dam's grandsire. Both Sir Archy and Whip were foaled in the same year.

CHAPTER SIX

Post-Revolution Short Racing

As THE QUARTER RUNNING HORSE moved west after the Revolutionary War, races tended to be less organized and more spur-of-the-moment things. In Virginia and the Carolinas before the war, there were annual meets and famous tracks, such as Nicholson's. When the war came, most racing ceased. In fact, the Continental Congress adopted a rather remarkable resolution, advising the people of the colonies to give up horse racing, cock fighting, and all other forms of gambling for the duration of the emergency. Most colonists obeyed, but after the war ended, the edict was discarded, and the nation continued its growth—and its diversions.

In the early years on the frontier there were the usual match races that always seemed to take place when two men with pride and fast horses met. As more settlers came in, and as farms, plantations, towns, and cities sprang up, once again purse races and permanent tracks began to appear. As the population in Tennessee, Ohio, Illinois, and Missouri increased, county fairs became popular. It was during these fairs that the first annual meets with straightaway paths occurred. But as more money became available, circular half-mile tracks were built. These were known as "bull rings," because the only suggestion of a grandstand was alongside the finish line of the racetrack. It was there that livestock was judged and paraded before the spectators.

George Washington was a man who enjoyed sports, especially cock fighting and horse racing. Because his personal integrity was widely acknowledged, he was often asked to judge a match or purse race. Most of his racehorse judging was done at the nearby track in Alexandria, where many of his friends came to try out the speed of their horses. Among them were some of the outstanding breeders of the day, such as Wyllie Jones, John Hoomes, John Tayloe, and John Goode. Washington was also well acquainted with the Randolph and Tasker families.

While the Tasker horses were winning most of their races, Washington was officiating at the Alexandria track. Tasker's domination is of interest, since he lived in Maryland. To eliminate some of the out-of-state competition, Virginia began limiting most races to Virginia-bred horses. Tasker then bought a farm in Virginia and bred racehorses there so that he could continue his winning ways.

Though Washington was involved in the purchase of *Ranger, as mentioned earlier, as far as we know, he did not buy, raise, or run many racehorses. There is only

Dexter. The illustration shows the straight-legged style in which jockeys rode during the eighteenth and early nineteenth centuries. From an engraving by T. Phillibrown.

one record of his participation in a match race. Naturally the general did not race with just anyone; this time his opponent was one of the few men in the country who could be considered his equal—Thomas Jefferson.

Washington's Magnolia according to Bruce's *American Stud Book*, was a chestnut stallion foaled in 1780 and sired by *Ranger (*Lindsay's Arabian) and out of a mare by *Othello.

Thomas Peters, writing in the *American Turf Register and Sporting Magazine*, is our source of information about this particular race. It was matched and run in 1788 at the Alexandria track that Washington frequented. We know little about Jefferson's horse, only that it was a roan colt—and that it ran away from Washington's chestnut. This was the first and probably the only time that men who were or would be presidents of the United States were matched in a horse race.

A well-known revolutionary period Quarter Horse was Black Snake. He was bred by a black freedman named Hugh Snelling, who lived in Granville County, North Carolina.[1] Black Snake was foaled about 1788, sired by *Obscurity and out of a running mare named Harlot, who was by Old Bacchus. As a young horse Black Snake enjoyed so much success that soon no local short horse men would match a race with him. Snelling did not have enough money, or perhaps the desire, to campaign him in new areas, so he sold him to a neighbor, who bred Black Snake, or matched him, for two hundred dollars, whatever the choice. A year or so later he was sold and taken to Petersburg, Virginia. There, too, it became impossible to get a race for him. He was just too fast. He was sold and taken to Philadelphia. Soon he was sold again, this time for five hundred guineas, and shipped to the West Indies (A guinea was worth twenty-two shillings at the time of the Revolution.)

At first Black Snake did well in the islands, but soon his reputation was established, and no good matches could be made unless they were for a mile or more. He was shipped back to the colonies and raced around Charleston under a new name. Patrick Nisbett Edgar, in his studbook, says that he was never beaten and won immense sums of money wherever he went. Finally, Edgar said, he became such a celebrity that he was publicly prohibited from running on any racecourse in South Carolina.

Andrew Jackson was, among other things, a quarter horse man from Tennessee, who was able to raise good horses because of limestone soil around Nashville, where his home, the Hermitage, was located. The general was one of the best horsemen of his day. Even at the age of fifteen he was recognized as an expert. It was then, according to some records, that he received a legacy of fifteen hundred dollars from his grandfather's estate and promptly blew it all at the Charleston racetrack.[2]

The story that he raised Truxton is not borne out by the *American Stud Book* or Edgar's *Stud Book*, both of whom list Truxton as being foaled in either Virginia or North Carolina.[3] One account has Truxton being brought into Tennessee for a match race with a well-known horse, Greyhound, owned by Lazarus Cotton. Truxton was beaten by Greyhound. Jackson witnessed the race and felt that the best horse had not won. He bought Truxton and rematched the race, and when Truxton was properly trained according to Jackson's orders, he beat Greyhound.

The general was not one to shy away from a bet on his own horses. In the rematch against Greyhound, he bet all his cash and most of his clothes. After the race he said that he was "eased in finances and replenished in my wardrobe."[4] A friend of Jackson's, Patton Anderson, also bet his all on Truxton. After his money was gone,

Anderson bet about fifteen saddle animals that were nearby. After the race was over, it was discovered that all the horses had women's sidesaddles on them and that they did not even belong to Anderson.

General Washington and General Jackson were examples of the fondness great military men have entertained for the horse down to the present. Although they were equally graceful riders in the field, General Jackson was the more successful at the racetrack. The record of his many victories attests to his success.

Maria was one of the best running mares of this period. She was generally referred to as Haynie's Maria to distinguish her from several other well-known Marias. Anderson said that Maria "was a most extraordinary race nag at all distances, probably not inferior to any that has appeared in America."[5]

Maria was bred by the well-known horseman Bennett Goodman, of Virginia. When Goodman moved to North Carolina, he took Maria's dam with him, and she foaled her *Diomed filly in that state in the spring of 1808. A little later, when Goodman moved on to Tennessee, he sold the filly to Captain Jesse Haynie, of Summer County.[6] She was one of the last of the get of *Diomed, who was foaled in 1777 and imported into Virginia by John Hoomes of Bowling Green in 1798, when he was twenty-one years old.

Maria's dam was sired by Tayloe's Bellair, by imported *Traveler and out of the great mare *Selima, owned by Colonel Tasker, of Maryland. Maria's second dam was sired by Symme's Wildair. Haynie's Maria was a dark chestnut, just barely fifteen hands high. She had the perfect disposition for a racehorse, because she was not high-strung. She began running as a three-year-old and did not seem to care what the distance was. She beat all comers from less than one quarter of a mile to four miles. Will Williams said that Grey Pacolet was taken to Tennessee with the idea of beating Maria. He added, "He did not do it, nor would any other horse, brought here, have done it, for she had beaten with ease, all rivals."[7]

Maria and the horse Saltram were trained by the famous quarter race horseman Green Berry Williams, who is generally referred to just as Berry. Saltram was an outstanding quarter horse, sired either by *Saltram or by *Sterling.

Berry Williams played an interesting part in the history of the quarter running horse. He was born in Burk County, Georgia, in 1778, at the time his parents moved away from Virginia to avoid the dangers of the war. Most of his life he called Gallatin, Tennessee, his home, although, because his occupation was running horses and matching races, he was almost always on the move in one state or another. His father also made his living running match races. Berry began riding his father's horses at an early age. It was to be his lifework from that time on.

Berry was a very successful jockey. He seemed to know and become a part of each horse he rode, and he was also in demand because his integrity was unquestioned.

A running mare and foal. During the early days of racing it was common practice to run mares before and after being bred. From W. H. Herbert, *Frank Forester's Horse and Horsemanship of the United States*, 1857.

When he was young, he could ride at fifty or sixty pounds for catch weights, and he never grew to be very large. Some of the better-known race horses he rode were Ready Money, a son of Goode's Twigg, and Hunter's String. From available records Ready Money and Berry never lost a race, although there was a dead heat with Georgia Bellair.

As he grew older, Berry began training horses and gradually rode less and less. Almost from the start he was one of the most successful trainers in the business. He seemed to know instinctively what a horse needed to be at its best in a race. For seventy years he was acknowledged to be at the top in his trade.

In 1806, Berry took Sally Friar by Jolly Friar to train and race. He ran her first at Goose Creek in a match for five hundred dollars a side. She won handily, and soon thereafter was bought by Patton Anderson. Berry also had great success with the horse Saltram, and later with Maria.

The ability of some early short horses, such as Maria, to run long is illustrated by

Robin Grey, who was by *Royalist and out of Bellariah, by Grey Diomed. In the winter of 1810, Robin Grey was run short against a very fast *Janus colt and won by twenty-seven yards. On July 19, 1810, going a full quarter, he beat one of the reportedly best quarter horses by six feet for five hundred dollars. Each horse carried 140 pounds. In the fall of the same year Colonel Abraham Buford won the second day's Jockey Club purse with him at Georgetown in two one-mile heats. Two weeks earlier he had won the first day's Jockey Club purse at Lexington in four one-mile heats! He beat Paymaster and four other good horses in that race. Then two weeks after he won a purse race at Versailles in one-mile heats, he ran at Harrodsburg, but there he got into difficulty. He was winning with great ease when, as John L. O'Connor says, he broke through a bridge, fell, crippled his rider, and lost the race. After recovering from the fall, Robin Grey was again matched short for five hundred dollars against Joe Woods's horse Bonester, for one quarter of a mile, carrying 140 pounds, and beat him by nineteen feet.

Another interesting race that took place in the 1820s also shows how the quarter horses were matched at almost any distance. The Tiger mare, Black Eyed Susan, who was successful on both the short track and the long track, was matched against the famous quarter horse stallion Cherokee, by Sir Archy. Black Eyed Susan was a brown mare, bred by George Burbridge, and foaled in 1821. At the time of the match race she was owned by Captain Viley. She was by Tiger, by Kentucky Whip, and out of a mare by Albert. Cherokee's pedigree is written up elsewhere in this book. He was one of the greatest sires of short horses of the 1800s, as well as an outstanding running horse. He was owned at that time by J. L. Downing. The race was held on the Daisy Hill Paths in Woodford County, Kentucky. The mare was to carry eighty-seven pounds, and Cherokee ninety. Black Eyed Susan was the crowd favorite before the start, but Cherokee won both heats in handsome style. He ran the first mile heat in one minute, twenty-nine seconds, and the second heat in one minute, fifty-one seconds. Both of these well-known sprinters ran a mile on occasion.

CHAPTER SEVEN

Great Sprinters, Great Sires

PRINTER

MANY of the best sources of information on the sprinting horse overlook the importance of Printer. The only time Bruce referred to Printer in *The American Stud Book* that I could find was in the obituary section, where he stated simply: "Printer, by imported Janus; foaled————; died in Virginia in 1828. He was a quarter horse."[1] John H. Wallace ignored Printer in his *Horse of America*. Edgar also left out Printer. Herbert, though he did not honor Printer by including him in his index, did mention this stallion (or a son) in the text. In surveying the horses going into Ohio in the early days, he wrote:

> In the adjoining vicinity of Fairfax County, was introduced a horse known as "Printer," a longish bodied, low and very muscular animal, a breed which old Mr. Van Meter says he knew when a boy in Virginia, and which he says, are nearly identical with the present Morgan stock. Many of these animals are excellent quarter nags—good in a short race, but with too little bone for the muscle. The oldest stallion of this strain in the country is now [1850?] owned near Lancaster, Ohio, and has won many a small purse in scrub races.[2]

Fortunately other information is available about the great short horse sire Printer. One of the most interesting versions of Printer's origin comes from Battel:

> *Printer*   Bay 15½ or less. Foaled 1795. Said to be a descendant of imported Janus. This horse was foaled in Kentucky, the property of Mr. Fernan near Lexington, from a fast racing mare that had been stolen from Virginia. The mare was reclaimed next year but her colt, Printer, bred in Virginia, remained in Kentucky. His stock were widely scattered and very notable for their speed, especially in quarter races. He died in 1827.[3]

There are several references to Old Printer in the *American Turf Register* during the year 1829. The Reverend Robert Breckenridge, of Kentucky, wrote that the true origin of Printer was unknown, surrounded by mystery. He thought that Printer possessed *Janus blood but doubted that he could have been a son. A bit later another correspondent signing himself R. J. B. (perhaps the same good reverend) gave the following account of Printer. He said that Old Printer was a deep bay about five feet, two inches tall. (This hardly sounds like a horseman talking, although he undoubtedly had seen Printer. Five feet, two inches would be fifteen hands, two inches.) He added that Printer was a striking-looking horse, with very fine body and quarters and neat legs, handsome and muscular. He said that Printer's withers were thick and low, and his hind legs straight and that he passed on these characteristics to his get. His stock distinguished themselves, the writer added, as quarter milers who could run less than a quarter but not more. The correspondent then told the story, from which Battel no doubt got his information, of how a Virginia mare was stolen and had a *Janus colt in Kentucky and how the mare was recovered but not the colt. He added that, when it came time to stand Printer, his pedigree was given as by *Janus and out of a Thoroughbred mare. The writer added that the quality and appearance of Printer's stock, and his own age and peculiarities, made the pedigree seem likely.[4]

Another contributor to the *American Turf Register*, writing from Lexington, gave the following details about Printer. He stated that Printer was foaled in Kentucky and from his looks and action appeared to be a *Janus colt. He added that Printer's get were speedy from three hundred yards to a quarter of a mile and observed that they almost universally had low withers and upright shoulders, were wide between the forelegs, and were not easy-riding animals.

In another newspaper a similar version of Printer's origin appeared under the date October 21, 1829:

> Enquiry is made in the American Farmer for the Pedigree of the horse Old Printer, of the neighborhood. His pedigree is unknown. His dam was brought to this State by a stranger and sold while in foal. It is however believed that either dam or sire was closely allied to the Janus stock. For strength, activity and fleetness for a short distance his foals and their descendants are very celebrated. Their compactness of form, good limbs and docility distinguished them as a class and rendered them valuable for domestic purposes, though they are not esteemed for the saddle.[5]

In the *Kentucky Gazette*, published in Lexington in 1825, was the following ad:

> Noted Remington Horse, Old Printer, in Jessimine County, Kentucky. Dark bay, black points, with such beauty, action and muscular strength as are seldom found connected with any horse. Colts sell for from $500 to $1500 each.
>
> Robert Simpson[6]

In O'Connor's book of stallion advertisements is an ad for a son of Printer owned by Eben Best, of Garrard County, Kentucky. The ad states that this Printer was by the quarter horse Printer, who was the fastest horse in America. In 1825 the following ad appeared in a Kentucky paper:

The Elegant Horse Old Printer

Will stand the present season at my stable in Jessamine C. three miles east of Nicholasville and one below the Union Mills, on Hickman Creek, and will be let to mares at $10. The season in commonwealth money $15. to insure a mare with foal. The season to commence the 20th March and end the 1st of July. Pasturage gratis for mares from a distance but will not be responsible for accidents should they happen.

Old Printer

Is a beautiful dark bay, black mane, tail and legs, with such beauty action and muscular strength as are seldom to be found connected in any horse. For the information of those who have not a thorough knowledge of Old Printer, suffice it to say that his colts are equal to any horse on the Continent of America and as many fine Stud horses have been produced by him as any other horse in Kentucky, which may be seen in various parts but particularly near his former stands—that is Mr. John Jones in Montgomery Co. had five Stud horses by Printer, Archibald Hamilton three, Frances Jones or Robin Moore one, Wm. Goodpaster two, Wm. Hammonds one, Jesse Jones, one, Nathan Roberts one, Jesse Hunter one, Edward Roberts one, Eben Best two, with many others too numerous to mention, which Studs are now as high as any other horse's colts in Kentucky from $500 to $1500 each. Any gentleman wishing to breed from Printer and not being entirely satisfied of his being one among the finest foal getters in the State, I will refer them to the different Counties where he has stood and I am pursuaded that they will find his colts equal to any horse's colts in Kentucky.[7]

Printer was probably not a son but a grandson of *Janus, but he had the *Janus conformation and inherited the *Janus ability to stamp his progeny with his own image and speed. Like so many short horse stallions, he had most of the faults, as well as the assets, generally found in the quarter horse then and now.

WHIP

One of the great quarter horses of the early 1800s was sired by an imported English Thoroughbred named *Whip. He adopted his sire's name and created a new strain of uniquely handsome sprinters that soon became the toast of Kentucky. *Whip never gained much fame. His son was taken from Virginia into Kentucky and there was recognized by the names Young Whip, Whip, Cook's Whip, and Blackburn's Whip. But more often and to most horsemen he was just plain Kentucky Whip.

In the *American Turf Register* a correspondent from Kentucky wrote as follows:

Before I dispatch this letter I will say something about Cook's or Blackburn's Whip; a complete genealogy of whom is a great desideratum with our breeders. He was the favorite horse in Kentucky for fifteen or twenty years and went to nearly all of our best mares, was a high form winner at one and two miles, of great speed, and incomparable beauty. Indeed it is questionable whether the world ever held his equal in smoothness, symmetry, and finish of form; and, moreover, whether any other horse has produced an equal number of beautiful stallions, mares, and geldings; many of them, too, of fine racing powers.[8]

*Whip, the sire of Kentucky Whip, was foaled in England. *The American Stud Book* recorded that *Whip was a bay colt who was foaled in 1794.[9] He was sired by Saltram, and his dam was by Herod, as good breeding as the times permitted. He was bred by a Mr. Durand and was sold and sent into Virginia in 1801. He lived until 1825.[10] Patrick Nisbett Edgar in his earlier studbook gave essentially the same information. Herbert said that Hickory, a prime four-mile racer, was his best son, adding that "his get in general were not of note." He chose to ignore Kentucky Whip, although he mentioned him elsewhere in his work many times, and Hickory's name was never mentioned before or after. Time has proved Kentucky Whip to have been far more important than Hickory or *Whip, his sire.

In Volume II, Herbert recounted the following about Kentucky Whip: "Before this time, the stallion known as 'Kentucky Whip,' was brought to the Sciota Valley, where he had left a fine progeny, and died at an advanced age."[11]

In another short article in the *American Turf Register*, written from Braedalbane (near Lexington), a writer discussed the outstanding blood horses in Kentucky, especially those originating in Virginia. Among those mentioned was "Blackburn's Whip, the Thoroughbred son of Imported Whip." In speaking of Blackburn's or Kentucky Whip, the writer said that, except for a defect in the withers, Whip was the most beautiful horse he had ever seen.[12] Perhaps he was a little low in the withers; many short horses were in those days. The writer from Braedalbane commented that Kentucky Whip's brother, Ree's Whip, and his sons, Tiger, Paragon, Whipstar and Kennon's Whip, were all wonderful horses and that the family was as extensive and handsome as any in America.

Kentucky Whip was foaled in Virginia on August 8, 1805, bred by John Patrick, of Charlotte County. William B. Cook took him to Kentucky as a young stallion, and he spent most of the rest of his life in Bourbon County, a few miles east and north of Lexington. Cook stood him for several years, beginning with the 1810 season. Before that he had been on the tracks for two or three years. His popularity in Kentucky was almost immediate, and soon Abraham Buford bought an interest in him. A few years later he was purchased by E. M. Blackburn and J. Kinkead, of Woodford County, although he continued to stand to mares in Bourbon County, about eight miles south of Paris. In 1822 he was taken to the Bourbon Agricultural Society Fair and took the purple ribbon as the best stallion shown. By 1827, Blackburn had purchased Kin-

THE CELEBRATED HORSE

PERRIANDER

Will stand the present season one part of his time at my stable in Pettis County, Mo., ten miles west of Georgetown, near the road leading to Warrensburg, and the other part at

and will be let to mares at the reduced price of $3 the single leap to be paid at the time of service, $4 the season paid by the first of February, $6 to insure a mare in foal, to be paid so soon as the fact is ascertained or the mare parted with, the following produce will be taken, to wit: young cattle, pork, hemp, tobacco, wheat, beeswax, tallow and dry hides, all of which will be taken at the above named stands by the first of February, 1845, if not the money will be expected. Season to commence the first of April and end the first of July, Sundays and public days excepted, great care will be taken to prevent accidents or escapes but no liability for either. Any mares coming from a distance will be furnished with good pasture gratis or corn fed on reasonable terms if desired.

DESCRIPTION & PEDIGREE

Perriander is a beautiful dapple bay, black legs, mane and tail, near sixteen hands high, 11 years old this spring, possessing as much muscular power as any horse in the State, it is unnecessary to make further statements about him as he is good recommendation for himself. Perriander was got by old Perriander, he by Big Printer, he by Old Printer Big Printer's dam was got by Kennon's Whip, he by Blackburn's Whip, he by imported Whip, he by Dunganon of England, Perriander's dam was got by one of old Hambletonian's best noted running Colts, and old Hambletonian by old imported Diomede.

March 18th, 1844.

SETH BOTTS,
SHADRACH DUNNING.

CERTIFICATE.

We the undersigned do Certify that we are well acquainted with the Celebrated Horse Perriander, and with his Colts and we belive them to be equal to any lot of Colts that we ever saw in Caldwell or Trigg counties Kentucky and we would rather breed to him than any horse in Pettis County, Mo.

ISAAC KENNEDY,
WM. WEATHERS,
WILLIAM REED,

JOHN. H. KENNEDY,
WHITNAL HOLLAN,
WILKESON REED.

Broadside for Perriander, an excellent example of the Kentucky Whip–Printer cross so popular during the 1840s. Courtesy of Jeff Edwards.

kead's interest in Kentucky Whip, and could brag in his advertisement in the *Kentucky Gazette* of March 14, 1827, that "I would just remark that in all the running last fall, in the Jockey Club races at Paris, four days, Lexington, three days, Versailles and Georgetown, there were but two winning horses except Whip stock."

Kentucky Whip's offspring were especially popular as quarter running horses, and many sons and daughters of this great horse found their way into Illinois, Tennessee, Missouri, and Ohio, where they were bred and raced. They produced some of the greatest of the early modern quarter horses. Tiger, one of his best sons, is discussed later in this book.

Short Whip was another well-known son of Kentucky Whip who became important to the quarter horse. Short Whip went to Illinois in later life. One of his first and best-known sons was Harry Bluff. One of Harry Bluff's sons, Steel Dust, would make history in Texas.

Kentucky Whip was extremely popular not only in his home state but also in nearby states. Many of his offspring were sold and taken to the newly forming states on the north and west. As a result of his popularity, one can find examples of advertisements carried in local Kentucky papers concerning Kentucky Whip's breeding arrangements. The following were selected from O'Connor's book or from *The American Turf Register*:

The Celebrated Running High Blooded Horse

COOK'S WHIP

Now owned by E. M. Blackburn and J. Kinkead of Woodford Co. will stand the ensuing season at my stable in Bourbon Co. about a half mile from the intersection of the Iron Works and Cleavland roads and eight miles south of Paris.

Whip is a beautiful mahogany bay, full fifteen and a half hands high and for beauty of form he is considered by the best judges a superior horse as to walking, trotting and running. I defy the state to produce his equal. Whip is also more distinguished for his colts than any other horse in Kentucky. They are superior for running also for the high price they command in market.

He was exhibited before the Bourbon Agricultural Society in Oct. last with other fine studs and the premium was given to him by the judges with one consent and without hesitation. For further particulars and pedigree see bills.

February 5, 1822. A. M. Buford.[13]

OLD WHIP

Will again stand the ensuing season at the same price as last year, and at the same stable at my farm where he stood at Maj. Buford's in Bourbon. I would just remark, that in all the running last Fall, in the Jockey Club races at Paris 4 days, Lexington 3 days, Versailles

Sir Archy, foaled in 1805, about twenty-five years after the death of *Janus, whose successor he became. Sir Archy's importance to the sprinting fraternity was demonstrated through his sons. Steel engraving from Herbert, *Frank Forester's Horse and Horsemanship of the United States*.

and Georgetown there were but two winning horses except Whip's stock. I have fine pastures and in addition have made about 50 acres more the last season; and I can say with propriety, that I have given as much or more satisfaction in my line of business than any man in Kentucky.

Mar. 14, 1827.   E. M. Blackburn.[14]

The Whip blood has been very important to the quarter horse and relatively unimportant to the Thoroughbred. While it is difficult to assess the relative importance of early-nineteenth-century sires on the modern quarter horse, Kentucky Whip belongs among the top half-dozen stallions. According to Bruce, he died in 1828 at the age of twenty-three years.[15]

SIR ARCHY

Sir Archy was foaled in 1805, some twenty-five years after the death of *Janus, and became his successor as the greatest Thoroughbred sire of quarter horse sires. Sir Archy and his sons were able follow-ups to the *Janus family. They added new and vigorous blood to the quarter horse. Sir Archy was bred by Colonel Archibald Randolph, from whom he eventually got his name (he began his career under the name Robert Burns). To be precise, he had two breeders. Sir Archy's dam was a blind mare named *Castianira. She had been imported into America by John Tayloe III, who turned her over to his good friend Archibald Randolph to breed on shares, so that any of her produce were half John's and half Archibald's. When Robert Burns was two years old, Archibald Randolph sold his share of the colt to Ralph Wormeley IV. Wormeley then bought Tayloe's interest for four hundred dollars and a good filly. It was Tayloe who began calling the colt Sir Archy, after Archibald Randolph. In contemporary literature the name is often spelled Sir Archie.

As a racer he was somewhat inconsistent, although it was not always his fault. Before his first race, the Washington Sweepstakes, which he entered as a three-year-old, he came down with distemper. To save the forfeit he was allowed to run in the race even though he had not fully recovered, and he was beaten. He was entered in another race at Richmond, still not entirely recovered, and he was beaten by True Blue. True Blue's owner, William R. Johnson, a shrewd turfman who knew all the particulars about Sir Archy's condition, and also knew how hard a race True Blue had just run, bought Sir Archy on the spot for fifteen hundred dollars. Sir Archy was given a year's rest to recover fully, and then returned to racing. By the time Sir Archy retired the second time, he had no equal as a racehorse. Johnson wrote to Herbert as follows: ''I have only to say that in my opinion, Sir Archy is the best horse I ever saw. . . .and [he] had not run with any horse that could put him half speed toward the end of the race.''[16] Since Sir Archy had raced all the best horses on the track during his day, this was full praise.

Sir Archy was sired by one of the best horses ever imported into the United States: *Diomed, who was by Florizel, by Herod, and out of a mare by Spectator, by *Crab. *Diomed blood is found in many of the best quarter running horses, as it is in many of the best Thoroughbreds. *Castianira, Sir Archy's dam, was by Rockingham, by Highflyer, by Herod and out of Tabitha, by Trentham, by Sweepstakes.

Sir Archy sired many fine running horses after he was retired to the stud. Among them were five who were responsible for some of the best quarter running horses of the period. They were Bertrand, Cherokee, Contention, Muckle John, and Timoleon. Perhaps Timoleon was Sir Archy's greatest son, so far as both long and short horses were concerned, although Bertrand was equally good in the production of sprinters, especially when crossed on Kentucky Whip mares. These five sons of Sir Archy are important not only because they themselves bred short speed but because their sons and daughters did likewise. A few other Sir Archy colts that were noteworthy for begetting early speed were Grey Archy, Pacific, Napoleon, Rattler, Copperbottom, Stockholder, Director, Sir Solomon, and Kosciusko.

One of the better descriptions of Sir Archy is found in Skinner's *American Turf Register*:

> Sir Archy is a rich bay color having no white about him excepting his right hind foot. He is a horse of commanding size, fully 16 hands high, with great power and substance. He is eminently superior in all those points indespensable to the turf horse, mainly contributing to strength and action. A shoulder, the most material part of a horse, strikingly distinguished, being very deep, fairly mounting up to the top of his withers and obliquely inclined to the hips. His girth is full and deep, back short and strong, thighs and arms long

THE CELEBRATED HORSE

SIR ARCHIE,

WILL STAND THE ENSUING SEASON

At my Stable in Northampton County, North-Carolina, about three miles from the Court-House, nine miles from the town of Halifax, and twenty-one miles from Belfield, Virginia.

He will Cover Mares at Fifty Dollars the Season, payable on the first of January next, or Forty-Five Dollars if paid within the Season, (with one dollar to the Groom in all cases.)

Such of Archie's Friends, that lives at a distance, will send their Notes with the Mares, payable on the first of January next—Also, feeding of the Mares to be paid when taken away.

The season will commence the first of February next, and terminate the Fifteenth of July — Extensive fields of Small Grain and Clover are sowed for the benefit of the Mares, (which may be left with the Horse) with the addition of grain feeding, at 25 cents per day.—Separate enclosures are provided for Mares with Colts.—No pains will be spared in taking the best possible care of Mares, &c. which may be left, but no responsibility for escapes or accidents.

SIR ARCHIE'S BLOOD, GREAT SIZE....Performance on the Turf, and celebrity as a Foal getter, are sufficient recommendations. WILLIAM AMIS.

January 1, 18

Broadside of 1817 announcing the stud service of Sir Archy. From William H. Robertson, *The History of Thoroughbred Racing in America*, 1964.

and muscular. His bone is good. His front appearance fine and commanding. His head and neck well formed, the latter rising well out of the withers. Take Sir Archy as a whole, and he has more size and substance than we often see combined in a full bred horse.[17]

Joseph Battel, in his *American Stallion Register*, said that as a racehorse Sir Archy was considered very superior, noting that, while he did not run extensively, he beat the best horses of his day. He is generally ranked by knowledgeable horsemen with the greatest stallions of England or America.

Turf, Field, and Farm gave an account of Sir Archy's last days. He died in Northhampton County in North Carolina, about two miles west of Jackson, the county seat. He was stabled on the farm of John D. Amis, who owned him when he died in 1833. He was supposed not to have shed his winter hair the last couple of years before he died, and looked pretty rough. He may have covered two mares in 1832, although only one was settled and produced Garrison's Zanganer. It was rather an undistinguished death for such a truly great stallion.

TIGER

There is little reference to Tiger in Bruce's studbook, and there is not much more in Edgar. Edgar said only that he was a Kentucky horse sired by Kentucky Whip and out of a Paragon mare by Hunt's Paragon. Edgar got his information from Elisha Winter in Kentucky in 1830. Bruce showed two colts called Tiger, out of Jane Hunt, one foaled in 1812 and the other in 1817 (?). Edgar and Bruce agreed that Tiger's dam was a Paragon mare. Bruce said that she was undoubtedly Jane Hunt.

Jane Hunt had been foaled right after the Revolution in 1796. She was by General Wade Hampton's Paragon, and her dam was Moll, by *Figure. She was bred by Daniel Hunt, of New Jersey, but her fame as a sprinter reached Kentucky, and John Harris bought her. She was raced for four years and then bred. Jane Hunt had fillies in 1802 and 1803 and then skipped two years. In 1806 and 1807 she had a colt and a filly. She was bred the last three times to Kentucky Whip, producing Tiger, Little Tiger, and a filly, Grecian Princess.

Tiger was one of Kentucky Whip's best sons and was able to establish a separate line of short horses known as the Tigers. He was foaled in 1812, about a month before war broke out between Great Britain and her former colonies. He ran his first race as the war ended. He is described in a stallion ad in the *Kentucky Gazette* in 1827:

The Celebrated Turf Horse

Tiger

A beautiful Mahogany bay fifteen and a half hands high now in high plight, will stand the ensuing season at our farm (Clark Co.) Kentucky 12 miles Southwest of Lexington and within half a mile of the Todd's road and immediately on the waters of Boone's Creek 8 miles west from Winchester 4 miles from Athens and 3½ miles from Chilesburg and will be let to mares at $10. the season, which will commence the 10th of March and expire the 10th of July following. Good pasturage gratis for mares from a distance and grain fed on reasonable terms if required. The strictest attention will be paid to mares and colts left with the horse to prevent accidents and escapes, but will not be responsible for either. Mares bred to Tiger in the Spring and proving not with foal can have the benefit of the fall season gratis. For further particulars see bills.

Feb. 28, 1827.   D. & D. W. Parrish.[18]

A few years earlier Tiger had been owned by Abraham Buford, the son of William Buford, who carried the following ad for Tiger:

THE MUCH ADMIRED AND CELEBRATED TURF HORSE

TIGER

A Beautiful dark mahogany bay fifteen and one half hands high, eleven years old this Spring now in high plight, will stand the ensuing season at my farm in Bourbon Co. eight miles South of Paris and within a mile of the intersection of the Iron Works and Cleavland roads, he will be let to mares at $15. the season. The season will commence the 1st day of April and expires on the 4th day of July; but the horse will remain at the stand until the 1st day of August. Good and extensive pasturage gratis for mares from a distance and corn furnished on reasonable terms if required. Great care will be taken to prevent accidents or escapes but will not be responsible for either.

Am. Buford[19]

John Harris owned Tiger's full brother, Little Tiger, and he, too, was an excellent racer. Another horse named Tiger, sometimes confused with Old Tiger, was a brown horse foaled in 1835 of Printer stock. This Tiger spent most of his life in Indiana in the ownership of Charles Love.

Many mares sired by Tiger produced sprinters, but none better than the bay mare bred by James Kieth, and later bought by George Thomas, both from Kentucky. This mare was by Old Tiger and out of a race mare with proven speed but unproven pedigree. The only way she might be faulted was that she produced only fillies, but they could fly. Bred to Birmingham she foaled Brown Kitty; bred to Boston, she produced Nellie Hardin, and bred to Wagner she foaled Model.

Tiger blood was taken west into Tennessee, Missouri, and Arkansas, and was mixed there with Printer, Cherokee, and Kentucky Whip blood to produce new generations of sprinters in Kansas, Missouri, Oklahoma, and Texas.

99

TIMOLEON

Timoleon is another example of an early stallion who contributed to both the sprinters and the stayers. Had he sired only the great Thoroughbred Boston, his fame would have been secure, but Boston was only one of his many influential sons. Others were vital in the formation of the modern short horse.

Wallace, in his *Horse of America*, said that Timoleon "had an impossible and untruthful pedigree on the side of his dam."[20] He concluded that, because of this, Timoleon was not technically a "Thoroughbred" but that he was certainly "distinctively running bred." A little earlier he had written that Timoleon was one of the most distinguished sons of Sir Archy.[21] Herbert continued along the same line, saying that, when a real turf man was informed that Timoleon, the son of Sir Archy, had for his great-great-grandsire a common cart stallion named Fallow, he would merely shrug his shoulders, satisfied that there had to be an error someplace.[22] A quarter horse breeder would not feel that way. He would recollect other cart horses, such as Traveler, of South Texas, who was discovered pulling a dirt scraper, or Old Fred, who was bought by Coke Roberds out of the traces of a freight team, and say, "It figures."

Will Williams said that "Timoleon, one of Sir Archy's best, was a horse of great size, correct proportions and finish, good even to the hoofs."[23]

Timoleon, a light chestnut, was foaled in 1813, by Sir Archy and out of a mare by *Saltram. His granddam was a mare by Simme's Wildair. The Saltram mare was a chestnut, bred and owned by Major Thomas Gibbon, of North Carolina. *Saltram was a brown horse, foaled in 1789, and imported into Virginia in 1800 by William Lightfoot. He was by O'Kelly's Eclipse. Timoleon was the third foal of the Saltram mare, who was about ten when he was foaled.

A description of Timoleon is found in Anderson's *Making of the American Thoroughbred*. Anderson wrote "Timoleon's hindquarters seemed higher than his forehand."[24] That is a common characteristic of the short horse. Anderson also said that his peculiar conformation and his uncommon strength gave him agility and stride. Timoleon was fifteen hands, three inches, and the only mark on his sorrel body was a small star on his forehead. He was bred by Benjamin Jones of Greenville County Virginia. He was run only in his third and fourth years.

Timoleon was not an especially good four-mile horse; a mile was about as far as he could go. At a mile he met and bested the top horses of his day. In February, 1818, he had an accident in a race and ran no more. But, he left no doubt that he was one of the best mile horses in Virginia. He won nine and lost only two of the seventeen races he was matched. The other six were forfeited for one reason or another.

As a three-year-old, Timoleon was sold to Colonel William Wynn, of Petersburg, Virginia, for $2500. The following year Colonel Wynn sold him to Robert

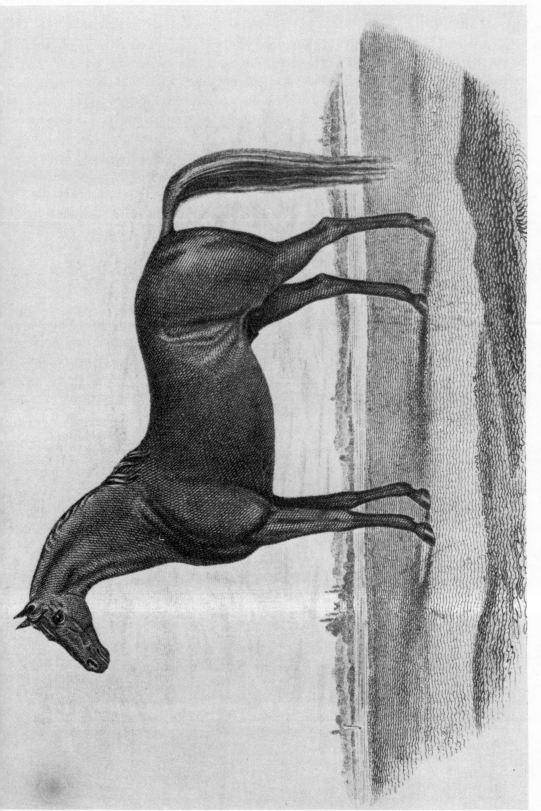

Timoleon. Engraving from John Hervey, *Racing in America, 1665–1865*, 1944.

R. Johnson, brother of W. R. Johnson, for $4000 and ten days later tried to buy him back for $5000. He believed him to be superior to any other horse that "turned" on a racetrack in the United States. Where starting gates were unavailable, the race horses were lined up facing away from the finish line and "turned" to start on the signal. After Timoleon broke down, he stood at Wynn's and Johnson's until he was sold for $4300 to Colonel David Dancy. Dancy later moved on into Alabama, taking Timoleon with him. In 1829, still the property of Dancy, Timoleon stood in Nashville, Tennessee, at the racetrack two miles south of town. He was handled by W. C. Davis, proprietor of the track. His stud fee was $50, and he had all the mares he could handle. During the breeding seasons of 1831 and 1832 he stood in Virginia; and during the later season he settled a Florizel mare for N. Rives. The resulting foal became famous. He was named after a popular card game of that time: Boston.

BERTRAND

From the quarter racing man's point of view, Bertrand was one of the best sires Sir Archy produced. He undoubtedly was not as well known among the long horse enthusiasts as his half brother Timoleon, but he was on a par with him in the production of sprinters.

Bertrand's dam was a mare called Eliza, foaled in 1804 and owned by the great South Carolina breeder William Alston. She was sired by *Bedford, a bay horse foaled in 1792, sired by the well-known *Dungannon, and bred by Lord Grosvenor and imported into Virginia by John Hoomes. Bertrand was Eliza's first recorded colt.

Bertrand was a bay stallion, foaled in 1821. Wallace, in his *American Stud Book*, said that Bertrand was as good in the stud as he was on the track. For a time he was owned by Colonel William Buford, of the Tree Hill Stud, Woodford County, Kentucky. He died in the ownership of James Lindsey and John Hutchcraft in Hopkinsville, Kentucky, in 1838.

Although he was originally named Bertrand, he was sometimes called Bertram in stud advertisements that appeared in Kentucky newspapers. The following examples add information about Bertrand:

Bertram (by Sir Archie)

Late the property of Col. John R. Spann of S. Carolina and now the property of John Hutchcraft and Company, will stand this fall season at my house nine miles south of Paris, seven miles from Winchester and seventeen East of Lexington and will be let to mares at $30. the season which may be discharged at $25. sent with the mare: $35. to insure. Good pasturage gratis, but not accountable for accidents or escapes of the season to expire the first of Oct.

July 19, 1826   John Hutchcraft[25]

The Race Horse and Unequalled Blooded Stallion
Bertrand

Will stand the present season, which has commenced and will end the first of July next, at my farm in Bourbon Co., at $40, which will in all cases be required to be paid within the season. Good pasturage gratis for mares from a distance and all possible care taken, but I will not be accountable for accidents or escapes.

Bertrand is at length at that very elevated rank which he has long merited and after my grateful acknowledgments to my friends and the public for their past patronage, I assure them that they have flattering prospects before them, in the selection of Bertrand as a stock horse who possesses numerous advantages—size and strength for the draft, beauty, gaiety and action for the saddle, and fleetness and durability for the turf. His colts are without doubt the very best from the same mares in the State. The largest portion of them are like himself, good bays—some are of a deep chestnut color, and among the whole of them I have never seen one of a pale sickly color. As racers they have far exceeded the most sanguine expectations. Capt. Viley's and Mr. Tarleton's colts that have run two and three miles, are believed by our best judges and sportsmen, who have witnessed their running to be equal, if not superior, to any colts of their age in the United States. Such an acquisition to the stock of the Country as Bertrand is rarely to be met with and as life is uncertain, gentlemen of all classes, the Religious, Lawyers, Doctors, Farmers and Sportsmen are invited to embrace the present opportunity of breeding from this justly celebrated horse. He who wishes to race horses is requested to send a good stock of the first order.

Bertrand will be offered the present season to eighty mares only.

Bourbon Co., Feb. 22, 1832.   In Feb. 28, 1832

                                                    John Hutchraft[26]

Bertrand was a popular horse all his life, on the racetrack as well as in the stud. John B. Irving, in his *History of the South Carolina Turf*, wrote that at one time Bertrand would have brought $35,000, if his owner had been willing to part with him. As it turned out, Bertrand, Tiger and Kentucky Whip furnished most of the quarter running horses that moved into the Old Northwest, especially Ohio, Illinois, and Indiana.

CHEROKEE

Cherokee was the name given to several related sprinters. It was an attractive name, and the horses running under it had a charisma so great that they caught the public fancy as it had not been caught since the time of Twigg. In each case a great sire was responsible; with Twigg it was *Janus, with the Cherokees it was Sir Archy. The Cherokee fans were true believers and would not hedge their bets against their favorite for any living horse. If a Cherokee lost—which was seldom—the fans remained convinced that their horse was faster and that some unusual circumstance had caused the loss.

The Cherokee primarily responsible for the name's popularity was a sorrel stallion foaled in 1821. He was by Sir Archy and out of Roxana, by Hephestion. He was bred either by Dr. Hayward or by Colonel Singleton. Bruce[27] showed Dr. Hayward as the owner of Roxana, while a stud advertisement in the *Kentucky Gazette* in 1826[28] claimed that Cherokee was bred by Colonel Singleton. Both agreed on his pedigree, however. Dr. Hayward's great interest in life was fast horses, and he raised his share of them. He took his mares to outstanding sires of short speed, such as Sir Archy, Buzzard, and Kosciusko, and he made his greatest cross when he took Roxana to Sir Archy. Cherokee was foaled in 1821.

Roxana's dam was by *Marplot. Breeding Roxana to Sir Archy showed considerable faith in that blood because Hephestion was Sir Archy's half brother—both were out of the great blind mare *Castianira. To repeat, Sir Archy was by *Diomed, and Hephestion was by *Buzzard. Hephestion was two years younger than Sir Archy, and both had been bred by John Tayloe.

In the *Kentucky Gazette* of August 3, 1825, appeared the following announcement:

Sportsman Attention

There will be run a match race over the Daisy Hill track on the 18 inst. for $300 in specie by the Black Eyed Susan owned by Messrs. Burbridge and Gillespie and the Cherokee owned by Mr. Downing. It is expected to be a hard contest. Those who are fond of the sport are expected to attend. The track will be in the best possible order and good accomodations furnished. Versailles

Aug. 3, 1825

Cherokee won the match. Black Eyed Susan was by Tiger, and was a well-known and successful speedster.

In O'Connor's book there is a stallion advertisement for Cherokee:

Cherokee by Archie

Bred by Colonel Singleton of South Carolina. Will stand this season at S. Cooper's Powder Mill one mile from Lexington, will be let to mares at $20. the season which may be discharged with $15. payable when the mare is put $25 to insure. Cherokee is six years old a good bay full fifteen hands three inches tall, of superior proportion, speed and power. His Pedigree and Performance will be given in bills. Mares from a distance will be under the direction of M. S. Cooper who will furnish good pasturage gratis and feed if required at a reasonable price.   March 10, 1826

J. L. Downing[29]

Cherokee sired many sprinters, some of whom were successful up to a mile, though most were quarter-mile horses. Whalebone was one of Cherokee's best running sons, and three of his mares showed class both on the track and as brood mares. One was Cherokas, a bay mare foaled in 1827 and owned by George Keene, of Fayette County. Another, called Cherokee, was owned by John Lewis, of Llangollen, Franklin County. Both of these mares were out of Kentucky Whip mares. The third mare was owned by William Buford of the Tree Hill Stud, and her dam was by *Archer. A filly out of Lewis' Cherokee mare is reported to be the dam of one of the last, and one of the best, quarter racing stallions to be named Cherokee. Even Bruce, no lover of the quarter horse, had to admit the existence of this Cherokee. He said of him in *The American Stud Book*: "Cherokee, quarter-horse, foaled 1847, died in 1872 at Council Bluff, Iowa, aged 25 years."[30]

Descendants of the first Cherokee gained fame on the short tracks and in match races. Big Davy, a bay stallion foaled in 1831, was an example. He was owned by James W. Fenwick, of Kentucky. Another was Lighthouse, foaled in 1831, by Cherokee and out of a mare by Quicksilver. Lighthouse was a half brother of Overalls Woodpecker. One of the fastest of the clan was Little Davy, a bay stallion foaled in 1836. He was bred by Joseph Shawhan. His dam was by Kentucky Whip. The Kentucky Whip–Cherokee cross was a favorite of the short horse breeder of that era.

OTHERS

There were a dozen or so additional stallions during this expansion period who deserve a few lines in any history of short racing. Most of them were famous, both for running and for their get. They are presented in chronological order.

Darius was born at the very beginning of this period. Burwell Jackson stood him at John Caldwell's place on Cartright's Creek, in Nelson County, Kentucky, in the spring of 1788. He was "let to mares at fifteen shillings the leap,"[31] according to an advertisement. This Darius was bred by Daniel Hardaway, of Amelia County, Virginia, and was sired by *Janus. His dam and granddam were also by *Janus. A note is appended to the advertisement saying that Darius would be for sale any time after the second Thursday in September, "at which time there is a race depending on him."[32] It

105

would have been interesting to know how the race came out. It no doubt affected the price asked for Darius.

Second on the list is Pilgarlick, foaled in 1780. Edgar had little to say about him, merely stating that he was got by *Janus and that his dam was by *Jolly Roger. Bruce had about the same information but added that Pilgarlick was bred in Virginia and owned in 1833 by "R. C.," of Virginia. Pilgarlick became a famous racing stallion. One of the few horses to beat him was Darius. In the *Kentucky Gazette* of February 16, 1788, is found the following interesting information about him:

The Famous Horse

PILGARLICK

Of a beautiful chestnut colour, full fourteen hands three inches high, rising ten years old, will stand the ensuing season on the head of Salt River at Capt. Abr. Irwin's, Mercer County, and will cover mares at the very low price of ten shillings a leap if the money is paid down, or fifteen at the expiration of the season: and twenty shillings the season in cash, or thirty shillings in good trade.

Pilgarlick was got by the noted imported horse Janus, his dam by Old Silver Eye, and is the swiftest in the district of Kentucke from one to six hundred yards, Darius (the property of Mr. Burwell Jackson) only excepted.

John Davenport

The next horse is Sweet Larry. Little is known about him except that he was one of the best of the Virginia short horses and owned by the racehorse man Henry Deloney (Bruce, incidentally, called him Henry Delancey). Sweet Larry was bred at Belfield, Virginia, and was sired by Wyllie Jones's Spadille and out of a *Janus mare. He was foaled about 1780 or 1781. He was a sorrel, very well formed, about fourteen hands, three inches high. Spadille was a celebrated quarter racer, by *Janus and out of *Selima by the Godolphin Arabian. It is not clear whether Deloney or Jones actually bred Sweet Larry, although Deloney owned him most of his life.

Then comes Lamplighter, who was foaled about ten years after Sweet Larry. He was a beautiful bay horse, fifteen hands, two inches high, and Edgar says he possessed as many running points as any horse. According to Bruce, he was sired by Old Medley but, the ad that appeared in the *Kentucky Gazette* of February 13, 1800, is as accurate as any information collected in later years by studbook compilers.

For Sale, Rent, or Exchange
for dry goods or other merchandise . . .
LAMPLIGHTER

A handsome bay, fifteen and a half hands high, well marked, free from all natural blemishes, was raised by Mr. Brock in Spotsylvania out of a mare got by imported Shandy. He was got by Young Celer, who were both good for a quarter, has produced the swiftest horses in Virginia and 'tis believed by Judges that Lamplighter can carry 150 lbs. and beat any covering horse in the state. He is eight years old.

The next horse of importance to this work was Woodpecker (a typical quarter horse name). He was a bay, foaled in 1796, bred and raised by one of North Carolina's premier quarter horsemen, Gideon Alston of Halifax County, North Carolina. Woodpecker was sired by Ashe's Roebuck and out of a mare by Galloway's Selim.

Woodpecker had four outstanding sons, all called Woodpecker after their sire. One was a bay horse foaled in 1834. He was bred by R. P. Snell of Kentucky, who brought a Saxe Weimer mare to Old Woodpecker. During that same breeding season of 1833, J. N. Overall, also of Kentucky, brought a Quicksilver mare to Woodpecker and her offspring was called Woodpecker Jr. In 1835, George Webb bred a Gallatin mare and the resulting colt was also dubbed Woodpecker. The last Woodpecker foaled in 1838 was bred by James Letton, of Bourbon County, Kentucky, and foaled in 1838. The dam of this Woodpecker was Mary Ellen by Snow Storm. Although the first Woodpecker was quite a runner in his own right, perhaps his greatest contribution was as a producer of dams. His mares produced many fast short horses.

Another good quarter running stallion was Contention, foaled in 1807 or 1808. He was sired by Sir Archy and out of a mare by *Dare Devil. His dam was owned by Edmund Irby of Nottaway County, Virginia. Her dam was by *Wildair. Besides Contention, his dam also foaled a full brother called Reaphook and three other foals with typical quarter horse names, Woodpecker (by *Dragoon), Snake, and Weasel.

Van Tromp was foaled about the same time as Contention. He was bred by Major John R. Eaton, of Granville County, North Carolina, and was foaled in 1809, sired by Ball's Florizel by *Diomed and out of Malbrook by *Mexican. The next Van Tromp, foaled in 1825, was by Eaton's Van Tromp and out of a mare by Sir Archy. He was bred by W. N. Edwards and owned by E. M. Wagoner, of Adair County, Kentucky. The third Van Tromp was foaled ten years later, in 1835. He was by Van Tromp and out of a mare by Muckle John, bred and owned by Beak and Williams in Georgia.

Buzzard, in common with other well-known sprinters, had to contend with rivals bearing the same name. The first *Buzzard was imported into Virginia in 1804 by John Hoomes. However, it was the Buzzard by Bertrand and out of a Hephestion mare that is of special importance to the quarter running horse. He was a bay stallion, foaled in 1837, and bred and owned during the early part of his life by J. C. Mason, of Kentucky. He proved to be an exceptionally fast short horse and later did well in the stud.

The next horse, Kosciusko, was named for the Polish military leader and statesman who came to America in 1776 to help the cause of freedom. Kosciusko, a chestnut, was foaled in 1815, sired by Sir Archy and out of Lottery by Bedford. He was bred by Colonel Alston, of South Carolina. After a successful racing career he was retired to the stud and got two equally well-known sprinters, both called Kosciusko Jr. The first was foaled in 1834, and his dam was by Ball's Florizel. The other was foaled in 1837, and his dam was by Bedford. Both of these stallions stood in Kentucky.

Another stallion popular with the sprinting set was Stockholder. He was foaled shortly before 1820, owned by Henry Cotton, of Halifax County, North Carolina. He was sired by Sir Archy, and his dam was by *Citizen, a stallion noted for the early speed of his get. Stockholder had three well-known sons who also bore his name: Dunbar's Stockholder, foaled in 1826, out of a mare by Bryan's Diomed; Young Stockholder, owned by a man named Perry, out of a mare by Wilkes Wonder; and Stockholder, foaled in 1829, whose dam was by Pacolet, owned by B. B. Pryor.

There were two well-known sprinters called Rifleman. The better of the two was owned by General Andrew Jackson. The general was known to match some of his horses at distances from a quarter mile to four miles. He did not like to lose, and seldom did. His Rifleman was a grey, bred and raised by him, and foaled on or about 1827, Rifleman's sire was Pacolet, a son of *Citizen, and his dam was by the General's most famous sprinter, Truxton, who was by *Diomed. There was one other Rifleman that sired quarter horses. He was foaled in 1835, sired by Woodpecker, and out of a mare by Potomac. He spent his life in the ownership of M. L. Hammond.

Veto was also foaled in 1827, at about the same time as Jackson's Rifleman. He was by Contention by Sir Archy and out of a mare by *Wrangler. He was bred by Mark Alexander of Mecklenburg County, Virginia. Then there was the Veto foaled in 1837, bred and owned by N. Harrison of Virginia, sired by American Eclipse, and out of a mare by *Diomed.

Medoc was a great breeder of early speed. He was a sorrel colt, foaled in 1829. He was bred by James Bathgate of Winchester County, New York, and later purchased by Colonel William Buford of the Tree Hill Stud in Kentucky. He was sired by American Eclipse and out of Maid of Oats by *Expedition. In 1839, Medoc broke a foreleg when he fell into a pit at Colonel Buford's and had to be destroyed. Another Medoc, occasionally confused with the first, is the Irwin Medoc, foaled in 1835 and owned by James Irwin of Kentucky. He was by Old Medoc and out of Pandora, by Ganymede.

Rattler, the last horse discussed in this chapter, was royally bred to run long, but he also left little to be desired when matched in the shorter distances. Rattler's owners claimed that he was the best-bred horse on the continent and equal to Sir Archy.[33] He was sired by Sir Archy and out of a Robin Redbreast mare. He was foaled in 1816, and bred by John Goode. There were only two sons of importance named after this Rattler. The first was foaled in 1825 and purchased by Edward Parker of Lancaster, Pennsylvania. The other was foaled in 1832, and his dam was by Tiger. Other stallions called Rattler were sired by Candidate, Comet, Kosciusko, and Thorton's Rattler.

CHAPTER EIGHT

Early United States Breeders

THERE WERE quite a few breeders producing fast quarter horses soon after the Revolutionary War. Most had started their breeding programs before the war. This was especially true of the quarter horse families, such as the Alstons, the Eatons, and the Bufords. Those breeders who were also active in national affairs, such as John Randolph, left detailed records about themselves and their families. The biographies of those who concentrated on private pursuits are difficult to unravel. It is often difficult to tell whether family members were brothers or cousins, fathers or sons. So, occasionally there may be an error in family relationships, but seldom in ownership of horses. Ownership was, as a rule, clearly stated. Several typical breeders are discussed below, with some mention of their best-remembered horses.

W. N. EDWARDS

W. N. Edwards was one of the better Kentucky breeders, but there is little record of his personal life. He was undoubtedly the son of John Edwards (1748–1837) and Penelope Sanford Edwards. W. N. Edwards was born on or about 1768. In 1780 the Edwardses decided to move, and they settled in the part of Virginia that was later to become part of Kentucky. John was successful and soon owned 23,000 acres of good land. He became a leader in Kentucky affairs, living first in Lincoln County and then in Fayette County. W. N. Edwards settled on some of his father's land in Adair County, and it was there that he bred and raised Van Tromp. Later, he sold Van Tromp to his neighbor, E. M. Wagoner. Van Tromp was by Eaton's Van Tromp and his dam was by Sir Archy.

JOHN R. EATON

The famous Eaton family, who bred the original Van Tromp, owed much of its prominence to John R. and Elizabeth Eaton. John R. was a maker of fine buggies and chaises in Halifax, North Carolina. He not only fathered a large family but was active in public affairs, serving as county coroner and a representative to the state assembly. In 1796 he acquired an estate in Williamson County, Tennessee, and one of his sons,

John Henry Eaton, settled there. Another member of the family was Charles R. Eaton, who farmed in Granville County, North Carolina. John R. bred Eaton's Van Tromp. Charles's best stallions were Garrick by Meade's Celer and out of a *Janus mare; Eaton's Little Janus, a full brother; and Purse Full, a gray stallion by *Janus and out of a mare by Brinkley's Peacock.

THE ALSTONS

The Alston family, discussed in Part I, was also prominent after the war, especially Colonel William Alston and Willis Alston. Both owned plantations in South Carolina. Willis Alston was a member of Congress. Colonel William bred Kosciusko, and Willis bred Andrew Jackson, foaled in or around 1820, sired by Timoleon out of a mare by Kentucky Whip.

EDWARD M. ("NED") BLACKBURN

Edward M. ("Ned") Blackburn was one of the truly great breeders of the period. When one realizes that he bred or owned such stallions as Kentucky Whip, Superior, Kosciusko. Red Eagle, Rattler, Buzzard, and Cracker, the reason for his success becomes apparent. He and his good friends the Bufords, the Harrises, and the Edwardses, were all gentlemen and sportsmen who liked nothing better than to race one another on the local tracks.

Ned Blackburn's father was George Blackburn, who settled a few miles south of Spring Station in the later 1700s. George first built a sturdy log cabin and then constructed a stockade around both it and the nearby spring to protect his family from Indian attacks. It was large enough for his family and the few nearby neighbors. Because of the stockade his home became known as Blackburn's Fort, and was so called years after all threats from Indian attack had passed. George's son Ned was born there near the end of the 1700s.

When Ned was ready to leave home, he bought some land nearby, alongside the Louisville and Nashville Railroad. He had a good eye for a horse, and his first love was short racing. One of his sons, Luke P. Blackburn, served as governor of Kentucky from 1879 to 1883. Another son, C. S. Blackburn, was a United States senator and was later appointed governor of Panama.[1]

Of all the famous horses owned by Ned Blackburn, none gained more fame as a quarter horse sire than Kentucky Whip. Whip was foaled in 1805 in Virginia and passed through several hands before Blackburn got complete ownership of him. Like *Janus, Kentucky Whip was extremely popular at stud and was also line-bred to his own daughters and granddaughters. For example, Rattler was by Kentucky Whip and

111

out of one of his daughters. Highflyer was by Rattler by Whip and out of a mare by Whip. His get, especially Short Whip and Tiger, were extremely popular in the new western states.

JOHN HARRIS

Just north of Woodford County, Kentucky, lies Franklin County, the home of another important breeder, John Harris. His farm was on the Forks of the Elkhorn, a few miles northwest of Lexington. Harris was friendly with the Bufords and the Blackburns, and they bred mares to each other's stallions.

John Harris was married in 1797 and soon thereafter moved to Franklin County. His wife was the daughter of another famous horseman, David Hunt, of New Jersey. John's wedding gift from his father-in-law was the great mare Jane Hunt.

Among the many outstanding stallions John bred or used were Paragon by Kentucky Whip; Apollo, a full brother of Paragon; Bob Collins by Thorton's Rattler; and Tiger.

Harris had other good mares besides Jane Hunt, such as Miss Obstinate by Sumpter; Morgiana by Thorton's Rattler; and Mary Norris by Medoc. His greatest mare however, was Jane Hunt.

THE BUFORDS

Another prominent family, famous for both their long and their short horses were the Bufords of Virginia and Kentucky. Some of the information that follows was obtained from a living descendant, Anthony A. Buford, of St. Louis, who, like his family before him, is raising sprinters. The family got its start in America when Richard Beauford left England and migrated to the colonies in 1635. He did well in the New World, accumulating much property. One of his many descendants was John Buford, who lived during the eighteenth century (by then the name had been Americanized). John's son, Abraham, was a famous Revolutionary War hero. Abraham was born in Culpepper County, Virginia. After the war, in 1788, he married Mary McDowell, and they moved to Kentucky. They settled near Georgetown in Scott County, and there he achieved a wide reputation as a breeder of fine horses and cattle. Another Buford, Simon, also moved to Kentucky a few years later and settled in Woodford County. Colonel William Buford, a son of Abraham and Mary Buford, lived in Woodford County, eight miles south of Paris.

The Bufords used many different bloodlines but especially liked the results they obtained when breeding to Tiger, Kosciusko, Bertrand, Kentucky Whip, and Medoc. With their good mares and stallions they were a racing family to be reckoned with in a

112

short match race or in a purse race at any distance from an eighth of a mile to four-mile heats. Most of the match races were run on their local tracks or at home tracks of their friends. Many longer races were run at the Lexington Association track, a few miles east of the Buford farm. William won his share of races but decided that he needed an outcross, for many of his mares were similarly bred. When he heard about a New York colt called Medoc, he sent to New York and purchased the stallion from James Bathgate, of Winchester County, for $10,000. Medoc proved to be worth every cent of the money. William Buford had fantastic luck with him and bred him successfully until the stallion broke his near foreleg. His colts could fly, and they made the Buford name a household word at all the tracks in the country. ''The get of Medoc produced a revolution in turf matters in the race horse region, lifting the Buford banner above that of their hitherto triumphant competitors.''[2]

Colonel William Buford's Kentucky farm, known as the Tree Hill Stud, was in eastern Woodford County. It was not far from the farms of his neighbors and racing rivals the Blackburns, the Burbridges, and the Harrises. All had training tracks, held informal meets, and were friendly, if serious, rivals on the turf. When Buford's get from Medoc were three years old, he had seventy-five winners. The colonel was a man of means, and if he thought he did not own the right stallion for a certain mare, he would buy a suitable stallion, if he could, or would send the mare to the horse.

William Buford liked Tiger and bought a full sister, Grecian Princess. Tiger, himself, was a great sire of sprinters. At the time Buford bred to Tiger, he was owned by D. W. Parrish, who had a farm a few miles south of Lexington. Grecian Princess was bred by Harris. Buford bought her to breed when she was retired from the track as a nine-year-old. Other examples of Buford's excellent breeding knowledge showed when he bred his good Archer mare to Morocco by Tiger; to Almanza, a grandson of Sir Archy; to Cherokee by Sir Archy; and to Grasshopper by Sumpter. He bred another of his fine mares, Elizabeth, who was by the Duke of Bedford, to Tiger in 1822, to Kentucky Whip in 1824, to Moses in 1824, to Cherokee in 1826, and to Sumpter in 1829.[3]

Another indication of the pattern of the colonel's breeding is indicated in an advertisement he ran in a Kentucky newspaper in 1827:

Valuable Stock for Sale

I have a number of young blood horses and fillies from the best stock in the Country, got by Sumpter, Whip, Tiger and Moses out of mares which were sired by Sir Archie of Va., the imported horses Spread Eagle, Speculator, Knowsley, Royalist, Archer and the American bred horses Whip and Faris' Diomed, who was one of the best sons of the imported Diomed as a stock horse. Being in the way of breeding on a large scale I am disposed to sell on moderate terms. Several of the mares from which I am raising stock,

Grecian Princess, full sister to Tiger; Nancy Taylor by Spread Eagle and Caroline by Sir Archie. Gentlemen desirous of improving their stock either for the saddle turf or harness may make selections well calculated to aid them in the design by an early application to the subscriber living in Woodford Co. Ky. on the old Frankfort road 14 miles from Lexington and 10 miles from Frankfort.

Apr. 24, 1827.   William Buford.[4]

Among his stallions, besides Medoc, Old Tiger, Bertrand and Kentucky Whip, were Cripple and Little Quicksilver. He raised Cripple, a bay stallion foaled in 1821, sired by Medoc, and out of a Kentucky Whip mare. Little Quicksilver was a gray stallion that Buford purchased from Samuel Davis in 1797 and owned jointly with John Buford. Little Quicksilver was sired by Old Quicksilver who was by Old Medley and out of a mare by Celer.

Abraham M. Buford, William's son, was perhaps as good a horseman as his father and grandfather. He farmed and raised horses with his father and then established his own breeding farm in Bourbon County, eight miles south of Paris. With his father he owned Kentucky Whip during 1810 and 1811 and Tiger in 1825. He stood Kentucky Whip on his farm in 1822 for Ned Blackburn, a family friend. The Buford clan was as successfull in breeding and racing horses as any American family before or since.

JOHN RANDOLPH

John Randolph (1773–1833) always added "of Roanoke" after his name to distinguish himself from his many relatives. He was the third and youngest son of John Randolph, of Cawsons, Chesterfield County, and was a descendant of John Rolfe and Pocahontas. He went to school at Williamsburg and then briefly attended Princeton and Columbia. He was well read, especially in the modern political and philosophical disciplines.

He served in the United States House of Representatives from 1799 to 1829 except for two terms (1813–15 and 1817–19). During Jefferson's presidency he was chairman of the House Ways and Means Committee. He was always a champion of state's rights. He also served in the Senate and while there fought a duel with Henry Clay. He always reserved the right to change his mind. In his will he provided for manumission of his slaves.

His horses, mentioned elsewhere in this book, were Randolph's hobby, and he allowed little to interfere with that hobby. He was an acknowledged expert in pedigrees, and his closest competitor as the "voice of the turf" was W. R. Johnson,

John Randolph of Roanoke (1773–1833), not only a statesman of note but also an important breeder of short horses. He was a champion of *Janus and realized the importance of his blood. He liked to run his horses both long and short. From Harrison, *The Background of the American Stud Book*.

who was a pure long horse breeder. Randolph liked to race both long and short. It has been the habit of Thoroughbred historians to criticize Randolph because, they claimed, he was "infatuated" with *Janus blood. *Janus' position today, as the foundation sire of the quarter horse and as one of the keystones of the modern sprinting Thoroughbred, takes the sting out of these criticisms.

PART III
WESTERING
1830–1880

An excellent way to fix a street is to plow a deep ditch across it. It prevents horse racing.

—*Neosho Valley Register* (Kansas), May, 1874.

QUARTER RUNNING HORSE SIRES

1830–1880

Superior horses in capital letters.

Alp, Little
Andrew Jackson
Anthony
Austin
Bald Hornet
BARNEY OWENS
Barton, Little
Bay Bill
Bay Dick
Bay Printer
Bear Meat
Ben Duncan
Berryessa
Bill Austin
Bill Garner
Billy Cheatham
BILLY, OLD
Blue Eyes
*BONNIE SCOTLAND
BRICK
BROWN DICK
Brown Elk
CHEROKEE
COLD DECK
COPPERBOTTOM
Cracker
Cripple
Dan, Old
Davy, Big

Davy, Little
Driver
Flying Dutchman
Freedom
Frogtown
Garret Davis
Gray Dick
Gray Eagle
Gray John
Gray Hound
Grey Rebel
Hard Bargain
HARRY BLUFF
Joe Hooker
John Adair
John Bacchus
John W. Horton
Kavenaugh
KENTUCKIAN
Kingfisher
LUKE BLACKBURN
MARION
MISSOURI MIKE
Missouri Rondo
Monday (Shannon)
Mose Brimmer
Mounts
OKEMA
OREGON CHARLIE

Pleas Walters
PONY PETE
PRINTER
REBEL
Red Eagle
Rheube
Rifleman
ROAN DICK
Rolling Deck
RONDO
Rupee
Sam Bass
SHILOH
Simtuck
Steamboat Charlie
STEEL DUST
Sway Back
Sweet Owen
Telegraph
Texas Ranger
Tiger, Magnum's
Tom, Blevin's Little
Tom Driver
Union
Veto
WALNUT BARK
Whalebone
WHITE LIGHTNING
Woodpecker

CHAPTER NINE

Crossing a Continent

THE SPEED with which quarter running blood was dispersed north, west, and south in the middle of the nineteenth century makes the story difficult to simplify. We can, however, trace some of the more prominent bloodlines, as represented by certain stallions, and tell how and when they moved into new territories.

Quarter running stallions were taken northwest into Ohio, Illinois, and Michigan. Simultaneously the same blood, representing Whip, Timoleon, Tiger and Printer, sifted into Arkansas, Missouri, Kansas, and Texas. From these last areas related stallions were ridden over the Oregon and Santa Fe trails to the Pacific Slope and the Southwest.

The first settlers had moved into the territory west of the Mississippi in the early 1800s. Then, after a few slow years, the migration turned into a surge that peaked from 1825 through the 1830s. As populations grew, territories became states. Even on the far side of the continent, new territories and states arose. Oregon became a territory in 1848 as the result of the movement that started in 1843, when one thousand settlers and two thousand animals followed the Oregon Trail west. In 1845 some three thousand emigrants used the trail. Farther south, when wagons replaced pack trains over the Santa Fe Trail in 1825, settlers began arriving, and by 1848, when New Mexico became part of the United States, ranches were being established and livestock, including quarter horses, were brought in from the east. California was settled slowly until 1848, but with the discovery of gold settlers swarmed in, and California became a state in 1850.

When we examine the states in a little more detail, we can see just what bloodlines were brought in. Ohio, especially the Scioto Valley, received excellent blood, brought from Virginia by John Van Meter. One of his stallions was Spread Eagle. Several sons of Sir Archy were also in the valley, and elsewhere in Ohio were descendants of Bacchus and *Diomed. According to David Gano, the following sprinters were available in Ohio in the 1830s: Colonel George Ramsey's Young Whip, by Kentucky Whip and out of a mare by *Buzzard; and Lehman's Salt Peter, by Tiger, by Kentucky Whip and out of the mare Blue Peg by Speculator. Also available to the breeders was Sir Solomon, by Sir Solomon.

The best-known Printer stallion in Ohio was owned by a breeder near Lancaster.

Around Steubenville, in eastern Ohio, Timoleon stallions were in great demand, and the cross of them on mares descended from Sir Archy was considered the best possible stock for utility and short racing. Another stallion, called Kentucky Whip after his sire, was brought into the Scioto Valley. This son of Kentucky Whip was foaled in about 1820. Bertrand blood also came into Ohio, usually from Kentucky. Joshua Clements wrote to Henry William Herbert on March 28, 1856:

> About the same time Mr. David Buchanan introduced some fine thoroughbred stock from Kentucky [1830], descendants of Old Sir Archie, and some of the most noted of his get, such as Bertram's, Kosciusko's, Whipster's, Whip's, Hambletonian's and Spread Eagle's. In the same year, Mr. Peter Voorhies brought from Kentucky a brown horse, Friendly Tiger, a descendant of Cook's and Blackburn's Whip.[1]

After the 1830s, Ohio had a good stock of quarter horses, and short racing became fairly common. As early as 1825 racecourses were in operation, and small annual meetings were held at Dayton, Chillicothe, Cincinatti, and Hamilton. The blood of the racing stock, according to racing programs and newspaper accounts, was primarily that of Bertrand, Sir Archy, Muckle John, Woodpecker, Sir Solomon, and Cherokee. Races were held until 1846, when through legislative action organized racing was discontinued. Match racing in the rural areas retained its popularity, however.

In the records submitted by the Hamilton County Agricultural Fair, held in Carthage, Ohio, in 1831, the following Quarter Horses are listed:

> Salt Peter, ch. h., by Tiger, dam by Speculator.
> Bay Medley, blood bay, h., by Old Medley, dam by *Janus.
> Young Solomon, b. h., 6 yr. by Old Sir Solomon.
> Ararat b. h., 5 yr. by Kentucky Whip, dam by *Diomed.
> Eclipse, br. h. 6 yr. by Kentucky Whip, dam by *Buzzard.
> Truxton, br. h. 5 yr. by Kentucky Whip, dam by *Buzzard.
> Laurel, b. f. 2 yr. by Bertrand, dam by Sir Solomon.

This list again confirms that the quarter horse sires, such as Kentucky Whip, Tiger and Bertrand, were popular in Ohio.

Good horses also moved into Michigan. When writing about the early Michigan horses, A. Y. Moore said, "There are many good horses in the State, called the Bacchus stock, got by Old Bacchus owned by Cone, who was shot at a race track. . . they are the fastest horses for short races, but are very strong and muscular."[2]

The Old Bacchus mentioned above is a reference to Cone's Bacchus. This Bacchus was foaled in 1825 in North Carolina, and his sire was a Bacchus sired by Sir

Archy. His dam was Crazy Jane, who at one time had had a reputation as a very fast race mare. Early tracks that featured short races in Michigan were found in Detroit, Adrian, Cold Water, Kalamazoo, Marshall, and Jackson.

Arkansas was the home of many well-known quarter horses, although perhaps Cold Deck and Bear Meat are the best remembered. Cold Deck stood in Van Buren for many years, open to the world for a short race, and bred to all comers, when he was not matched. He was bred by Nathan Floyd of Carthage, Missouri, and was owned at one time by Foster Barker. Bear Meat was a bay stallion, bred and owned by Captain T. T. Tunstall. He was foaled in 1837, sired by Bertrand and out of a mare by American Eclipse. He never left Arkansas. While Bear Meat was not campaigned, he did not dodge any races on his home track.

Missouri had many outstanding quarter stallions, and it was also the source of many horses taken over the Oregon Trail into California and Oregon. Examples are Blevin's stallion Little Tom, who was by Veto, and Brown's Mare, the dam of Old Dan. Old Dan was by Selim and out of Brown's Mare of Brimmer stock. Both were led or ridden across the Great Plains, over the Rocky Mountains, and down into Oregon, where they propagated a family of fast short horses along the Pacific Coast.

Missouri Mike, by Printer, by Cold Deck, was foaled near Carthage, Missouri, and Barney Owens, by Steel Dust, by Jack Traveler, was bred by John Hedgepeff, of Joplin. Bill Stockton bred Missouri Mike. The Alsups and Joe Berry lived in Missouri for a time, and they, too, used Steel Dust and Cold Deck blood.

Kansas also owes much to Missouri. Mike Smiley, of Sylvan Grove, bred several mares to Missouri Mike and to Barney Owens. H. A. Trowbridge, of Wellington, and Uriah Eggleston, of Garden City, used Cold Deck, Steel Dust, and Barney Owens blood.

Illinois seemed to prefer Whip horses, and, for that matter, so did Texas. Short Whip, a son of Kentucky Whip, had a great influence on the Illinois breeders, as did his son Harry Bluff. The blood of Medoc and Reputation was also used.

Texas received much of its early blood from Kentucky and Tennessee. Steel Dust was from Kentucky, Shiloh from Tennessee. It must not be assumed however, that Steel Dust represented the first blood of Kentucky Whip to appear in Texas. In fact, Whip, Tiger, and Bertrand were represented and active on Texas quarter paths before Steel Dust ever ran a race. There were three descendants in North Texas, not far from Dallas, all advertised in the *Clarksville Northern Standard*.[3] These stallions were Bodoc, by Bertrand, dam by Whipster; John Bill, grandson of Sir Archy, dam by Kentucky Whip; and Woodpecker. Woodpecker was the most famous. He was owned for a time by Thomas D. Lee. Before he was sold, he stood during alternate weeks at two farms about ten miles from Clarksville, one John Robbin's farm, the other, John Style's farm, east of town. Each Sunday Woodpecker was ridden through town from one farm to the other. He was also quite a racehorse. The Texas Woodpecker was sired by Missouri Woodpecker, owned by John Webb. Missouri Woodpecker was by J. C. Mason's Buzzard. The Texas Woodpecker's dam was Lady of the Lake by Kentucky Whip.

Joe Mangum, of Nixon, Texas, used Tiger blood he received from the famous mare he bought, May Mangum, so through her Whip blood was also present in South Texas. Milam, whose dam was a full sister of Tiger, was also in Texas.

California undoubtedly got blood directly from the East, as well as from Oregon. It just happens that we have more records of fast quarter running horses springing from Oregon sires, for example, Oregon Charlie, who was a mixture of Brimmer and Printer blood, and Old Dan, who carried Whip blood. John Adams, of Woodland, California, used blood from both of these stallions and also from Blevin's Little Tom, another Oregon horse who was a grandson of Sir Archy. We also find that the movement of blood in these days could reverse itself. California's Joe Hooker, Theodore Winters' stallion, is a case in point. Mares by him were found not only in Oregon but also as far east as Wellington, Kansas, in the mare band of H. A. Trowbridge, who was certainly one of the best breeders of the day.

New Mexico did not have a large number of short horse breeders during this period. In fact, none of the mountain states or the northern plains states had many breeders for rather obvious reasons. In the land where the quarter running horse got his start, row crops like cotton or tobacco were the accepted pattern of life. People lived reasonably close together and knew the relative merits of their neighbors' horses. Adequate crossbreeding and match racing were possible.

This same neighborliness moved westward with the short horse when it left the Atlantic Coast and moved into Illinois, Ohio, Tennessee, Missouri, Arkansas, Kansas, and Texas. No material changes took place in the life-style of these settlers. They continued with intensive farming, breeding, and matching-horses, much as they had in their home states.

The next advance west, however, was something else again. Now the short horse was to leave his familiar surroundings and take root in the mountains and on the plains, and deserts of the American West, where row cropping was still far in the future. The bawl of a calf and the lonely call of the coyote replaced the raucous bray of the mule and the muted voices of the field workers.

The quarter horse found a new home on the immense ranches that sprang up after the Civil War on the Great Plains and in the mountain areas. In these locations the quarter horse spent half a century begetting cow horses for the western ranches. The old neighborly contact almost disappeared, for neighbors were few and the nearest ranch might be several days' ride away. While some exchange of blood and some matching did occur they were not daily or weekly events as they were in the East.

CHAPTER TEN

Creating Legends

AS THE SETTLERS and their horses moved into new states and territories, the basics of match racing remained the same—one man believing that his horse was faster than another's and then trying to prove it. The more professional the racehorse man was the more factors had to be spelled out. If the match was between neighbors or friends, all that was really necessary was to agree on a time and place. Sometimes distance and weight to be carried were discussed before the race. If the race involved a man who made a business or a serious hobby of matching his horses, complexities developed. Each sportsman tried to see that the conditions of the match favored his horse. The following factors were deemed essential and were spelled out clearly in front of witnesses or, better yet, agreed to in writing by both parties.

When and where the match race was to be run was always the first consideration. A neutral track was generally decided upon, for neither side liked to run on the other's home track. The distance to be run was the second consideration, and then weight to be carried, third. The distance might be anything from fifty feet to ⅝ mile. Most short races were run 200, 220, 300, 330, 400, or 440 yards.

Each side tried to lengthen or shorten the best distance of the opponent's horse. An attempt was also made to gain the advantage of weight. If a horse was sturdy and mature, the owner would hold out for as heavy a weight as he could get, and if the horse was a slender two-year-old, his owner would want to run with "catch weights," which meant that each owner could use as heavy or as light a jockey as he wished.

After time, place, distance, and weight were finally agreed upon, then further details, often even more complex, were settled: the amount of money that each owner would put up and the amount that would be forfeited if one horse could not or would not run. This was necessary to guarantee that the time, training, and travel involved would be paid for if one side refused to run. It was also necessary to select someone acceptable to both sides to hold the stakes and pay any forfeit. The selection of judges was a major problem, especially when bets were placed at different distances along the track.

It was also necessary to decide on the start: lap and tap, ask and answer, or any of several other customary ways of getting a race going. Also, did the track have to be dry, and even more important, who would decide if it was wet or dry? All in all there were many details to be settled, some more important to some horses than to others. Misunderstanding on any point resulted in many a fight and even fatal gunplay.[1]

ANDREW JACKSON AND BERRY WILLIAMS

Quarter racing in the early 1800s was highlighted by the story of two men whose racing activities covered the period from the close of the Revolutionary War until the Civil War. The only thing they had in common was the love of good horseflesh. One was a jockey and a trainer, the other a frontiersman and a President. Their love of quarter racing brought them together many times, and the jockey-turned-trainer bested the President each time they met—a feat that no other person was able to achieve. The jockey turned trainer: Berry Williams, mentioned in an earlier chapter. His opponent: General and later President Andrew Jackson.

The best accounts of their various races are found in Anderson's *Making of the American Thoroughbred*, in the appendix entitled "Reminiscences of the Turf by Balie Peyton." Peyton had talked to Williams in the 1870s, when the latter was ninety-five years old.

Andrew Jackson had grown up with horses. They were hobbies and playthings for the General, while for Williams they were his business. Jackson not only raised horses but raced them, and he was often asked to be an official at match races. When he said that a contested start was fair or that a certain horse had won, few cared to argue the point with the fiery general. Among his better-known horses were Truxton, Rifleman, Pacolet, and Bolivar. According to some, the General raised Truxton. He was a bay, foaled in 1800, sired by *Diomed and out of Nancy Coleman, by Batte's Fearnought. Jackson would match Truxton at almost any distance, from 440 yards to four miles.

There were two well-known sprinters called Rifleman. The better of the two belonged to Jackson. He would race Rifleman as short as 400 yards. He disliked losing a race and seldom did. Rifleman was a gray horse, foaled about 1827. He was definitely bred, raised, and raced by the General. Rifleman was sired by Pacolet, a son of imported *Citizen, and his dam was a mare by Truxton. The other Rifleman that sired short horses was bred and owned by M. C. Hammond, of Georgia. He was sired by Woodpecker and was foaled in 1835.

On the track Jackson would often intimidate his adversaries by the boldness of his defiance, when he might not have won by the speed or bottom of his horse. Many men brought horses out of Virginia and North Carolina satisfied that they could in full assurance beat the General in a match race, but he was seldom, if ever, beaten on his own course.

The only races of the General's that are of interest here were those between

Haynie's Maria, trained by Williams, and the various horses Jackson used in a vain attempt to beat the mare.

Maria's speed was as great as necessary. She ran fast against fast horses and slow against slow horses. A good example of this was evident when Berry Williams worked her out against Saltram, who was also in his training. When he put them together, they always came in locked with Maria just a fraction ahead.

After one of Jackson's first endeavors against Haynie's Maria he bought a race horse he thought fast enough to beat her. He went to Georgia and got Stump-the-Dealer from Colonel Alston. However, when he got "the Stump" home, he found that, although he was fast enough to win most races, he was not quite in Maria's class.

Disappointed, Jackson looked around for another horse. He heard that a Mr. DeWett in Kentucky had a fast mare, so he sent him a letter suggesting that he come to Tennessee and that they match Maria. DeWett brought the mare to Tennessee and trained her on Jackson's track at the Hermitage. She had the reputation of being the swiftest nag in the United States up to a mile. The race was matched for $1,000 to be run in the fall of 1814, a mile run on a neutral track, the only place Berry would consider matching a Jackson horse. It was run at Clover Bottom and Berry and Maria easily took the race. General Jackson immediately rematched the two horses for another race at half the distance, for $1,500 for the leader at the end of 440 yards, $500 for the leader at 600 yards, and $500 at the finish of the race. This time the race was run at the Nashville straightaway, and again Maria won at all distances. As Skinner so aptly put it, although General Jackson conquered the Indians, defeated Packenham, beat Adams and Clay, crushed the Bank of the United States under the heel of his boot, he could not beat Berry and Maria at any distance.

OTHER MATCHES, OTHER STATES

Not all quarter races were as famous as Maria's, but many similar ones were held in all the states. A few will be mentioned here as samples, starting with some held in the foundation states, Virginia and South Carolina.

An interesting challenge for a match race was announced in the *American Turf Register* for 1833. It involved a Virginia horse, African Lion. The owner offered to run his horse, for any amount up to $500, against any horse in the world. The only stipulation was that the other horse must be near his horse's height and weight. The distance was to be a quarter mile. The offer was to remain open for one year. The owner said that he expected all racehorse men either to accept his challenger or to "leave off abusing my horse." The article was signed George Hume. After the signature there appeared a postscript that provides the punch line: "P.S. I forgot to mention the height and weight of African Lion, he is 19 hands high, and weighs, by the hay scales, 2147 pounds. As I am not disposed to set any unnecessary difficulties in the way, produce a horse weighing 2000 pounds and I will give the 147."[2]

In the same journal is an account that shows the ingenuity of the black population in Virginia. Two black boys wanted to race their master's horses, but one lacked experience in turning and starting a race horse. He also had difficulty in handling the high-strung horse when they tried to start side by side. They arrived at an entirely logical and practical way to overcome this difficulty. They decided not to try to start side by side but to start at the same time from different ends of the track. The first to reach the halfway point would be the winner. Two posts marked the halfway mark. They started and fairly flew toward the center. Within a few feet of the posts the two horses hit head on, and both horses were killed on the spot. The boys escaped without serious injury. Nothing is mentioned about their master's reaction to the race and its outcome.[3]

Match races were still being held in the Carolinas in the 1840's, as indicated by the following items from the *Spirit of the Times* of March 23, 1844.

Challenge for $500 or $1000

James B. Barclay of Columbia, S.C. offers to run his horse Jack, with featherweights on each at any horse in the world, one quarter of a mile, for $500 or $1000, half forfeit. Mr. Barclay's challenge at length will be found in our advertising column. Jack is said to be but 14½ hands in height. Mr. Barclay's challenge is open for acceptance until May 20th.

An ad in the same issue follows:

To Owners of Quarter Stock

My Chestnut horse Jack, 14½ hands high, with feather weights on each, can beat anything of horseflesh kind in the U.S., one quarter of a mile, for $500 or $1000 cash up. H.F. at Columbia, South Carolina, at any time to be agreed on by the parties. This proposition to be open until the 20th day of May next.

Columbia, South Carolina,
March 13, 1844
Jas. B. Barkley

Quarter racing was popular in Pennsylvania during the middle of the 1800's. The leading short liner of the 1850s was the celebrated Reading mare. Her owners would back her for any amount, it was claimed, in a race 600 yards or less. Examples of some Pennsylvania races follow as they were reported in the *Spirit of the Times*.

Columbia Flats   Friday Mar. 19, 1852
Match for $40   carrying 140 lbs.   440 yards

E. Tookers chestnut horse Canada Bill 1st
Mr. Tinkers brown horse Emancipation 2nd

Seidels Lanes   Thurs. Mar. 25, 1852
Match $200   catch weights   350 yards
Limber Jim   1st   Mr. Derr's mare   2nd
[This was Limber Jim's first appearance in Pennsylvania.]

                                                      Thursday, April 15
Match $200   carrying 110 lbs.   500 yards
C. R. Harmon's chestnut horse Canada Bill 1st
Mr. Bond's gray gelding Blue Dick 2nd
Time 28 seconds.   Won by 28 feet.

The last race above resulted in a match between a horse named Prince and Canada
Bill:

Match $200   carrying 120 lbs.   400 yards
Pike and Dixon's roan gelding Prince 1st
C. R. Harmon's chestnut horse Canada Bill 2nd
Time 24 seconds.[4]

After the above race the owners took Canada Bill to New York to find some fresh
money. At a straightaway track called Union Course a match was set up for May 6,
1852, for $50. Canada Bill raced a horse named Printer and he won with ease. Then
the owner of Bay Coachman challenged Canada Bill to run 500 yards with the purse to
be $200 at 440 and $200 at 500 yards. Canada Bill won at both lengths. Blue Dick and
Polly Brown now moved into Union Course from Seidels Lanes in Pennsylvania. Blue
Dick ran Polly Brown 550 yards for $400 and got beat. Then on March 20 came the big
match, Canada Bill against the New York favorite Lancaster Gray, owned by a man
named Skyles. This was the race Canada Bill's owners had been waiting for. He had
not been allowed to run his best before that race. It was run over 440 yards, carrying
110 pounds, and for $1,000 a side. C. R. Harmon, the owner, and his friends cleaned
up; Canada Bill came in with 20 feet to spare. There was an immense crowd to cheer
on the local favorite, Lancaster Gray, but they went home poorer and wiser.

Ohio was the site of many a great match race during the period 1830 to 1880.
Many were of an impromptu nature and were held at small crossroads towns. Local
county fairs were often utilized as a site for matches, and some fairgrounds even had
tracks.

A correspondent to the *Spirit of the Times* told about a short race held in
Monroeville, Ohio, on Saturday, October 20, 1853. The race was matched for $200,

catch weights and was to be run eighty rods (440 yards). The favorite—and also the winner—was Great Bacchus, a colt owned by John Tuttle.[5] The other horse was Kate Lawrence, owned by H.W. Hopkins. The mare was ahead at the halfway mark but could not hold her lead. Hopkins was not convinced that the mare was slower, so he matched another race, also to be run on Tuttle's straightaway in Monroeville. Again he lost. The match was run Wednesday, November 2, for $300, catch weights. This time the Bacchus colt led all the way and won by about 30 feet.

A quarter race that attracted great attention during this period in Ohio was run between Ida Mae and Kitty Clyde. Ida Mae was considered a superior quarter mare and was open to the world except for the great California horse Comet, who had defeated her. A man named Price, of Tuscora County, raced the black mare, Ida Mae. A Mr. Clark, of Pittsburg, agreed to a match for $2,000 if Price would give him the world to find his horse. Price agreed, barring only Comet, and gave Clark six weeks to bring the horse to New Philadelphia Track ready to run. The money was posted, and Clark left.

Six weeks passed, but Clark did not return with a horse. On the evening of the day of the race the forfeit money was turned over to Price. Several hours later Clark arrived with the then unknown nag Kitty Clyde, but he was too late; the $500 had already been paid to Price. Clark was was not happy with the situation, saying that he had been unavoidably delayed because the railroad schedule had prevented him from making the deadline. Price wanted to run and was not too happy to get only $500, so he was willing to compromise. He gave Clark $250 back, and Clark agreed to new terms, $1,100 to $1,000, the race to be run two days later. There would really be two races in one, half the money being paid at 440 yards and half at 600 yards.

Both horses were on the score at the starting time, 2 P.M. Kitty did not appear to be fresh, probably because of the railroad trip, confinement and travel. Ida looked ready to run. After about an hour of turning, Kitty Clyde broke loose, but the black mare stayed at the score, so Kitty was called back. After another long try, Ida Mae broke and ran through the race alone. It was dark by then, so the race was postponed until Monday.

The black, Ida Mae, had shown such a burst of early speed when she broke loose Saturday evening that on Monday the backers of the sorrel, Kitty Clyde, were a little hesitant to bet any more money on the 440. Kitty was still the favorite at 600 yards. The added two days' rest had helped the sorrel mare. It was again difficult to get them started, and the sorrel, Kitty, broke twice when the black, Ida Mae, was held up. Finally after the black had reared, plunged, and backed for two long hours, she was coaxed to the scratch and they were tapped off. Kitty had a two-foot advantage. One observer said, "Ye Gods such a start. Such a run never was witnessed in Ohio."[6] By the time they reached 150 yards, the black mare had the lead by daylight, but from that point on the sorrel gradually gained until at the quarter mark less than two feet separated the two mares, which, by the rules agreed upon, made the race a dead heat. From that mark on it was all Kitty Clyde's race.

Regular races were held in Michigan during the 1800s. Fairs, such as the Michigan State Fair held in Detroit, regularly scheduled short races. Three examples follow:

Wednesday, September 28, 1853   Match $50   80 rods
Mr. Morris   bay horse   Printer   1st
Mr. Townsend's chestnut mare   Lady Woodpecker   2nd
time 24 flat

Thursday, September 29, 1853   Match $25   80 rods
Mr. Frost's chestnut horse   Napoleon Bacchus   1st
Mr. Ruben's chestnut horse   Phillessey-my-Joe   2nd
time 25 flat

Saturday, October, 1853   Match $50   80 rods
Mr. Dewey's chestnut horse   Eclipse   1st
Mr. Frost's chestnut horse   Napoleon Bacchus   2nd
time 24 flat[7]

Turf, Field, and Farm told about a quarter race to be held in Mississippi in 1871. It seemed that two quarter horsemen, a Mr. Larkin of Oak Ridge and a Captain Hardy, of Brooklyn, Mississippi, matched a race to be run on October 12 for $5,000 a side. Each put up $2,500 forfeit money. Larkin's horse was a dun mare named Lilly Hamilton, and the Hardy horse was a bay gelding named Bob Lee. The correspondent who sent in this information stated that although it was only a quarter race, it was exciting no little interest, because of the size of the purse and the forfeit.[8]

A quarter horse race held in Iowa was described in a sporting journal. The item was dated July 2, 1872 at Council Bluffs. The race was held at the straightaway track next to the Rock Island Railway Depot. The writer said that a couple of mares were matched for a quarter race. One mare, named Flora, owned by a Mr. Campbell. The other mare, Sage Hen, was owned by a Mr. Hatcher. Sage Hen was a well-known speedster, and most of the betting was on this mare. By the time they approached the line, the odds were two to one. The race, over 400 yards, was won by Flora in twenty-four seconds.[9]

In the October 13, 1838 issue of the *Spirit of the Times* is an excellent report of some match races held at Fort Gibson, in the Cherokee Nation, about 350 miles west of the Mississippi. The races began on September 1. The straightaway track was laid out by the officers of the fort, and the work was done by the enlisted men. Captains

129

Dawson and Moore of the 7th Infantry Regiment were in charge of building the track. The only available level stretch was crossed by several roads used by wagons bringing hay and timber to the fort. As a result there were some bad places on the track.

The races were well attended considering the remote location. One visitor estimated the crowd at several hundred. He added that the variety of colors, diversity of costumes, and contrasts in manners produced an interesting scene. A great deal of betting took place even before preparation was made for the first race. The day started with a match race for $500 a side, to be run a mile out. A Lieutenant Simmons' sorrel gelding won the race. The second match race was run for a suit of clothes. The distance was 600 yards. A chestnut gelding named Red Fox owned by a Mr. Almsted won that one beating Mr. Doyle's brown gelding. No time was announced. The bet, intended to be a suit of clothes to be purchased by the loser, turned out to be a little more. The winner went into the store and equipped himself from the inside out, even putting in the vest a pocket knife and a pencil. The total bill, including the overcoat, ran to a little over $180.

The next match, 300 yards, was run for a hat. Lieutenant Simmons' sorrel gelding won this race, beating Mr. Musgrave's Bugler. Several other races were matched on the spot. One buffalo hunter had a black pony he thought was fast. He got a race for $10 a side, to run a mile against Jupiter. Even though the black pony was just in from the Comanche country, fresh from chasing buffalo, he was easily beaten. Another race was run 100 yards for $40 a side. In this race a chestnut gelding defeated a dun gelding named Pumpkin Slinger. Pumpkin Slinger was the favorite, having won previous races, but in this one he was overmatched and lost. The races were finally terminated when the sun went down.

Fifteen years later, in 1853, short races were reported at Fort Smith, Arkansas:

> Dear Spirit. We had quite an exciting race on Saturday, October 1, between Blags mare and Crop. Six hundred yards with Blag (124 lbs. on the mare) and Little George Kenny, 73 pounds on Crop. The track was heavy, having rained all the day before. Betting was equal on both sides for some time, even up to 4 pm, when Crop became the favorite, and about sundown, two to one was offered on him by some knowing ones, and taken at a word. Horses were on the track a little before sundown, and a little after the word was given, and away they went. The mare was ahead for about 140 yards, then Crop locked her and passed her soon after.[10]

Regular short races were held in Fort Smith and elsewhere in Arkansas during this period. In the fall of 1853 a Fort Smith correspondent to a New York sporting journal wrote that long and short straightaway races were held during the fall meet.

Quarter racing was also recorded in Kansas Territory some years before statehood in 1861. At the time of the race described below, there was bitter rivalry between the "free soldiers" from the North and southern slaveholders who had moved in, bringing slaves and good short horses. On June 2, 1857, in Paola, Kansas, several short races were held. One that attracted special interest was between an Indian and a white man for 600 yards. The Indian's name was Kil-son-zah, and he was racing a black mare called Prairie Fawn. The white, J. C. Smith, had a bay horse named Revelry. Each put up $500, and Prairie Fawn won.

Just north of Wichita, Kansas, in view of the city, was a very popular race path where matches were held on most weekends. After the war, on July 6, 1872, there was a race between a Texas horse and the local champion:

> The local mare won and it is said more than a thousand dollars changed hands. It is estimated that more than 1,000 men were present, besides five carriage loads of 'soiled doves.' So great was the rush that main street, for an hour or so seemed almost deserted.[11]

TEXAS

Steel Dust may not have been the greatest quarter running horse, but he certainly was one of the best known. Like so many of the fastest short horses of the period, he crossed two of the most popular sprinting families: Sir Archy and Kentucky Whip. He was brought to Texas from Kentucky and was stabled near Lancaster.

Not many miles north another stallion was becoming as well known. His name was Monmouth. Steel Dust and Monmouth ran at McKinney, Texas, in 1855. The match attracted wide attention, and all businesses closed for the event. Even in neighboring Sherman and Jefferson, business came to a halt so that everyone could see the race. So many people turned out that the main hotel in McKinney, the Foote House, was turned over to the ladies. The men slept where they could.

Both horses were carefully trained for the match. Henry Ellis, a thirteen-year-old boy, was to ride Steel Dust. Henry was a brother-in-law of the owner of Steel Dust. He was so light that he would have to wear a money belt filled with shotgun pellets to meet the 110-pounds weight. A straightaway path was cleared across the road from the Ellis home, and there Steel Dust was worked out. When Henry's mother, a devout Baptist, found out that the race was to be run on Sunday, she put her foot down and refused to let her son ride. Henry was brokenhearted. To take his place a lightweight black youngster, Tom McKnight, was chosen. Since the boy had not had much chance to practice on the fast-breaking Steel Dust, blackstrap molasses was smeared on the horse's back to help the jockey stick on.

The way to McKinney looked like a general moving day, so many wagons and riders went north with Steel Dust. One of the better-known horsemen in attendance was Jack Batchler. Many other notable people were already waiting, including J. W. Throckmorton, a future governor of the state. C. A. Williams, the county clerk, saw Steel Dust arrive and reported that the stallion was closely guarded by a half-dozen men, who allowed no one to approach. The twelve-year-old bay seemed quiet, almost sleepy, and because of his years and intensive training, his ribs were showing. After reports of Steel Dust's less-than-outstanding appearance circulated among the crowds, the Collin County people were even more ready to bet. The entourage that arrived with Steel Dust were willing to meet them halfway.

Finally the race started, and Steel Dust no longer seemed gaunt and sleepy. He left the mark like a telegraph going over the wire downhill, and in less than twenty-three seconds Collin County was nearly broke. Steel Dust was the toast of Dallas County.

Another famous match was the one between Shiloh and Steel Dust. Shiloh was owned by Batchler, and was by Van Tromp, by Thomas' Big Solomon, by Sir Solomon, a son of Sir Archy. He was foaled in Tennessee but taken to Texas by his owner, who settled near Lancaster. Since he and Steel Dust lived so close, it was inevitable that eventually they would meet. Probably the reason they did not lock horns earlier was because their owners were neighbors and the best of friends.

The race was to be run on the neutral Dallas straightaway, at the eastern edge of town. It has long since been covered with cement and houses, but in those days it was the site of many a thrilling race. Dallas even then had a few thousand people and a small weekly newspaper. Its main hotel was the Crutchfield House, where venison and wild duck were on the daily menu.

What happened when the race time came was described by Wayne Gard. Jack Batchler's son Henry was at the track for the race, and Henry described what happened as follows:

> Steeldust was so eager for the show, that he reared and plunged all the time he was in the chute. When he made his leap to clear the stall, he struck the wall and ran a splinter into his shoulder, which disabled him. Father galloped Shiloh over the track and claimed the forfeit, to which the judges decided he was entitled. As a result of the injury to his shoulder Steeldust went blind and never raced again.[12]

It is doubtful that Steel Dust's "moon-blindness" (ophthalmia) was caused by the splinter. More likely it was the cause of the accident.

Shiloh, was then eleven years old, but he continued to be raced by Batchler. Considerably more about Steel Dust and Shiloh appears later in the book.

No western state or territory was able to dominate the quarter running horse industry as Virginia had in the early days, until Texas began to breed and run the short-liners. Several states were outstanding in the quality of their quarter horses, notably Missouri, Arkansas, and Illinois, but they lacked that certain something that brings notoriety and breeds legends. In the Lone Star State, Steel Dust, Shiloh, Billy, Pan Zarita, Della Moore, and Miss Princess all had that certain something that leads to immortality in the minds of the quarter running horse fan. Just as Virginia dominated in the production of sprinters during the first hundred years, so did Texas dominate the field from the middle 1800s until the 1950s. Oklahoma has played a role similar to South Carolina's, in that both states ran their neighboring rivals a tight race for dominance in the short-racing industry, and both led in certain respects.

The first quarter horses who went to Texas were used for many things besides match racing. Many a Texan owed his life to the speed of his horse when he encountered Indians. Not a few outlaws lived to continue their roguery for a while longer because they were mounted on first-class sprinters when the law began closing in. Obviously the stakes for the winner in such predicaments were high. As the Indians retired west and north and the frontier began to calm down a mite, short races became common—so common that soon after the Civil War the Texas legislature outlawed match racing in the streets of any town.

Along the the Río Grande border additional zest was added with the opportunity to run against the Mexicans, who had some pretty decent quarter horses. At first many Texans thought that running the Mexicans would be as easy as matching the Indians. The Indians were proud of their ponies, who had great endurance, and a ruggedness that allowed them to thrive with a minimum of feed and care, but they were no match for the descendants of Kentucky Whip and other sires of his quality. The Mexicans had a better grade of horses, because they had obtained good stock from Europe and from the United States. It did not take the Texans long to realize that it paid to be mounted when you crossed the border.

Malcolm D. McLean, in *Fine Texas Horses*, tells of a quarter horse race in the 1840s, held at the Dayton Grove Track, which was about a mile out of Clarksville. One of the participants was Alfred Bailes, a man very prominent in Texas racing in the mid-1800s. He matched a horse he called Rackmaroleon against Berkshire's Boar, owned by James Boerland. Berkshire's Boar was undoubtedly Flying Dutchman under a new name, although the dates do not agree exactly. Each man put up $1,000. The race was supposed to be run at one o'clock, but it took about two hours to get the horses started, while each side jockeyed for position. Bailes's horse got the jump on the Boar, but by the 200-yard mark the Boar had passed Bailes' horse, and the race was not close. Bailes, who always wanted the fastest horse, bought Berkshire's Boar on the spot.

Berkshire's Boar (or Flying Dutchman) had been bred in Kentucky by Webb Ross, of Scott County, by Grey Eagle, by Woodpecker, by Bertrand and out of the famous mare Blinkey, also known as Mary Porter. Blinkey was by Muckle John, by

133

Sir Archy and out of a son of the Old Printer by *Janus.[13] Berkshire's Boar campaigned in Kentucky, Missouri, and Mississippi as Flying Dutchman, and gained such a reputation that James Boerland had difficulty getting races for him. He changed the horse's name, went to Texas and got the race with Bailes mentioned above. Berkshire's Boar was a red bay, about fifteen hands, with dark spots on his rump, his markings being somewhat reminiscent of a Berkshire Boar's. After Bailes had all the races he wanted out of Berkshire, he and his partner, a man named Oliver, sold the Boar to Frank Lilly, of Throp Spring. The Boar was a full brother of Sweet Owen, Viley, and Bay Printer.

Alfred Bailes spent most of his time on the road running quarter horses. He was partners with Oliver in Guadalupe County until after the Civil War, and he also must have had a ranch or a partner on the South Fork of the Sulphur River, near the old town of Tarrant.[14] Bailes later owned another speedster, Brown Dick. There is today some confusion owing to conflicts in dates, but probably the brown stallion, Brown Dick, that Bailes ran against Steel Dust was the same one that was later owned by Colonel Bailey, of West Texas. Bailes sold Brown Dick to Jack Bridges, of Sulphur Springs, and sometime later Brown Dick or a similarly bred and named stallion was standing at stud for Colonel Bailey.

When Bailes matched Brown Dick against Steel Dust, Steel Dust was being trained by Jack Batchler. The race was run at Lancaster. In the late 1930s, I received a letter from a Mr. Shelton about the race. While his recollections did not agree with all the known facts, his observations about Steel Dust are interesting because he was a direct descendant of the people involved. The Sheltons met the Perrys on their way south to Lancaster and settled on a farm near that of Middleton Perry. A Shelton married an Ellis, the other family connected with Steel Dust. When Shelton died, his widow married Alfred Bailes. Here is the account as given in the letter from Shelton:

> In the fall of 1857, two miles west of Lancaster, Jack Batchler and Alfred Bailes staged the race. The Unbeatable Brown Dick went down in defeat, beaten by an unknown horse 13 years old, who had just run his first and last race. After the race, Alfred Bailes sold Brown Dick to Jack Bridges of Hopkins County for $2,500 in gold, so Brown Dick returned to the place of his birth.
>
> After the race, Jack Lilley and a man whom we will call Lightfoot had a quarrel over the race. Lightfoot backed up. That night after Jack Lilley had gone to bed and was asleep, Lightfoot entered the room and shot him through the heart with the muzzle of the gun so close that there were powder burns on Lilley's underclothes.
>
> Mid Perry was so upset over the killing, which had taken place after the first race of the bay stallion, he never let him run again. The horse lived in peace and plenty until 1863 or 1864, and was then buried on Mid Perry's old place five miles southeast of Lancaster on the north side of Ten Mile Creek. So here lies the most talked of, written of, argued over

horse with the least positively known origin of any that Texas ever had—the original Steel Dust of Texas.[15]

There is a good description in the *Spirit of the Times* of a Texas straightaway race held in Corpus Christi. There was a large crowd, which included many women. Some of the ladies remained on horseback during the races. This way they could see better, and they were kept away from the too-familiar jostling of the crowd. The ladies and some of the wealthy townsmen turned out in the latest finery. The carriages were equally fashionable. The splendid carriage of Mrs. Kenny, drawn by four superbly matched horses, attracted great attention. Present too were army officers and also several Mexicans, Indians, border chiefs, ranchers, and frontiersmen. One or two of the ladies entered their horses in the mile race, which made the event even more exciting. All started well, and for the first 800 yards all the horses were grouped, the *Spirit* says, "like a flock of sheep." Then a general stampede took place. One of the ladies' horses bolted across the track, while some others headed for higher country. All of this happened to the great amusement of the crowd, who rent the air with their shouts and hurrahs as Mr. Colton's bay horse came in an easy winner in 1:57.[16]

Earlier I mentioned Alfred Bailes and Brown Dick. A prominent son of Brown Dick raced in two great matches with a quarter horse called Gray Wonder, owned by a Mr. Haley, who lived near Lancaster, Texas. I have been able to find direct references to only the first of the races between these speedsters. It was held at the Lancaster straightaway in June, 1857. The horses ran 500 yards for $2000 a side. Brown Dick's son was just a two-year-old, but he had won every race he had run. Haley had equal success with his beautiful little gray gelding, Gray Wonder. Both horses went into the race undefeated, and the racehorse gang gathered from miles around. Not since Steel Dust and Monmouth had run a few years earlier on the same track had such a crowd been drawn to Lancaster. Every man and boy on the ground picked a winner, and all seemed sure that their horse could not be beaten. There was more money on the local horse, but enough money came in from West Texas to keep the wagering even. There appeared to be no favorite; every man just bet all he had or could borrow.

When the horses arrived, one could hear a murmur run through the crowd. When the jockeys were given a leg up, they seemed too little to trot a saddle horse, much less ride a race. Then the interminable process of turning, asking, and not answering began. First one was ready, then the other, but neither seemed in the mood to start. At last, "Go!" was heard from the jockey on Young Brown Dick in answer to the "Ready!" that had been given by the rider on Gray Wonder. Young Brown Dick, according to the account, gave a mighty leap at the word and had a bulge on the gray. The colt ran, according to the observer, like "a small dog on high rye with two or more tin kettles tied to his tail."[17] Gray Wonder followed close in his wake. Neither seemed

135

to gain or lose an inch for about 400 yards, at which time Young Brown Dick was about twelve feet in front of Gray Wonder. At this point the gray began to gain a little every jump, and his backers began to have some hope that he might pull the race out of the fire. The race was a bit short, or the colt had a little extra, for he crossed the finish ahead of Gray Wonder.

Another famous race, this one involving a Steel Dust filly, occurred when Sam Hildreth's father took his family to Texas to match a race with Jim Brown. Sam Hildreth's father raced horses. The family lived in a small Missouri town. Down at the general store one evening Hildreth, Sr., heard some fellows talking about horse racing in Texas. "There's a horsemen named Jim Brown down in Texas who's got some mighty sweet ones; and say, boy, how that little devil will bet on his horses," one of them told Hildreth. Hildreth had a very fast horse called Red Morocco in his stable that he would run against any horse. When he got home that evening, he told his wife to pack up, kids, horses, and all—they were going down to Texas on a matter of important husiness. The news didn't faze Mrs. Hildreth; she was used to her husband.

A few days later the whole Hildreth family, with their belongings, were on the move. They had four wagons, ten or twelve race horses, and six or seven riding horses. When night fell, Hildreth and his sons tended the horses while Mrs. Hildreth and the girls worked around the campfire.

Sam Hildreth was only about five years old at the time, so he could not remember where in Texas they found Jim Brown (it was at Giddings, Texas). Sam described Jim as a little bit of a whippersnapper, leather-faced, thin, and wiry, and as courageous as they made them, even in that country, where a fellow couldn't get by unless he had his nerve with him.

According to Hildreth the people of Giddings elected Brown sheriff to clean up the county. The first thing Jim Brown did was go after the gang belonging to Wesley Hardin and Bill Langley. Brown picked up Hardin's trail and followed him on horseback through Texas, the Indian Nations, Kansas, and then back to Lee County. There he captured him and took him to the town jail.

But Lee County didn't really get cleaned up until three horse thieves stole the best racehorses in Brown's string, including Gray Alice, by Steel Dust, his fastest horse. Brown started out after the gang. One evening, two hundred miles from Lee County, he came face to face with them. Everyone reached for his gun at the same time, but the three horse thieves never had a chance. With his first shot Brown killed one of the thieves, and with his seond he wounded another. The third knew when he was beaten and gave up.

When the Hildreth family arrived in Giddings, Sam's father hunted up Jim Brown as soon as they made camp. He told the sheriff that they had come all the way from Missouri just to match some races. Brown was cordial. He told Hildreth that he had a mare named Gray Alice that was just about as speedy as anything on four legs in that section. Brown said that he would be glad to race Gray Alice against Red Morocco for a side bet up to $5,000.

They didn't have any telephones or radios down there then, but in less than ten days the cowboys and ranchmen for miles around began pouring into town. All they talked about was the coming match between the Texas and Missouri mares. They began betting big money on the race, with Gray Alice the red-hot favorite, which led to some troubles for Hildreth. Some of the bigger backers of Gray Alice got to Hildreth's jockey and gave him several hundred dollars to disappear. This he did, leaving Red Morocco with no rider and the race only a few days away. Some of the Texans told Hildreth about a jockey who lived nearby. On their say-so, Hildreth sent a messenger after the jockey, who sent word that he would come.

The course was laid out over a quarter-mile stretch of smooth ground on the prairie. It was typical, with two narrow pathways running alongside each other on a straightaway and a narrow strip of green turf between. The people of Giddings had made the paths by hitching a team of horses to a big iron cauldron and dragging the kettle along a straight line upside down. Then they raked the grass from the loose earth and packed down the dirt a little on the sides, and the track was ready. Running from the start was a rail separating the paths about eighty yards along the course. There was also a temporary fence to keep back the crowd.

About five or six hundred cowboys and ranch owners lined the course when Gray Alice and Red Morocco took their places for the ask-and-answer start. The start meant a great deal in quarter-mile races. If you got left at the post, in a short race you didn't have a ghost of a chance.

The new jockey got Red Morocco away to an even start with Gray Alice. Before they had reached the end of the fenced-in part of the track, she was two lengths in front and widening the gap. Old Red was running straight and true, and it looked like she could win by eight or ten lengths, even in that short distance. There didn't seem a chance she could lose.

But when she reached the end of the rail between the paths, something happened. She moved out to the strip between the two pathways. That ground was hard and uneven, and she wasn't plated for that kind of footing. Gray Alice pulled up on her fast and moved ahead of her a few steps from the finish. The Hildreths' mare lost. Their $5,000 was gone. Gray Alice was a daughter of the great Steel Dust that lost very few races, and she didn't lose this one. Sam Hildreth had this to say about losing the race:

> And the worst part of it was we'd been cheated. The gamblers had got to our new jockey that night before the race and paid him to do just what he did—pull Old Red out to the hard turf so she'd have to stop. From the day we set foot in that Texas town we'd never

had a chance to win that match race with Jim Brown's horse. And in later years old John Huggins, who was well known around the New York and Chicago tracks in the eighties and early nineties, and who had once been Brown's racing partner, told me that it would have been like pulling teeth to have got that five thousand if we'd won. But I will say for Sheriff Jim that he was pretty white when he saw how discouraged the whole thing had made my father. He gave us five thousand dollars, a herd of cattle, and some other race-horses for Red Morocco before we left Texas. That squared things some, though it nearly broke my father's heart to leave that grand old mare in strange hands.[18]

Jim Brown later moved to Chicago and continued racing. Sam Hildreth grew up to become one of the very best Thoroughbred trainers who ever lived.

CALIFORNIA

During the Spanish and Mexican periods of California history there were many recorded two-horse match races. It seems safe to say, however, that quarter racing, with quarter-bred horses, did not begin until the influx of United States citizens in the 1840s.

In the January 3, 1885, issue of the San Francisco sporting magazine *Breeder and Sportsman*, Joseph Cairn Simpson pretty well summed it up when he wrote:

> The short-horses who came with the multitudes which the gold discovery brought, were muscled, powerfully built animals, who could break from the score like an arrow from a bow, and beat the earth with such force and rapidity of stroke as to carry them from 400 yards to half a mile in very fast time.

The quarter horse came to California with the argonauts from Illinois and Ohio, from Kentucky and from Arkansas, from Missouri and Kansas, and especially from Oregon. When they reached California, their owners reacted in the normal way: they raced them. As Simpson said, "Bags of coined gold, buckskin sacks of dust, were wagered, and not infrequently the sharp notes of the revolver and the gleam of the bowie knife gave an emphasis to the sport."

It was during this period, while gold was still the object of frantic search in California, that the first references to quarter racing were made. The accounts often left out details that we would like to know, such as pedigrees, owners, and other interesting data, but much can be read between the lines. According to the March 15, 1848, issue of the *Californian*, a newspaper published in San Francisco:

> A horse race came off at the Dolores Mission course on Monday, March 6, between a horse of W. A. Leidsdorff, Esq. of this place and one of Mr. Hedspeth's of Sonoma. The

138

judges decided in favor of Hedspeth's, he being a little ahead of the other at the coming out place.

Hedspeth's horse was named Doc, and he had been running with great success. Not long after the race described above, Doc ran against Andreas Pico's horse 600 yards for $5,000 a side. The race was run on the outskirts of Sonoma. Later the two horsemen met again, in a race run at San Jose on April 3, 1850, for $10,000 a side. The story was told in the *Alta California*.

San Jose was then the capital of California. It had acquired that distinction by offering about thirty acres of land as a capital site and by arguing that it was more centrally located than Monterey, its primary rival. Probably what influenced the decision as much as anything was the fact that San Jose had a fine, commodious building, seventy feet long and thirty-five feet wide. The residents also bragged about their "salubrious climate." So the race was run in San Jose, the capital. It was attended by a huge throng. The Sonoma horse once again beat Andreas Pico's horse.

A short time later a race of just a little over one-eighth of a mile (300 varas) was held in Santa Barbara. Again it was an American quarter horse against a native California horse. The California horse was owned by Francisco Noreiga. The principal stake was 300 head of cattle. There was also a lot of betting on the side by both participants and by their friends. They bet money, cattle, horses, sheep, hogs, cloths, wine, and anything else agreeable to the bettors. The American horse, Old Breeches, won handily, and everyone was invited to a fandango that night.

One of the earliest references to match racing is found in the letters of a pioneer family to their people back east. In a letter dated April 15, 1851, is found the following paragraph: "Tell the boys we have one that is a fast nag. We, not being betting characters, one of our neighbor's ranch men had her and is open for all bets from $100 to $500, had a race in her Saturday." This letter was found in *The History of Yolo County, California*, edited by William O. Russell.

There was so much racing in Yolo county that in the 1860s a horseman's association was formed. Land was purchased a little north of Woodland, and a track and stables were built for future races. The track was on a little-used ranch road going east and west. It soon picked up the name Race Track Road, and it is still so called today by long-time residents of the area, although the street sign says Kentucky Avenue. Perhaps it got the later name because the original landowners along there were mostly from Kentucky.

In the middle fifties there was also a fine track for short horses at Knights Landing and at Cacheville. The Knights Landing track was owned and operated by I. W. Brownell. In 1854, Curey Burney, a racehorse man, bought the track and modernized it. A meet was held there in 1855 that old-timers were still talking about at the turn of the century. The festivities lasted a week, and the bars never closed during that time. Unfortunately, the results of the races and the horses involved were not recorded. I found only one reference to the races there: "Henry Williams in 1854 brought in 'Owen Dale' by Belmont, and during that year Carey Burney laid out a track near Knights Landing, where for years the fastest horses were trained and speeded."[19]

One of the first recorded accounts of a short race in California is found in a sporting magazine published in New York:

Racing in California

San Francisco, California		Saturday, April 12
Match for $2000.	½ mile	Each to carry 90 lbs.
C.R. Hill's h.	Bearmeat	1st
W. Bowman's m.	————	2nd
Time	51½ sec.[20]	

The *Alta California*, the first English-language paper in California, described this match race as follows:

The day being beautiful, there was a large attendance, including a number of ladies. The betting for a number of days, however, had been even. After being stripped, and moved by the judges stand, the odds changed from even to 100 to 75 to 100 to 50, and taken. A cry was now heard from the crowd "they are off," and they were off. A good start for Bearmeat, who cleared two lengths at the word, which fully proved that his trainer was "some pumpkins" at training a race horse, and had been there before. Bearmeat maintained his position to the home stretch when his jockey let out a link, and opened the gap to five lengths, and came by the judges stand under a strong bracing pull, winning the race and money like an old stager, as he is, in fifty-one and a half seconds.[21]

Another early race, this one at Cacheville, was especially interesting to me because I attended grammar school there in the 1920s. The race was briefly recorded in the *Spirit of the Times*:

Racing at Cacheville, Yolo County

Friday, June 19, 1857   Sweepstakes $50 each   700 yards
Woodpecker 1st   Moro 2nd   Bumble Bee 3rd
      Time not taken

Racing in Cacheville, Yolo County

Friday, August 14, 1857   Match for $1500 a Side

Catch Weights	300 yards
S. Oldham's Eagle Grey Bird	1st
J. Couple's Bay mare Hummingbird	2nd

Won by three feet[22]

The next race in which Oldham entered a horse in Tehama County was certainly one of the most important quarter races ever matched in California before the 1940's. Oldham carefully campaigned his horse for the race and never let him win by too much, so that the setup would be favorable not only for a big stake but also for side bets. The results of the race can found in two places; the one given in the *Spirit of the Times* on November 21, 1857, is the more detailed. Oldham let the gray run in this race since it was for all the apples:

Quarter Racing in Tehama County, California

A great quarter race for the large stake of $10,000, $5,000 a side, came off September 26 in Tehama County, California, between a Mr. Simeon Oldham's California Grey mare and a horse well known there under the sobriquet Paddy. Distance was 400 yards. There was an immense crowd in attendance to witness the race. The mare won by 37½ feet. Over $100,000 was bet on the result, including cattle, ranches, and everything else that could be turned into money.

Summary. Saturday, September 26, 1857

March $5000 a side	400 yards
Mr. Oldham's grey mare	1st
Mr. ————— horse Paddy	2nd

Won by 37½ feet

Purses and betting of this caliber would constitute quite a match race. One should remember that money today is not as valuable as it was in the middle of the nineteenth century.

Before we leave Tehama County, we might mention one more race, which was run on December 16, 1857. It was between Lum Ward's gray filly, Jane McCumber, and Dr. Bett's bay gelding, Lollypop. It was close; the filly won by only two feet. It is interesting to note that the names of the quarter horses were as colorful in those days as they are now.

The town of Mariposa in the mining region was another locality that either had a lot of quarter racing or at least people willing to sit down and write letters to editors. There were three reported quarter races in Mariposa in the middle of September, 1837, and one in October of that same year. They were reported in the *Spirit of the Times* as follows:

141

Racing in Mariposa County, California

Thursday, September 17, 1857	Purse $200	
3 year olds	600 yards	
H.C. Long's chestnut filly, Anquintum		1st
Capt. Boling's chestnut horse, Reube Chandler		2nd
H. Beagles' chestnut horse, Quien Sabe		3rd

Friday, September 18, 1857	For a saddle value $100
California Horses	
W. Suttonfield's chestnut gelding Henry Clay	1st
3 others 0	

Saturday, September 19	Purse $1350	
2-year-olds	600 yards	
C.C. Overton's chestnut horse Billy Blaine		1st
H.C. Long's chestnut horse Tom Long		2nd
N. Farren's Bay horse Harry the West		3rd

Thursday, October 1, 1857 Purse $300 400 yards	
Fanny Baling	1st
Gregory Horse	2nd

   Won by 12 feet.

There were other races held in California, but only a few reported. Among those whose results appeared in print were:

Racing at Iowa Hills, California

Monday, October 5, 1857	Purse ———
	300 yards
William Crutcher's grey gelding	1st
J.W. Johnson's roan gelding	2nd

Tuesday, October 6	Purse ———
	300 yards
Jo's Colgan's roan mare Dolly	1st
Mr. Crutcher's grey gelding Dobbin	2nd

   Won by 8 feet.

From the reports of these two races it would appear that Bill Crutcher should have taken his winnings and gone home after the first race. Dolly was just a little too much for old Dobbin.

   Still another race in 1857 was reported in the *Alta California* of October 11. The meet was held in Stockton. The first race on the program was not a short race, so it will not be reported here, but after the account of the race we find the following: "After this race, a match race for $100 a side was run between two sorrel horses, which afforded an opportunity to the 'knowing ones' to pocket a considerably amount of loose change, in the way of odds on the winning nag." Things stay about the same.

Some two years later, in still another sporting magazine, more short races were reported. This time they were carried in *Wilkes' Spirit of the Times*. This sporting magazine was edited by George Wilkes in 1859, after the death of William T. Porter, who had founded the original *Spirit of the Times*. One way or another this journal continued publication in New York until 1915. The record appeared in the issue of November, 1859:

Quarter Racing in California

Visalia, Tulare County, California
Saturday, September 24, 1859
Match for $500   600 yards
Tow String   1st   Roach Pony   2nd
Tow String won this race by 20 feet.

Same Place   Monday, September 26
Purse ——   Distance 600 yards
Roach Pony   1st   Picaynne 2nd

In a later issue in 1860 we find:

Racing at Marysville, California

Sewells Track   March 3
Purse $2400   600 yards
Steve Ford's b. h. Overland   1st
Mr. Reese's b. h. Buss Roarer   2nd
Tim Murphy's b. h. Billy Mudge   3rd
    Won by 30 feet.

An interesting account of a quarter horse and an outlaw is found in Asa Merril Fairfield's *Pioneer History of Lassen County*, published in 1916. While compiling this book, Fairfield spent considerable time traveling and talking to the old-timers who were still living. The quarter horse he wrote about was named Bald Hornet. He was a bald-faced sorrel weighing about 1,000 pounds. Fairfield said, "He was a quarter-horse, and as he had run at Quincey in 1857, and made a good showing, he was quite a noted horse."

143

Bald Hornet belonged to John Mullen, of Honey Lake Valley. Mullen murdered "Frenchy" Henry Dordier in 1858 and then traded horses with another outlaw named Bill Edwards, who was also involved in the slaying. The posse caught Edwards and Bald Hornet on June 19, 1858. The next morning the posse started back home for Honey Lake, taking Edwards and Bald Hornet. Edwards was not tied, and all the way home he rode along and talked just the same as the others. Edwards was found guilty and hanged. A man named Elliott claimed Bald Hornet and later sold him to a Captain Hill, who kept him until he died.

CALIFORNIA QUARTER HORSE TIMES BEFORE 1900
(Under 23 seconds)

Time	Date	Town	Horse	Owner
21¾	Oct. 2, 1891	Fresno	April Fool	J. H. Walker
22	Oct. 29, 1891	San Bernadino	Rosie	
22	Oct. 2, 1891	Fresno	Queen	J. H. Walker
22	Oct. 29, 1891	San Bernadino	Minnie B	Dennison Bros.
22	Nov. 28, 1891	Fresno	Sally Brown	E. A. Ducker
22	Oct. 3, 1895	Fresno	Bonnie	J. M. Capps
22½	Apr. 10, 1883	Los Angeles	Suspender	
22½	Oct. 6, 1891	Visalia	Spring Water	F. Work
22½	Oct. 6, 1891	Visalia	Lady Blanche	A. Ellis
22½	Sept. 26, 1893	Susanville	Ten Cents	
22½	Oct. 11, 1893	Hollister	Gypsy	
22½	July 5, 1896	Fresno	Plowmare	J. W. Kane
22½	Oct. 10, 1896	Fresno	Buckhorn	B. Dean
22¾	Dec. 18, 1886	Visalia	Sleepy Dick	W. H. Rielly
22¾	Mar. 28, 1891	Fresno	Red Light	A. Bertrandias
22¾	Sept. 26, 1893	Ione	Toots	A. Bertrandias

NEW MEXICO

It is a little difficult to determine horses' names, times, and tracks for the mountain states during the 1830s to 1850s. The newspapers that considered short horse races important enough to write about were almost nonexistent. The Rocky Mountain states from New Mexico to the Canadian border were very active after the 1850s because rich ore deposits had been discovered. The miners, mountain men, and cowboys all loved a horse race; next to poker it was the favorite sport.

The report on one match race is found in a sporting magazine published in New

York in 1871. In this account we learn that Lucien B. Maxwell, of Fort Sumner, New Mexico, had a racehorse named Fly; and he thought she could. He offered, through the papers, to run her against any stallion, mare, or gelding up to 400 yards for any amount of money between $5000 and $40,000. He suggested catch weights and said that if the challenger would put up at least $20,000 he would put up $1000 traveling expenses. The race was to be run on the Las Vegas straightaway in New Mexico.[23]

The ad got results, and a Texan named Dowell agreed to run Maxwell, putting his mare Kit against Fly. They matched for $10,000 and agreed to run at Franklin, Texas. The following facts are known about the first race, which was run on January 6, 1872. Maxwell had wanted to run at Las Vegas, New Mexico, but Dowell would not leave Texas, so Fly was taken there. They were to run 400 yards, each carrying 100 pounds. Dowell put up $5,000 to the other's $4,000 and gave an additional $500 as a traveling bonus for Maxwell. Each side put up $1,000 forfeit to assure the race. Judges were placed at the outcome and a man at the start to see that no "jockeying" was done and that the word was given and answered. Kit won the race by 25 feet. Later that afternoon Dowell's stallion, Ned Hughes, ran against a sorrel gelding owned by Maxwell, for 500 yards. The sorrel gelding won by 30 feet.[24] You win some, and you lose some.

CHAPTER ELEVEN

Fabled Sires

COPPERBOTTOM

COPPERBOTTOM, on his arrival in Texas in 1839, was not the first, or the last, of Sir Archy's get to make Texas their home. In fact, during most of the 1800s Texas horsemen thought the ideal cross for a sprinter was the Sir Archy–Kentucky Whip cross. Copperbottom furnished much of the Sir Archy blood in the eastern part of Texas.

Copperbottom was bred by Edward Parker, of Lancaster, Pennsylvania, sired by Sir Archy and out of a daughter of *Buzzard. His second dam was by Rattle. In 1839, General Sam Houston had Copperbottom sent to Texas, by way of New Orleans. From New Orleans he was transshipped to Galveston. He was ridden from Galveston into Chambers County and then later to Huntsville. There he was sold and taken to Hopkins County, where he lived near Sulphur Springs until his death in 1860.

Father Benedict, a French priest who arrived in Galveston in 1848, noted that on Sunday afternoons Negro slaves matched their masters' Copperbottom horses in short races along the sandy beach.[1] A little later Copperbottom was taken to Chambers County, his second stop, where he also left progeny. Elmer Barber, of Barber's Hill, had great success with Copperbottom mares. In Coryell County, Blue Kelly, the grandfather of the late R. L. Underwood, of Wichita Falls, also bred and owned Copperbottom horses.

STEEL DUST

Steel Dust was the first of the legendary sires of the modern quarter running horse. Steel Dust never became as influential as several of his contemporaries, but he did more than any other sire to glamourize the quarter running horse. He was foaled in Kentucky in 1843 and died in the late 1860's, at Lancaster, Texas. His sire was Harry Bluff, by Short Whip, by Kentucky Whip and out of Big Nance, a granddaughter of Timoleon, who was by Sir Archy. He thus was a cross of the two most popular bloodlines of the day.

He went to Texas as a juvenile, and in the mild southern climate, with abundant

146

forage, he rapidly developed into an outstanding specimen of horseflesh. He stood a little over fifteen hands, was a beautiful bay color, and weighed at maturity 1,200 pounds. He had the short, chunky body of the sprinter. Dan Casement said that "the most noticeable thing was his immense muscular development which seemed to reach a climax amounting almost to a positive deformity in his bulging jaws. . . . This appearance is characteristic of the Steel Dust strain."[2]

Steel Dust's name has led some writers into the mistaken belief that he was a gray horse, named for his color. As Bratcher pointed out, his name was undoubtedly derived from the nineteenth-century medical concoction known as steel dust or anvil dust. It was a rust color, much closer to a bay than a gray. Steel dust was also used in charms and was supposed to bring good luck, especially in gambling.

Steel Dust was bred to many mares, but only a few of his offspring have left reputations that can be verified today. Gray Alice, Bill Fleming, Tom Driver, Rebel, and 80 Gray are some of them. Bill Fleming was a son of Steel Dust and out of Gray Alice. Gray Alice was owned by Jim Brown, of Giddings, who raced her before he bred her. 80 Gray was by Bill Fleming and out of a sister of Wolf Catcher. She raced in several states as well as in North Texas. Steel Dust also sired Ram Cat, the dam of Old Billy; and Jack Traveler, the maternal grandsire of Barney Owens and the great-grandsire of Weatherford Joe Bailey. He also sired the dam of Old Dutchman, the dam of Ace of Hearts and Bill Garner, who was the sire of Rocky Mountain Tom. Sykes Rondo was by McCoy Billy by Billy, and Billy was out of Ram Cat. Old Joe Bailey of Weatherford traced to Steel Dust on both sides of his pedigree. Rebel was especially noted for his fillies, who had speed and produced speed. Steel Dust blood is found in the Billy, Cold Deck, Rondo, and Peter McCue families. Tom Driver was bred by Henry T. Batchler. He was by Steel Dust and out of Mammoth by Shiloh.

Jim Brown also ran a Steel Dust colt named Pat, who could scat for 600 yards, and the colt Rebel, by Steel Dust. His best Steel Dust, though, was Gray Alice. Her reputation spread far and wide when she defeated the well-known mare Gray Dick, owned by the Thomason family of Denton. In fact, the Hildreth family came all the way from Missouri just to match Gray Alice. That story was told in Chapter 10.

Sam Bass, one of Texas' most famous outlaws, owned a well-known Steel Dust racing horse commonly referred to as the Denton mare. Bass was an orphan who showed up in Denton in 1870. He worked hard and never wore a suit of clothes that cost over five dollars. "But unfortunately for himself, on an evil day in 1874, he became the owner of a little sorrel mare. This was the beginning of a downward career, which has made Bass one of the most noted criminals of this or any age; for the mare proved to be fast, and Bass soon became faster than the mare."[3]

Bass purchased the Denton mare in 1874 from a farmer named Mose Taylor, who lived in the Hilltown neighborhood, later called Little Elm. When Sam first saw her,

147

she was about two years old. She had one white hind foot. Since Steel Dust died in the late 1860's, the Denton mare was more likely a granddaughter than a daughter. She was quite a race nag and won many more races than she lost, and more than once, she carried Bass to safety from determined pursuers.

SHILOH

Shiloh was foaled in Tennessee in 1844, one year after Steel Dust, and he was brought to Texas in 1849. He died there in 1874. He was sired by Van Tromp, by Thomas' Big Solomon, by Sir Solomon, by Sir Archy. Helen Michaelis said that his dam was by Union. Van Tromp was out of Barbette by Sandbeck.

Batchler, along with many other free spirits east of the Mississippi, decided to go to Texas after it was annexed to the United States. It already had a reputation as a wonderful land with cheap, good soil, and it was expected to develop rapidly. With his wife, two children, and Shiloh, Batchler headed west. He saw his friend Mid Perry beat Monmouth with Steel Dust, and was impressed but not afraid. When people urged him to run Shiloh at Steel Dust, he agreed. The outcome of that race is told in another chapter of this book. Not enough information has come down for us to understand why he borrowed Steel Dust when he matched Alfred Bailes' Brown Dick. It would seem that Shiloh would have been a better selection, but we will never really know, although several possibilities come to mind.

Shiloh ran many races, before and after the Steel Dust encounter. Sometimes the jockey was one of the Batchler boys, sometimes a featherweight Negro. Stakes were not large, but then money was not easy to come by in those days. Horses, gear, and produce were the most common wagering materials between neighboring horsemen.

Some records were kept of Shiloh's breeding activities. Wayne Gard quoted two: "Bred old Jenni to Shilow," and "Bred dun mair to Shile."[4] Batchler's records give the last known date for Steel Dust: In April, 1865, he recorded that he bred his big filly to Steel Dust.

Shiloh met his death in the same fashion as his great-grandson, Dan Tucker. One day when Jack Batchler was away on business, Shiloh managed to get into a corral with another stallion. Mrs. Batchler heard the commotion and came running with her broom to separate the two horses. She was too late. Shiloh died of a ruptured blood vessel soon after she got them apart and into their own stalls.

*BONNIE SCOTLAND

After 1850 an imported stallion appeared in America that spawned a whole new school of shortliners. He was *Bonnie Scotland, foaled in England in 1853 and brought to the

148

*Bonnie Scotland, painted during his lifetime. Courtesy of the American Quarter Horse Association.

United States in 1857. He was raised by William I'Anson of Yorkshire, and his sire was Iago. He was out of Queen Mary by Gladiator. Iago was by Don Juan and out of Selim. *Bonnie Scotland was never really sound, but still became one of the best racers of his day. He broke down completely during his third year, so, hoping for a good sale, his master sent him to America.

Henry W. Herbert went down to the waterfront to see the new import. He reported that *Bonnie Scotland was a blond bay, black-legged, without a spot of white on him except for a star on his forehead. He stood a full sixteen hands high with the longest shoulder, deepest heart, best forehand, shortest saddleback, and most power-ful quarter of any horse then available. Others who saw *Bonnie Scotland said that he was a little too short in the pastern and that he toed out a little.

*Bonnie Scotland had many difficulties to face in America. First it was hard to

149

find a buyer for him. Then, when he was sold, he was taken out of Thoroughbred country into the Great Lakes region, where it was almost impossible for him to show his worth. His good colts had no place to run, because the Civil War was in progress. His stay in Lancaster, Ohio, and Waukegan, Illinois, did not help him. Eventually a few of his get found a track to run on, and they spoke a world for their sire. When *Bonnie Scotland was nineteen, General W. B. Harding, a first-class breeder, ferreted him out and took him south to replace his senior stallion, who had died. For the first time *Bonnie Scotland had some class mares to work with. At Belle Mead, the general's farm, he realized his potential. By the time he died, in 1880, he was the leading sire, his get winning 137 races that year. His record superseded that of another good horse, Lexington.

Except for height, the description of *Bonnie Scotland reminds one of *Janus. His ability to transmit speed was also similar. His compact build, deep heart, loaded forearms, and broad rear quarters all bespeak a sprinter, whether Thoroughbred or quarter horse. Bramble, Luke Blackburn, and Bonnie Rose carried these characteristics and passed them on to their foals. Some of his better descendants, whose names will be familiar to the quarter horse breeder, are Bonnie Joe, Pan Zarita, Carrie Nation, Uncle Jimmy Gray, Billy Sunday, Dewey, Joe Blair, Useeit, Joe Reed, Jiggs, and Major Speck.

BILLY

As far as South Texas is concerned, Billy, or Old Billy as he is generally referred to, so as not to be confused with other stallions with the same name, was an outstanding sire of this period. He was a Steel Dust and Shiloh cross, born about the time the Civil War was getting under way. His first owner was probably some black-soil farmer living in Dallas County, for both Shiloh and Steel Dust stood at Lancaster. He was sired by Shiloh, and his dam was Ram Cat, a daughter of Steel Dust.

His first owner decided to fight for the South. Before he left, he chained Billy to a tree to keep him from running away or being stolen. His wife fed and watered the colt, but Billy was in sorry shape when his owner came home.

Bill Fleming, too, was returning to Texas from the Civil War when he found Billy and bought him. The neglected colt had hoofs so long they had to be sawed off before they could be filed down. When the chain was taken from around his neck it left him with a scar for the rest of his life, and the hair never grew back.

In the *Breeders Gazette* of August 3, 1922, there was a discussion of Billy horses by H. T. Fletcher, who claimed to have a friend who had known Fleming and Billy. This friend said that Fleming got the colt in Kentucky, which is an error, although his sire was foaled in Tennessee. He said that Billy was descended from Steel Dust, but he was actually sired by Shiloh. Fletcher added that Billy was supposedly a registered Thoroughbred, which, of course, he was not, though Billy and many of his close relatives, including Steel Dust, can be found in the Appendix of the *American Stud Book*.

Fletcher's friend went on to describe Billy as a dark bay, fourteen and three-fourths hands high, weighing around 1,000 pounds. He said that his body was heavy, his hips sloping, and his legs comparatively short.

Fleming bought Billy for $580. During the next three decades Billy horses were recognized wherever short horses ran. By 1900 his colts were running in Oklahoma, Kansas, Missouri, Colorado, Arkansas, and Old Mexico. Fleming sold eleven racehorses in a group to some Mexican gamblers for $40,000. They were lost in a chicken fight the very night they reached Mexico.

Billy was at his best when crossed on the mare Paisana. Fleming bought her from Oliver, who with his partner Alfred Bailes raised short horses in the Seguin area before the Civil War. Paisana was by Brown Dick, who was by Berkshire Boar, and out of Belton Queen, by Guinea Boar.

Paisana's best colt sired by Billy was Anthony, the sire of Billy Dribble, Alex Gardner, Little John Moore, Fashion, and Lemonade. Other well-known foals of Old Billy were Jenny Oliver, Rover, Dora, Sweet Lip, Little Brown Dick, Pancho, Joe Collins, Brown Billy and McCoy Billy.

COLD DECK

Cold Deck was foaled at Carthage, Missouri, in 1862. He stood a scant fifteen hands and was a dark-sorrel color. Foss Barker told Coke Blake that Cold Deck was sired by Steel Dust and related the following story. One day while Steel Dust was racing, he was left in the care of a groom while his owner went out of town. The groom immediately got into a poker game. One of the players had a mare he wanted to breed to Steel Dust, but the stallion's owner had given orders that his horse was not to be bred under any circumstances. Soon Steel Dust's groom had lost all of his money—and had also promised to allow Steel Dust to be secretly bred. The colt that resulted bore the telltale name Cold Deck. Whether this story is true or not is unknown, but who could pick a better sire for the great Cold Deck than Steel Dust?

Except in the Blake horses the Cold Deck family has not been an independent line for many years. It has been mixed into the modern blood of the Joe Baileys, Rondos, Sykeses, and Peter McCues. Some of Cold Deck's fastest get found their way into the *American Stud Book*, and many horses listed in the Appendix claim Cold Deck as their sire. His blood was passed on through his sons Printer, Diamond Deck, Berry's Cold Deck and Gray Cold Deck.

PEDIGREE

—OF—

RED DECK.

He is by Diamond Deck, half mile record, 49 seconds; he is by old Cold Deck, the boss quarter horse of America. Cold Deck sired Lone Siss, Gold Dust, Little Danger, Big Em., Burntfoot, Don, "the warm colt," Barney Slippers, Deck, and many others too numerous to mention---all cracker-jacks. Red Deck's dam was sired by old Mike, the sire of more fast quarter horses than any horse living, or dead; the sire of Surprise, who held the world's record at Chicago for half mile heats; three heats in 49 seconds, and better. Red Deck comes of the two best families of quarter horses living, given up by all good horsemen.

Red Deck should be a great breeder of race horses. His sire, Diamond Deck, was a great race horse; he won nearly all the races he started in, and one of the finest lookers on earth. Old Cold Deck and old Mike have gotten the fastest lot of quarter horses in the United States. He is by Diamond Deck, and he is by old Cold Deck. Old Cold Deck comes from a family of horses called Steel Dust, and old Mike comes from a family of horses called Printers and Brimers.

Broadside issued by Tom Stephenson, of Gonzales, Texas, in 1910 (?), advertising Red Deck, a Missouri-bred stallion he was standing. The Old Mike mentioned in the pedigrees is Missouri Mike. Courtesy of the American Quarter Horse Association.

BARNEY OWENS

Barney Owens was the best-known son of Steel Dust in Illinois, which, strange as it may appear, was thronged with running quarter horses near the end of the nineteenth century. Barney was foaled around 1870. One account says that he was sired by Cold Deck; another says by Steel Dust.[5] He was not a large horse, only fourteen hands, three and one-half inches, but he weighed 1,200 pounds. He was bred by John Hedgepeff, of Joplin, Missouri, trained by Bill Cassity, and owned and raced by James Owen, of Berlin, Illinois. When his racing days were over, he was sold to Sam Watkins, of Petersburg, who used him for several years and then sold him to Thomas Trammell, of Sweetwater, Texas, who owned him until he died.

OTHERS

Besides the stallions treated individually above, there were others almost as important that were active between 1830 and 1880. Brick was a California horse, foaled in 1871. He was sired by Oregon Charlie, and his dam was by Pilgrim. His second dam was Choctaw's Sister, by Obe Jennings. Obe Jennings was by Patete's Ariel, by Simpson's Ariel and out of Betsy Baker, by Welden's La Blanch. Patete's Ariel was out of Eden Best's Ladyfoot. Brick was owned and bred by John Adams, of Woodland, California. Two of Brick's best-known sprinters were Pearl and Ita, both of whom were campaigned throughout the West.

There were two prominent Brown Dicks foaled during this period. One was a brown colt foaled in 1850 by the imported *Margrave and out of Fanny King, by *Glencoe. He was bred by T. B. Goldsby, of Alabama. The better-known Brown Dick was foaled in 1852. He was by Berkshire Boar (also known as Flying Dutchman) and out of Old Mary. He was, as indicated by his name, a brown stallion. He was owned first by Oliver and Bailes, of Seguin, and then was taken over by Alfred Bailes, who raced him and sold him to Jack Bridges, who finally sold him to Bailey in West Texas. There was still a third Brown Dick, foaled in 1887 and sired by Cold Deck.

Kentuckian is another one of those influential stallions about whom we know very little. He was a bay stallion, foaled in 1833, by the great Bertrand and out of a mare by Kentucky Whip. He was owned, and perhaps bred, by James Shy of Kentucky. Another dominant stallion was Luke Blackburn, but again very little information about him has come down to us. We do know that he was a bay stallion, foaled in 1877 and sired by *Bonnie Scotland and out of a mare named Nevada, by Lexington.

Missouri Mike was a sorrel stallion, foaled in 1876. He was by Printer, by Cold Deck, and his dam had been sired by Alsup's Brimmer. He was bred in Carthage,

153

Missouri, not far from the foaling place of Barney Owens. It is uncertain who bred him, but he was owned by Bill Stockton, of Lockwood, Missouri, and run by Jack Weir, of Weir City, Kansas. He was sometimes referred to as Little Mike, or Old Mike in later life. Alsup's Brimmer was probably by Tennessee Brimmer, who was by Club Foot, by *Janus.

Okema's reputation was not hurt by his owner's good name as a breeder of sprinters and owner of some excellent mares sired by Cold Deck. Mrs. H. A. Trowbridge was one of the best breeders of the last half of the nineteenth century. Okema was by Reform, out of Maggie, both found in the *American Stud Book*. He was purchased by Mrs. Trowbridge and taken to her stud at Wellington, Kansas.

Oregon Charlie was one of the foundation sires of the Pacific Coast. He is generally acknowledged as having been sired by Old Dan. Old Dan, who lived from around 1850 to 1870 was by a stallion called Selim and out of a mare of Printer or Brimmer stock. Selim was related, since he was by Barne's Black Whip. Oregon Charlie was probably foaled about the year 1860. He was bred in Oregon, and while there was also called Old Charlie and Jenkin's Charlie, after his one-time owner. He was sold in his later years to John W. Adams, of Woodland, California, who was very successful in using Oregon Charlie as a stallion. While Adams had him, he sired Adams' best-known stallion, Brick, out of a Pilgrim mare, and Berryessa, out of Jennie Gipson.

Pony Pete was a colorful racehorse and the best sire in his area. He was foaled in the 1870s and was by Barney Owens, by Cold Deck, and his dam was of Printer breeding. He was owned and probably bred by Mike Smiley, of Sylvan Grove, Kansas. Smiley also owned Printer Tom, another prominent stallion of the period.

Printer Tom was by Pony Pete and out of Cherokee Maid, by Cold Deck. The earlier Printer was foaled about twenty years before Tom and was by Cold Deck and out of a mare who was a direct descendant of Gold Printer. Printer was foaled in either Illinois or Missouri, and later stood in Texas, where he sired some speedy sons and daughters.

Rebel was one of Steel Dust's last colts, owned by Jim Brown, of Giddings, Texas. He proved to be almost as good a sire as he was a match racer. Brown bought the colt from Mid Perry, of Lancaster, on one of his trips to the Dallas area. Some of Rebel's better-known get were Texas Ranger, Charley West, Boner, Endora, Miss War, Rebel Line, and Molly Moore.

Roan Dick was foaled in 1877 and died in 1904. He was sired by Black Nick, by Stewart's Telegraph, and he was out of a mare by Greenstreet's Boanerges, who was a grandson of Old Printer. He was bred by Robert T. Wade, of Plymouth, Illinois, and later owned by Charles Neeley, of Littleton, Illinois, and Grant Rea, of Carthage, Illinois. Rea bought Roan Dick and old Nettie Overton at a public sale.

Rondo was an extremely popular name for a quarter running horse. Four of the better-known ones were foaled after this period (1880). The two of interest are Alsup's and Fleming's. Alsup's Rondo was foaled about 1854 and lived until 1870. He was sired by Alsup's Brimmer and bred by Ben Alsup in Tennessee and was taken to Missouri when the Alsups moved to Douglas County, Missouri. Fleming's Rondo was a Texas horse, probably sired by Steel Dust in the 1850's. He was a small, heavily muscled horse, branded all over according to John Bouldin. The one fact that has come down clearly is that he was almost unbeatable at 300 yards or less. He also gave his name to later Texas Rondos.

The California Walnut Bark was one of John Adams' main stallions, taking his place beside Brick, Steam Beer, and Uncle Billy. Walnut Bark was by Blevins' Little Tom. Little Tom was by Veto, by Old Veto, by Contention, by Sir Archy. Walnut Bark's dam was Bessie Tar Tar, by a son of Tarter. The *American Stud Book* says that he was a chestnut, foaled in 1853.[6] He was the sire of Jenny Gipson and Nellie, both speedsters.

CHAPTER TWELVE

Early Western Breeders

THE PERIOD of western expansion was a particularly interesting time for the quarter running horse. During this period the country from the Mississippi River to the Pacific Ocean was explored and settlement begun. The region included the Great Plains, the Rocky Mountains, the western desert lands, and the fertile Pacific slope. To complicate the picture, the period also included the Civil War.

The war hampered, but did not stop, the breeding and racing of short horses by those who were remote from the action. Transportation still depended on the horse and buggy, and if you were 500 miles from the fighting, that was remote. During the Revolutionary War almost everyone was crowded into the area along the Atlantic Coast so the threat of action was always present. In the Old South, where the Civil War was fought, long horses had become the rule, as short horses had been during the Revolution. By the time of the Civil War most of the better breeders of the short horse lived far away in Illinois, Missouri, Arkansas, Kansas, Oklahoma and Texas, and consequently their breeding programs were not seriously affected.

TEXAS

Middleton Perry and Jones Greene

Middleton Perry and Jones Greene, the owners of Steel Dust, were reared on the southern edge of Greene County, Illinois. They bought the colt Steel Dust from Old Man Bill Greene before they started for Texas in two covered wagons. That was in the fall of 1844. They liked the colt's looks and knew that a good stallion prospect was always worth the money. Their Greene County farm was in west-central Illinois, a region that was to be famous for many great short horses. So, with Steel Dust tied to the back of a wagon, they headed south for fresh land and new neighbors.

Middleton Perry was the son of a stonemason from Virginia who had a love and knowledge of horses that he gave to his son. The family first stopped in Indiana, where Middleton was born. His father then moved on into Illinois. Middleton, or Mid as he was called, made a trip to Texas in 1837 and liked the good cheap land. Texas was still a republic in 1844, and it gave grants of land to those who had fought in the Texas War of Independence. The soldiers, in turn, sold the land for as little as twenty-five cents an acre. Back home again, Perry married a neighbor, Ellen McKee, the daughter of Mr. and Mrs. Thomas McKee Ellis.

Jones Greene was born in Illinois. His father came from Kentucky. Shortly before the two men left for Texas, they became brothers-in-law: Jones married Ellen's sister, Mary Ann. Perry and Greene, although young, were seasoned farmers and horsemen.

It took a little over a month for the two prairie schooners to reach Texas. They stopped first in Lamar County, where the Ellis girls' had an uncle named Witt. The men left their wives and the wagons at the uncle's farm and rode on to look for land.

This story about Perry and Greene follows very closely the account given by Wayne Gard. He said that the pair went down past Dallas, which was then a little cluster of log cabins on the east bank of the Trinity River. There those who wanted to cross the stream without getting wet could use a crude ferry. The ferry was made of split logs fastened across two canoes hollowed from the trunks of cottonwoods. It was pulled across the stream by a rope made of twisted buffalo hair.

The two men traveled and asked questions until they found land they liked in what was then Robertson County. It had rich black soil and a few trees to remind them of Illinois. They each bought 320 acres and returned to their wives at the Witt farm. Early the next spring they loaded up and moved south to their new home. There was a new president in 1845, Polk, and Texas was about to become the twenty-eighth state of the Union. Soon a new little town, Lancaster, grew up near their farms. As soon as they settled on Ten Mile Creek, the Perrys and the Greenes wrote home and persuaded the Ellis family to come down to Texas to live.

The new life was an interesting, if hard, one. A bear stole the settlers' pigs, so they killed the bear and made soap out of the tallow. They saw a bobcat near the spring, but he got away. Indians dropped by on occasion, but were never welcome because only two or three years earlier Indians had killed and scalped five men in a survey party just a few miles away. The women cooked, cleaned, and made clothes from wool grown on their own farm. But there were also barbecues, hunting trips, picnics, and short races. They had their own quarter-mile track, across the road from the Ellis cabin, and it was there that Steel Dust first showed his speed to the new settlers.

Jack Batchler

Soon after Texas joined the Union, Jack Batchler, of Tennessee, decided to move to the new state, where good land was cheap and adventure was everyplace. In 1849 he loaded up a wagon and with his favorite stallion, Shiloh, and his wife and two children

157

took the road for Texas. He first settled in Rusk County, but he did not like the red soil, so he loaded up again and moved west, looking for black dirt. He crossed the Trinity River at Porter's Bluff and moved on up the valley to the southern edge of Dallas County. There he rented a farm and set up a blacksmith shop. He shod several horses for Perry and Greene, and the two owners of Texas' greatest short horses became neighbors and friends.

Both Steel Dust and Shiloh established themselves as popular sires. Horsemen from many miles away brought their mares to the two stallions. In 1857, Batchler bought some land a few miles south on Bear Creek, in Ellis County, and moved his family to their new home.

The Civil War came and disrupted the families. In 1862, Perry formed a company of Confederate cavalry. After two years of fighting he returned home. Poor health and eye trouble kept Jones Greene home, where he died in 1864.

No stud records were kept for Steel Dust, but some scanty ones remain for Shiloh. Horses came from as far away as San Antonio, and were noted in Batchler's blacksmith records. While not complete, surviving pages list breedings to Shiloh from 1860 to 1865. They indicate that at least twenty to forty mares were bred to him from out of the county. The record also indicates that Batchler and Perry did not hesitate to breed their mares to each others' stallions.

Henry Batchler, Jack's son, raised Tom Driver, a son of Steel Dust, out of a Shiloh mare named Mammoth. I have several letters in my files from the descendants of men connected with Steel Dust and Shiloh, two of which follow (H. T. Batchler was Jack Batchler's son, and Will Williams was the son of Alex Williams, the deputy county clerk of Collins County who saw the Steel Dust–Monmouth race and told his son, Will, about it):

Mr. Bob Denhardt,   10/14/39
c/o A&M College,
College Station, Texas.

Dear Sir:—I've read with interest, an article in Star-Telegram by you, which I will add to my scrap book, kept for many years, on Steel Dust, and the Quarter Horse. I am enclosing a letter from my old friend 'Uncle Henry Batchler' for your attention, and feel that no one could say different, as the Batchler Family of Ellis County, was one of Texas most prominent racing families and "uncle Henry" was with the horses from the time he could walk until he retired a near ninety years of age. I want you to return this letter promptly, as it is one of my keepsakes.

My father was a young man in Collin County when the first race Steel Dust started in, and it was with Monmouth (owned by the Stiff's, also a racing family), and Steel Dust won the race. This was a great event—they adjourned Federal Court at Jefferson and Sherman, and Governor Throckmorton was there. When my father went into the army, he and two of his close friends, Will O Medlin of Denton County, wanted to be well mounted (they had to furnish their own mounts, and the Confederacy was to pay them when the war "was won") so they got one mare, and two geldings by Steel Dust and rode to the front. When they happened to meet up with another command of the armies, they at once got to matching horse races, and I've heard them say that they seldom lost a race, and at times had more confederate money than could take care of. I attended the special morning showing of Quarter Horses and Palominos, at last Ft. Worth Show, and consider it the best horse show I ever saw.

Very truly yours
Will Williams

P S Please return "Uncle Henry's" Letter

Here is the letter from "Uncle Henry Batchler" that Will enclosed:

Dallas texas 7-12-1922

Mr. Wm Williams
Denton texas

Dear Sir

I received your letter   have Been from home just returned from (ky)   in regard to steeldust he was Brought to texas by Ellis and green   they came from (Ill)   steeldust was a quarter Bred horse   he was sired by Harry Bluff   I dont rember his Dam   I knew the stiffs Back in 1861 and 62   the best one of steeldust get was a mare called gray alice   he sired a great many good quarter horses   But gray alice was the best one—My father Brought shiloh to this country in 1849 from (tenn)   he was all so a quarter Bread horse and I think the Best horse I ever saw   I saw steel Dust   I raised a very fast colt called Tom Driver by steel Dust and out of a shiloh mare

yours truly
H. T. Batchler[1]

Harrison Stiff

North of Dallas County, in Collin County lived Harrison Stiff. He owned the famous sprinter Monmouth. Harrison was a Kentuckian by birth, brought up at Breckenridge. A brother moved to Texas and sent back such a good report about the possibilities of the new land that Harrison decided to go west also. He had won many races with Monmouth in Kentucky. He never said how his stallion was bred. Perhaps he thought it might be easier to get races if he said he did not know Monmouth's breeding. One report said that he was a Whip. If so, he probably was a grandson of Kentucky Whip.

Stiff traveled by boat to Alexandria, Louisiana, and gradually worked his way north to McKinney, Texas. He arrived on Christmas Day, 1850. About two years later he married a local girl, Mary Ann Nelson. Mary Ann disapproved of racing on religious grounds but had no objection to the gold pieces that Harrison won when he matched a race. The best-known horse Stiff owned was Monmouth, and his match with Steel Dust furnished the quarter horse fraternity with one of its great legends.

Jim Brown

Lee County, Texas, was organized in 1873, and was named for General Robert E. Lee. Giddings, the county seat, was named in honor of Colonel D. C. Giddings, of Brenham, Texas. The first election was held in November of that year, and James McKoewn was elected sheriff. The following year Jim Brown, a short horse man from San Saba, arrived in Lee County with a string of racehorses. He bought a farm from Campbell Longly, of Giddings, and built a race track on the place.

In 1875 some of Jim's friends talked him into running for sheriff. He won by a large majority, because he had become well known through the success of his horses. Gray Alice, whom he owned, was a daughter of Steel Dust. She never lost a race, and his gelding, Pat, who was killed accidentally in a boxcar while being shipped to Brenham, also never lost a race. Brown's stallion Rebel, a son of Steel Dust, was great on the straightaway and in the stud. Jim Brown had four children—two boys, Galen and Ed—and two girls—Luna and Annie. Most of my information about Jim Brown comes from an interview Helen Michaelis had with the Brown children.[2]

Luna, the story goes, had two suitors, Virge Woolley and John Owens. Her father wanted her to marry Woolley, but she loved Owens. Owens' friends advised him to leave town, saying that Brown would kill him rather than see him marry his daughter. Owens took their advice and left town. He got as far as La Grange, about thirty miles away. Brown learned where he had gone and wrote him a note signing Luna's name to it, telling him to come back and they would arrange to run away and get married. He gave the note to Woolley and told him to follow Owens and bring him back. Woolley did so. After Owens returned, Brown wrote another note to him, again signing Luna's name, telling him to meet her in the stable in the backyard that night to run away. That night Luna was sitting in the parlor playing cards with Woolley when a shot rang out in the backyard. Woolley tried to hold her back, but she broke away. As she entered the yard, she saw her father coming out of the stable. She rushed in and found her sweetheart lying there, dead, with Woolley's pistol beside him. She came out of the stable abusing her father unmercifully. He knew that he could not do anything with her and that she would get him convicted if he did not get her out of the country at once. He gave her money to go to El Paso that night with her friend Lydia Lawrence. Luna opened a sporting house in El Paso, made a lot of money, and invested it all in diamonds, from which she became known all over West Texas as the "Diamond Queen."

After Brown killed Owens, his best friends criticized him, and he knew that he was done for in that county. He took his horses to Chicago, and his family followed him later.

Sam Hildreth said that Brown owned some good horses when he left Texas. Among them was Bobby Beach, a sprinter with a great flight of speed. Bobby Beach had won his first race on Futurity Day at the fall meet at Sheepshead Bay in 1890, romping away from the seven-to-ten favorite, Meridan. He had gone to the post at six to one, and Brown and his friends had cleaned up a fortune. In his next start the Brown sprinter was beaten by Mabel Glen, but on his third try he again returned a winner, leading Clarendon home, and the Texas betting crowd walked off with another huge killing. That year Bobby Beach won every other race but one, a total of fifteen firsts out of eighteen starts. In 1891, Brown owned the two-year-old Addie M, winner of twelve races, afterward bought by Pierre Lorillard for $9,000. In 1892, Brown owned the best two-year-old colt and the best two-year-old filly in the West: G. W. Johnson and Red Banner.

In the years after he left Texas, Brown became known as a fellow who was either a good friend or a bitter enemy. There was no halfway business with him. Hildreth used to see him often with big Ed Corrigan, the master of Hawthorne Race Track in Chicago and one of the best-known turfmen of the West. A strange pair they made, Brown a small bundle of nerves who barely reached to the shoulder of the stolid Corrigan. At times they were on the best of terms; at other times Jim Brown would shake his fists at Corrigan. Hildreth described the scene as looking like a terrier snapping at a great Dane.

Hildreth went to Chicago during the first week of September, 1892, on his honeymoon. On September 5 he went out to the track to arrange stable room for his horses, which were on their way from Saratoga. About three o'clock that afternoon Hildreth happened to be standing near the entrance to the track. The streets were filled with policemen. He could see their uniforms through the gates. His wife was watching it all from the third-story window of a hotel across the way. She told him afterward that the police appeared so suddenly they seemed to spring up out of the ground. Hildreth was not eager to be riding around Chicago in a police wagon on his honeymoon, so he ran to the hotel entrance. The following is a direct quote from Hildreth:

> The police had been warned to be on the watch especially for a little man in gray clothes; a sage-brush killer who would cause trouble, they had been told. That was Sheriff Jim Brown. The policemen found him over near the stables standing with Bob Rice, another well-known horseman, taking in the whole scene and cursing the police for their

interference. They ordered him to throw up his hands. He refused, but began backing away from them. Then one of the policemen started shooting at his feet. If he'd ever have known the little sheriff as I did he would never have taken a chance like that. It fired Brown into a frenzy. There was a flash from his gun and policeman John Powell lay dead in his tracks, shot through the mouth with Brown's first bullet. Brown started running toward the Fortieth Street gate of the track. Policeman Henry McDowell followed in pursuit, circled a building, and overtook him. He seized the little sheriff by the throat and was overpowering him when Brown pressed his 44-calibre revolver to McDowell's abdomen and fired, mortally wounding the policeman. By this time a dozen policemen were on the scene. They brought Brown down with a volley of bullets, but there was still a spark of life in his body. Jim Grant, a friend, ran over to him. As he approached Brown pointed his revolver in Grant's direction.

"For God's sake, Jim, you're not going to shoot me, are you?" Grant cried.

"No, but I'm going to shoot the snake hiding over there in the celler," Brown replied, referring to a policeman who had taken refuge in the window of a basement and had then fired on him. But Sheriff Jim never fired that last shot. He fell back dead before he could pull the trigger.[3]

Sam Hildreth ended his remarks about "Wild Jim" Brown with words that may as well end this brief survey:

Gone are the old quarter horses that fought in their way for the same things their pampered descendants of today struggle for in theirs, gone are the quarter mile tracks out on the prairie, so utterly different from the great plants of luxury and comfort that have come to take their place, and gone are the Sheriff Jim Browns who gave to the game a thrill and a touch of color that will never return.[4]

William Fleming

William Fleming, known to his friends as Billy, or "Uncle Billy," was born in Georgia on November 18, 1830. He died on April 30, 1911. Much of the information in the next few paragraphs comes from an account that appeared in a Seguin, Texas, paper soon after his death.

William Fleming, as a young man, moved to Mississippi from Georgia, and then on to Texas. There he joined the Texas Rangers and served for several years along the frontier, fighting the Comanches. At the time of his death he was drawing a pension from the government for his frontier services. He also fought for the Confederacy in the Civil War, enlisting in Texas and serving four years. He was decorated for bravery and was wounded several times. He carried a deformed hand and arm as a badge of the war for the rest of his days. He never married.

A quote or two from the clipping on his death shows the place he held in his community:

Many of his old neighbors from Belmont, and from over and down the river, were present to pay their last regards, and many women to place flowers upon the grave of one who had fought back the Indians in early days and stood for the South in her bitter struggle. Rev. T. J. Dodson paid tribute to his worth and life as a citizen and soldier, and his old comrades with gray beards and bent forms, with a large company, stood as Mr. Horton spoke at grave of time being nearly up with them; that they had better hasten their preparations to 'cross over the river and rest under the shade of the trees.' Tearfully the friends covered the mound, the benediction was pronounced, and all departed for their homes, leaving the body of a brave old soldier and worthy citizen to await the resurrection morning.[5]

Billy Fleming was not a big man, but rather short and slender. He wore a beard and moustache and was a little self-conscious about his deformed hand. He looked somewhat like pictures of Buffalo Bill. After the war, he started breeding horses, using as his brand the ace of clubs. For a time he was in partnership with Tom King, who sold horses for him. According to Red Hysaw, Fleming's farm was near Leesville, about ten miles south of Belmont.

Fleming's most famous horse was Billy (Old Billy) and the stallion was named for him. Billy was by Shiloh and out of Ram Cat, by Steel Dust. He is listed as the sire or grandsire of many famous horses, such as Pancho, Joe Collins, McCoy Billy, and Sykes Rondo. His name is also prominent in the pedigrees of both Joe Baileys.

Another good Fleming horse by Anthony was Little John Moore. He was out of Little Blaze. Billy Dribble was still another Anthony colt, purchased by R. T. Nixon, whose strain of horses produced Joe Bailey. Little Brown Dick, a son of Old Billy and Paisana, was raced all over Texas by Ruff Herring. He was borrowed from Fleming and never returned. Little Brown Dick sired mares who produced Little Ben and Aury. Aury was then bred to Little Ben and produced Susie McQuirter, the dam of Weatherford Joe Bailey. Joe Collins, a Billy-Paisana cross, was bought by Alex Gardner, who later sold him to Clay McGonigle. Pancho, another Billy stallion, was also purchased by Alex Gardner. Pancho was open to the world for any distance less than a quarter mile. Pancho also sired Jim Ned, who sired Concho Colonel for Billy Anson, who sold him to Dan Casement.

Ott Adams once told J. M. Huffington an interesting story about Bill Fleming. Bill had to breed an inferior mare for a friend and neighbor. It was one of those deals a horseman finds himself in once in a while. When the cold-blooded mare foaled, the little stud colt was called Red Rover. Eventually Red Rover was sold to a partner of Sam Bass, who took the colt to El Paso.

While in El Paso, Red Rover was used to pace some racehorses at the fairgrounds. He outran them. So without telling the owners, the hands proceeded to match Red Rover against the horses, one at a time, and beat them all. Making the matches was not difficult because Red Rover showed his cold blood and was rough-looking.

163

Some years later Red Rover was tken back to Fleming's community, and before long Uncle Billy was talked into matching one of his fillies against him. As you have probably guessed, Fleming lost the race. He was, to say the least, upset. According to Ott Adams the story points out one thing: A cross-blooded horse may be fast, but they are not potent. The blood of Fleming's stallion, Billy, comes down through the generations and into the quarter horse studbook, but who ever heard about Red Rover's offspring?

In 1907, Billy Fleming was seventy-seven years old, and his horses had got to be too much for him to take care of. He sold his six mares and Little John Moore to Fred Matthies. When his horses were driven off, he could not stand it. He moved to the Matthies farm with his beloved horses and stayed there, a welcome guest, until he died in 1911.

Shelby Stanfield

Although relatively unheralded, Shelby Stanfield, of Thorp Springs, in Hood County, Texas, was almost as successful as his younger contemporary, C. B. Campbell, of Oklahoma. Stanfield and Campbell exchanged horses and maintained a good friendship. Campbell's best acquisition from Stanfield was the great stallion Pid Hart. Both men were active during the late 1800s, though in the 1890s Stanfield sold out and moved west to Eastland County. Some of Stanfield's better-known horses besides Pid Hart were Anti Pro, Bill Garner, Eureka, Thurman, and Rocky Mountain Tom.

Shelby Stanfield was a pioneer in Hood County, having moved there with his brother Jake before the Civil War. Shelby worked as a stonemason, with his brother as his assistant. Some of his buildings, like Bernard's Mill in Glen Rose, became landmarks and are still standing. Soon Jake and Shelby became prominent citizens, influential in community activities. For several years they built homes and businesses, and by 1861 Shelby had accumulated enough capital to invest in a farm and concentrate on one of his first loves, fast horses. His holdings were along the Brazos River, a few miles above Thorp Springs.[6]

One of his better-known race mares was Corn Stalk, who was very fast, but very nervous, especially when lined up with another horse for a race. She always knew when it was race day. When taken to the track, she would not stand or turn to come to the line. She became so upset when lined up by another horse, that she would run in any direction, regardless of who the jockey was or how many men were holding ropes looped through the snaffle-bit rings. Shelby finally got around this problem by matching her against time only. According to reports he would bet any amount that she would beat twenty-three seconds, and lesser amounts down to twenty-two and one-fourth seconds. He won as much as $10,000 on one race with her in this fashion.

Stanfield was a student of pedigrees and racehorses, so he often got in touch with other breeders for new blood. He worked with the best short horse breeders of his day, including C. B. Campbell (mentioned above), in Oklahoma; Mike Smiley, in Kansas; Mrs. H. A. Trowbridge, in Kansas; and Bill Stockton, in Missouri.

MIKE SMILEY OF KANSAS

Mike Smiley was as colorful a character during the last part of the 1800s as Henry Deloney was during the Revolutionary War period. They both enjoyed a good "endeavor." Of the two Smiley was the better breeder and was just as capable of throwing a prospective competitor off guard.

Michael T. Smiley was born in Missouri about 1855. As a young man he moved to Kansas and bought almost a section of farmland about six or seven miles north and a little west of Denmark. The closest town was Lincoln, about thirty miles west of Salina. It was a beautiful piece of land overlooking the lush green grasslands below. A few years later he married and built a fine two-story home of limestone blocks. He also erected his outbuildings of limestone, including a three-hole "Chick Sale" that was an architectural gem. Included in the buildings were a granary, two barns, a chicken house, and a smokehouse, all constructed of limestone blocks. According to the probate of his will, filed in the court house at Lincoln, he died on January 11, 1928. His wife, adopted son, Charles, and three granddaughters survived him. None are now living on the farm or own any part of it.

Most of the following information came from either Walter W. Urban, a lawyer of Lincoln, or Harry Nelson, a horseman living near Denmark. Urban, seventy-two when he was interviewed, had grown up in the Sylvan Grove area. Nelson, sixty-nine, had been a close friend of Charley Smiley, Mike's boy. Dan Casement, who bought horses from Mike, and his son Jack, also added to my supply of Smiley tales.

Smiley bred and ran many horses and made money with them. He led what some might consider an ideal life. He spent all of his time either hunting or working with horses. Every year he and his hunting partner, John Burton, spent the winter months hunting in the Cheyenne Bottoms. They even made money out of their sport, shipping barrels of ducks and geese to the eastern markets. When spring came and the hunting tapered off, Smiley would look over his horses and select six or eight to train for the coming racing season. Generally they were about equally divided between two-year-olds and seasoned campaigners. After a month of work he would hitch up his self-designed and built covered wagon, complete with a wood range and bunks, and head out to match a race.

The wagon was described by Harry Nelson, who said that until recently it had been stored in a shed on the Smiley farm. It was gone when I was there in 1977. Inside

Mike Smiley's old homestead north of Sylvan Grove, Kansas. It was used by him during the last half of the nineteenth century for raising such quarter horses as Little Steve, Croton Oil, and Pony Pete. Photograph by the author, 1977.

the wagon were a kitchen and sleeping facilities and along each side were feed racks for the horses with grain above. Prairie grass was free and plentiful.

He never followed a regular route. If he heard about a fast horse somewhere in Oklahoma or Colorado that had backers with money, that was where he headed. Situated as he was in north-central Kansas, he could easily go to anywhere in Kansas and surrounding states.

Mike's boy, Charley, was adopted, and many stories have been handed down about Mike and him. According to one story, the baby boy was left on Mike's doorstep by a determined woman who left a note with the baby saying that Mike could just rear the boy himself. Another story, also perhaps just a legend, was that Mike had had a lot of trouble with his jockeys and decided to raise one of his own. He looked around for a baby boy to adopt that was small but athletic. When he found what he wanted, he took

166

Mike Smiley's barn with the lean-to where he fed his colts. Photograph by the author, 1977.

the baby boy home and reared him as his son. Whether or not that legend is true, Charley became an expert rider and won many races, all of which did nothing to stop the tales. Charley began riding quarter horses as soon as he could hang on. Mike would strap him onto the horse bareback, throwing a surcingle around the horse and tightening it up with the boy's knees underneath the strap. By hanging onto a throat collar and the reins, Charley was ready to ride.

Many were the interesting races that Mike matched and won. One time Mike all but cleaned out a general store and had to head for home with the wagon so full of merchandise that they had to sleep and eat on the ground. The other horse's owner owned the country store. He bet more than he should and put up the store as collateral. After Mike won, the man did not have the money to cover his bets, so Mike backed up his wagon to the store and loaded up suits, hams, saddles, bolts of cloth, hardware, and anything else that would fit that he could use.

One of Mike's better-known racers was Croton Oil. Mike put about five or six brands and counterbrands on him so that he looked like a much-traded cowhorse. When Mike was traveling across the plains with his wagon and horses headed for anywhere, he would often come across a trail herd or a bunch of cowboys working cattle. Mike would saddle Croton Oil, who was not all that bad as a cowhorse, and help out a little. Before long he would have a race matched with the rancher or a cowboy. Often Mike would rub sand into Croton Oil's hair to make it look irregular and to cover up his sleek racehorse lines. Needless to say, he didn't lose many races with Croton Oil.

One fall a racehorse man from Arkansas came by. He apparently underestimated Mike or did not know him. He had a gray racehorse that Mike thought looked like a good prospect. Mike let Charley work out with the gray but told him always to keep a tight rein and to allow the gray to edge him out at the finish. Before long the owner of the gray was suggesting a race. Mike was slow to accept, but after the race was run, he ended up with the gray, the wagon, and everything else the man had of value. Mike loaned the man a horse to get to Abilene.

Mike liked to start his horses from an incline, a fairly common start at the time. He always whip-trained his horses for the start. He would stand to one side and move the whip back and forth in front of the horse's face. As long as he did this, the horse would stand still. When the signal for the start came, Mike would drop his whip by his side, and the horse would be off like a shot.

Of the many horses Mike owned or bred, he favored Croton Oil, Guinea Pig, Johnny Corbett, Pony Pete, Printer Tom, Red Texas, and his favorite, Little Steve. Little Steve was purchased by Dan Casement soon after 1880. Mike's best mares were sired by the Thoroughbred Frank James. Mike knew how all his horses were bred, but he kept no written records, so there is room for error in the pedigrees of his horses. That also explains the differences in the pedigrees given for his horses. One old-timer said that it was easier to match a horse of unknown parentage. Mike agreed. His training track was across the road from his home on the level grassland. He worked his horses diligently and intelligently. He bred most of them, although he bought the best mares available from breeders like Campbell and Stanfield.

His best breeding stallion was Pony Pete, by Barney Owens and out of a mare by Ricket's Printer. A son of Pony Pete, Little Steve was also a top racehorse and stallion. His dam was a Cold Deck mare named Cherokee Maid. Johnny Corbett was sired by Little Steve and bred by Charley Walker, although he was owned by Mike for a time. Guinea Pig was also by Pony Pete and out of Cherokee Maid, making him a full brother of Little Steve. Guinea Pig, too, could run. Printer Tom was another full brother. Red Texas, who was also called Smiley after his breeder, was by Little Steve and out of a mare by Croton Oil. There seems no doubt that Smiley and the

Trowbridges were the best short horse breeders Kansas has produced, and that includes a large number of excellent horsemen.

BILL STOCKTON AND ALEX CHOTE OF MISSOURI

Bill Stockton and Alex Chote were from the southwest corner of Missouri, another hotbed of sprinting quarter horses during the 1800s. It was there that the Alsups bred and raced their Brimmers and Lightnings; it was there, too, that Nathan Lloyd bred Cold Deck, and his friend John Hedgepeff, of Joplin, took one of his good mares to Cold Deck and got Barney Owens. So it was there also that Bill Stockton in 1876 took a race mare he had bought from the Alsups, bred her to a son of Cold Deck and was rewarded with (Missouri) Mike. His friend Alex Chote did about the same thing in 1880 and got a colt he called (Missouri) Rondo. The blood of these horses spread rapidly into all the areas where short horses were popular.

The Stocktons were, and are, a numerous and well-known family in Dade County, Missouri. Most of the following information was obtained from Francis Stockton Brown and from the papers of the Dade County Historical Society.

Clayton Stockton was the family patriarch. He married Nancy Patton while living in Virginia. After a brief stay there, they moved to Kentucky, then to Tennessee, and on to Missouri. Along the way Clayton obtained some of the best short horse blood to be found. By the time they got to Missouri, they were driving more race horses than they had children, and they had eleven of the latter. Issac D. was to become the father of William Wan Stockton, commonly referred to as just Bill Stockton.

A number of years before he died, Clayton, on impulse, had a coffin made for himself. On occasion, Bill and the other grandchildren would play in it, in the attic. That family legend ends with a story that Clayton took on considerable flesh in his later years, and it was only with the greatest difficulty that they were able to wedge him into his coffin.

William Wan ("Bill") Stockton was born on April 24, 1836. He inherited his love of race horses from his father and grandfather. He married Nancy E. Cantrell, and they had just one child, John, commonly called "Race-Horse" Stockton. "Race-horse's" grandson was named Finish Brown, and in 1977 was still living in Mariposa, California. Bill was killed in Lamar, Missouri, while shipping a carload of racehorses. They were shunting the cars around rather roughly and Bill was afraid that one of his race horses might get down. He was watching his horses so closely that he did not see another train backing down the track toward him, and a boxcar ran over him. He was buried in the Round Grove Cemetery, about six or eight miles south of Lockwood, Missouri.

Like their friends the Stocktons, the Chotes were interested in fast horses. Alexander Chote was about ten years younger than his friend Bill, but they used each other's stallions and were always friendly rivals in the racehorse business. Alex married Lena Ann Norvell on August 2, 1874.[7] Coke Roberds' famous Old Fred was bred by Chote. He bred a pacing mare he owned to his stallion Missouri Rondo and got Black Ball, a black stallion foaled in 1888. Later he bred Black Ball to an old yellow race mare he had picked up, and she foaled Old Fred in 1894. Old Fred grew into a large horse and was trained for the harness when he showed no great speed. However, the trained eye of Coke Roberds recognized the great potential of Old Fred, and he became a great sire of quarter horses in Colorado.

JAMES OWEN OF ILLINOIS

James Owen, of Berlin, Illinois, was one of several successful breeders west of Springfield. It was an outstanding group that included Sam, Hugh, and Walter Watkins; Robert Wade; Grant Rea; and Joe Brown, to name a few.

Jim Owen was born near Berlin on March 10, 1843 and died on September 5, 1899. He was buried in Ashland, Illinois. Most of his best horses were bred before 1880, so he is included in Part III of this book, although, like some of the others mentioned above, he could have been as easily placed in Part IV, since he was still active after 1880.

Most of my information about Jim Owen comes from W. B. ("Bill") Robertson, of New Berlin, whose father was a long-time friend of Owen's. The elder Robertson went to Berlin from Kansas, looking for a teaching job. That was in the early 1880's, when he was eighteen years old. He was headed out to see Jim Owen, who was a member of the school board, when he met Owen and one of his friends at a bridge. He asked for the job, and Jim told him he wouldn't last one day. That made Robertson mad, and he gave them a cussing and wheeled his horse around and started back for Berlin. The other man with Owen, a Mr. Watts, was also a trustee. He and Owen called the young Robertson back and gave him the job. Owen told him he had better lick every big kid the first day so that there would be peace thereafter.

Jim Owen lived on a farm of 720 acres in Cartwright Township, a few miles northeast of Berlin. Although he never married, he had a large, three-story home with a cupola on top. He had several rather impressive barns and sheds to house his brood mares, racehorses, work horses, and stallions. It was a going concern and much admired by the people of Sangamon County. Robertson believes that Owen's family originally came to Illinois from Kentucky, bringing a few good mares with them.

Owen raised a large number of horses and during his best years had horses on the tracks in Chicago, New Orleans, and even Cuba and Jamaica. He mostly bred, raised,

170

and trained, running only a few himself. Most of his horses were loaned out to others for a share of the purses.

Owen had his best luck with his stallions, Reputation Jr. and Fib. Among his top mares were Marchie A, a daughter of Fib, out of a son of Voltigeur; Gertrude W., similarly bred; and Vologne, by Voltigeur and out of a granddaughter of Lexington. Vologne's third dam was June Bug, by Harry Bluff, a Watkins bloodline. Another top mare he had was Polly J, by Spinning and out of Dell, by Cold Deck. Still another was by Spinning and out of a Jack Traveler mare. He also owned Dell, a mare by Cold Deck, and he raced Barney Owens for a time. As can be seen, he had many of the same bloodlines the Watkinses had, which is really not surprising seeing that they lived fairly close together and that they both had the habit of breeding winners.

CALIFORNIA

John Adams

The John Adams operation was southwest of Woodland, California. The family was active in racing from the 1860s to the 1880s. There are listed in various turf publications over sixty short racehorses that Adams bred, raised, or raced. A listing of a few stallions and mares is all that is needed here:

Stallions:
  Walnut Bark ch. c.f. 1853 by Blevin's Little Tom
  Brick ch. c.f. 1871 by Oregon Charlie

Mares:
  Bess ch. m. f. 1872 by Oregon Charlie
  Ella T. ch. m. f. 1881 by Shannon
  Lillie W. ch. m. f. 1887 by Joe Hooker
  Maud B. b.m.f. 1889 by Uncle Billy

John Adams and his family loved horses and short races. A good account of one of their races appeared in 1885 in the San Francisco sporting journal *Breeder and Sportsman* (published between 1882 and 1919 and edited by the well-known horseman Joseph C. Simpson). Adams raised his horses in Berryessa Valley but maintained a residence in Woodlawn. The Big Mare referred to below was his fast mare Ella T:

Equine Sprinters

The great match for $5,000 between Big Mare, owned by J. Adams, of Berryessa Valley, and Blue Mountain Belle owned by S. J. Jones, of Portland, Oregon, was decided

171

in the rain and mud of last Saturday. The match raised a great excitement among the ''short horse'' fraternity, and even those who profess an utter abhorrence of quarter-racing were somewhat exercised at the meeting of two such renowned animals. Big Mare was thought at one time to possess phenomenal speed. She defeated Jim Douglas so easily in a run of six hundred yards at Scarmento during the Summer, that it was held by the experts of this kind of racing that she could outrun any animal—faster, in fact than all of the famous heroes and heroines of the quarter-paths in any era of any country. She is a large and remarkably handsome mare; a bronze chestnut in color and of immense muscular development. Blue Mountain is smaller a great deal smaller as was evident when brought together, and is of a deeper chestnut-like bronze. She, too, is very well formed and has run some notable races. It could scarcely be termed a fair trial when the mud was fetlock deep, and there was a shower of sloppy clay flying from their feet as they took their preliminary gallops.

The betting was heavy. At first it was dollar for dollar, but then Blue Mountain became the favorite at $100 to $75, as a majority of the speculators fancied that her chances would be better in the mud than her long-striding competitor. There was a good deal of money back of Big Mare, and this brought the betting to even again. There was no wasting of time at the starting point, the half-mile pole, as the jockeys were fearful that there might be danger in pulling up should they get away before the flag fell. So at the first attempt a capital send-off was given, there being scarcely a foot of difference when the signal was given. Blue Mountain Belle was rather the quickest at getting away, and having the benefit of the inside, the other had further to go, though all the way around the turn the contest was very close. When straightened into the stretch Blue Mountain Belle commenced to draw away with clean, resolute action, while Big Mare was all abroad and the last furlong was only a big gallop for the Oregon championess, she winning very easily by many lengths in 53 seconds. It is very likely that defeat will not be accepted by the losers without trying to retrieve the lost laurels on a ''good day and a good track.''[8]

When the race was rematched for a shorter distance on a dry track, Ella T. won. When the entire story of the Adams racing and breeding operations are told, it will add an important chapter to short racing in the West.

Theodore Winters

Theodore Winters and John Adams were influential in the development of California quarter running horses, but each went at it in a different way. One reason may be that Winters was very wealthy and never let money stand in the way of obtaining a horse he wanted.

Theodore Winters crossed the plains in a covered wagon as a young man, on the way to the California gold fields. He arrived at Sutters Fort on October 29, 1849. Unlike so many other forty-niners, he brought his wife and child with him. It must have been difficult for his young wife to leave their home in Illinois, where Theodore's

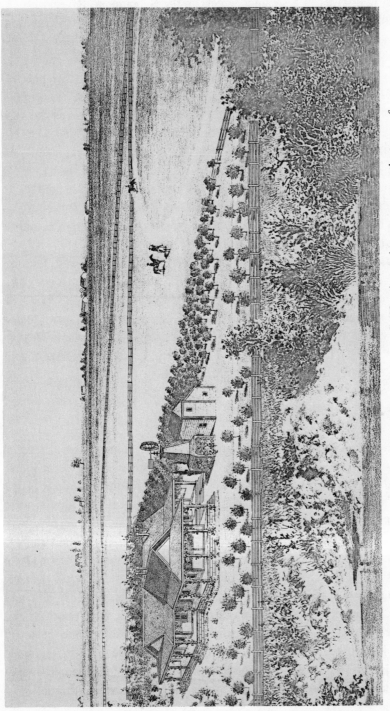

The home and ranch of Theodore Winters, an early California racehorseman, near the town of Winters, which bears his name. From *Illustrated Atlas and History of Yolo County, California*, 1879.

father was a wealthy stage-line operator. The move proved to be a tragic one: both she and her child lost their lives in a steamer wreck on the Sacramento River.

Winters spent several years working along the streambeds and saved the gold he panned. In 1857 he spent some of his savings on land. He heard that the Mormans were being recalled to Salt Lake and that those who had settled in Nevada were selling out cheap. He went to Nevada and purchased 1,700 acres near Carson City, which became the foundation of his livestock empire. He soon owned land in various sections of the West. In 1864 he went east and bought the great horse Norfolk, perhaps the best stallion (and certainly the most expensive) imported into California by that date. He soon discovered that the winters were too cold on his Nevada ranches to raise and train racehorses, so he bought land along the north bank of Putah Creek in western Yolo County, California. He had Norfolk shipped there by boat via Panama. He paid R. A. Alexander, owner of the Woodburn Stud, in Kentucky, $15,001 for Norfolk. Alexander told Winters that he had paid $15,000 for Norfolk's sire Lexington, and he wanted to get just a little more for Lexington's best son.

Winters' best sire of sprinters was Joe Hooker, but he preferred to raise Thoroughbreds, since it was easier to get them on the tracks. Joe Hooker was by Monday, by Colton and out of Mayflower by *Eclipse. He was foaled in 1872; both he and his dam were natives of the Golden State. Mayflower was a chestnut sorrel foaled in 1867, purchased by Winters from James and Chase. Winters' best-known long horse was Salvator, who ran a mile in 1:35½. Mrs. H. A. Trowbridge purchased several Joe Hooker mares to breed to her stallion Okema.

LUCIAN MAXWELL OF NEW MEXICO

Lucian Maxwell was born in 1818, about seventy miles south of St. Louis in Kaskaskia, Illinois. He was the grandson of the French-Canadian aristocrat Pierre Menard, who had a rather adventurous life. Kaskaskie was a small town just across the Mississippi from Missouri, and in those days both Missouri and Illinois were quarter horse states. No doubt Maxwell had more than a passing acquaintance with short racing before he left Illinois. His ambition was to be a mountain man and trapper. He was almost immediately successful and became an associate of Kit Carson, John Frémont, Charles Brent, Dick Wooten, and other famous frontier characters. In fact, much of Frémont's fame as an explorer was gained when Carson was his guide and Maxwell his official hunter. In 1842, Maxwell returned to Taos, which both he and Carson considered home. Before long he married Luz Beaubien, the beautiful daughter of a local grandee. Lucien was twenty-four, and his bride thirteen. The story has Maxwell kissing his bride good-by at the church door (Lady of Guadalupe Chapel in Taos) and promising to come back for her when he had made his fortune.

Lucian B. Maxwell (1818—75), trapper, guide, hunter, Indian fighter, sutler, merchant, banker, judge, cattle raiser, businessman of note, and, notwithstanding, the leading quarter racing man in New Mexico in his heyday. From *Old Mill Museum* (pamphlet), Las Vegas, 1968.

Lucien joined Carson and Frémont for more exploring and stayed on to help Frémont in the conquest of California. When Maxwell returned, he settled down with his bride to help manage her family estate. He built a fabulous home in Cimarron in 1858, and it became one of the most famous stops on the Santa Fe Trail. It was destroyed by fire in 1922. The ranch itself consisted of some 1,714,774 acres, a fair-sized plot. It just may have been the largest single privately owned, one-unit ranch in United States history. The original grant had been made to two men, Guadalupe Miranda and Carlos Beaubien, Maxwell's father-in-law. The grant, when later surveyed by United States surveyors, was found to cover a large portion of northern New Mexico and even parts of southern Colorado.

In 1864, Maxwell's father-in-law died, and Maxwell became sole owner of the grant. From that time on, the ranch was known as the Maxwell Grant. In 1870, Maxwell sold the grant for $650,000 and moved to Fort Sumner with his family and a few horses. He died in 1875.

Lucian Maxwell's mill. His home is in the background. Maxwell ruled with uncontested power, like a feudal lord, over 1.7 million acres, probably the largest single piece of real estate ever held by an American citizen. Photograph courtesy of Les Davis.

The Maxwell Land Grant continued to figure in the history of New Mexico's quarter horses. The new owners wanted to improve the livestock on the ranch. In 1881, to upgrade the horses, they went to England and purchased, for a small fortune, twenty of the finest Thoroughbred mares available in England. As a group they were in foal to thirteen different English stallions. Also included in the shipment was the French stakes winner Uhlan. The horses were shipped to New Mexico and at first stabled at the large barn that Maxwell had built along the river. Many of these buildings are still standing. The blood from this importation was to be mixed with American short horse blood brought into New Mexico, and the resulting horses produced many of the outstanding quarter horses raised thereafter in northern New Mexico. New Mexico and the quarter horse industry owe much to Frank Sherwin, president of the Maxwell Land Grant Company at the time the English horses were purchased, and to Frank Springer, who became president and saw that the blood was fully utilized.

One of the best examples of how the Maxwell Land Grant Company's importation helped improve the short horses of New Mexico is found in the Springer strain of quarter horses. The CS Ranch was established in the early 1870s, and is still operated by the Springer family.

PART IV
THE EARLY MODERN PERIOD
1880–1930

Everyone proficient in equine pedigrees knows that these wonderful beasts run through a long list, that exists in a direct line, between them and the patriarchal pair that munched corn in the ark.
—*History of the Turf in South Carolina*, Charleston, 1857.

QUARTER RUNNING HORSE SIRES

1880–1930

Superior horses in capital letters.

Ace of Hearts
A. D. Reed
ALAMO
Arch Oldham
Billy Sunday
Black Ball
BOBBIE LOWE
Bob H
BONNIE JOE
Booger Red
Brown Dick
Buck Thomas
CHICARO
Clabber
DAN TUCKER
Dedier (D. J.)
DEWEY
Eureka
FLYING BOB
Guinea Pig (f. 1922)
HARMON BAKER
Hermus
Hickory Bill

Jack McCue
Joe Bailey (Weatherford)
JOE BLAIR
JOE REED
John Wilkins
KING (Possum)
Leadville
Little Danger
LITTLE JOE
Little Steve
Lucky (f. 1914)
MAJOR SPECK
Mark
Master Gould
Missouri Rondo
Mose (f. 1914)
MY TEXAS DANDY
OKEMA
Oklahoma Star
Old Sorrel
Old Fred
PETER McCUE

PID HART
Plaudit
PONY PETE
PORT DRAPEAU
Primero
RANCOCAS
Remolino
ROAN DICK
Rocky Mountain Tom
Rondo (Locks)
Royal Ford
Sam Watkins
Silver Dick
Steam Beer
THE SENATOR
The Sheriff
Texas Chief
TRAVELER
UNCLE JIMMY GRAY
Yankee Doodle
Yellow Gold
Zantanon

CHAPTER THIRTEEN

The Quarter Horse Comes of Age

THE PERIOD

IN THE quarter racing story, in many ways the period 1880 to 1930 was one of quiescence and to some extent rebirth. There was a lull while the great effort was made to settle the Great Plains and Rocky Mountains, and widespread interest in racing and breeding was not rekindled until the development of organized short racing, which started in the late 1930s and early 1940s.

For the most part racing is maintained and nurtured by those who have some wealth and leisure time. During this period the average man was busy gaining the former in hopes of enjoying the latter. That helps explain the lack of organized racing in the American West during the last part of the nineteenth century and the beginning of the twentieth.

There was, nevertheless, some racing, and some outstanding sires and dams were produced. The breeders were widely scattered. Travel was still basically a horse-and-wagon affair. The first continental trains were moving, linking the East Coast to the West Coast. But it was still a several days' buggy ride for many westerners to reach a railroad. Today's transportation by highway and air makes it easy for racehorses to get from track to track. The most widely separated tracks are only hours apart.

Such was not the case before 1930.

Yet, though the movement of horses was limited by distance, it was not stopped. The horses were driven, led, or carried to populated centers where races were held and money to bet was available. Capitals, mining towns, resort areas, and border towns were likely to have race tracks, and if so, quarter horses found their way there. Short races were held in Hot Springs, Arkansas; Juárez, Mexico; Butte, Montana; Denver, Colorado; and elsewhere.

During this period the most active states were probably Illinois, Arkansas, Missouri, Kansas, Oklahoma, and Texas. Somewhat surprisingly, until you consider the availability of pari-mutuel betting, Arizona, New Mexico, and Colorado made rapid gains during the early years of the 1900's. Arizona was the first state to organize quarter racing and to hold purse, allowance, and handicap races. Tucson, ramrodded by Melville H. Haskell, featured what were called, with some justification, World's Championship Races.

179

THE PROBLEMS

Quarter racing has always been a colorful spectacle, with those interested coming from miles around. For the majority of those attending a match race, the machinations that took place went unheeded. The spectators just rooted for and bet on the horses they liked, with no idea of the designs of the owners, trainers, or jockeys. It was not uncommon for the greenhorn, or even a knowledgeable horseman, to lose heavily in a fixed race. This was perhaps the greatest drawback to match races: the best horse did not always win. The only thing that approached rules or conditions was the set of terms agreed to by the match makers, often in private. But even then there was no way of enforcing the agreement except through violence or a long court battle. The local courts, if any, were feeble because the defendant had probably already left the state or territory or proof was unavailable.

These conditions caused many breeders to concentrate on regulated races run on recognized tracks. During the years that the Jockey Club had appendix listings, many owners registered their quarter horses for racing purposes. By the 1900s, after the appendix was eliminated, that was no longer possible. Some horses that were less than thoroughly bred crept into Jockey Club records. One such was Peter McCue. For this reason the quarter horse breeders, frequented the more liberal tracks at Chicago, St. Louis, New Orleans and Juárez.

The problems inherent in match racing might seem to imply that there were no honest races. There were many. The middle western states, such as Ohio, Indiana and Illinois, had county fairs where racing was held. Some towns in Missouri, Arkansas, Oklahoma, and Texas held good annual race meets. The one common problem that all these races had was the absence of necessary information to card a good race meet. The racing secretary had to look over the horses that showed up and more or less guess which ones were of equal speed. There was no quarter horse organization to provide this information or to record and publish race results and times. Also lacking was pari-mutuel betting to pay for the track and its employees and provide the purses. No state was about to authorize pari-mutuels to a track that knew nothing about the horses that wanted to race. If they did, there would be no way to protect the public, which is generally reputed to be one of the functions of the state.

THE MEN

Arizona was a territory of the United States until 1912, and, as was true on the other frontiers, many local match races were run. The nearest organized racing was across the border in towns like Juárez. Some individuals took sprinting seriously. One of them was James J. Kennedy, of Bonita. He was a rancher who was more interested in racing horses than in raising cattle.

For a time Kennedy raised or bought his racers locally but soon saw that that was not the way to have a winner. He needed the best available blood. The year Arizona became a state, Kennedy imported Traveler's famous son King from Texas. For reasons best known to the Kennedys, they changed his name to Possum once he was in Arizona. They also bought several other racehorses and a string of mares. Kennedy then obtained the services of Berry Gardner to train his horses. Unfortunately Kennedy went broke a few years later, his ranch began to disintegrate, and the horses and cattle were turned out to roam. W. D. Wear was hired to try to keep things together. Out of the job he got Tony, a grandson of Possum and also a granddaughter of Barney Owens. Quite a few of the best horses Kennedy owned were scattered during that time, and it caused considerable confusion when their descendants were being put up for registration and exact pedigrees became important. Some of the stallions handled by Kennedy and Gardner were King, Guinea Pig, Apache Kid (often called Lucky), Doc, Duke, Monty Cross, Bulger, Baby King, and Strawberry.

Colorado had its Casements, Roberds, Dawsons, and Peavys, well-known horsemen and breeders. It also had important individuals like Kirk Williams, D. B. Turner, and Henry Leonard. Kirk Williams, of Mancos, bred Billy White and stood his sire Billy Caviness, a grandson of Billy. D. B. Turner sold all the horses he could raise, the fastest to racehorsemen, the others to polo players. He got his foundation stock from the Trammells and the Newmans of Sweetwater, Texas. He had Booger Red and a fine young stallion by Rancocas. He bred Fallacy, Red Boy, Red Devil, and La Plata. Henry Leonard had Leinster, by a Thoroughbred stallion and out of a Senator mare; and Nell Gray, by the Thoroughbred *Bluecoat and out of a mare tracing to Steel Dust.

In Illinois, the Watkinses were probably the best-known family, especially Samuel Watkins. When you bred horses of the caliber of Dan Tucker and Peter McCue, you were bound to attract some attention. There was an equally successful branch of the family living a few miles away at Oakford, among them Hugh, Bill, and Beverly. This branch bred Duck Hunter, Jesse Hoover, Carrie Nation, and Buck Thomas. Farther west, in Carthage, Grant Rea lived, and a few miles south, in Plymouth, lived Bob Wade. Both are famous for having stood Roan Dick, and Bob Wade for the horse named after him.

Kansas has much the same story. Uriah Eggleston, of Garden City, had a great band of quarter mares that he bred to his stallion, Elk Horn, by Uncle Tom. H. A. Trowbridge, of Wellington, bred Little Danger by Okema and out of a Cold Deck mare. Mike Smiley, of Sylvan Grove, bred Guinea Pig and Pony Pete, by Barney

181

Owens. He also had or raised Johnny Corbett, Printer Tom, Red Texas, and Little Steve. Joe Lewis, of Honeywell, bred Doe Belly by a son of Cold Deck and Rolling Deck by the same stallion.

In Missouri, Bill Owen had Bay Cold Deck and Boanerges, while a relative, James Owen, of Berlin, Illinois, with his good mares, bred Reputation and Fib. In New Mexico there was Ed Springer with Old Joe by Harmon Baker.

During this period Oklahoma was second only to Texas in the number of active breeders. They included Coke Blake, of Pryor; C. B. Campbell, of Minco; the Armstrongs, Trammells, Kellems, and Meekses, around Sayre; and John Harrel, of Canute.

Oregon's great accomplishment was to supply California with basic quarter blood. These horses came overland on the Oregon Trail, mostly from Missouri. Later many settlers moved down into California, taking their quarter horses with them. The foundation stock for Oregon was provided by Old Dan, by Selim; Oregon Charlie, by Old Dan; Oregon Eclipse, by Joe Hooker; and Oregon Lummix, by Simtuck.

Texas had so many breeders that it is difficult to single out a few to mention. There was John Wilkins, in San Antonio; Clay McGonigle, in Midland; Trammell and Newman, in Sweetwater; Shelby Stanfield, at Thorp Springs; Henry Pfefferling, of San Antonio; Dow Shely, of Alfred; Webb Christian, at Big Spring; and so on.

Wyoming also had some men interested in breeding sprinters, as did its sister state, Montana. Earl Moye, of Arvada, Wyoming, bred Dutch Martin, and C. A. Allison had Jim Rex and Pearly Bells. In Montana, R. H. Baker had Red Buck in Helena, and H. Kirkendall, of the same city, had Panama.

A more detailed account of the best breeders of this period will be found in later pages.

CHAPTER FOURTEEN

Matching and Pari-Mutuels

TURN-OF-THE-CENTURY RACING

THE ONLY satisfactory way to tell a race horse's class is by the time if takes him to run a certain distance. For many years Bob Wade held the world's record for the quarter mile, running it in twenty-one and one-quarter seconds. That time showed class because no other horse had run as fast before or would run as fast for years afterward. That the record was probably set with an elevated starting post is beside the point. While I was talking to an elderly man who used to live on the ranch adjoining the race track used by Bob Wade, near Plymouth, Illinois, he said that he remembered the elevated start used by the quarter horses running on that track. So Bob Wade learned to start from an inclined plane, and he may well have used one at Butte, Montana, when he set the record. If he did, so did his opponents, and they could not run that fast.

In the early 1960s the modern quarter horses began to close in on Bob Wade's time. Earlier, Rainbow, a Senator filly, was supposed to have run about as fast, and Peter McCue was rumored to have equaled Bob Wade's time, but these times were by hand-held watches, for the most part unverified. When Jet Deck set a record of 21.49, it was electrically timed and not open to question. In 1977, Dash for Cash was clocked in an amazing 21.17, for a new world's record. That shows class. Man o' War is said to have run one first quarter in twenty seconds flat. That time was made with a score, or a running start, so is not comparable with a quarter horse's time made from a standing start, the watch starting as the gate opens.

Bob Wade's time may be questioned today because of the probable start and because of the probable use of hand-held watches. However, one can not say that he was not a class horse. Six days before he set the world's record, he ran a quarter at Butte in 22¼. A month after he set the record, he ran a quarter at Salem, Oregon, on a level track in 22½. In July, 1891, again in Butte, he ran a race in 22¾. These are all times that can be run only by a sprinter of the very best quality. That is true even today, three-quarters of a century later.

Before 1900 some horses were almost as fast as Bob Wade, and were probably equal to, or a little better than, modern horses. The reason for this claim is that the horses were running under greater handicaps than their modern counterparts. They had inferior tracks to run on; they had inferior transportation from track to track; they had inferior medication and less scientific feed and mineral-vitamin supplements; and racing plates and veterinary attention were not as scientifically sound.

Below are listed some of these superior quarter running horses, all of whom ran the quarter in under twenty-two seconds before 1900:

Belle, Galveston, Texas, July 3, 1880	21¾
Jim Miller, Deer Lodge, Montana, August 16, 1888	21½
Sleepy Dick, Kiowa, Kansas, November 24, 1888	21½
Nettie S. Helena, Montana, August 23, 1890	21¾
April Fool, Fresno, California, October 2, 1891	21¾
Lark, Butte, Montana, August 15, 1896	21½

A great many horses ran the quarter in twenty-three seconds or less, and their names are recorded in Goodwin's annual turf guide. They made these times not just on the superfast tracks but in different states and on different tracks in California, Missouri, Montana, Nevada, Oregon, and Texas. Five had times of 22¾, ten others ran in 22½, and seven ran in the excellent time of 22 seconds flat. Since the times are just those recorded by Goodwin, they represent only races run on those tracks he felt worthy of recording. Hundreds of other races were run, some undoubtedly in fast times.

One could wish that Goodwin had tried a little harder to obtain the pedigrees of the horses he chose to record. The publisher of the guide says in the index that they could not guarantee the correctness of the pedigrees that did not trace to the *American Stud Book*. That includes all six of the quarter running horses listed above, and, for all intents and purposes, all other quarter horses, including Bob Wade.

Bob Wade was foaled in 1886. He was sired by Roan Dick and was out of Nettie Overton. Goodwin lists races by him in several states, and he is also known to have run in Illinois, Montana, Tennessee, Colorado, Oregon, Utah, Missouri, and Texas. His most dangerous rivals were his own half brothers and sisters.

The other horses running under twenty-two seconds were headed by Belle. She was a bay filly foaled in 1872. She was owned and probably bred by L. T. Porter, of DuPre, in Hays County, Texas. She was by Pilgrim, and her dam was a quarter mare, T. Belle, by Rupert.

Jim Miller was a sorrel colt foaled in 1885. He was sired by Roan Dick and so was a half brother of Bob Wade. Jim Miller's dam was Amanda Miller. Jim set the world's record for 440 yards in 1888, when he ran the distance in 21½ seconds. Another half brother of Bob Wade, Silver Dick, ran a quarter in 21½ seconds in 1902.

Sleepy Dick was a sorrel gelding, sired by Ironclad, by Woodburn and was foaled in 1882. Nettie S. was a gray, sired by Roan Dick, foaled in 1885. She set a world's

Joe Blair, sired by Bonnie Joe and out of a *Bonnie Scotland mare. He was foaled in 1911 and bred by C. B. Campbell, of Minco, Oklahoma. He will always be remembered for three things: his match race with Pan Zarita, his time of 39 seconds for 3½ furlongs, and his siring of Joe Reed. Photograph courtesy of Franklin Reynolds.

record for 600 yards in 30¼ seconds. When her racing days were over, she was bred back to her sire, Roan Dick, and foaled Bay Billy. April Fool was a sorrel gelding foaled in 1887, bred by L. A. Blasinggame, of Fresno, California, and by Confidence, by Walnut Bark; this Oregon stallion was owned by John Adams. Lark was a bay gelding foaled in 1888. His sire was Young Dasher, but his dam and breeder were unknown.

JOE BLAIR and PAN ZARITA

Mexico was the setting for one of the most dramatic races ever held by Thoroughbreds, quarter horses, or any other variety of running animals. Perhaps it was written that a sprinter and a long horse, a stallion and a mare were to be involved so that nobody could take all the credit for that "memorable chapter in sprinting history."[1]

The two contestants were Joe Blair and Pan Zarita. Joe Blair was an extremely well bred Thoroughbred, carrying the best sprinting blood available at the time. He was sired by Bonnie Joe, by Faustus, by Enquirer, and his dam was a daughter of *Bonnie Scotland. Bonnie Joe was then owned by C. B. Campbell, of Minco, Oklahoma. Joe Blair was foaled in 1911 and campaigned hard all his life. He could have been a great sire, had he not been in training most of the time. He was bred once in San Antonio to Della Moore without his (or her) owner's or trainer's permission. The exact circumstances are unknown today, although the following story was told to me by Boyd Simar, who trained and ran Della Moore for most of her races. Some of the stable hands were playing cards. Della Moore was in heat, and Joe Blair was nearby. To keep the barn quiet so that they could play cards, they let Joe cover Della Moore. The colt that was born of this illicit union was Joe Reed. She later foaled Joe Moore for Ott Adams.[2]

Joe Blair was considered as fast as any sprinter of his day, and his times bear it out. On February 5, 1916, carrying 115 pounds, he ran three and a half furlongs in thirty-nine seconds. On oval courses that record has stood for many years.

Pan Zarita is especially interesting to short horse breeders. She, like Joe Blair, was bred by a breeder of both long and short horses: Jim Newman, of Sweetwater, Texas. She was sired by the Thoroughbred Abe Frank and out of the quarter mare Caddie Griffith.[3] Both traced to *Bonnie Scotland. Her feats on many tracks have never been equaled. She spent her relatively short life running, and she became the greatest drawing card of her time. The bettors loved her. She started 150 times and took 76 firsts, 31 seconds, and 21 thirds. She was out of the money only 23 times.

Her most famous race was the match race she ran against Joe Blair in Juárez, Mexico, on February 10, 1915. Times were taken and bets made at every furlong. She won the ⅝-mile race in world's record time—1:57$^{1}/_{5}$. Her other times were 220 yards in 10$^{1}/_{5}$; quarter mile in 21$^{3}/_{5}$; ⅜ mile in 33$^{2}/_{5}$; and half mile in 44$^{4}/_{5}$. And she was carrying 120 pounds, not catch weights. If that does not seem like much, take out your best horse, use catch weights if you wish, and see if your horse can equal any of those times. Suppose she had been trained for just one of those distances, what might her time have been?

Pan Zarita was named for Pansy, the beautiful daughter of the mayor of Juárez. Jim Newman was a friend of the mayor's, and many of his horses raced in that city. As John Hendrix wrote, "In the short span of her meteoric career, covering the years 1912 to 1917, she set records on race tracks of America that stand unbroken to this day."[4]

When she died suddenly, it was called a tragedy. Her remains were buried in the

Pan Zarita, a sorrel mare foaled in 1910. She was bred and owned by the Newmans, of Sweetwater, Texas. She was sired by the Thoroughbred Abe Frank and out of a quarter mare. Pan Zarita was probably the fastest mare up to ⅝ mile that ever lived. Author's collection.

center of the infield of the New Orleans Race Track. The only female that might have replaced her, the great Thoroughbred filly Ruffian, also died suddenly, without the chance to equal Pan Zarita's records.

TEXAS SPEEDSTERS

During the years immediately preceding pari-mutuel racing, Texas had more than its share of speedsters. Some of the better-known runners were Texas, owned by Webb

Christian; Mamie Sykes, owned by Bill Taylor; Felix Jones, owned by another Bill Taylor; Pleas Walters, owned by Pleas Walters; and Gray John, owned by Sampson Haile.

Pleas Walters was a brown stallion sired by John Crowder. Crowder was a sorrel stallion sired by Old Billy and out of Paisana. Pleas Walters' dam was Dutch, a quarter mare raised by Joe Mangum. Pleas Walters was bred by Pleasant Walters, of San Antonio, Texas, and ended his career with Dow Shely, of Alfred, Texas. Texas was probably by Bobbie Lowe and out of a Thoroughbred mare. Both soon established a reputation for short racing and clamors arose for them to match a race. When the match was made, to be run at the Llano County Fair in 1905, it was the talk of the quarter horse fraternity throughout Texas.

Pleasant Walters, a butcher by trade, had bought the brown horse to use on his delivery wagon. He soon discovered that he had bought a better racehorse than cart horse. At both Junction and Lampasas, where Pleas Walters was first run, it was discovered that he could not only race but also win.

Most of the betting for the match was on Texas, for Webb Christian was a well-known and respected racehorseman with a world of experience. Also, Texas had been running extremely well. As often happens, however, the favorite lost. Pleas Walters won the race by half a length.

The Gray John race had been run a couple of decades earlier. A gray stallion, he was said to be by Steel Dust, although he must have been sired by a son of Steel Dust. He was foaled in 1874, bred and raised by John Watson, of Burnet County. At the time of the race he was owned by Sampson Haile, of Llano. Gray John weighed about 860 pounds and stood fourteen hands, three inches tall. Watson was a staunch Baptist, and when he found out that his boys were secretly matching Gray John, he sold the horse to Haile. Vance Faris, of Llano, a grandson of Sampson Haile, told Hazel Bowman that Gray John was the fastest horse in the country at the time.

One race that was much talked about was Haile's race with the notorious Jim Brown, of Lee County. Brown brought an unbeaten horse to Lampasas just to outrun Gray John. It took several hours to get the race started, as jockeys turned their horses, each striving for the advantage. When they were tapped off, Gray John won—not by much, but he won. After the race Brown tried to buy the gray horse, offering up to $2,500, a lot of money in those days, but Haile would not sell. Later the horse was raced in Arizona and ended up in California.

Another outstanding racehorse during this period was Charley Wilson, a sorrel stallion foaled in 1889. His sire was the Thoroughbred Buck Walton, and his dam was a quarter mare named Daisy. He was raised by John R. Nasworthy at his Bridgeview Stud near San Angelo. William Anson said that he was never beaten up to three-fourths of a mile, when raced by his breeder. Charley Wilson became notorious for a scandal on a Chicago track and was ruled off the turf. However, he continued to win many races after that on unrecognized tracks throughout the West.

Although Traveler is primarily known for his offspring, he was an honest racehorse himself. He was foaled about 1900; his parentage is unknown. He ran his best race when Brown Seay, of Granbury, Texas owned him. He was matched against the top horse in that area, Bob Wilson. When he defeated him, he was mighty hard to match short. He was soon retired to the stud.

Many of Traveler's colts turned out to be fast, such as Judge Thomas, Judge Welch, Buster Brown, Little Joe, and King (called Possum in Arizona). Little Joe was bred by Dow and Will Shely, but George Clegg raced him. In his first race he beat Carrie Nation in San Antonio, George Clegg told me that Little Joe was the fastest horse he had ever handled and was probably as fast as any that ever ran in Texas. King began running as a two-year-old, and is supposed to have won his first match race, at San Antonio, in 21½ seconds. Later, running at Kyle, Texas, he beat the excellent horse Yellow Jacket on the O. G. Parke track. Zantanon, a grandson of Traveler, raced widely in Mexico under the control of Eutiquio Flores. He was never trained properly—just led out and raced when the occasion presented itself. He made his owner a wealthy man in his village. Benevides Volpe purchased him when his racing days were over and took him back to Texas, where he gained new fame as a sire.

Carrie Nation, mentioned above, was one of Peter McCue's fast fillies. According to William E. Boeker, she was raised by George Watkins and Ed King, of Oakford, Illinois. King, who had a grocery business in Oakford, had a neat mare that pulled his delivery wagon. He bred her to Peter McCue, who was being handled by George Watkins, a friend. When the mare foaled, they named the filly Carrie Nation. Her speed soon made her a marked horse, and Ed and George sold her. In Oakford every Saturday, according to old-timers, was Carrie Nation day. She defeated all comers, including such well-known horses as Burnt Black, Coyote, and Gatlin Gun. She was never defeated on the Oakford track. She was never started in a walk up, or by a turn when facing away from the starting line but from an open chute with her nose on the starting line. She would stand quietly in the chute to wait for the starting signal. She did not care how her opponents started as long as they were not past the starting line when the signal was given.

She drew crowds from as far away as Springfield and Peoria. When Jim Thomas, who owned her during most of her career in Illinois, died in 1906, her new owners took her to Texas. She was one of the very best sprinters of her day.

OKLAHOMA SPRINTERS

The land that was to become Oklahoma was set aside as an Indian reserve by the

189

federal government in 1834. It was to serve as a permanent home, primarily for the "Five Civilized Tribes," as the Cherokees, Creeks, Choctaws, Chickasaws and Seminoles were called. Demands for land by white farmers on the borders of the tribal homelands of these Indians forced Congress to move them from their ancestral soil in the southeastern part of the United States. The land north of the Red River was, for the most part, uninhabited and seemed to Congress the place to send them, since it lay in the southern part of the unorganized Indian territory.

The first important movement by white settlers into Indian Territory came in 1889, when the Oklahoma "run" took place. The government had given in to pressure and agreed to open part of it to white settlement. Two years later the homesteaders organized the western part of the region as Oklahoma Territory. The two territories joined together and in 1907 entered the Union as the forty-sixth state. Its late settlement and statehood explain why Oklahoma got a slow start in the cattle and horse business. It probably should be mentioned here that there were some exceptions, for cattle and horse-breeding operations were carried on legally or otherwise before 1889. However, while Oklahoma land remained Indian Territory, most operations were assumed to be temporary. The activities of the Waggoners and the Burnetts could be used as an example. They got along well with the Indians and the Department of Indian Affairs and leased thousands of acres of Indian land on which they ran cattle before 1889. However, they maintained their headquarters and their horse breeding operations south of the Red River in Texas. A few smaller cattlemen married Indian girls and settled down permanently.

Once the territory was opened to homesteading, the rolling grasslands proved ideal for horse raising. The settlers were also fortunate that just across their borders in the older states, Missouri, Arkansas, and Texas, lived some of the best quarter horses in the world—Steel Dust, Shiloh, Cold Deck, and Missouri Mike, plus the Bertrands, Brimmers, Printers, and Whips. Oklahoma was surrounded by the best blood available, and she made good use of it.

When the American Quarter Horse Association was organized in 1940, it was determined that the first horses registered should be, as far as possible, outstanding foundation animals, all bred before 1925. There was only one exception: number one was to be given to the winner of the purple ribbon at the Fort Worth Livestock Show in 1940. The decision about which horses were to be given low numbers was left entirely in the hands of the Board of Directors of the AQHA. The board was composed of seventeen Texans, two Arizonans, one Kansan, two Coloradans, one from Mexico, and one from Oklahoma. But when the nine foundation sires were selected, five of the nine were stallions that were bred or stood in Oklahoma: The horse registered as number three was Joe Reed, whom J. J. Slankard stood in Elk City. The horse registered as number five was Chief, who spent his entire life in Hammon. Number six

190

was Oklahoma Star, who was bred and raised in Oklahoma. Number eight was Colonel. Colonel was bred on the CS Ranch, at Springer, New Mexico, but was taken to Wewoka, Oklahoma, by Jim Minnick. Last was number nine, Old Red Buck, bred by John Dawson, of Talala. Five out of nine is quite a record and helps explain Oklahoma's success in raising some of the very best running quarter horses.

Oklahoma Star was an outstanding sire of Speed, and he could run. He was sired by the Thoroughbred Dennis Reed and registered as out of May Matteson. His real dam was the quarter mare Cut Throat. Cut Throat was by Gulliver, by Missouri Mike and out of a Dan Tucker mare. She could fly. Oklahoma Star took after his dam and as a two-year-old showed that he could run short. He was matched in his first race against Slip Shoulder at Covington, Oklahoma. He won. He was next matched against Kate Barnard and beat her in the 220-yard race in eleven flat, according to those who were timing the race. For the next ten years he ran all comers as far as 600 yards and won most of his races. During his racing career he beat Duck Hunter, Henry Star, Jimmy Kicks, Ned S., and a host of others.

Badger, foaled in 1912, was another Oklahoma horse. He was by Peter McCue and out of Mazie Marie by Tom Campbell. He was kept in training most of his life, and so did not cover many mares while he was entire. Reed Armstrong, who generally called him Gray Badger, ran him for six years. When he was nine years old he began slowing down, so Reed sold him to a farmer friend who, wanting a light draft and buggy horse, gelded him.

There was a fast Oklahoma mare called Nellie Trammell. She had a club foot, but like others with this affliction, she did not let it slow her down. When she had some age on her, she came into the possession of Jess Cooper. Cooper took her to the best racehorse he knew, Badger, and talked Armstrong into giving him a breeding to Badger. Nellie foaled in 1916. The foal was black and was immediately dubbed Midnight. He looked so good that Jess's brother bought a half interest in him. Together they broke and trained Midnight. His first race, in 1920, was against a pretty fair horse imported from Cuba, and when the race was over, the Coopers had the money.

Armstrong had kept his eye on Badger's colt, and hearing that the Coopers were mighty high on Midnight after beating the Cuban horse, he decided that he might as well have some of those Cuban pesos for himself. He selected A. D. Reed to get the job done for him. A. D. Reed was a bay stallion, a half brother of Badger, foaled the same year as Cooper's horse. Armstrong expected to beat Midnight easily with him. But Midnight did not know all this, and he ran away from A. D. Reed. Now Armstrong dollars jingled with the Cuban pesos in Jess Cooper's pocket.

It soon became difficult to match Midnight, so the Coopers sold him to Red Whaley. To match him, Whaley knew that he had to go to the best, so he challenged the Waggoners, of Fort Worth, Texas. When he won the race, the Waggoners bought Midnight. He was then five years old. After running for them for a while, he was purchased by the JA Ranch. After serving the JA's, he was purchased by Aubra Bowers. Walter Merrick, of Cheyenne, bought Midnight's last colt and called him Midnight Jr. With him he won sixteen straight match races. Merrick now lives at Sayre, Oklahoma.

A CAJUN DYNASTY

People who have not been in the quarter running horse business over a long period are surprised to find that Louisiana has played an important part in the revival of the sprinters. The golden age of Louisiana sprinters began when Dewey was imported in 1900 and reached its peak in the 1930s when Flying Bob began producing colts and fillies with blazing speed. It did not take the Southwest long to realize that if you couldn't beat them, you'd better join them, and a long train of buyers began beating a path to the Cajun country for horses. There was a period during the late thirties and forties when Cajun sprinters dominated the racetracks all the way through Texas, New Mexico, Arizona, and on to California.

Louisiana's short racing had its own individual flavor, just as unique as its cooking and its coffee. They never ran an eighth, three-sixteenths, or a quarter. Their most popular distance was 256 yards. They also featured milk races for colts that were still suckling their mothers.

The first important stallion to influence Louisiana sprinters was Dewey. The Cajuns in St. Martin's Parish had an extremely fast mare they called Louisiana Girl, and a traveling racehorseman beat her with Dewey. When that happened, two of the better quarter running horse families, the Stemmans and the Broussards, put up the money to buy Dewey. A son of Ludovic Stemmans bred and raised Della Moore, who won her first race when she was still suckling her mother. Some neighbors had put on a milk race. Such a race served two purposes: it gave them a line on their prospects, and it was a good excuse to bet. The colts were taken to the racetrack and held by their owners along the start. The mothers were then led up the track. After a short wait the colts were released, and they ran for their mothers down the track, who had been whinnying to them.[6]

Dewey was undoubtedly the Thoroughbred Dewey, a bay stallion foaled in 1899, by *Sain and out of Sister, who was by Uncle Bob, who was by Luke Blackburn. The Broussards thought Dewey unbeatable. However, the same man from whom they bought Dewey went back to Louisiana the next year and matched Dewey with a horse called Dedier (when the Louisianans pronounce the name, it sounds like "Deejay"). Dedier is reported to have been sired by the Thoroughbred Henry Star. Dedier defeated Dewey, and so they bought him. Now the Cajuns had two stallions to breed to their mares, both of whom had class.

Flying Bob, who was sired by the Thoroughbred Chicaro, was at his best when crossed on mares by Dedier. This family of sprinters made waves all the way to the Pacific Coast, and the only way to beat them was to buy one. Flying Bob died in 1946. Until Three Bars appeared on the scene, he was the greatest sire of sprinters of this century, begetting offspring with matchless speed.

ORGANIZED SHORT RACING

Quarter horse races had seen some organization and regularity since colonial days, but scheduled meets were definitely the exception. Consequently, records of the abilities of the short liners were almost impossible to obtain. This never proved to be a drawback when it came to matching a race between two horses, but handicapping was impossible. You cannot handicap a horse (except by age, sex, and size) without some information about his past performances.

The one book that provided some meager facts, *Goodwin's Official Turf Guide*, was not readily available. But most of the quarter running horses listed were widely separated and would never show up at one track at one time so that a racing secretary could write a race for them. It fell to one state, Arizona, and one man, Melville H. Haskell, to change all of this.

In the late 1930s and early 1940s a small group of men living in or near Tucson were drawn together by a mutual interest in short racing, the kind in which they, as individuals, could participate. The man who had the track was R. C. ("Bob") Locke, of Hacienda Moltacqua, so his ranch became a sort of unofficial headquarters. One of the most active of these owners, all of whom raised, trained, and raced their own horses, was J. Rukin Jelks. He operated the Moltacqua racetrack for Bob Locke. Equally interested was Melville H. Haskell, who wanted everything down in black and white. The last of the inner core of horseman was probably the best natural horseman of the bunch: A. M. ("Jake") Meyer. He was willing to do anything to help promote Arizona stock horses and running horses. At one time or another he was starter, steward, announcer, and public relations man for the race meets and the Southern Arizona Horse Breeders Association, which all four horsemen ramrodded.

A few more individuals should be noted. One was that incomparable short horse enthusiast Jo Flieger. Then there was C. C. ("Clancy") Wollard, Olin Sims, and Smokey Bonner. All put their shoulders to the wheel, and they were all that Tucson short racing needed. Mel Haskell saw the need for records. Only when sufficient information was available could purse races be run without some unknown fast horse taking all the money. His plan was to have records kept wherever short races were run and, when these were compiled, to have them available to any short track in the country. In those days that was just a dream, though today it is a reality.

The first track on which the group ran races was the Moltaqua track. It was an oval track half a mile long. The races were run on the track across from the spectators, with a 220 gate and a 440 gate on a chute entering the track on the far side. Both races finished at the judges' stand at the quarter pole. Longer races were run around the track. The track was completed for quarter horses in 1941, and nine meets plus the first speed trials were held. The second year about fifteen meets were scheduled, and additional match races were run. In 1943 races were held almost every Sunday afternoon, and the now-annual speed trials attracted widespread attention.

It did not take many afternoons of racing to convince Haskell and his friends that more rules were needed to avoid chaos. It was agreed that certain rules had to be adopted so that straightaway racing could be run without interference that would cause a horse to lose his position. The track was dragged after each race, and the marks made by the horses' hoofs were studied so that any horse guilty of running out of his lane and bumping another horse could be identified and penalized. They did not have any films to look at in those days. Their aim was to promote the speed of the horses and eliminate luck, accidents, and jockeys' tricks.

Moltacqua had a six-stall, mechanically sprung closed gate, exactly on the starting line. The idea was to walk the horses quietly to the stalls and back them in against the tail bar. Then Jake Meyer would pull the lever, and the horses would break as one.

Before long, handicapping was done by grading the horses. Any horse that could run a quarter in 23 seconds was graded AA and limited to racing in match races, specials, stakes, or open races. Horses that could run between 23 and 25 seconds were divided into grades A, B, and C and given handicap weights within each grade. These handicaps were about ten pounds for each $1/5$ second. Horses were continually being reclassified on the basis of their races. All untried horses, or those of doubtful class, started in grade D, an amateur or cow horse division.

The fastest horses running in those early days were Shue Fly and Clabber. Shue Fly ran 220 in 13 seconds flat and 440 in $22^3/5$. Clabber ran the 220 in $12^4/5$ and the 440 in $22^4/5$.

Other fast times made by horses on the Moltacqa track during its few years of operation were as follows: 220 yards, Red Man, $12^3/5$; Painted Joe, $12^4/5$; and Chicaro, $12\frac{3}{4}$. For the full quarter there were Joe Reed, $22^4/5$; Alex the Great, $22^4/5$; and Nobodies Friend, $22^4/5$.

A little more about some of these horses might be of interest. Shue Fly was foaled in 1937, and she was bred by Lloyd Miller, of Santa Fe, New Mexico. Most of her racing was done after she was purchased by Elmer Hepler, of Carlsbad, New Mexico.

Shue Fly, World's Champion Quarter Horse in 1942, 1943, and 1944. She was onwed by Elmer Hepler, of Carlsbad, New Mexico. Author's collection.

She was by Cowboy, by Buck Thomas, by Peter McCue and out of Lady Luck by Booger Red. When Hepler took her to Moltacqua in December, she was matched against Clabber, the then reigning champion. Clabber broke out of the gate first and was leading by daylight at the eighth pole. At this point Shue Fly shifted into high gear and finished almost a length ahead of Clabber. She set the track record in the race.

Clabber was also foaled in 1937, sired by My Texas Dandy, by Porte Drapeau, a Thoroughbred. He was out of Golden Girl by Uncle Jimmy Gray. He was a big, strong, rugged horse who was always worked hard. He was bred by Claude Smith, of Big Foot, Texas, and purchased by A. A. Nichols. Clabber loved three things above all others: to eat, to run, and to rope. His only training was hard work on an operating cattle ranch. In Eagle Pass in 1941, he ran three races in one day, and won all three in the same time: twenty-three seconds flat.

At the end of the 1942 season Melville Haskell issued a booklet listing the horses with necessary data. It was titled *Racing Quarter Horses*. Six more booklets were published in the series.

The annual quarter horse speed trials, which developed into the championship races began to attract out-of-state horses. The winner carried the title World's Champion Racing Quarter Horse.

Haskell was determined to interest other states in keeping adequate records of their races so that, looking forward, they could, in an organization of tracks, exchange this information and so be able to handicap horses properly, regardless of where they

195

The paddock at Rillito Racetrack in Tucson, which during the 1930's and 1940's was the center of quarter horse racing. The guiding spirit for those races was Melville H. Haskell. Photograph courtesy of Melville H. Haskell.

came from. In 1944 the group was finally able to operate as the Tucson Racing Association. Rukin Jelks was president, Bob Locke was vice-president, and Mel Haskell had the title secretary-registrar.

The organization of the American Quarter Horse Association in 1940, and its rapid and solid growth, helped the Tucson group by providing assistance in identification of registered horses. Use of the closed starting gate also made racing much more satisfactory.

The success of the racing program encouraged the building of a new track at Rillito, by Rukin Jelks. It was designed just for the short race. It was completed in time for the 1943 racing season. The Tucson group never put a limit on the length that would be run, so an oval was included, as well as a straightaway leading into the oval. The straightaway ended on the south side of the oval coming in from the west. The chute was ⅜ so that for straight races the gate could be placed anywhere from 220 yards to 660 yards. The oval was one half mile around, and the track was forty-five feet wide. The stands could hold 1,500 spectators, although most preferred to stand along the rail or move around. There was also a mutuel room for wagering. The paddock was unique and characteristic of the track. There was a round center, about five feet in circumference, rimmed with cedar posts, with a flag in the center. From this radiated six heavy logs about fifteen feet long, resting on forked tree stumps standing about three feet high. A four-foot woven log fence, in the best corral tradition, surrounded most of the paddock area. Each horse could be seen by everyone while being saddled for the race.

The new Rillito track was an immediate success, made so primarily by the integrity and the enthusiasm of its officials. Rukin Jelks was the president, Clancy Wollard the racing secretary, Mel Haskell the presiding steward, and Jake Meyer the starter. Their first meet was run during 1943, and the group operated under its own organization, the Tucson Racing Association. Mel Haskell was even then planning to organize an American Quarter Racing Association, which would be responsible for registering horses for racing purposes only and keeping the necessary statistics from tracks all across the country. He wanted a publication available for all tracks, containing records of the races held each year and sponsored by a new multistate racing organization.

Rillito track racing was conducted informally, much like a family affair, although no basic rules were ignored. It was conducted entirely by local, nonprofessional race horsemen. They were cattle and horse breeders. The pari-mutuel department might be considered an exception, for a state tax commission accountant was in charge of it. Horsemen helped around the track and shared the profits, because the net profit from the mutuels was given out in the purses. Most of the officials served without pay.

The grading of horses was gradually improved and corrected by experience. Grade A horses now were those horses capable of running 440 yards in 23½ seconds or better. Grade B horses were those horses that could run a quarter between 23½ and 24 seconds. Grade C was for horses running between 24 and 25 seconds. Weight for age was the general rule for these horses. Grade D was for cow horses and other would-be race horses that could not run in C time.

Celebrated American Quarter Running Horses, a term picked up from Patrick Nisbett Edgar, was the title now given to the very best horses. At Rillito, 23½ seconds for the quarter was used as the minimum qualifying time for this honor. During the 1943–44 season, only 18 of 130 horses that started in races at three-eights and under earned the right to be called Celebrated American Quarter Running Horses.

Following is a list of some of the horses that became Celebrated American Quarter Running Horses:

Rumpus, a chestnut gelding, foaled in 1940, sired by Master Bunting, a
    Thoroughbred, who ran 440 yards, carrying 135 pounds in 23$^1/_5$ seconds
Rosalita, a chestnut mare, foaled in 1939, by Doc Horn, a Thoroughbred, who ran 440
    yards carrying 125 pounds in 23$^1/_5$ seconds
Shue Fly, mentioned above, who ran in 23$^1/_5$ seconds

Shue Fly defeating Rosita in the famous match race at Tucson in 1944. Shue Fly was owned by Elmer Hepler, and Rosita by Helen and Maxie Michaelis. Author's collection.

Texas Lad, a brown colt, foaled in 1941, sired by Monte, by Yellow Boy, by Yellow Jacket, who ran 440 carrying 125 pounds in $23^2/5$ seconds

Piggin String, a bay colt, foaled in 1942, sired by Ariel, a Thoroughbred, who ran 440 yards carrying 120 pounds, in $23^2/5$ seconds

Rosita, a chestnut mare foaled in 1939, by Doc Horn, a Thoroughbred, who ran 440 yards carrying 117 pounds in $23^2/5$ seconds

Punkin, a bay mare sired by Flying Bob, who ran 440 yards carrying 115 pounds in $23^2/5$ seconds

The 1945 booklet carried a subtitle: *Year Book and Register of Merit of the American Quarter Racing Association*. Haskell had been successful in organizing a multistate racing organization. In this booklet results of races at Eagle Pass, Texas, and Corona, California, are listed, as well as the races held at Rillito. Other races were obviously held, but were not reported or did not follow the rules and regulations that would have ensured comparable figures.

The American Quarter Racing Association was organized at Tucson on February 1, 1945, in the picturesque Old Pueblo Club, with representatives from most of the states that held organized quarter races. The officers and directors selected at the Pueblo Club were as follows: J. Rukin Jelks, president, representing the Tucson Racing Assocation; Ivan Brower, of Corona, California, vice-president, representing the Southern California Quarter Horse Breeders Association; Melville Haskell, secretary-treasurer, representing the Rillito track in Tucson; Bob Denhardt, of Wharton, Texas, representing the American Quarter Horse Association; Helen Michaelis, of Eagle Pass, Texas, representing the Eagle Pass Quarter Track; H. G. McKinsey, of King City, California, representing the King City Quarter Track; Felix Hickman, of El Paso, Texas, representing the El Paso Quarter Track; Bill Lamkin, of Westminster, California, representing the California Horseman's Association; Dewey Wilbanks, of Tampa, Florida, representing the Florida Quarter Horse Association; and F. B. Rigdon, of Carlsbad, New Mexico, representing the New Mexico State Fair quarter racing (Albuquerque). Also elected directors were Bob Locke, of Tucson, Arizona; Elmer Hepler, of Carlsbad, New Mexico; J. O. Hankins, of Rocksprings, Texas; A. E. Harper, of Edmond, Oklahoma; and Jack Casement, of Westplains, Colorado.

The rules and regulations set up by this first national association of quarter racing groups were relatively simple but adequate. Mel Haskell had spent many hours on them and had anticipated most of the problems, since he had already experienced them at Moltacqua or Rillito. The main purpose was to adopt and enforce basic rules and regulations to govern short racing. The group accepted the fact that it would have to register for racing purposes all horses that wanted to run on member tracks. There was no other way to provide identification or to classify them properly. Membership was open, and registering a racehorse made membership automatic. The association expected to be financed by a fee of one dollar per entry for all races at recognized tracks. The fee proved hard to collect.

Of greatest importance in providing adequate records for classification of horses were the uniform racing rules. All starts had to be from a closed gate, and the horse's head must be exactly over the starting line. All races must be straightaway or otherwise noted. Multiple watchers and conservative timing were indicated. All races were to be timed to the closest one-tenth of a second. One-half length was to be considered one-tenth of a second in estimating the time of nonwinners. The second horse, even if beaten by a nose, was always given a time one-tenth second slower than the winner. The association sent out detailed racing rules to all tracks, although it expected local conditions to make some alterations necessary. Performance was the only qualification for registration of the quarter running horses. Bloodlines, or their

199

absence, made little difference as far as registration was concerned. The description of the horse was much more vital than his pedigree.

By 1944 the following track records had been set (all were straightaway races from a closed gate): The 220 record was set by Lady Lee, who was by Baby Ruth, by Flying Bob. She ran the 220 at Corona, California, carrying 127 pounds in 12.3 seconds. Six other horses ran that distance in 1943 in 12.4. Flicka, who was by Major Speck, by Uncle Jimmy Gray, ran 300 yards under catch weight in 16 seconds flat. Jeep B by Clabber, by My Texas Dandy, ran 330 yards carrying 128 pounds in 17.4 seconds. Nettie Hill, by Dodger, by Harmon Baker, also ran the distance in 17.4 seconds, Punkin, mentioned above, ran 350 under catch weights in 18.2 seconds at Eagle Pass. Shue Fly, also mentioned above, now held the 440 record at 22.6.

After 1949, Tucson and Melville H. Haskell, no longer dominated quarter racing in America. The American Quarter Racing Association had undertaken to convince state racing officials that quarter horses were here to stay and that provisions must be made so that they could run on state-controlled pari-mutuel tracks. California, New Mexico, and other western states began building short tracks and holding one or two short races on long race programs. Most of the problems that arose in connection with these new ventures had to do with proper identification of horses arriving at the tracks.

Ultimately the success of short racing depended upon accepting one national organization to provide this service. It turned out to be the American Quarter Horse Association.

By 1946 the work was getting too much for one man, and so Mel Haskell obtained the services of Van A. Smelker, a young Tucson veterinarian who was a died-in-the-wool short horse enthusiast. By the time the 1947 yearbook was out, Van Smelker became the paid executive secretary and remained in that position while the AQRA gained over 700 members, over 2,000 registered horses and 22 member tracks in Arizona, California, Nevada, New Mexico, Oklahoma, and Texas.

By this time the competition had resulted in better horses making better times. Woven Webb, by Bold Venture, a Thoroughbred mare bred by the King Ranch in Texas, had come on the scene. She ran on the short track under the name Miss Princess. She lowered the quarter-mile record to 22 seconds flat. She also held or equaled the world marks in the 400 at 20.6 and the 350 in 17.8. Miss Panama, by Ace of Diamonds, held the 330 record at 16.9; Barbra B, by Bar Hunter, held the 300 mark at 15.8; and Tonta Gal, by Clabber, and Texas Jr., by My Texas Dandy, jointly held the 220 mark of 12.1 seconds.

CHAPTER FIFTEEN

Outstanding Sires

IT IS an extremely difficult task to select a few horses from this period to write about. So much is known about so many. Some of the well-known stallions that produced sprinters were purchased and used primarily by ranchers to raise cow horses. Had they been bred to a different type of mare, they could easily have made the list. Raising stock horses is an interesting and useful pursuit, but it is not the focal point of this volume. That is why excellent stallions, such as Concho Colonel, Joe Bailey, Joe Hancock, and Mark are missing from these pages. There were other important stallions during this period, some that we know quite a bit about, and others that are known only through the excellence of their offspring. Some were Thoroughbreds, and since information about them is available from the Jockey Club, not much information will be given here. Examples of these are Bonnie Joe, Chicaro, Henry Star, Leadville, Major Speck, Master Gould, Port Drapeau, Rancocas, Remolino, and Royal Ford. Another factor that had to be considered in the selection was when they lived. It was desirable to have representatives that covered the period 1880 to 1930. Consequently, we start with Rondo, foaled in 1880, and end with Plaudit, a foal of 1930.

RONDO

W. W. Lock is known to most quarter horses breeders as the owner of Rondo. Rondo was bred by Charles R. Haley, of Sweetwater, Texas. In the winter of 1885 he was shipped from the racetrack at Fort Worth to Kyle, Texas, by Tom Martin.

In a letter dated April 2, 1942, W. W. Lock's son wrote Helen Michaelis the following explanation concerning Rondo, Tom Martin, and the Fort Worth race. Here is the story, somewhat condensed, in Lock's own words.

Lock wrote that his father, W. W. Lock, died in 1908:

> . . . and we boys scattered up. So the race horses were dropped. . . . I can look back now and see a big mistake in not holding on to those good fillies and raising some real horses a man could travel with.
>
> My father sent me to Crawford Sykes with Daisy L. in 1892. She brought a stud colt just like the old Sykes horse who was almost a dun. After we moved the horses and Rondo to

Greer County in 1895, this Sykes colt was a two-year-old. The Sykes colt got very vicious on the range and someone shot him with a 30-30 and killed him. About the same year that Rondo died, I think that was in 1897.

Now as to Rondo. Sometime in the fall of 1885, Old Man Jim Brown matched a race with the Haley Brothers, and both of these horses were two-year-old fillies; one owned or handled by Jim Brown, the other by the Haley boys. The match between the two was to be run in the fall of 1885 in Fort Worth for $1000 a side for one quarter of a mile. Jim Brown was a good friend to Old Man Tom Martin of Kyle, Texas. After the race was matched, the Haley Brothers wanted to double the bet. Jim Brown began to get cold feet and he wrote to Tom Martin to come to Fort Worth and look them over. After Martin got up there and looked both fillies over, Tom told Brown that he was going to lose the race.

Tom Martin found out that the jockey who was going to ride the Haley filly had ridden a lot of races for him. He got the jockey off to one side and told him that a lot of his money was up on the Brown filly, and that if she didn't win he was broke. Arrangements were made and Martin and Brown put down more money. The Haleys bet all of their money and all they could borrow, and then bet the stallion Rondo against $2000 more. When the race was over, the Haleys were broke and Jim Brown gave Tom Martin $1000 and Rondo for his help in winning the race.

Martin shipped Rondo to Kyle, Texas, in the fall of 1885, and stood him in the spring of 1886. The next spring Dad bought Rondo for $1000 and bred Mary Lee to him and got Blue Jacket. I don't know if the Haleys raised Rondo or got him from someone else. Rondo was five years old when the race was run.

Rondo was a sorrel son of Whalebone, by Billy, by Shiloh, and out of Mittie Stephens, who was a daughter of another son of Shiloh. Rondo was foaled in 1881, and he was a reported to be a beautiful quarter horse. He stood on the Lock ranch near Kyle until 1895, when he was taken to Greer County, then a part of Texas. He died there in 1897, one year after it became Greer County, Oklahoma Territory.

PID HART

Pid Hart, a sorrel, was bred by Shelby Stanfield, of Thorp Springs, Texas, and foaled somewhere between 1885 and 1887. His sire was Tom Driver, by Steel Dust, and he was out of Jenny Capps, by Little Jeff Davis, by Shiloh. His second dam was Bay Puss, by Mounts, by Steel Dust. Pid Hart was sold as a colt to the man who gave him his name, Pid Hart, of Cleburne, Texas. He was later owned by John C. Platt of Sipe Springs, Texas, and then by C. B. Campbell, of Minco, Oklahoma. He was a great racehorse and sire, his first foal being Rocky Mountain Tom. Pid Hart was running at St. Louis during the early 1890s, when he was purchased by C. B. Campbell. After using Pid Hart for several years, Campbell sold him to the Trammells, of Cheyenne, Oklahoma.

Pid Hart's first race was run in 1887 or 1888 against Gray Wolf, whom he beat

202

handily. He then campaigned in Idaho, Montana, and Oregon, ending up in St. Louis in 1894. Pid Hart died in the ownership of George Little in 1905, on Little's ranch west of Durham, Oklahoma.

DAN TUCKER

Barney Owens was no doubt one of Cold Deck's greatest sons, and it is equally true that Dan Tucker was one of Barney's greatest sons. Just siring Peter McCue would have made Dan Tucker famous, but he also sired other outstanding sprinters, such as Barney Lee, Log Cabin, Tommy Tucker, Hi Henry, Hattie Shipley, Harry N, Hazel Hughlett, Katie Wottle, and Nona P.

Samuel Watkins owned a good mare that he raced called Butt Cut.[1] During the same time a friend of Watkins, James Owen, of Berlin, Illinois, had a fast stallion named Barney Owens that was cleaning up all competition. Watkins took his fast mare Butt Cut to Berlin and bred her to Barney Owens. The result was Dan Tucker, who turned out so well that Watkins later bought Barney Owens. Dan Tucker was foaled on April 20, 1887, and grew into a big horse, standing over fifteen hands and weighing over 1,200 pounds.

Watkins began running Dan Tucker as a two-year-old. His first race was a match against a local champion in Menard County. He did so well as a two-year-old that Watkins sent him to recognized race meets at three. *Goodwin's Turf Guide* shows him entered in races at nearby Springfield and also at St. Louis. In 1892 he started eleven times, won once, and placed six times. He won a half-mile race in forty-seven seconds.

Dan Tucker soon left the organized race tracks and spent his time matching racing, where he was at his best. He looked too big to run a short race, but when the signal was given, he came off the post like a hoop rolling. One of his most famous races was with a half brother named the Sheriff, a sorrel stallion foaled in 1890, three years younger than Dan Tucker. He was by Barney Owens and out of a paint quarter mare. His breeder had taken his mare to Barney Owens while Watkins was standing the stallion. The owner raced the Sheriff for a year and then sold him to Fred Wood, of Abilene, Texas. Wood had great success with his horse, running him in Texas, Oklahoma, and Kansas. He matched a race with Dan Tucker in St. Louis for a quarter of a mile. Dan Tucker won the race in twenty-two seconds flat, according to reports, and everyone agreed that it was quite a match.

A few years later Dan Tucker was retired to the stud. He developed periodic ophthalmia and had to be watched very carefully. The Duke of Highlands, who was in the adjoining paddock, got in with Dan Tucker one day and almost killed him before he was driven off. In 1898 an agent for Trammell and Newman of Sweetwater, Texas,

Peter McCue, who ranks with the best sires of speed horses of all time. He was bred by Sam Watkins, of Petersburg, Illinois, and was sired by Barney Owens. His dam was a Thoroughbred named Nora M. Photograph courtesy of George Dorrill.

purchased Dan Tucker and his sire, Barney Owens, and took them to Texas. They used Dan for a number of years, but one day another stallion got into his paddock and killed him. Dan Tucker was too old and blind to protect himself. It was a tragic way for a foundation animal of the American quarter horse to die.

PETER McCUE

Much has been written about Peter McCue, most of it justified. One factor that helped establish his reputation was that he stood at stud in several states after his racing career was over. He had rather long stands in Oklahoma, Texas, and Colorado. Since his colts were great, his reputation as a sire became widespread. He was already well known for his racing successes.

Peter was a somewhat ungainly bay stallion foaled in 1895. He died in Colorado in 1923. He was sired by Dan Tucker, and his dam was Nora M, by the Thoroughbred Voltigeur, who was owned by his breeder, Sam Watkins, of Petersburg, Illinois. His second dam was a quarter mare named Kitty Clyde. Peter's sire was a large horse, but Peter was even larger. He stood sixteen hands and weighed 1,430 pounds in good flesh. Those who knew him said that he was one of the fastest short horses that ever lived. He was caught in twenty-one seconds for the quarter, a time that seems a little fast, although the present record is just a couple hundredths of a second slower. A little while later three watches again caught him in this time.

Peter McCue's principal owners besides his breeder were John Wilkins, of San Antonio, Texas; Milo Burlingame, of Cheyenne, Oklahoma; and Si Dawson and Coke Roberds, of Hayden, Colorado. Some of his more famous progeny are Carrie Nation, Buck Thomas, Harmon Baker, Sheik, John Wilkins, Hickory Bill, Duck Hunter, Chief, Jack McCue and Badger. Among his better-known grandsons are Joe Hancock, Paul L, Sam Watkins, Old Sorrel, Nick, Midnight, and New Mexico's Little Joe.

THE SENATOR

Leadville was a better-than-average Thoroughbred stallion running on the Colorado racetracks. He broke down at Overland Park in the early 1890s, and State Senator Casimiro Borilla, who had been watching and admiring his early speed, bought him and took him home to his ranch near Trinidad, Colorado. The senator bred his new stallion to a number of mares, but when he was bred to a small bay quarter mare named Woolly, the nick was just right. Woolly was fourteen hands, two inches at the withers and about two inches more over the rump.[2] She achieved a brilliant quarter racing career and was well regarded. She was raised and raced by Charley Walker of Kiowa, sired by Little Steve.

The colt foaled by Woolly and sired by Leadville turned out to be the stallion who became famous under the name the Senator. He was foaled in 1897, and as a mature horse he stood a fraction over fifteen hands and weighed 1,100 pounds. One thing that was noticed instantly were his short ears, which he had inherited from his dam. The tips turned in like half moons. According to those who knew him, he had plenty of heart and a world of sense.

Frank S. Byers, who had wide interests plus a newspaper, liked to race horses. He learned of Woolly's good colt and went to Trinidad and bought him. He named the colt the Senator, after his breeder, and took him to Hot Sulphur Springs in the Colorado Rockies, where he had a hotel and stables. There was much quarter racing in the area, especially at Granby and Steamboat Springs.

Before long the Senator had set a track record, carrying 145 pounds, running a

205

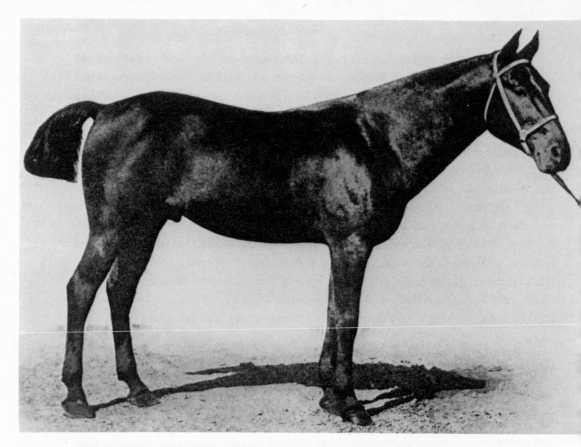

Little Steve, the well-known Colorado short horse raised by Mike Smiley, of Kansas, and owned by Charlie Walker, of Kiowa, Colorado. Photograph courtesy of Dan D. Casement.

half mile in forty-nine seconds. No other horse was pushing him, or he might have run faster. Agnes Wright Spring tells about a race the Senator had when he was trained by Ed Galbreath. A race was matched with Charley Walker's Little Steve, and at the starting line the Senator took a deep breath and broke his girth strap (an old one), just as the race started. With no help from the jockey, who was holding onto the neck strap for dear life, the Senator managed to beat Little Steve to the finish.

TRAVELER

Traveler was a sire who came out of nowhere to establish a strain of Texas quarter horses. It is useless to speculate on his probable breeding, as the first we know of him was when he was working on the right-of-way of the Texas and Pacific Railway, in Eastland County, Texas.[3]

206

When Traveler was bought out of the band of work horses, he was already a mature horse at least eight. This would have him foaled about 1900. He had never been broken to the saddle, although he had been worked all his life. All authorities agree on the next part of the story of Traveler. He began racing very successfully, and from that time on the legends and stories evaporate, and we have facts. One of his first races was against a mare named Mayflower. Will Crutchfield rode Mayflower in that race. His friend Bob Berry remarked afterwards, ''Crutchfield could not have thrown a rock off Mayflower and touched Traveler's dust.''[4]

A man named Brown Seay owned Traveler after he started racing. One of his best matches was against Bob Wilson, who had a reputation as one of the fastest horses in Texas. Traveler beat him. Traveler ended up with Will and Dow Shely in Alfred. His best colts were Little Joe, King (Possum), Judge Thomas, Judge Welch, Buster Brown (Jack Tolliver) and Texas Chief.

KING, OR POSSUM

Many a quarter horse has had several names. Undoubtedly the name was changed on occasion so that a speedster's identity could be concealed in an area where his name was known but where he had not been seen in the flesh. It certainly made it easier to match a race. Or perhaps the new owner just did not like the original name. Whatever the reason, King had three names altogether: King, King Cardwell, and Possum. He was generally called King in Texas and always Possum in Arizona.

King was as well bred as a South Texas quarter horse could be. He was by Traveler and out of Jenny, by Sykes Rondo. Jenny was a daughter of the best mare South Texas has produced, the fabulous May Mangum. Some feel that King was Traveler's greatest son. He was bred at Alfred, Texas, by Dow Shely and foaled in 1905. King died in 1925, respected and admired by horsemen in a half-dozen states. He was a light sorrel with many roan hairs.

Dick Herring, of Devine, Texas purchased King from Shely and, after he grew up, sold him to J. J. Kennedy, of Bonita, Arizona. He ran some races in Texas before going to Arizona. Ed Echols saw his race with Yellow Jacket at O. G. Parks track, near Kyle, Texas. King was also said to have beaten a horse at San Antonio running the quarter mile in under twenty-two seconds. All agreed that he was a good racehorse, even if he did not beat twenty-two seconds.

He never raced in Arizona. According to the accepted account, he was crippled en route to a match race at Wilcox. He was led up to a water tank that had overflowed, and was surrounded by wet earth. Possum sank into the mud and in the struggle to get out pulled a leader in one of his hind legs. It later got well enough so that he was practically sound, but it took the edge off his speed. From then on he was used only at stud.

Melville Haskell, the founder of modern organized short racing, found out some interesting facts about King. Of the approximately two hundred horses that ran between 1940 and 1944 on approved American Quarter Racing Association tracks, only thirty-nine qualified for the title Celebrated American Quarter Running Horse, the highest honor given the fastest horses. Of these thirty-nine honored horses, the Traveler line, headed by King accounted for nine, almost one-fourth of the entire list.[5]

King's best offspring in Texas was undoubtedly Joe Bailey of Gonzales. In Arizona it was Red Cloud, Guinea Pig, and Blue Eyes.

UNCLE JIMMY GRAY

Uncle Jimmy Gray's progeny dominated the "bull rings" and short tracks of America during the early 1900s. Jimmy was a brown horse, foaled in 1906, who inherited speed and prepotency from his great-grandsire, *Bonnie Scotland. His sire was Bonnie Joe, by Faustus. Bonnie Joe's dam was Bonnie Rose, by *Bonnie Scotland. Bonnie Joe was bred by James B. Gray, of Marysville, Missouri, and foaled in 1894. C. B. Campbell, of Minco, Oklahoma, bought Bonnie Joe, and the horse made Campbell and Minco in Oklahoma as famous as Watkins and Petersburg were in Illinois, and at about the same time. However, Campbell never received the publicity that came to the Watkins family. Bonnie Joe got Useeit, who in turn foaled Black Gold, who won the Kentucky Derby. Useeit was also the dam of Beggar Boy, Ronald Mason's famous stallion. Campbell also bred Joe Blair, who was by Bonnie Joe and out of Miss Blair, by Bowling Green. Joe Blair was the sire of Joe Reed.

Uncle Jimmy Gray was both a noted runner and one of the most prolific breeders of short sprinters since *Janus himself. People joked that you could breed him to a boxcar and get a race horse. Two mares were listed as possible dams, Mary Hill and Bettie Campbell. The way he ran and reproduced himself made the dam of little importance. He was registered by the Jockey Club as out of Mary Hill, by Bowling Green. The controversy was the same that arose among many short horse breeders who kept both quarter horses and Thoroughbreds. Bettie Campbell was by Bob Peters, by Old Bob Peters, by Pony Pete. Both Bettie and Mary were first-class race mares.

Uncle Jimmy Gray was raced till 1918, when he was twelve; then he was purchased for stud by the Army Remount Service. Within a few years Ed Pfefferling, of San Antonio, who had a stable and horse barn, took Uncle Jimmy and stood him for the rest of his life. Jimmy had been condemned to be destroyed by Army Remount inspectors in 1929 because, they insisted, he was too old and had outlived his usefulness. However, Pfefferling had grown fond of the old horse, who was also returning him a great deal of money each year in service fees. Even at twenty-three Jimmy was being bred heavily to as many as four mares a day during the season. At

Uncle Jimmy Gray, a brown stallion foaled in 1906. He was sired by Bonnie Joe and out of Bettie Campbell. He was bred by Charles B. Campbell, of Minco, Oklahoma. From Robert Moorman Denhardt, *Quarter Horses: A Story of Two Centuries*, 1967.

twenty-five he covered sixty mares, fifty-six of whom foaled. Pfefferling hated to lose the old horse, so he talked the service into leaving Jimmy with him. He kept and bred him for three more years, until he died in 1932, at the age of twenty-six. The only horse as popular among the racing fraternity of Texas was Peter McCue.

Uncle Jimmy Gray had many get and grand-get running on the short tracks. To list just a few: Tommie Gray, the sire of Chain Lay; Major Speck, the sire of Flicka; Major Gray, the sire of Silver; Alamo, the sire of Pal, Cyclone, and Go Forth, who in turn sired Twist; Golden Girl, dam of Flicka; My Pardner, the sire of Mariposa; and Bull Dog, the sire of Chubb. In 1947 the yearbook of the American Quarter Racing Association shows Uncle Jimmy Gray at the top of the list of maternal grandsires of Register of Merit horses. The progeny of Uncle Jimmy Gray dominated the short tracks during the 1920s and 1930s, just as Flying Bob's did during the 1940s.

JOE REED

Joe Reed was sired by Joe Blair, whose race with Pan Zarita is discussed earlier in this book. Joe Blair's dam was another great race mare, raised in Louisiana. A book could be written about short racing in Louisiana because that state produced as many fast short horses between 1900 and 1940 as any other single section of the country.

209

Della Moore, held by Ott Adams. She was sired by Dedier and out of Belle, by Sam Rock. When bred to Joe Blair, she produced Joe Reed; when bred to Little Joe, she produced Joe Moore. Photograph courtesy of Ott Adams.

Della Moore, the dam of Joe Reed, was foaled a few miles north of Scott, Louisiana, on the farm of Ludovic Stemmans. Stemmans, like many of his friends and neighbors, loved a short race, and he had a mare named Bell, a daughter of Sam Rock, who was seldom defeated. When it came time to breed her, he took her to Dedier. The offspring of Bell and Dedier was Della Moore. Della Moore raced all through quarter horse country, and was bred, during her racing days, to Joe Blair without her owner's permission. More information on how Della Moore happened to be bred can be found in the section on Pan Zarita and Joe Blair.

Della Moore was owned at this time by John Lindsey, who bought her from Boyd Simar. He was eager to have her running so that he could complete some match races he had arranged. Joe Reed was taken from Della Moore right after birth. When Lindsey returned home after the racing season, he found Joe Reed in pitiful shape, running loose in a cotton field and practically starved. Lindsey got him up and in shape, trained him, and ran him. Later he sold him to J. W. House, of Cameron, Texas, who kept him for about twelve years and then sold him to Dr. J. J. Slankard, a veterinarian living in Elk City, Oklahoma. Slankard kept Joe Reed until he died on May 19, 1947.

My Texas Dandy, foaled in 1927. His sire was the Thoroughbred Porte Drapeau, and his dam was a quarter mare, Sadie May, by Little Dick. From Denhardt, *Quarter Horses: A Story of Two Centuries*.

While House owned Joe Reed, he sired Joe Reed II and Red Joe of Arizona. Other well-known horses sired by Joe Reed are Joe Darter, Little Fanny, Two Timer, Sue Reed, Catcher, Reed McCue, Joe Sunday, Joe Bob and Jim Reed.

MY TEXAS DANDY

My Texas Dandy was a sorrel with a wide blaze and one white hind foot. He was bred by C. F. Myers, of Ellinger, Texas, out of his quarter running mare, Sadie May, by a Thoroughbred Myers admired: Port Drapeau, owned by Dr. A. J. Clark, of Schulenburg, Texas. Sadie's sire was Little Dick, and her dam was a bay Thoroughbred mare named Nellie, sired by Panmure. In the spring of 1927, Sadie May dropped My Texas Dandy, named for My Dandy, another Port Drapeau colt that was running on the big tracks at the same time with considerable success.

My Texas Dandy was trained by Charlie Brenham, of Hondo, Texas, and ran a few races at La Grange and New Braunfels, but was too slow. His greatest fault was that he just could not run around the "bull rings," the half-mile oval tracks so popular at the time. He would start fine but fail to turn properly and have to be pulled up.

When it was seen that he would never be a racing prospect, he was sold to J. C. Smith, of Big Foot, Texas. My Texas Dandy was five when Smith began breeding him. In 1932, Colonel Clyde was foaled. The next year Captain White Sox appeared. A few years later the great runner Clabber was foaled, out of an Uncle Jimmy Gray mare. Other horses sired by My Texas Dandy include Free Silver, Golden Slippers, Ginger Rogers, Texas Dandy, Little Texas, Nancy Hanks, Texas Star, Texas Jr., and Shadow.

FLYING BOB

When Melville Haskell began organizing short racing in Tucson in the late 1930s and early 1940s, it seemed that all the fast ones were Flying Bob's. Lucky held the 220-yard record, Lady Lee was coholder of the 330-yard record, Punkin was the coholder of the 350-yard record, and the 440-yard record was held by Queenie. All were sons or daughters of Flying Bob.

Flying Bob seemed to get his fastest colts when he was crossed on the daughters of Dedier (often just called Old D. J.) In an indirect way, John Dial of Goliad, Texas was responsible for the appearance of Flying Bob. He bought the great Thoroughbred Chicaro in New Orleans in 1928 and started home with him. He spent a night in Abbieville, Louisiana, and while there, Chicaro covered Zerengue's Belle, who in due time foaled Flying Bob. Chicaro was by *Chicle, and he bred sprinters other than Flying Bob. His son, Chicaro Bill, out of a Little Joe mare, was the sire of the quarter horses Chicaro, Arizona Girl, and Senor Bill, while Tony McGee, another Chicaro colt, sired Peanut, Jughead, and Double Cross. Daughters of Chicaro produced Don Manners, Maggie, and Pokey for the King Ranch.

As a mature horse, Flying Bob stood fifteen hand, one inch, and weighted 1,100 pounds. He was a beautifully formed dark-bay horse, with the same round compactness of body and limb as his sire Chicaro, although not as tall. He died in Texas in 1946. Besides his get mentioned above, there were also Dee Dee, Danger Boy, Babe Ruth, Black Beauty, Bay Annie, and Effie, all high-class sprinters.

ROCKY MOUNTAIN TOM

Rocky Mountain Tom was raised by that outstanding breeder of sprinters, Shelby Stanfield, of Thorp Springs, Texas. He was by Pit Hart, by Shelby, by Tom Driver, by Steel Dust. Pid Hart was out of Jenny Capps by Dash, by Little Jeff Davis, by Shiloh. The dam of Rocky Mountain Tom was Lady Gladys, by Bill Garner, by Steel Dust. Rocky Mountain Tom was an unusual color for a quarter horse—black with a star on his forehead. He was foaled May 20, 1890. He was raced extensively while owned by Sam Payne, of Quanah, Texas, and George Rummins, of Springtown. He was advertised at stud in 1914 by J. G. Helm, of Newark, Texas:

> Rocky Mountain Tom will make the season of 1914 at my place one mile west of Newark, Texas, Terms: Services to insure mare with foal, will be $15.00   Money due when mare

Chicaro, the Thoroughbred stallion sired by *Chicle and out of Wendy, by Peter Pan. He sired the short horses Flying Bob, John Dial, and Chicaro Bill and some fast mares.

Flying Bob, by Chicaro and out of a Dedier mare, the great sire of Louisiana quarter horses in the 1930's and early 1940's. From Denhardt, *Quarter Horses: A Story of Two Centuries*.

Queenie, by Flying Bob and out of a Dedier mare. In spite of her club foot she ran a quarter mile in 21.8 seconds at Albuquerque. She was foaled in 1939 and was World's Champion Quarter Horse in 1946. Photograph courtesy of Melville Haskell.

Rocky Mountain Tom

Above is an exact picture of Rocky Mountain Tom

The Famous Race Horse, was foaled by Shelby Stanfeld, and was once owned by George Tummins at Springtown, Texas. Now owned by J. G. Helm and Son.

Rocky Mountain Tom is a beautiful black, with star in forehead, and was foaled May 20, 1890. Sired by Pid Hart. Pid Hart was sired by Shelby, he by Tom Driver, and he by old Steel Dust and out of Mammoth, and she by old Shyloe. First dam of Shelby: Mattie Stephens, the mother of the celebrated Governor Roberts; she out of Nellie Gray and by Pierce's Young Shyloe, he out of Old Puss, she by Freedom, he by imported Emancipation. Sire of Nelly Gray: Dan Sacres, he by Old Joe Chalmers, the celebrated four-mile horse owned by Capt. Tom Haley; Dan Sacres' dam, Mary Cook. Pid Hart's dam was Jennie Capps, she by Dash he by Little Jeff and he by Old Shyloe and out of Mary Cook. First dam of Jennie Capps: Bay Puss, owned by Frank Menefee, she by Mounts, he by Old Steel Dust. Jennie Capps' grand dam on sire's side, out of Caddo Maid, by Joe Chalmers. Tom's dam was Lady Gladys, she by Bill Garner, and he by old Steel Dust. First dam of Lady Gladys was Mancoe's big filley, and she was sired by Little Bert, and dam by the Old Mancoe roan race mare.

Rocky Mountain Tom will make the season of 1914 at my place 1 mile west of Newark, Texas, Terms: services to insure mare with foal, will be $15.00. Money due when mare proves to be in foal, is traded or moved. Lien to be retained on mare and foal until services are paid. Not responsible for accidents.

J. G. HELM AND SON.

Broadside for Rocky Mountain Tom, the famous stallion bred by that outstanding short horse man Shelby Stanfield, of Thorp Spring, Texas. Early pedigrees are worked out from such advertisements as these. Courtesy of Mose Newman.

proves to be in foal, is traded or moved. Lien to be retained on mare and foal until services paid.[6]

The heading on the bill was "Rocky Mountain Tom, the Famous Race Horse." It was an accurate description.

Rocky Mountain Tom's dam, Lady Gladys, was also a race mare of note. She was good enough to be campaigned throughout the West. She was running in Oregon when bred to Pid Hart, who was also on the short racing circuit. Lady Gladys was sent home to Stanfields at Thorp Springs to have her foal. Rocky Mountain Tom was trained as a two-year-old by Stanfield and then sold. Some reports have Tom Trammell of Sweetwater using him for a few years.

LITTLE JOE

Little Joe was a common name, and several horses bore it. The most important Little Joe was a brown stallion foaled in 1904, one of the best colts sired by Traveler, who was owned by Dow and Will Shely, of Alfred, Texas. His dam was Jenny, making him a full brother of King (or Possum). Jenny was by Sykes Rondo; her dam was May Mangum, by Anthony, by Old Billy.

George Clegg, of Alice, Texas, bought Little Joe as a yearling, broke, and trained him, and ran him first as a long two-year-old against Carrie Nation in San Antonio. Carrie Nation was a proven mare, and the victory made Little Joe a marked sprinter. Later Ott Adams bought Little Joe and kept him as a stud until he ran short of money and sold him to O.W. Cardwell, of Junction, who had him when he died. Little Joe sired some great horses, such as Ada Jones, Plain Jane, Adalina, Nita Joe, Rainbow, Clear Weather, Joe Moore, Zantanon, Grano de Oro, Pancho Villa, Jim Wells, Pat Neff, and Cotton Eyed Joe.

HARMON BAKER

Harmon Baker was sired by Peter McCue, foaled in 1907, and died in 1925. He was a brown stallion that showed his Thoroughbred blood. He was out of Nona P by the Thoroughbred Duke of Highlands, and was raised by Samuel Watkins, of Petersburg, Illinois. Harmon Baker's second dam was Millie D, a half sister of Peter McCue. Harmon Baker was a full brother of Hattie Jackson, Tot Lee, the gelding Buck Thomas, and the stallion San Antonio. Harmon was registered in *The American Stud Book*.[7]

William Anson, who bought Harmon Baker, said:

216

Harmon Baker, who is thought more of than any horse since the days of Steel Dust, has just the right mixture, and perpetuates his own wonderful conformation and disposition more truly than any stallion I ever knew. I can not remember the exact date, but he ran a race in Oklahoma City, somewhere in 1911, 1912 or 1913. There was a short race on the program every day. They offered one particular purse for a three furlong race which attracted race ponies from Kansas, Illinois, Oklahoma and Texas. They knew Harmon would win if left to himself, and a horse was put in for the purpose, which was accomplished, of knocking him off his feet at the start, for which the jockey was set down for the rest of the meeting. Almost, you might say, left at the post, he came through and won in 34¼ seconds. I never race him myself. I let a reliable man take him out after breeding season is over; just to let him make a reputation, and his name has become a household word among Texas horsemen.[8]

A. D. REED

A. D. Reed was foaled in 1916 and was bred by A. D. Hurley, of Canute, Oklahoma. Hurley had the excellent quarter mare Good Enough, who was by Ned Harper, by Old Bob Peters. He took her to Peter McCue, who was standing in nearby Cheyenne, and the resulting foal was A. D. Reed. Hurley and Reed Armstrong were good friends, and when he gave the colt to Armstrong to run, he said, "Let's call him A. D. after me, and Reed after you," and so the colt got his name.

Midnight beat A. D. Reed once, but he won many more races than he lost. When A. D. Reed's running days were over, he was sold to John Harrel, of Canute, and while Harrel was standing him, A. D. Reed sired Oklahoma Shy, Doctor Blue Eyes, Billy the Tough, Whiskaway, and Jeff Self. Harrel later sold A. D. Reed and Whiskaway to Gallegos and Baca of Gallegos, New Mexico.[9]

ZANTANON

Zantanon was one of Little Joe's best get, and his dam was Jeanette, by Billy, by Big Jim, by Sykes Rondo. Zantanon had three ancestors tracing to Rondo and the fourth to Traveler. South Texas could offer no better blood in 1916. Zantanon was bred by Ott Adams, of Alfred, Texas, and was foaled on March 27, 1917. The next year a man from Mexico came by Adams' place, looking for racehorses. He bought three, one of them young Zantanon. The buyer was Erasmo Flores of Nuevo Laredo. He sold Zantanon to his uncle, Eutiquio Flores, for a profit, and his uncle put the colt in training. For years Zantanon's winnings kept the Flores clan living in a fashion they appreciated. When Zantanon was fourteen years old, Manuel Benevides Volpe went to Nuevo Laredo and bought the old horse.[10]

217

Zantanon's last race was against Conesa, a daughter of Ace of Hearts, in 1922, and he won. Zantanon's best-known get include Jess Hankin's King, Ed Echols, Chico, Cucuracho, San Simeon, Sonny Kimble, and Quatro de Julio. Ed Echols sired seven AAA Register of Merit sprinters in Arizona.

PLAUDIT

Plaudit was a palomino quarter horse who sired some mighty fast horses, and his fillies have been the dams of many more fleet quarter horses. Plaudit was sired by the Thoroughbred King Plaudit, by Plaudit, whose dam was Wild Thistle. Plaudit's dam was a quarter mare named Colorado Queen, who was by Nick, by Old Fred. Plaudit was foaled on July 8, 1930.

Tom Meeks, of Meeker, Colorado, bred Plaudit, and sold him as a colt to Coke Roberds, of Hayden. Roberds later sold him to Warren Shoemaker, of Watrous, New Mexico. Shoemaker sold him to the Philmont Ranch. After changing hands a couple more times, he ended up in the ownership of Leon Harms, of Albuquerque.

Plaudit looked the half-breed he was. He stood a little over fifteen hands and weighed about 1,000 pounds. He was a beautiful palomino color, which he got from his dam. His greatest son was probably Question Mark, who got his name from the shape of the white blaze on his face. Question Mark will never be forgotten by those who saw his race with Shue Fly at Trinidad in 1940. He ran an officially scored quarter mile in $21^4/5$ seconds, and the the three-eighths mile in $33^1/5$ second.

It was a purse race, and Joe Lewis was also in the race. There were bets at every eighth pole, and since Question Mark led all the way, he won all the bets. Near the finish he popped a sesamoid bone in his left front foot. He finished the race on three legs and heart. Another son of Plaudit that made a name for himself was Hank Wiescamp's Scooter W. That horse gave Hank a boost toward the nationwide reputation he now enjoys as a breeder of excellent allround quarter horses.

CHAPTER SIXTEEN

Outstanding Breeders

IT IS interesting that certain areas in the West appear to have had more than their share of great quarter horse breeders. There are several reasons why these concentrations appeared. For one thing there were talented horsemen living in that area who loved the sprinters. Another equally important factor was the appearance of one or two great sires in the region. As Coke Roberds used to say, any intelligent horseman can raise good horses, but only God can create a great sire. The third reason for these centers is a spinoff from the first two: neighboring horsemen and ranchers benefited from their association with the first two so that they in turn became better breeders, perpetuating and crossing the blood of the foundation stallions that appeared in their locality.

Although most of the western regions that were developed between 1880 and 1930 had few or no organized races for the quarter horse, that did not mean that there were no breeders or races. There were some men who had the time and money to indulge in their love of racehorses, even if it meant sending them a long way to get a race. For example, Thomas Trammell had horses running in Europe, and James Owen had horses running all over the United States and in the Caribbean.

These not-to-be-discouraged breeders can be catalogued into two groups: those who raised large numbers of horses and either sold them or sent them off to run under the supervision of a trusted trainer; those who raised a few horses and personally took them into several states to arrange matches or attend meets. C. B. Campbell, of Oklahoma, would be an example of the first kind of breeder, and Mike Smiley, of Kansas, an example of a breeder who campaigned his own horses.

Although state lines meant little or nothing to the breeders, for consistency we will discuss the breeders by states. It should be remembered that the better breeders were well aware of each other's activities and often exchanged and purchased horses from one another. Also, for years, organized race meets were for Thoroughbreds, that is, horses registered in *The American Stud Book*. As mentioned earlier, there was no regular pari-mutuel racing for quarter horses until Melville Haskell started it in Tucson in the late 1930s. There was one answer to this lack of racing meets. Almost all the better breeders kept some Thoroughbreds to provide sprinting blood. Having a Thoroughbred stallion also provided a way to ensure that their best horses would be eligible to run on the organized tracks. It was only a matter of filling out a registration application in the desired manner.

ARIZONA

Among the better-known early-day quarter horse enthusiasts in Arizona were the Kennedys, the Gardners, Dock Pardee, Mark Dubois, Chester Cooper, the Parkers, and the McGonigles. They were responisble for such well-known stallions as Possum, Blue Eyes, John Crowder, Brownie, Lucky, Mark, Guinea Pig, and Red Cloud. Texas contributed generously to the good Arizona horses. For example, probably the greatest single import during this period was Jim Kennedy's Possum (called King in Texas). Dick Herring's nephew Van Hastings moved to Arizona from Texas, and the mares he took with him had some of the best short horse blood in Texas.

Possum produced a great horse when he sired Red Cloud, who was owned most of his life by Mark Dubois. Red Cloud was bred by Jim Kennedy, of Bonita. He was out of Dottie, by No Good, by Barney Owens. Red Cloud was also used by Ernest Shillings and R. A. Pride, of Wilcox, and A. V. Mercer, of Mammouth. Red Cloud was foaled in 1919, and his best son was Mark, who produced good cow horses as well as respectable racehorses. Mark was bred by Burns Blanton, of Wilcox. Some of his best get were Lucky; Buster Brown; Red Clouds, the dam of Jeep; and Ruby, the dam of both Red Racer and Pay Dirt. Guinea Pig, foaled in 1922, was another great son of Possum. Jim Kennedy bred him, and he was later owned by Doc Pardee, of Phoenix, and by W. D. Wear, of Wilcox.

Another import, probably second only to Possum, was Joe Reed II, bred by J. W. House, of Texas. He was brought in by Bert Woods, in October, 1941. When he beat Clabber for the stallion championship at Tucson in 1943, his fame was secure, and he was retired to the stud. There he sired Leo, Bulls Eye, Lady Gray, and many other good, fast horses.

Another pioneer breeder was Chester Cooper, who settled in the Tonto country when it was still the wide-open kind of country Zane Grey wrote about. His best stallion was Brownie. He first attracted notice when he outran Coal Oil Johnny, by Peter McCue. In the early 1930s he bred a race mare he owned called Silver to Doc, by Possum. Silver was by Blue Eyes, by Possum. Her foal was Peggy C. Later he bred Silver to Doc and got Duchess. Between Peggy C and Duchess they produced Sleepy Dick, Tonto Girl, Little Wolf, Prissy, Buster, Twilight, Miss Atomic, and Betsy Ross.

Van Hastings, who lived until 1950, was associated with short horses all his life. Besides Possum and Blue Eyes, he also had a part in developing Lucky Mose, by Old

Mose, by Traveler. For forty years Hastings' Quarter Circle Diamond Ranch bred some of the best quarter horses in Arizona.

Dave Parker and his sons, Dink and Bud, also were closely tied in with the sprinters of Arizona. Dink had Ben Hur, by Rainy Day, by Lone Star for years. He was bred by Eugene Schott, of Riomedina, Texas, but like Possum became a great Arizona sire. The Parkers brought him from Texas. Ben Hur ran a quarter in 22.5 seconds, which was respectable time considering the tracks and training available during his day. The Parkers raised Glass Bars, Ed Heller, and Black Easter, and for a number of years Dink stood the good stallion Ed Echols.

Other Arizona breeders that deserve mention are Everett Bowman, of Hillside, who had Snooper and Sonny Boy. Ernest Browning, of Wilcox, always had good horses. One of his early stallions was Bally, by Possum, whom he sold to his brother-in-law, W. D. Wear. Later he bought the good colt Billy Byrne, foaled in 1933, from the Casements in Colorado. W. D. Wear also bought a Casement colt, called Frosty at the same time. Wear later sold Frosty to Chick Logan, of Tucson, who also had Riley.

Mayburn Gardner bred Fuzzy in 1911. Fuzzy was by Three Finger Jack, by Traveler, and his dam was by Brown Billy, by Pancho. In the early days Jim Kennedy probably had more good quarter horses than anyone else. They included Apache Kid, Little Brother, Bulger, Doc, Duke, Guinea Pig, Monte Cross, Red Cloud, and Strawberry.

COLORADO

Charley Walker

Charley Walker's best-known quarter horse was probably Little Steve, bred by Mike Smiley and foaled in Sylvan Grove, Kansas. Smiley took Little Steve into Colorado to beat a local favorite. Walker saw that race and bought Little Steve, because his main business was racing horses, and he needed another fast one.

Charley kept a fast horse or two tied behind his Studebaker wagon and drifted through several states, making the most of the short race meets and matching a race wherever he could. He used Denver as headquarters, although he kept his horses on a ranch on Kiowa Creek, in Elbert County.

There were some brothers named Peterson, all horsemen, who lived out on the plains east of Denver. They raced together, ate together, and fought together. It was one man against a bunch when you matched a race with the Petersons, and so you had better win the race in convincing fashion. At that time, in the late 1890s, the Peterson's were running a horse called Never Seen. Walker matched Little Steve against Never

Seen for a quarter mile. They just could not believe that a horse that stood only fourteen hands, two inches at the withers and maybe fifteen hands over the hips could outrun Never Seen. They were not happy the first time Little Steve ran away from their horse, and they kept trying to beat him seven more times. Little Steve won the first seven races without trouble, but the eighth was something else. The jockey was pulling Little Steve's head around almost to his knee at the finish, but the race was lost by the part of his neck that was folded back. The time was 22¼ seconds. Walker looked around at all the Petersons and decided not to say anything.

Charley Walker always kept a few mares, and because all their foals could run, they were popular with the polo players. It seemed easier to make a living raising and selling polo ponies than to match races, so Walker trained, rode, and even played some polo with Little Steve. Soon the stallion became well known in polo circles. Much of Charlie's time was spent in Colorado Springs and Glenwood Springs, two polo centers. Little Steve was matched many a race from goal post to goal post. The best-remembered post-to-post race was held at Glenwood Springs. In this race a Thoroughbred, backed by the Palmers of the Broadmoor in Colorado Springs, ran at Little Steve for $1,000, not counting side bets. Charley had partaken of too much local "sulfur water" and was too sick to ride, but Bryant Turner, a socialite rancher, jumped into the breach and rode Little Steve. Despite being left at the start, Little Steve won by a nose.

A few years later, with the increased desire for Thoroughbreds by polo players, Walker bought the Senator. He was by the Thoroughbred Leadville, the same stallion that had sired Coke Roberd's early stallion, Primero. After a few colt crops from the Senator, Charley Walker decided to sell him. In 1911, Dan Casement, then living in Colorado Springs, looked at the Senator but decided against buying him. He bought Concho Colonel instead.

Dan Casement

Dan Casement's father, General John Stephen Casement, for whom Dan's own son was named, helped build the Union Pacific. The general was also one of the first to run steers on the northern plains. In 1878, when Dan was about ten, his father obtained land in the valley of the Big Blue, just north of Manhattan. A little later he also acquired land in western Colorado near the Utah border. The former occupants, the Uncompahgre Utes, moved further west into the Utah Territory. Headquarters for this ranch was established on Fall Creek, about halfway up the Unaweep Canyon. A cabin was built, and the Triangle Bar Ranch, which was to become famous as a home of top Herefords and quarter horses, was begun. Dan took over and operated both of these ranches soon after 1890.

In 1900, Dan settled down and began to devote his time to agricultural pursuits. He soon became a standout figure in the livestock industry. He was always present at the major livestock shows and meetings. His greatest pleasure, outside his horses, was derived from fitting, showing, and selling calves of his own breeding. He bred, raised, and promoted quarter horses for over fifty years. He and his son, Jack, helped organize the American Quarter Horse Association in 1940.

John Stephen Casement

Dan's son, John Stephen ("Jack") Casement, was equally well known in the livestock world. He too was a strong character, although an entirely different individual from his famous father and grandfather. Being the third in line of prominent Americans did not faze him at all. He just went on in his own inimitable way. When he took over the ranch on the Unaweep in western Colorado, he was the third generation to manage it. Jack had a well-rounded early life, which included attending an eastern "name" college and cow-punching for the Matadors in Texas and the Bell Ranch in New Mexico.

Jack took over the Triangle Bar about 1931. It had been only eight years since he and his dad had mounted up and ridden down the winding wagon trail to Whitewater to pick up sixteen mares Dan had purchased from Ed Springer. These mares were sired by New Mexico Little Joe. They gave the quarter horse manada at the Triangle Bar a fresh infusion of Peter McCue blood to comingle with the blood of Little Steve, Balleymooney, and the Senator. The careful Casement breeding plan paid dividends. In just one spring the foals included Red Dog, Frosty, Deuce, Billy Byrne, and Buckshot, who were to start new families in Arizona, Wyoming, Kansas, and Colorado. At the same time the ranch was producing top Herefords for the feeders' market.

During the late 1930s, Jack became interested in promoting a Steel Dust or quarter horse registry. He worked with a small group that included a Texas A&M professor interested in the same project. Jack Casement's articles in the late 1930s helped arouse the interest necessary to form a breed organization.

In 1943, Jack sold the Triangle Bar and moved temporarily to a half section of irrigated pasture on the Elk River, in Routt County. A major factor in the move was that Marshall Peavy, another quarter horse breeder and a close personal friend, lived nearby at Clark. A little later both men moved lock, stock, and barrel to the plains of northeastern Colorado. Jack bought land near Padroni, and Peavy near Westplains.

Jack raised many famous horses that could do it all. Although he won any number of conformation classes, performance to him was paramount. He never wanted to buy a top horse; his satisfaction lay in raising one. He bred, raised, and trained two consecutive champion quarter mares, She Kitty in 1962 and Chloe in 1963. She Kitty was coholder of the world's record for 400 yards. Other well-known horses he raised were Cherokee Maiden, Little Meow, and Alfaretta. For three years in a row he won the Rocky Mountain All-Around Championship, in 1948, 1949, and 1950. At the first quarter horse show held in Tucson, Marshall Peavy had the Grand Champion, and Jack had the Reserve Champion. In Denver in 1949, Peavy had the Champion Stallion, Gold Heels, while Jack had the Reserve Champion mare, Cherokee Maiden.

Si Milton Dawson

Si Milton Dawson and Coke T. Roberds (below) were friends of the Casements. They ranched near Hayden, Colorado. Like Ott Adams and George Clegg of Texas, even their friends couldn't agree which was the finer horseman of the two. Like most friends and rivals in the horse business, Si and Coke always did a lot of good-natured joshing and swapping. When they were together, you could bet the topic was horses, and sooner or later they would match a race, sometimes against one another, but more often the two against some other racehorse man.

Si was born in New Mexico Territory on March 31, 1870, on his father's ranch about eighteen miles north of Cimarron, near present Dawson. He was a direct descendant of Thomas Dawson, who fought with the first Virginia Infantry in the Revolutionary War. Si went to the Yukon in 1898. He and his brother decided to drive some stock up and sell them in the gold fields. When they got to Seattle, they chartered a boat to Skagway, and from there successfully drove their animals over White Horse Pass to the Yukon River. There they built flatboats and rode the rapids to Dawson and sold their animals.

According to Delphine Dawson Wilson, Si's daughter, Si bought Peter McCue for himself and had him shipped to Hayden. Later, when he decided to go to Brazil to manage a large ranch, he left his mares and Peter with his friend Coke. She said that he may have given Peter McCue to Roberds at that time, in 1916. Dawson died while he was in Brazil, and when his wife returned, she sold all of his mares. Peter McCue stayed with Roberds.

Si bought Peter McCue from Milo Burlingame in 1911 and did apparently give him to Coke in 1916, although the stories of several people vary in detail. All agree that Peter McCue died in 1923 at the age of twenty-eight. The Dawson horses were better known than Roberds' horses during the early 1900s. His best stallions were Wild Cat, by Jim Ned, by Pancho, by Old Billy; Silertail, also by Jim Ned; Peter McCue; and Booger Red by Coke's Old Fred. Si and Coke often bred to each other's stallions.

Coke Roberds, of Hayden, Colorado. He and his partner, Si Dawson, put Routt County on the map as far as fast horses were concerned. They did it with the help of Peter McCue and Old Fred. Author's collection.

Coke Roberds

Coke Roberds began his horse-breeding operations in 1898, a few years after Dawson. He started in Oklahoma Territory, and when it became a state in 1908, he decided to move to Colorado. While in Oklahoma he bought the nucleus of his mare band: eight Steel Dust mares, seven sorrels, and a bay. On his trip to Hayden he lost his principal sire, Primero, who was by Leadville. He soon replaced Primero with Old Fred. Later he raised and bred Sheik, who was by Peter McCue and out of a Primero mare. After several years he sold Sheik to Marshall Peavy. From Peavy, Sheik went to the Matador Ranch in Texas and finally ended up back with Coke in 1941.

225

When he moved from Oklahoma to Hayden, Colorado, Coke's outfit was primarily a summer steer setup and horse-pasture operation. In that mountainous country every rancher needed good horses to keep track of the livestock in the summer and to feed with in the winter. At first his steers made him the most money, but soon his horses were in great demand, and he sold over $100,000 worth between 1920 and 1952, the year that he sold out and moved to Denver. He had grown old, and the long winters and hard work proved to be too much for him.

It was men like Dawson, Roberds, and Marshall Peavy who put Routt County on the horse map. The speed and popularity of their horses soon created enough enthusiasm that the local racehorse buffs scraped a short track out of the large mountain near Steamboat Springs. County meets were held in Craig, Hayden, and Steamboat, and horses sired by Old Fred, Peter McCue, Wildcat, and other stallions belonging to these two men were always favorites. Squaw, raised by Coke, was so good they could not get a race for her in northern Colorado. She may have had too much white on her face, but she could fly.

Other Breeders

Many other breeders besides these more famous ones were found in Colorado. Leonard Horn, of Wolcott, raised some good quarter horses. He had Red, by Billy Sunday, by Roman Gold, and Young Peekaboo, by Bob H and out of Snip, by Si Ding. R. J. Hurruish, of Littleton, had a fine stallion he raised called Senator Jr. He was sired by the Senator and was out of an Oregon race mare. R. P. Lamont was proud of Surprise, a sorrel stallion by the Thoroughbred Tad H and out of a Concho Colonel mare. Henry Leonard raised a whole string of fast horses, such as Leinster, by the Thoroughbred Helmet and out of Rainbow by the Senator. Other stallions included Neel Gray, by the Thoroughbred Blue Coat and out of a Steel Dust race mare from New Mexico; Rainmaker, a full brother of Leinster; and St. Damian, sired by the Thoroughbred Dark Friar and out of Rainbow.

Marshall Peavy, of Steamboat Springs, raised Nick S, by Sheik and out of Sylvia by Bob H; Saladin, by Ding Bob and out of Fleet, by Bob H, by Old Fred; and Time, a Saladin colt out of a Thoroughbred mare. A. E. Peterson, of Elbert, raised Gold Coin by the Senator and Mont Megellon by Gold Coin. Bryant Turner, of Colorado Springs, raised a whole string of horses sired by Booger Red, such as Red Boy, Red Devil, and Red Lion. Kirk Williams, of Mancos, had Billy White by Billy Caviness, Columbus by Silver Dick, Dutch by Billy Hubbard, and Silver Dick by Billy Caviness, who was a grandson of Old Billy.

ILLINOIS

Robert Torian Wade

Robert Torian Wade's parents came into Hancock County, Illinois, in 1831. They had a large family, and there were many branches of the Wade family in the Hancock area.[1] Bob Wade's father, David, and his mother, Nancy Trammell Wade, were popular with all their neighbors. The David Wades had fourteen children, of whom Bob Wade was number eight. He was born on October 10, 1838, in Schuyler County, and died in Plymouth on November 29, 1904. He married Mary Fowler, who was born in Schuyler County in 1837. They were married in Hancock County in 1859. Their children were Sarah, Celestia, George, Mary, David, Ethel, and Ester.

Some of Robert Wade's best-known horses were Bob Wade, Sirock, Silver Dick, and Roan Dick. Roan Dick was his best stallion and the sire of the famous sprinter Bob Wade, raised in Plymouth and bred by Robert Wade. The racetrack used by the Wades was about halfway between Augusta and Plymouth. There is a golf course there now. The track was built along the crest of a flat-topped hill. There was a rather steep bank on each side, and trees and brush grew in the ravines. When races were run there, which was almost every Sunday during fair weather, the crowd lined the track and spilled down the sides of the hill.

The Lawton family, who owned the land that bordered the track, were also interested in sprinters. A grandson told me that his mother would not allow him to attend the races while he was a child, and his father backed her up on the prohibition.[2] One Sunday he said that he was going swimming but instead sneaked over to see Bob Wade run. The first person he saw when he got to the track was his father.

The horse Bob Wade was gelded and so does not have a special section in this book. Bob Wade's dam was a mare owned by Bill Smith, of Plymouth, according to Jim Barger, Robert Wade's grandnephew. He said she was Nettie Overton. Smith owned the Plymouth livery stable. Bob Wade was broken by Dick Huddleston, an Indian jockey employed by Robert Wade, who finally sold Bob Wade to Jim Sutton, who took him to various states to run, including Butte, Montana, where he set the world's record. Later he was owned by Forest Grover.

Bob Wade was normally started from a ramp. Barger said that he saw the ramp south of Plymouth many times and that it was downhill for about thirty feet. There were two paths worn in the ramp, about fourteen inches into the turf, where the horses would run.

Robert Wade eventually sold Roan Dick, one of the best sires he ever raised, who was responsible for a large number of fast horses. Roan Dick was foaled in 1877 and

227

died in 1904. Robert Wade started breeding in the late 1860s and continued until his death in 1904.

Grant A. Rea

Grant Rea's parents, John and Clestina Huckens Rea, came to Rock Creek township in Hancock County, Illinois, in the late 1850s. John was born in Chester County, Pennsylvania, and Clestina on the border between Vermont and New Hampshire. Grant A. Rea was born in Rockcreek Township on November 22, 1863, and attended the Lincoln District School. In 1889 he married Minnie Bell, a daughter of early settlers in the county. After their marriage they moved onto eighty acres that Grant owned in Section 20.

Grant made all the improvements on his farm and added to his holdings as he became prosperous. He and his wife had a family of one girl, Clestina, and three boys, Emil, Dee, and Frank. He soon specialized in running horses and raised them on an extensive scale. He bought the noted sprinter Roan Dick in 1902 and raised Young Roan Dick, He worked closely with Bob Wade, of Plymouth, and James Owen, of Berlin, and also got some mares from the Watkins family, of Oakford. Most of his horse operations were carried out near Carthage and Adrian, Illinois. Many of the Roan Dick horses on the short tracks of the West were bred and raised on his farm and sold as yearlings or two-year-olds to racehorse men throughout the West.

The Watkins Family of Oakford

Much has been written about the Petersburg branch of the Watkins family of Illinois, because Samuel was responsible for Peter McCue.[3] Very little has been said about the equally active group that lived a few miles northwest, in and around the town of Oakford. These family members raised similarly bred horses, some of which have been improperly credited to Samuel Watkins, if William E. Boeker's research is correct.[4] According to Boeker, Peter McCue was first leased to Charlie Watkins, who was the son of Sam's brother Bill. It was Charlie who first trained and raced Peter McCue. Later Charlie's brother George leased Peter McCue and stood him. During his stay in Oakford he was kept by Harmon Baker, and there he sired Carrie Nation, Buck Thomas, Harmon Baker, Cricket Ray, and Oakford Queen.

The Watkins were pioneer settlers in Menard County. The first Watkinses were the brothers Thomas and Joseph, who came to Clary Grove, bringing short horses with them from their home in Kentucky. All their descendants were horsemen, but those mentioned above are Tom's boys, Sam and Bill, and Bill's boys, Charlie and George.

Bill Watkins lived southeast of Oakford. Some of his best-known racing stock

Contemporary drawing of the Watkins farm. Courtesy of Gene Boeker.

were Rhome Sam and Barnsdale. Beverly Watkins lived southwest of town and challenged the world to race against his Steel Dust horse through an ad in the local paper. Beverly's son Crit Watkins also raised short horses and sold almost as many to California as his Uncle Sam sold to Texas.

Sam's brother Bill also raised fast horses, and his son-in-law Kay Ray got started when William gave him some mares. His best sprinter was a mare, sired by Peter McCue, named Cricket Ray. She was one of the last famous short horses to come out of Oakford. In 1907 she was matched against a Blakely horse named Peter McCue II, who had little if any Peter McCue blood. The race was run at Long Branch, and the

229

Sam Watkins' home in Petersburg, Illinois, called Little Grove Stock Farm. There he bred such outstanding horses as Peter McCue, Barney Owens, Dan Tucker, and Jack Traveler. Photograph courtesy of George Dorrill.

crowd was so large that several officers were needed to maintain order. Her last race in Menard County was at the fair grounds, in 1908, when six thousand spectators came to see her run. Violence and gambling caused the village of Kilbourne to rule against any more races, and the city council of Oakford voted the town dry, ending racing in that community.

Other Breeders

There were other short horse breeders in Illinois. One, briefly mentioned above, was Edwin Blakely, of Kilbourne, who also ran two Peter McCue colts, one called Menzo Shurtz and the other Kilbourne. Joe Brown, in Petersburg, raced his fastest horse, Johnnie Brown, who was by the Thoroughbred Star McGee and out of Bessie Keough, by Peter McCue. About twenty-five miles northwest of Oakford, at Lewiston, Harry Stuart had the fine horse Barney McCoy, who was by the Thoroughbred Floyd K and out of Bridget McCue, by Peter McCue. Earlier, breeders in this period were Grant Rea and James Owen, both discussed earlier. Illinois was full of sprinters during the late 1800s and early 1900s.

KANSAS

H. A. Trowbridge

There were six or seven Trowbridges living in Wellington, Kansas, between 1877 and 1890, but the name is not remembered today. The family either died out or moved away. They were there, because the deeds recorded in the courthouse show them buying and selling property almost every year during that period. Three transactions, in 1880, 1885, and 1889, were recorded by H. A. Trowbridge, one of the largest and most successful quarter horse breeders of the period. Modern historians have seen the name H. A. Trowbridge as the owner of outstanding stallions like Little Danger, No Remarks, and Okema, and of such mares as Vergie, by Cold Deck; Belle H, whose dam was by Jack Traveler; Deck, another Cold Deck filly; and Miss Murphy, whose dam was by Harry Bluff.[5] They show that Trowbridge was in touch with the breeding operations of Floyd Nathan, of Carthage, Missouri, and the Watkins family, of Petersburg, Illinois. Trowbridge also bought a horse or two from Theodore Winters, of California, of Joe Hooker breeding. What these historians did not know was that H. A. Trowbridge was a woman.

Unfortunately we do not know H. A.'s first name or her maiden name. In all her official correspondence and paperwork she used only the initials. The first courthouse record encountered was dated March 31, 1880. She bought some lots in Wellington. On March 8, 1878, her husband, Samuel, sold his eighty-acre farm, probably to move into town and join his wife. This may very well have happened the year they were married. Seven years later she bought more lots and on July 3, 1889, purchased two more. The last two led to the discovery of her sex: on November 4, 1889, she sold the lots, and the papers required the signature of her spouse. The indenture carries these words: "H. A. Trowbridge and Saml. Trowbridge, her husband."[6]

In those days raising and maintaining horses within the city limits was no more unusual than having a garage with one or more cars in it today. Since she owned a block of lots, she had several acres of land, and there is little reason to believe she carried on her operations anywhere else, since there are no records of other land holdings. It would seem that she ran the show herself, for all the deeds were in her name, except for the sale which mentions her husband almost incidentally. Even at the bottom of the indenture, the notary public lists her first and Samuel second, calling them wife and husband, in that order.

One can surmise several things about H. A. Trowbridge. She had to have wealth because of the caliber of the horses she bought, and she spent her money in her own way. Today, several women run racing and beeeding stables, but H. A. Trowbridge lived in a much stricter society in the late nineteenth century. Convention, morals, and even the laws of that time did not recognize women's rights in this business—or most others, for that matter. She must have had the backing of Samuel, for he stayed with her, and she certainly was successful.

Other Breeders

John Day, of Asawata, was another important Kansas breeder. He bred many short horses, but is best remembered for Little Pete, who was foaled in 1878 and sired by Pony Pete, by Barney Owens, owned by his friend Mike Smiley. He was the best sire Day bred and raised. Uriah Eggleston, of Garden City, was probably the number-three Kansas breeder after Smiley and Trowbridge. He registered most of his horses with the Jockey Club in the Appendix. His band of mares, headed by Ella Mitchell and Molly McCreary, were as good as any band west of the Mississippi. Molly McCreary was a chestnut mare, foaled in 1875, bred by Albert Snapp in Illinois. She was by Zero, by Boston, and out of Lucy, by Humboldt. S. E. Lawrence, of Maple City, had Pawhuska. Pawhuska was by Okema and out of Lady Lawrence.

Joe Lewis, of Honeywell, had three outstanding colts by his stallion Bobby Cromwell, by Old Cold Deck: Doe Belly, Joe Lewis, and Rolling Deck. Their dam, Grasshopper, was a full sister of June Bug and was apparently also the dam of Sykes Rondo. More research needs to be done on Joe Lewis, whose breeding and racing career covers the period between 1870 and 1890. Lewis was a good friend of both Mike Smiley and Sam Watkins. He used their bloodlines, and they his.

NEW MEXICO

Frank Springer

Frank Springer arrived in Cimarron on February 22, 1873, after a long trip from Burlington, Iowa. Perhaps he had not come west to buy a ranch, but he proceeded to do so. On the evening that he arrived, he purchased a 1,600-acre spread east of Cimarron that was to become the nucleus and headquarters of the CS cattle and horse operations, which are still active today.

Frank was followed west by his brother Charles in 1878, and before many years the cattle operations assumed Charles's name. From that time on the Charles Springer Cattle Company and the CS brand (carried on the right side of many good cows and on the right shoulder of many good horses) were famous throughout the West.

232

Frank's law practice helped start the cattle venture. He soon was fighting to save the Maxwell Land Grant Company (he was their lawyer) from the many litigations that arose. To preserve the grant, he carried the fight to the United States Supreme Court. At the same time he was also the lawyer for the Santa Fe Railroad. By 1890 he was president of the Maxwell Land Grant Company. Before this he and his brothers introduced the first herd of purebred Herefords into New Mexico.

In 1885 the Maxwell Land Grant Company decided to dispose of some of its imported horses. Frank Springer bought ten fillies and two stud colts. The two colts stayed in service on the CS for many years. They did much to provide the base for the superior horses produced by the ranch after the 1890s. One was *Ute Chief, who came to America inside his dam. He was sired by Maxmillian and out of Angelic. When foaled in New Mexico he had been dubbed *Ute Chief. The second colt was Uhlan II. He had been bred and dropped in New Mexico. He was by the French stallion *Uhlan and out of the English mare *Anapolis.

Frank Springer had three sons: Ed, Hank, and Wallace. Charles had no children. Of all Frank's children Hank was probably the best horseman and cattleman. From 1905, for many years, he was general manager of the CS Cattle Company. He was such an extraordinary horseman that Buffalo Bill Cody tried to get him to leave the ranch and join his wild West show. However, Hank loved ranch life too much to leave it.

In 1912, Hank heard from Frank Hatton, the foreman at Vermejo Park, that he had seen a stallion at the Trinidad, Colorado, fair that the CS should buy. The horse proved to be a beautiful sorrel stallion sired by Billy Anson's Harmon Baker, who was by Peter McCue. Arrangements were made to buy him for $1,000, and the purchase took place at 7,800 feet, on top of Raton Pass, a few miles north of Raton, New Mexico. The stallion's name was Little Joe. John Brewer, one of the top hands of the CS, threw a saddle on him after the exchange and rode him to his new home on the CS at Cimarron. There he was crossed on the ranch mares of *Uhlan, Si Dawson, and Deck breeding and did much to make the CS horses famous throughout the cattle country. One of his very best colts was Springer's Little Joe.

In the 1920s, Ed Springer and his friend Dan Casement, of Colorado and Kansas, formed a loose partnership to exchange quarter horse blood. The Springer mares that the Casemonts got from the CS furnished a foundation on which they bred many of their best animals. T. E. and Albert Mitchell also obtained blood from the CS Ranch.

Thomas Edward Mitchell

Thomas Edward Mitchell was born in Fairplay, Colorado, on September 8, 1863. His parents were pioneer settlers in Colorado, who traveled by oxcart from Independence,

Missouri, to Santa Fe, New Mexico, and then on to Fairplay. As T. E. Mitchell grew up, he showed his interest in a cowman's life by working on several cattle ranches in Colorado and New Mexico.

The cattlemen in southern Colorado showed their faith in the young man by employing him as their "trail cutter." It was a job that called for a cool head and a heap of nerve. His success in this job gave him a reputation for integrity and fairness that followed him throughout his life. It was also the indirect means of his successful move into New Mexico. He was invited to work for the Dubuque Cattle Company, and he soon became its manager. The ranch was in the northeastern corner of New Mexico, lying east of the Maxwell Land Grant and north of the Pablo Montoya Grant. It covered most of Union and Colfax counties. The company branded the Bar T Cross and they carried around 100,000 head of cattle the year around. Mitchell was its most successful manager.

In 1895, Mitchell bought the deeded land owned by the Dubuque Company. The advent of barbed wire and windmills made homesteading possible and brought settlers into the areas where the company ranged its cattle. The writing was on the wall for all the old outfits that had prospered during the open-range days. The land Mitchell bought lay in the Tequesquite Valley. *Tequesquite* is the Indian word for the salt deposits along the creekbed.

Two years before Mitchell bought the ranch on the Tequesquite, he married Linda E. Knell, the daughter of one of the valley's original settlers. Andrew Knell, her father, ranched near Albert, a small town he founded and named for his son, who was killed in a roping accident while working on a roundup in the early 1890s. T. E. Mitchell's son Albert Knell Mitchell was also named for that young man.

In 1914 T. E. and his son Albert K. bought out Andrew Knell's ranching and cattle interests and established the present Tequesquite Ranch. Thomas Edward Mitchell died, on December 1, 1934, while still actively engaged in the cattle business at the age of seventy-one.

By the time of his father's death, Albert K. Mitchell was almost as well known as his father. His father had been a state senator, a deputy United States marshal, and a member of various commissions and boards. Albert followed in his father's footsteps. Albert was schooled, along with his sisters, by governesses brought to the ranch for that purpose. Later he went to Occidental College, in Los Angeles, and then to Cornell University, where he got a degree in agriculture. In August, 1928, he married Juli Sundt, of Las Vegas, New Mexico. They had three children: Linda Elisabeth, Thomas Edward, and Albert Julian. Linda is now Mrs. Les Davis, wife of the president of the CS Cattle Company.

Down through the years the Mitchells showed their awareness of the importance of good horses. Their remudas carried some of the best sprinting Thoroughbred blood, as well as top quarter horse blood. Their quarter horse blood came from the Springers; from John Zurick, of Rosebud, New Mexico; and from several Texas breeders.

Francisco Gallegos and N. T. Baca

Francisco Gallegos homesteaded his ranch in 1876 and began raising horses for cow work. He named his ranch Rincon Colorado and branded Z and ZZ on the left thighs. After Francisco's death, in 1890, the ranch was managed by Filiberto and Enpacio, his two sons. Francisco also had a daughter named Sara, and one-third interest became hers. The ranchlands surrounded Lite Creek, and the town of Gallegos grew up as part of the ranch. By the time Francisco died, the holdings amounted to 150,000 acres.

Just north of the Gallegos' spread was a ranch, owned by the Baca family. They had a son, generally known as N. T. Baca, who was born on the ranch in 1889. The nearest town to the ranch was Endee. Later the elder Baca bought another ranch sixty miles north of Tucumcari. This was the Black Hills Ranch, which took its name from some black lava buttes along Ute Creek on the ranch.

There were few fences in those days, and the cattle drifted with the weather. Some Baca cows occasionally turned up on the Gallegos ranch. N. T. Baca was the representative attending the Gallegos roundups. At one of these gatherings he met and fell in love with Sara Gallegos. In 1909 they were married, and N. T. Baca moved to the Rincon Colorado Ranch to take care of his wife's interests. He and Filiberto, manager of the Rincon Colorado and Sara's oldest brother, became close friends.

In those days there was no quarter horse registry, and so no quarter horses as such. However, the good quarter horse type was the kind the best ranchers looked for in their stallion purchases. In the early 1900s the Gallegos and Baca families were using four stallions: George, Jack, Frosty, and Chief. George and Jack were of Trammell and Newman breeding and came out of Texas. Gallegos bought them in Portales. Chief was a Thoroughbred, foaled in 1902 and registered as Chief Bush. Filoberto bought him at a racetrack where he had been injured. Jack was a black quarter horse out of Texas. The ranch knew nothing of his breeding. One day a man, obviously in a hurry and probably an outlaw, stopped by the ranch riding Jack. He traded him for a fresh horse and was gone. In 1910 the ranch bought some Peter McCue blood and two years later a Chickasha Bob stallion they called Old Mike.

When World War I came along, the ranch was split three ways. N. T. Baca and Sara moved to Brantine, south of Gallegos. N. T. took with him a stallion named Sunday School, who was by Billy Sunday, by Peter McCue, and Old Mike, the Chickasha Bob stallion. Filiberto and N. T. Baca remained the best of friends and exchanged stallions freely. In 1930, Gallegos bought Whiskaway, a double-bred Peter McCue. He was by A. D. Reed and out of Good Enough, by Peter McCue. They liked this horse so well that they bought old A. D. Reed himself.

235

In 1932 both of the Gallegos boys died, and N. T. Baca became administrator of the estate. The two families had brought into New Mexico some of the very best quarter horse blood available.

Milo Burlingame

Milo Burlingame's story could appear under Texas or Oklahoma just as well as under New Mexico, but he spent the last half of his life residing in New Mexico.

The first letter I had from Milo was dated October 25, 1939. It read as follows:

> Words can't express how surprised I was to pick up your *Cattleman* and find my picture and old Peter McCue which I think was the grandest sire of all horses, and the fastest horse that ever faced a flag and I had the pleasure of riding him in St. Louis and Chicago in 1893 and 1894 up to the time he broke his leg. I always said that if I was ever able to own a good horse some day I would own Peter McCue. I can't imagine how you came into possession of that picture. I thought I had the only one left.[7]

Milo was born on January 21, 1874, in Illinois. When he was young, his family moved to Texas and helped found the town of Clarendon; they later moved to Mobeetie. In that Texas town there lived a short horse man by the name of W. J. Miller. From him Milo learned the ways of the quarter running horse. Because of his small size Milo became a jockey and soon was an owner as well. His best race mare was Nellie Miller, whom he got from W. J. Miller (incidentally, Milo's father clerked for many years in the old Rath and Hamburg Store in Mobeetie).

In 1911, Milo bought Peter McCue from John Wilkins. Peter was then sixteen years old. Milo had had a good year campaigning Nellie Miller and Corn Stalk, and with his winnings he bought the Palace Royal Saloon in Cheyenne, Oklahoma. Tom Caudill stood Peter McCue for him for twenty-five dollars. Milo bought a few Thoroughbred mares and hoped to raise some racehorses and, with his son as jockey, make the circuit again. He invested quite a bit of his stake in bringing a railroad to Cheyenne but never got any return for his money. When he was almost broke, he moved to New Mexico, taking Peter McCue with him. He settled first in Magdalena, and it was there that he sold Peter McCue to Si Dawson, In 1920, Milo moved to Albuquerque, where he became a cattle buyer. He lived there until his death, not too many years after the formation of the AQHA.

Other Breeders

There are more breeders that should be mentioned. Among these certainly is Warren Shoemaker, of Watrous. In 1940, he was one of the four or five best breeders of quarter horses in the United States. He owned Plaudit and Nick and the dam of Bright Eyes. He raised Nick Shoemaker, who was Hank Wiescamp's foundation stallion. He sold Plaudit to Waite Phillips, the Oklahoma oilman who owned the Philmont Ranch west of Cimarron. From the CS Ranch, Waite bought ten good mares of Little Joe Springer breeding. Later he turned the ranch over to the Boy Scouts of America.

M. E. Andres, of Portales, New Mexico, had Jack of Diamonds and Red Wing, both of them by Jack McCue. J. W. and Charles Francis, of Floyd, New Mexico, also had good horses: Texas Jack by Jack McCue and Shorty by Barlow, by Lock's Rondo. The third Francis, W. J., of Elida, owned Jack McCue. Teddy, by Billy Dick, was owned by J. W. Ashcroft, of Ramah, and bred by Albert Harrington, of Correo. A. T. Hayes, of Greer, bred Miacho, by Yellow Wolf, by Old Joe Bailey. Jim and Earl Kelly, of Las Vegas, raised some good ones, including Kelly, by Star, by Hermus, by Tom Campbell. They also raised Star Shoot out of Little Deer by Idle Boy. Roy Kimbell, of Clayton, bred Reincocas, by Mose, by Traveler. Oliver Lee of Almagorda bred Lee Bay, Lee Sorrel, and Trouble, all descendants of Dan Tucker. Young Chickasha Bob was bred by J. C. ("Cliff") Neafus, of Newkirk, and was sired by Chickasha Bob, by Pid Hart.

Some of their best short horses were raised by A. P. Saunders and his son. They included Wandering Jew, by the Thoroughbred Set Back and out of Fay Larkin, by Barney Lucas, by Traveler; Robert A, by Set Back and out of Noo, by Barney Lucas, by Traveler; Nooblis, by the imported Thoroughbred *Batchlor's Bliss, by the same Noo; and Mud Lark, by Set Back and out of Fay Larkin, by Barney Lucas. Last but not least was J. W. Zurick, of Stead. One of his best-known horses was Pancho, by the Thoroughbred Peace Buddy and out of Miss Sleepy, by Star Shoot, a grandson of Tom Campbell.

OKLAHOMA

C. B. Campbell

C. B. Campbell was a wealthy rancher who lived a few miles southwest of Oklahoma City in Grady County. He was born just before 1805, and by 1880 he was one of the top breeders of sprinters in America. Only two or three other breeders were his equal. He also ran cattle on thousands of acres of Indian land, and some claimed that he did not know how many horses and cattle he owned. If his accounting was lax, he was a good judge of horseflesh and human nature, for he owned the best horses and hired the best trainers in the business.

One of his best moves was to hire three young fellows who showed up for work at the ranch one day. They were Reed, Dan, and John Armstrong. Their success with sprinting quarter horses is taken up elsewhere in this book. After the Armstrongs moved on, Campbell hired James Gray and his son to look after his racing stock. Under their management the Campbell stud soon had a national reputation.

C. B. Campbell's best-remembered horses are Bonnie Joe, Pid Hart, Tom Peters, Tom Campbell, Denver, Jeff, Minco Jimmy, and Uncle Jimmy Gray. Uncle Jimmy Gray was named for James Gray, who was in charge of the racehorses. Everyone called him Uncle Jimmy. Campbell and Gray exchanged blood with the other top breeders, such as Mike Smiley in Kansas and Shelby Stanfield in Texas. It was not at all unusual to find the best breeders cooperating. For example, take Barney Owens. Barney was bred and first used by John Hedgepeff, of Joplin, Missouri. Then he was raced and used at stud by Bill Owen, of Berlin, Illinois. After this Sam Watkins, of Petersburg, Illinois, used him as a stud. Later he was sold to the Trammells in Sweetwater, Texas. He produced some great offspring for all of his owners.

Little information on Campbell as an individual is available. Some of what follows was obtained from Bruce Horn, who once worked for Campbell, and from Alma Thompson, a relative of Campbell's wife. Both live in Minco. I interviewed them there in 1977.

Campbell's headquarters were on his ranch a few miles north of Minco, where he lived with his wife. Mrs. Campbell's maiden name was Mandy Williams. They were married in the 1870s. Their family consisted of two boys, Milton and Bud, and five girls, Belle, Effie, Stella, Ella, and Bernadine. The old home in Minco is still standing. Most of the deeded land of the old ranch north of town is now owned and operated by the Mason family. Campbell's horse barn is still standing on the ranch.

When the depression came after World War I, Campbell was unable to keep the ranch, and everything was auctioned off: horses, cattle, land, and equipment. Alma Thompson said that Campbell and his wife moved south to Chickasha and that he died a few years later. I made a search of the courthouse in Chickasha for a deed or probate, but could find none. A search of cemetery records was also fruitless; however, cemetery records are almost nonexistent before 1920. Regardless of when or where he died, Campbell was one of the greatest breeders of quarter horses since the Civil War.

Coke Blake

Coke Blake moved to Oklahoma from Arkansas, where he was born in 1862. With him he brought a knowledge of short horses and their bloodlines that helped him throughout his long career as a quarter horse breeder. In 1888 he married a Cherokee girl, and they settled not far from Tahlequah in the Cherokee Nation. His quarter horse breeding program was dictated by his preference for certain bloodlines, the Bertrands, Brimmers, White Lightnings, and Cold Decks. He liked Cold Deck on the top line of

SHILO

The Blake Horse

Shilo was sired by Red Man, he by Idle Jack, he by Tu-Bal-Cain, he by Old Cold Deck (the Joe Berry horse), he by Old Cold Deck (the old race horse), he by Old Steel Dust.

1st. The Dam of Red Man was Bell Starr sired by Big Danger, he by Young Cold Deck, he by Old Cold Deck (the Joe Berry horse), he by Old Cold Deck (the old race horse) and he by Old Steel Dust.

2nd. The Dam of Idle Jack was Lady Blake sired by Young Cold Deck, he by Old Cold Deck (the Joe Berry horse), he by Old Cold Deck (the old race horse), he by Old Steel Dust.

3rd. The Dam of Lady Blake was Gray Meg sired by Possum, he by young White Lighting, he by Old White Lighting.

4th. The Dam of Big Danger was Lucy Maxwell.

5th. The Dam of Young Cold Deck was a Bertran mare sixteen hands high, a bay with black mane and tail.

6th. The Dam of Tu-Bal-Cain was Lucy Maxwell.

7th. Dam of the Joe Berry horse was sired by Ben Alsup's Red Buck, he by Grinder, he by the Todd horse, he by Old Snort (the Burris horse), he by Big Mulatto, a full brother to Old Brimmer.

8th. The Dam of Red Buck was sired by Big Joe, he by Chrisman's Sway Back, he by Old Brimmer.

9th. The Grand Dam of Red Buck was sired by Shelt Alsup's Broke Leg, he by Steel Dust, he by the Coontz horse, he by Old Snort.

10th. The Dam of Broke Leg by Steel Dust was Emmily Walker, sired by Old Mose Brimmer, he by Burris' Old Brimmer.

11th. The Dam of the Coontz horse was sired by Winahen's Old Jeff.

12th. The Dam of Grinder was out of a mare by the noted race horse driver of Marion County, Arkansas.

"I will say here that I knew the above named breeding horses owned or run by myself or family and they were of the above named breeding"—Lock Alsup.

The Blake horse was founded in Mayes County, Oklahoma, by S. C. Blake in the year of 1900. These horses soon became known all over the world, on account of their superiority to all other horses. As an all-purpose horse, they do everything other horses do, and do it better and on less feed. They are the strongest horses for their weight and are most intelligent. They can be taught almost as if they had reasoning facilities.

They are the fastest horses in the world and unexcelled for roping and polo. They can start and stop quicker than any other horse. They are also the best plow horses in the world and the plow is the beginning and the end of civilization.

Shilo is a Chestnut Sorrel, 15 hands high and weighs 1200 pounds when in good flesh. He is a good saddle, driving or work horse and has an eye like an eagle and a step like a deer.

Shilo will make the season of 1938 on the Blake Horse Ranch, 10 miles southwest of Pryor, Oklahoma.

TERMS: $10.00 to insure colt to stand and suck. If mare is traded or about to be removed from neighborhood, season becomes due, colt or no colt.

W. H. Stamps

President and General Manager of Blake Horse Ranch.

Broadside issued by Coke Blake in 1904 (?), advertising Shilo, one of his stallions. It is interesting for the pedigree information it contains. Courtesy of Coke Blake.

his pedigrees and was happy to be able to buy Young Cold Deck from N. B. Maxwell in 1896. Later he acquired Berry's Cold Deck, who sired Young Cold Deck. Both Young Cold Deck and Berry's Cold Deck were bred by Joe Berry, of Mount Vernon, Missouri. The Old Cold Deck stallion, by Steel Dust, to which Coke's stallion traced, was foaled in 1862 (the same year Coke was born) in Carthage, Missouri. Blake got his White Lightning blood from "Small" Baker, of Peggs, Oklahoma.

Coke Blake learned to respect the Cold Deck blood from his early friendship with Foss Barker, who raced and stood Cold Deck for many years. One day, after he had not seen Foss for some time, Coke ran into him under circumstances that today might seem questionable, but were par for the course in those days. He and his Cherokee wife, and a relative of hers, S. H. Mayes, a chief of the Cherokee Nation, were eating supper at his house, not far from Pryor. There was a knock on the door, and another Indian asked to talk to Coke. He claimed he had an old work horse that could run a little and he wanted a short race of not over 350 yards. Coke, not wanting to appear too eager, told him he would sleep on it and give his answer in the morning. When the Cherokee left, he told his wife and her relative that he was going to run the race, and if he lost he would just put in another patch of cotton. He found the Indian where he said he would be, camped in a small grove of trees north of the ranch. Who should be there with him but Foss Barker, who was using the Indian as a front man. Coke said, "I knew when I saw Foss that the animal with the trace marks was a race horse." He didn't match the race as he planned, but he and Foss did trade a couple of horses.

M. S. ("Small") Baker

M. S. ("Small") Baker was a racehorse man from who laid the chunk. He moved about Texas, Colorado, Kansas, Missouri, and Arkansas every spring and summer, trailing a few fast horses behind his wagon. His wife stayed home and kept the fire going. According to available records, which are mighty scarce, he really had some outstanding match races with "Old Man" Smiley in Kansas and with Charley Walker in Colorado and H. A. Trowbridge of Kansas.

"Small" Baker's home was not far from Muskogee, and he lived into the twentieth century. Perhaps his fastest horse was a mare he called Gray Jennie. H. A. Trowbridge tried to outrun Jennie with a Cold Deck filly she had named Vergie. Vergie was a sleek brown mare foaled in 1886 and registered with the Jockey Club for racing purposes only. Her dam was by Cherokee Bill.

The Trammells

The Trammells were a large family, like the Wades of Illinois and they first moved to the Sweetwater, Texas, area from Navarro County. Tom Trammell liked Sweetwater, but some of his brothers, Frank, Phil, and Ted, decided to go north into the Cheyenne and Arapahoe country in the Indian Territory. Other members of the family, such as Lewis, also went north. The Trammells made contracts with the neighboring Indians so that they could run their cattle and horses on Indian land. Their contracts were made in 1892, before the land was open to white settlers.

Tom Trammell married Jim Newman's sister. Jim and Tom were unofficial partners and bred their horses like pardners. Walter Trammell was Tom's son. Phil Trammell married Bettie Newman, a cousin of Mose Newman. These relationships are mentioned here because much of my information came from either Mose Newman or Walter Trammell. According to Mose, most of the horses that Frank, Phil, and Ted took north carried the blood of Steel Dust and of Shiloh. One of the stallions was Eighty Gray, who was by Bill Fleming and out of Gray Alice, by Steel Dust. Every few years the Oklahoma Trammells would drive a group of their best mares south to Sweetwater to be serviced by stallions owned by Tom and Jim. After a year or two they and their offspring would be driven back overland to their home in Oklahoma. A few years later Peter McCue was available to them when Burlingame stood him in Cheyenne. It is little wonder they raised such excellent horses.

The Armstrongs

There were five Armstrong brothers in the Cheyenne country: Frank, Bob, Reed, Dan, and John. All of them specialized in sprinters, although we hear most about Dan, Reed, and John. Dan established himself at Doxey; Reed, at Foss; and John, when he was home, at Elk City, the nearest town. John really became a Texan because he spent so much of his time racing there, as well as training horses for the rich ranchers of South Texas. Shortly before 1930, Bob Kleberg, of the King Ranch of Texas, prevailed upon John to train the ranch's short horses. It was a smart move in two ways. Kleberg got a top trainer and two of his best quarter mares, Lady of the Lake and Johnny's Bay.[8] At the time Johnny was training for Alonzo Taylor, of Hebbronville, and he moved to Kingsville from Hebbronville.

Early in the 1890s, Dan, Reed, and John Armstrong had pulled up their stakes in Iowa and moved west to the Oklahoma frontier. The oldest of the three was not twenty years old. The three boys stopped at Minco, Oklahoma. They had heard about C. B. Campbell and his horses, and they needed jobs. They found out that Campbell was a big operator and "had every acre of the Caddo and Chickasha Indian Nation's land under lease."[9] They hesitantly asked for jobs and got them. Johnny only weighed about ninety pounds, and he soon became one of Campbell's favorite jockeys and he rode many of Campbell's horses in their races. Reed became Campbell's trainer.

241

After a few years Reed met Nancy Meek, fell in love with her, and married her. She was the daughter of a frontiersman and buffalo hunter named Jake Meek. After Reed and Nancy were married, the Armstrong boys and Jake Meek became fast friends, as well as relatives. Meek wanted to get some land in the Cheyenne country and settle down, and the boys decided to go with him. Since Meek was a freighter, the move was no problem. Campbell hated to see the boys leave, for he had grown fond of them. However, they went with his good wishes and more: he gave them Bob Petters, Tom Campbell, and Nellie Hart, three fine horses.

Reed and Nancy had four children: Cyrus, Sarah, Nilla, and John. I got most of my information from Nilla, who now lives in Elk City. According to Nilla, Dan married a Bonds girl and had eight children. Frank had four, and John had four. Some of the better-known horses that were raced by the Armstrongs were Fear Me; Hermes, by Tom Campbell; Dr. Blue Eyes, by A. D. Reed; Goldie McCue, by Peter McCue; and Nettie Stinson, by Jeff C.

The Harrels

The Harrel family settled in Canute, Oklahoma, not far from the Armstrongs. John Allen Harrel went to the Cheyenne country from Texas in 1903. He arrived during a winter snow storm with three dollars in his pocket. His wife, Nancy Moore Harrel, was also from Texas. Their children were Budy (pronounced "Boodee"), Cecil, Peter, Pearl, Orville, and William.

Most of the Harrels' racing was done at country fairs. When the crops were in, they would get out the wagon, tie on the racehorses, and make the county fairs that had racing meets (which most did). One of their best-known stallions was A. D. Reed, whom they bought from A. D. Hurley, of Canute, and later sold to the Gallegos family, of New Mexico. They also had Duck Hunter, Jack Dempsey, and Red.

The Meeks Family

The Meeks family, of Foss, also raised short horses. They raised and raced Jeff Self, a well-known sprinter. His dam was a Peter McCue mare named Casino. They also raised Santa Claus, by Red Buck out of Polly, by Tom Campbell.

The Cheyenne area of northwest Oklahoma teemed with quarter horses, and still does. In addition to the breeders mentioned above, it was to become the home of a great present-day breeder, Walter Merrick. There must be something in the red dirt of that area that is good for quarter horses and quarter horse men.

Other Breeders

Other Oklahoma breeders included Mike Beetch, who raised the horse named for him that was purchased and popularized by Tom Burnett, of Texas. Beetch also had Smokey and Gray Eagle. George Doty, of Afton, had Chicken Smart, a good short horse he raised by the Thoroughbred Belamous and out of Goldie, by Big Jim. Joe Adolph ran Chicken Smart. John Dawson, of Talala, always had good horses, such as Muskogee Star, by Oklahoma Star. Early in the 1900s, Clyde McClain, of Leedy, had some of the very best blood available. His stallion, Joy, foaled in 1912, was sired by Jeff, a grandson of Printer, by Cold Deck and out of Lou Trammell, by Peter McCue. His Keeno was by Joy and out of a good unnamed quarter mare. Bill Patton also had the same blood in his Red Lightning stud.

William Francis, of Elk City, had Red Bird; Smith Kellum, of Cheyenne, had Old Bob Peters, by Pony Pete, and bred Young Bob Peters. Johnny Parvis, of Elk City, raised Gray Badger, who was by Peter McCue and out of Mazie Marie. W. J. Miller, of Sweetwater, bred Idle Boy, by Long Tom.

TEXAS

Dan Waggoner

Dan Waggoner was born in Lincoln County, Tennessee, on July 7, 1828. His family moved to Hopkins County, Texas, and there Dan married Nancy Moore. Their son, Tom Waggoner, was born on August 31, 1852.

Dan Waggoner, with the help of one Negro boy, drove 242 head of cattle from Hopkins County to Wise County, where he found plenty of free grass two miles east of Decatur. Within a few years he had a 10,000-acre ranch eighteen miles west of Decatur. In 1864 he located on a large ranch on the Wichita.

The famous Waggoner brand was registered in 1871, in Wise and Clay counties, and a little later in Wilbarger County. By the 1890s, Dan Waggoner and his son were selling about 40,000 head of cattle each year. By this time they grazed cattle on the Kiowa and Comanche lands as well as on their own lands. It has been said that the Waggoners placed 10,000 head of cattle on the Comanche reservation in the early 1880s, at $2.50 per head per year. At the same time they were building up their ranches in Archer, Baylor, Foard, Knox, Wichita and Wilbarger counties in Texas until they owned more than 500,000 acres. In 1900 oil was discovered on their land, and money became secondary.

Dan Waggoner died around 1900. His son W. T. (Tom) died on December 11, 1934. Today the business is run as an estate for the descendants.

Paul Waggoner, one of Tom's sons, showed the most interest in quarter horses. Paul turned the Three D stock farm at Arlington, Texas, the old Thoroughbred race track, into a quarter horse breeding operation. He hired as foreman Pine Johnson, one of the top quarter horse trainers of all time, and they were in business. He bought Pretty Boy, by Dodger, by Harmon Baker, and with him raised Pretty Buck. He also purchased a King colt called Poco Bueno, who by himself could have made almost any man a breeder of note. He selected ranch mares rich in Yellow Jacket blood to breed to his stallions, and the continuing quality of the Three D horses was assured.

Crawford Sykes and Joe Mangum

Crawford Sykes, with his partner and relative, Joe Mangum, were horsemen in the best tradition of Billy Fleming and W. W. Lock. Indeed, they owed their best stock of horses to those earlier breeders. They moved ahead and created new bloodlines from the older ones. The following words of Crawford Sykes are contained in a letter sent to H. T. Fletcher in 1922:

> I raised the horse [Crawford Sykes] you speak of, and sold him to Billy Anson as a two-year-old for $150.00. His sire was Arch Oldham. I gave $1000.00 for Arch. His sire was Gallantry. Arch was a race horse from the word go to five-eighth mile. His dam I do not know. The mother of your horse was sired by Rondo, the best horse to sire Quarter Horses—I mean one fourth mile race horses—that ever was between the San Antonio and Guadelupe Rivers. The first I ever knew about Billy Horses was about 45 years ago, owned by Bill Fleming on the Guadalupe, near Belmont. The old original Billy was the sire of McCoy Billy the sire of Rondo. Rondo sired your horse's mother.[10]

Crawford Sykes spelled his name with a *y*, but other members of the family sometimes used an *i* instead. Whether it was due to personal idiosyncrasies or poor spelling is difficult to say. Mangum Sikes wrote in answer to an inquiry by Joe Huffington in 1946 that the Sykes and Mangum horses his two grandfathers (Joe Mangum, Crawford's partner, and Christopher Sykes, Crawford's brother) raised were mostly of Billy Fleming and Rondo stock. In speaking of Rondo, Mangum Sikes wrote that he had heard his father say that he had seen Rondo when he was so full of pear thorns that you could hardly tell what he was. Crawford Sykes would work wild cattle on him all week and then go to the races and outrun everybody. That sounds a little like the style of Ab Nichols and Clabber. One thing for sure, Crawford Sykes and Ab Nichols had using horses—and used them.

Perhaps Sykes and Mangum just drifted into partnership. They were related by marriage, and both were raising outstanding quarter horses. Mangum married Mattie Gillespie in 1876, and so Mangum was related to Crawford Sykes's brother Christopher. When the partnership was joined, a blend of Billy, Swagger, and Tiger blood produced a large number of outstanding short horses. Rondo proved to be their best stallion, and their best mare was May Mangum, a Tiger mare. This cross produced Jenny (the dam of Little Joe), Baby Ruth, Nettie Harrison, Kitty, and Blue Eyes.

Crawford Sykes picked up his mail at Nixon, Texas, although his home ranch was a few miles west, nearer Pandora than Nixon. Joe Mangum and Christopher Sykes also lived west of Nixon, although Christopher's place was closer to Stockdale than to Pandora. Crawford Sykes was born in 1843, and died in 1925. Joe Mangum, a few years Crawford's junior, preceded him in death. Both had large families.

Samuel Burk Burnett

Samuel Burk Burnett was born in Bates County, Missouri, on January 1, 1849. Jayhawker raids in 1857 and 1858 finally forced the family to give up and move to Texas. Burk's father, Jerry, was soon up to his neck in the cattle business. When the Kansas market opened up at Abilene, he was in a position to profit from the sale of his cattle. It was also about this time that his Denton County herds began carrying one of the best-known brands of all time. the 6666. Although there is a popular legend that the brand originated in a poker game, such may not be the case.

The Burnetts generally gathered steers in the south and drove them to winter on the Osage Reservation, an area that even today has some of the best grass in the United States. As the Burnetts prospered, they purchased new land in Texas. Burk established his headquarters about where Wichita Falls now stands. He hauled the lumber for his home on wagons all the way from Fort Worth.

Burk Burnett married Margaret Loyd, the daughter of a Fort Worth banker. The Burnett family, like their neighbors and friends the Waggoners, made money during the 1880s and 1890s. They soon owned a great deal of land in several surrounding counties, and they leased an additional 300,000 acres from the Kiowas and the Comanches. Burk took a prominent part in the negotiations with the tribes, for he was a close personal friend of Quanah Parker, the foremost chief in the Kiowa-Comanche country.

The Indian country provided cheap grass, and Burk Burnett and Dan Waggoner made maximum use of it. With their profits they bought Texas land. When Oklahoma opened to settlement, they had enough land to move back into Texas. As luck would have it, soon after they returned, oil was discovered on their lands. The oil boomtown Burkburnett sprang up near the Red River line of Wichita County.

Burk Burnett spent the last years of his life in Fort Worth. He built a large, beautiful home and an office building there. He continued his interest in his ranches and made many trips between Fort Worth and the various headquarters. He had two sons, Tom by his first wife, Margaret Loyd, and Burk Burnett, Jr., by his second wife, Mary Couts Barradell, of Weatherford, Texas. Burk Burnett died in Fort Worth in June, 1922.

Tom L. Burnett was very active in ranch affairs as well as quarter horse breeding. He spent most of his time in Iowa Park. He died there on December 28, 1938, at the age of sixty-eight.

It would take far too much space to tell about the Burnett horses. In earlier years considerable Thoroughbred blood was used. When Dow and Will Shely sold their horses in South Texas, most of them went to three breeders: the Burnetts, the Waggoners, and Ott Adams. A man named Henson, acting directly or indirectly for the two North Texas cattlemen, is said to have bought all the Shely horses that Adams did not outbid him on. Most of them were mares, and they were put directly into the breeding manadas of the two ranches, where they disappeared.

W. W. Lock

Unfortunately we have very little biographical information about W. W. Lock. That he was a character there can be little doubt, as witness what A. R. Hamilton of Pittsburgh, Pennsylvania, wrote about him to Dan Casement in 1922:

> I picked up a band of quarter-mares that had been raised by Old Man Lock, one of the famous old characters of the Southwest and brought them out here and raced them for two or three years at the fashionable meets then in Vogue in the East. One was a little mare called Bonnie Bird.[11]

The famous old character he was referring to must have been W. W. Lock, because he raised Bonnie Bird and she had his LO brand on her shoulder. Minnie Lee and Bonnie Bird were sold by Lock in Roswell, New Mexico in the early 1900s.

In the mid-1890s, W. W. Lock decided to move north into Green County, Oklahoma, closer to the short tracks of Kansas, Missouri, and Arkansas, where it was easier for him to match his horses. He brought his horses with him, including Rondo, Texas Chief, Daisy L, and probably Bonnie Bird. W. W. Lock died in 1908. His widow lived until 1924, survived by five sons and two daughters: John Lock, of Marfa, Texas; O. A. Lock, of Mangum, Oklahoma; A. W. Lock, of Austin, Texas; W. W. Lock, Jr., of Riverside, California; and Frank Lock, the youngest.

James F. ("Jim") Newman

Jim Newman came to the Sweetwater area from Navarro County in 1879, and soon

This Texas Chief was a sorrel stallion bred by W. W. Lock, of Kyle, Texas, and foaled in 1890. He was a son of Rondo, by Whalebone. His dam was Daisy L., by Project. This picture was taken on April 4, 1896, after he won a race at Mangum, Oklahoma. Author's collection.

had ranches in Nolan and Fisher counties. He began to feel a little crowded in his ranching ventures, so he moved part of his outfit into New Mexico, centering his operations near Portales. He built his spread, branding DZ, into a 15,000-head cattle ranch. He continued to live much of the time in Sweetwater and spent so much time traveling that in 1905 he sold his New Mexico holdings to Bill Curtis, who branded the Diamond-Tail. Jim Newman was sheriff of Nolan County for a time. His reputation as a horse breeder kept pace with that of his friend and brother-in-law Tom Trammell.

The Newmans had three sons, A. T., called "Cap"; H. S., called "Auti"; and Moses, called "Mose." As mentioned before, Jim's sister married Tom Trammell. With Trammell he had around one hundred head of good brood mares in the racehorse

247

manadas. Until around 1900 they were primarily interested in short horses, but after that they raised Thoroughbreds along with quarter horses to make racing easier.

Jim Newman died in 1914, at the outbreak of World War I. Two of his sons, Auti and Mose, selected some of the better racing prospects and moved down to Juárez, Mexico, where there were legal betting and good purses. There, in 1915, Newman's Pan Zarita ran a world's record five furlongs. If the Newman horses were not known before, they were world-famous from that time on.

In addition to the stallions mentioned in the section on Trammell below, the following studs were used by the Newmans: Charley Wilson, by Rancocas; George House, by Black George; Grover, by Barney Owens; Kid Weller, by Rancocas; No Good, by Barney Owens; Casey Jones, by Peter McCue; and Ace, by Peter McCue.

Thomas Trammell and Jim Newman were not partners in the strict sense, although horsemen invariably link their names because they used each other's stallions, centered their activities in Sweetwater, and had families that intermarried.

Tom Trammell

Tom Trammell was an outstanding horseman and well-known breeder. Some of the stallions he used in his program were Barney Owens, by Cold Deck; Dan Tucker, by Barney Owens; Black George, a grandson of Steel Dust; and Rattler, by Sam Bass. He established one of the first ranches in the Sweetwater area and branded the 9R, using his brand from 1866 until 1913. When Trammell was ranching north and west of Sweetwater, the Comanches and Kiowas were still troublesome. As Trammell began making more money, he devoted more and more of his time to breeding horses. His fame soon spread across the country, and his Thoroughbreds had great success in Europe. He was also interested in banking and community betterment.

In 1892, Trammell pastured 10,000 head of cattle on his ranches in Borden and Scurry counties. About that time he married Jim Newman's sister. The Trammells were a large family, and some of them moved north into the Indian Nations. They are discussed with other Oklahoma breeders.

Dow and Will Shely

Ott Adams, a friend and neighbor of Will Shely, once told me that he felt the Shely brothers were as important in establishing the South Texas quarter horses as Fleming or Lock. However this may be, the Shely's Palo Hueco Ranch in Jim Wells County was the center of quarter horse activity during the early 1900s. Will spent his time on the ranch, while Dow lived part of the time in San Antonio. While both were involved in the business, Will did the breeding, and Dow did the buying, selling, and racing.

Will Shely, well-known breeder of South Texas speed horses. His full name was Colonel William Almond Shely, and with his brother Dow he made South Texas famous for its horses. Blue Eyes, Traveler, Little Joe, Texas Chief, and King (Possum) are some of the horses they stood or bred.

They started out with some Crockett mares, and for their first stallion they purchased a prospective sire from Crawford Sykes, Blue Eyes, by Rondo and out of May Mangum. They sold most of his colts but kept some of the better fillies if they showed speed. Blue Eyes himself was a wonderful individual and a top racehorse. Ott Adams said that he established a world's record on the Dallas track that stood for a number of years. According to *Goodwin's Turf Guide*, the fastest time Blue Eyes made in Dallas was 48¼ for one-half mile, made on October 25, 1893, which could hardly have been a world's record.

The next stallion Shely used was another great racehorse, John Crowder. Crowder, a sorrel was foaled about 1880. He was reported to be by Billy and out of Paisana. His fastest recorded time was in a match against Sorrel Kate at Phoenix, Arizona, on December 12, 1886: one-half mile in 50½ seconds. He had a great reputation as a racehorse, but he made even a greater reputation as a sire when crossed on Blue Eyes' fillies. Two of them, Mamie Crowder and Lady S, must have been fast because George Clegg and Ott Adams both said they were never outrun. Later John Crowder mares were crossed on Shely's last stallion, Traveler. Traveler sired Little Joe and King (Possum).

When the Shelys gave up the ranch in 1914, Traveler was dead. According to Elizabeth Shely, Will's daughter, "He had to be destroyed by Dad just a few years

249

Texas Chief, by Traveler, foaled in 1905. Will Shely is on his back. Photograph courtesy of John Almond.

before we left the ranch due to an infection they were unable to cure.''[12] The Shelys moved to Corpus Christi, where Shely became sheriff. He died on January 2, 1939.

A quote from Ott Adams makes a good conclusion:

> The Shely brothers finally dissolved partnership. At the sale I purchased the famous Mamie Crowder, Julia Crowder, Moselle, and Little Kitty. A man by the name of Henson took most of the other Shely horses to north Texas. The old stallions purchased by Will and Dow Shely were proven sires, and the cream of the quarter horse world.[13]

Ott Adams

Ott Adams, of Alfred, Texas, was one of the great breeders of South Texas, standing alongside the Sykeses, Mangums, Shelys and Locks. Ott was born and raised in Llano County, Texas, but moved south to Jim Wells County because he heard so much about the horses being raised by Will and Dow Shely. His father was born in England, and his mother in South Carolina. Ott lived for ninety-four years, and died in 1963.

The first great Adams stallion was Little Joe. When Little Joe grew old, Ott bred him to a mare named Della Moore. The result was his second great stallion, Joe Moore. He bred and raised many famous horses: Zantanon, Grano de Oro, Pancho Villa, Jim Wells, Pat Neff, Cotton Eyed Joe, Bumps, Less Moore, Lee Moore, Hobo, and others. He bred mares that were also household names, such as Lady of the Lake, Monita, Stella Moore, Texas Rose, Kitty Wells, Ada Jones, Plain Jane, and Big Liz.

Dow and Will Shely were his friends and patrons. Ott said that much of his early

Ott Adams, a South Texas quarter horse breeder who owed much of his success to the Shelys. He owned Little Joe and bred Joe Moore. From Robert Moorman Denhardt, *The King Ranch Quarter Horses: And Something of the Ranch and the Men That Bred Them*, 1970.

knowledge came from information they gave him. He also got from them his excellent start in the horse business. His most famous sire, Little Joe, was bred by the Shelys, and the first stallion he used, El Rey, was also a Traveler colt bred by them.

A horseman once asked Ott which horse was the greatest he had ever seen, thinking he would say Little Joe. Adams had seen many great horses, such as Chicaro, Bold Venture, and Traveler. He never hesitated, but said Rondo, referring to Sykes' Rondo. To Ott, a good horse always had early speed. Conformation always took second place with him. He would breed speed to speed and let the conformation and quality take care of itself. He had no objections to beauty in a horse—to symmetry or to a good head—he just saw no value in them if there was no speed.

When Ott died, he left most of his horses to the hired man who came to live with him after his second wife left him. The man was a Mexican-American, and his Mexican wife cooked for the two men. Ott told them that if they would take care of him until he died he would leave them half of everything he owned. He did. The other half he left to his brother Jim's grandchildren.

William Anson

William Anson was the first breeder to sense the future destiny of the quarter horse. Earlier breeders were just as enthusiastic, but they did not take time to research the history of their breed or to write letters and articles to popularize them. Anson was also one of the first to suggest a studbook. For these reasons he can be considered a founder of the modern quarter horse.

Unfortunately, most of his personal breeding records were lost in a flood. I first learned of this loss in a letter from Mrs. Anson dated February 15, 1940.[14] She wrote: "Any papers I have are put away at the ranch. Some may have been destroyed in the flood as I had safekeeping articles in trunks, and everything simply disintegrated." The house was searched from top to bottom, but, except for some papers in the library, little was intact. The papers that were found were tear sheets of articles Anson had written or saved from various livestock magazines, especially the *Breeders Gazette*, together with some historical memorandums.[15]

William Anson was born in England on April 17, 1872, the seventh son of the Second Earl of Litchfield. His mother was Lady Georgiana Louisa, oldest daughter of the First Duke of Abercorn. He spent his early days in Shugdorough Hall, in Stafford County, England, where his family had lived since the 1600s. Generations of Billy Anson's forebears had owned and raced horses as a hobby. He was educated in England and then came to America to join his two older brothers, Claude and Frank. Both had purchased cattle ranches.

Anson arrived in Texas in 1889, still in his teens. He lived with his brother

William Anson, one of the first breeders to urge the establishment of a quarter horse registry. His ranch was at Christoval, Texas, and he owned such horses as Sam Harper, Harmon Baker, and Jim Ned. From Denhardt, *Quarter Horses: A Story of Two Centuries*.

Claude for a few years. Claude lived on the old Jim Ned Ranch, near Coleman. Then Billy Anson leased the old Cleveland Ranch near Valera, Texas, and got his first experience managing a western cattle outfit. He found plenty of time to play polo, and for that reason decided to find a ranch closer to San Angelo. In 1903 he purchased land on the headwaters of the South Concho, about twenty miles south of San Angelo, which became his permanent home. The family still lives there. He named the ranch Head of the River Ranch. The closest postoffice was Christoval.

Anson spent considerably more money than he made on his ranch, until the Boer War created a demand for horses, which he agreed to furnish. While he was traveling around Texas buying horses, he also had the opportunity to look for and buy good quarter mares. The following is a direct quote from Anson's personal notes mentioned above:

In 1899, after the outbreak of the Boer War, I commenced to supply Texas ponies to the English government. These ponies gave such good service that at the close of the Boer War I had sold over 22,000 head. In 1899, having already acquired a few Quarter Horse Mares, I acquired a Quarter Horse stallion, sired by the original Rondo, and in the succeeding years, up to May 1902 during which time probably over 100,000 Texas ponies

253

came under my observation, I acquired the nucleus of my original stud of Quarter Mares.[16]

Anson shipped the horses he bought direct to Cape Town, South Africa, from Galveston.

In 1917, Anson married Louisa Goddard Van Wagemen, the daughter of Mr. and Mrs. Frederick Devoe Van Wagemen, of Fulton, New York. She was a descendant of some of the original Dutch settlers in New York. Mrs. Anson had graduated from Smith College in Northhampton, Massachusetts in 1910. She had also appeared on the stage. She and Anson moved to San Angelo and lived there until 1923. They spent a lot of time on the Head of the River Ranch. In 1923 they made a long visit to England, and while there, in 1926 William Anson died at the age of fifty-three.

David Webb Christian

David Webb Christian was one of the great breeders of quarter horses and Thoroughbreds in central West Texas. Within a hundred miles of his home in Big Spring were such breeders as Walter Trammell, Clay McGonigal, Tom Haley, William Anson, John Nasworthy, Jim Newman, and Alex Gardner. Webb did not need to take a back seat to any of them. His Barney Lucas, Bobbie Lowe, Eddie Earl, and Dusty Brown were on a par with the superior horses his older neighbors were producing.

Webb Christian was born near Goldthwaite, in Mills County, Texas, on August 1, 1896, and went to Big Spring in 1902. He died on January 12, 1956, at the Big Spring Hospital. He was survived by his wife and two sons. At the time of his death his son Weldon was living in Tulsa, and Lee was living in Lubbock.

Horses were always Webb's first love, and as soon as he could he devoted his full time to raising and racing horses. He owned the noted Traveler for a time, and stood a son, Cunningham's Traveler. While Webb had Traveler, his best colt was Barney Lucas. Barney Lucas was out of Webb's good mare Annie May. Before he used Traveler, his best horses were sired by Bobbie Lowe. Sometimes Webb is given credit for breeding Bobbie Lowe, but he was still a youth when Bobbie Lowe was foaled, and it is much more likely that his father was responsible. The dam, Suzie McWhorter, he did own. One of his better Thoroughbred sires was Palm Reader. Christian also took mares to the Trammells to obtain Barney Owens blood. Barney had been bred by John Hedgepeff in Missouri, raced by Jim Owen, used in the stud by Sam Watkins, and then sold to Tom Trammell. This all goes to show how the best blood found its way to the hands of the top breeders. Webb always had good mares, and they were much in demand by other breeders. Jim Newman, of Sweetwater, got several good broodmares from Webb, including Cintilla, by Jack De Mund. She raised fast colts by Bobbie Lowe and Barney Lucas. Western Beauty went to Louis Sands, of Glendale, Arizona. Webb also sold Dusty Brown to Jack Cunningham, of Comanche, who traded a Traveler colt for him.

John Dial

As a young bachelor John Dial courted two young ladies. He had not yet established his name as an outstanding breeder and horseman, and so neither girl's parents were particularly enthusiastic about him. He was working as a hired hand in a livery stable, so under the circumstances, when he did make his choice, he was unable to get the father's permission to marry the girl. One night the couple eloped, spending the night with one of John's best friends, George Clegg, in Alice. The next day they found a minister and were married. It was a long and happy marriage, and they eventually received her family's blessing.

Like most young men then and now, John and George liked to travel fast. Each wanted to own the fastest horse. When it came to horses and horsemanship, neither of them would admit that the other had the best of it. It was always nip and tuck, first one winning and then the other.

John Dial was a little more openminded than many of his friends, because he liked the Thoroughbred as much as the quarter horse. Unlike his friends Ott Adams and George Clegg, he did not stay with short horse bloodliness. Dial was more like another mutual friend: Bob Kleberg. Doc Northway, the King Ranch veterinarian and no mean horseman himself, listed John as the fifth-best horseman he had known, in a list that included Will Shely, George Clegg, Ott Adams, and Bob Kleberg. Northway remembered Dial's two favorite and oft-repeated statements. One was, "I don't know anything about horses, but they sure as hell can run." The other was, "If it's free, you better not take too much."

Bob Kleberg liked to tell about the time John Dial took a horse into Mexico for a race. It was to be a match race with a well-known Mexican quarter horse. A lot of money was up on each side. Dial's horse ran true and straight and won by a couple of lengths, the jockey standing in the stirrups. Dial was standing beside the Mexican general who was the finish judge. After the horses thundered by, Dial turned to the general and said that he was glad to win that one. The general replied: "I am very sorry, Mr. Dial, but just as the horses came to the finish line I dropped my pencil. In stooping to pick it up, I missed the finish. We can either go to the house and have a chicken dinner, or run the race over." Dial accepted the dinner.

Some of Bob Kleberg's best quarter horses and Thoroughbreds can be traced to blood he obtained from John Dial. It was while Dial was running Thoroughbreds in

New Orleans that he picked up Chicaro in 1928. Dial took Chicaro home and later sold him to Bob Kleberg.

Dial was a real help to Bob Kleberg when he was establishing his strain of sorrel quarter horses. Kleberg needed some good quarter horse blood—blood strong enough to use as an outcross. Among the mares of this kind that Dial helped the King Ranch get were Ada Jones, Lady of the Lake, Plain Jane, Big Liz, Old Queen, and Johnnies Bay. Three were by Little Joe, and two were by Ace of Hearts. Dial either sold these mares to Kleberg or told him where he could buy them.

It is mentioned above that John Dial had the Thoroughbred Chicaro. He also had a large number of quarter horses, especially in the early days. Dial did not seriously run Thoroughbreds until the 1920s, but he always kept his interest in quarter horses. Dial was friendly with most South Texas horsemen, all of whom were generous with their horses. An example was Ed Rachel, of Falfurrias, Texas. He and Dial were always swapping horses, and exact ownership was often hazy. Dial owned or at one time or another had an interest in Ace of Hearts, Little Joe, Jim Wells, Billy Sunday, Jiggs, Spokane, Chicaro Bill, Grano de Oro, and many other well-known quarter horses.

When he died in 1969, the horse world lost a top breeder and a great man.

Other Breeders

Among other outstanding Texas breeders was Dick Baker, of Weatherford. He was responsible for Old Joe Bailey. Old Joe was by Eureka, by Shelby, by Tom Driver, and out of Suzie McQuirter, by Little Ben, by Barney, by Steel Dust. He also bred Yellow Bear, Yellow Wolf, and Little Ben. Then there was Dick Baker, who specialized in the bloodlines used by Shelby Stanfield. Leeman Barker, of Boerne, popularized the Kingfisher horses. Jim Brown, of Karnes City, had the popular Karnes City Jim and would match any short horse with him (this is not the Jim Brown, of Giddings).

J. M. (''Monty'') Corder raised and raced many good ones, such as Fun Powder, Muy Pronto, Pedro Rico, Rambling Sam, Robin Hood, Shooting Star, and Stepping On It. One of his top stallions was the Thoroughbred, Esquire. He also had Red Seal, by Sealskin, by Harmon Baker. Another good breeder was Alex Gardner, of San Angelo. He had Billy Bartlett by Traveler; Brown Billy, by Pancho, by Billie; and Chief Wilkins, by John Wilkins, by Peter McCue. Gardner stayed with the old bloodlines. Dick Gray, on the other hand, mixed Thoroughbred and old bloodlines. His Honest Dick was by Barney Lucas, and his Willrun was by the Thoroughbred Runmore and out of a Barney Lucas mare. The Habys and the Schotts, of Riomedina, raised one good sprinter after another. Tom Haley, of Sweetwater, was not quite the breeder Jim Newman was, but he was good, as Dash, Old Dutchman and Shelby attest. Stanfield bought from Tom Haley the colt named Shelby. Shelby became one of Stanfield's better stallions. He was foaled in 1878, and was by Tom Driver, by Steel Dust, and out of Mittie Stephens, by Shiloh Jr. J. W. House of Cameron, has already been mentioned in the discussion of Joe Reed and Joe Reed II. He also bred many other fast horses, such as Joe Butler and Jonas.

Jap Holman, of Sonora, was still another outstanding breeder of sprinters. Most people remember him for Yankee Doodle, but he also raised and raced Diamond, Jap, Johnny, Keggy, Moser, Red Wing, Ruby David, Top Hat, and many more. G. Berry Ketchum, of Sheffield, cannot be left out. He ran many, including Damit, by Red Rover, by Billy; and Old Mineral. Tom Martin, of Kyle, had Bell Punch, Cold Deck (by Old Billy), and Rattler (Martin's). John Nasworthy, of San Angelo, was also a superb breeder of sprinters. He had, for example, Charley Wilson, Hal Fisher, and Nigger, all runners sired by his stallion Buck Walton. He raised some top mares also, such as Grey Nellie, Laura Lee, and Little Sister. O. G. Parke, of Kyle, is mentioned elsewhere in this book. He too was a top breeder.

Henry Pfefferling, of San Antonio, ran Gurinsky's Horse and Mule Barn. He had many horses, but no doubt his best was the onetime remount horse Uncle Jimmy Gray. Others he had were Eddie Gray, Highball, Jack of Diamonds, Major Speck, and Tommy Gray. The several Renfros moved often, but still had a fistful of sprinters, such as Concho Kid, June Bug, Kinch, Moon Mullins, Pecos Pete, Rio, and Tom Polk. They were racehorsemen and then some.

The Waddells, of Kermit and Odessa, were breeders of the very top class. They used Thoroughbreds such as Dennis Reed and quarter horses like Moss King, and they raised a whole string of fast horses: Dinero, Johnnie Reed, Muskrat, Pete King, Powder River, Stand Pat, and Woodpecker. John Wilkins, of San Antonio, was also a well-known racehorseman, always interested in racing and horses, and also a respected citizen. He was city marshal of San Antonio around 1900 and later assessor of Bexar County. One of his better-known horses was Billy Sunday, who was by Horace H and out of Carrie Nation. Billy Sunday was registered as Huyler, and Carrie as Belle of Oakford. John Wilkins bought and stood Peter McCue and bred Charlie Howell by Peter out of a Thoroughbred mare.

If any state had more than its share of breeders, it had to be Texas.

Epilogue

They could run four miles, or they could run a quarter of a mile, like an arrow from a bow.

—*The Horse of America,* New York, 1897.

THE PERIOD COVERED by this book ends in the late 1930s and early 1940s, when modern short racing began. But the history and development of the quarter running horse did not stop then—far from it. The quarter running horse moved forward like a rush telegram on a downhill wire. The growth was simply phenomenal. Today the American Quarter Horse Association is the largest breed registry in the world. According to one report the AQHA has more registered horses than all of the other breed associations combined. To understand this growth, one needs to review the changes that took place in the organization, in the race meets, and in the horse itself.

The original officers that the AQHA elected in 1940 were a president, a first vice-president, second vice-president, a secretary, and a treasurer. At that time all the officers were directors, all owned quarter horses, and all lived within a few hundred miles of one another. Since that time the organization has grown so large that it is now run by professional, paid administrators, who have brought it to its present position in the industry.

There were originally twenty-five directors from five states. Of this original group two, Ernest Browning and I, are still active. At the second annual meeting the number of directors was increased to thirty. In 1977 there were 144 directors, representing all the states and several foreign countries. At the end of the first year there were 556 registered horses. In 1977 all fifty states had registered Quarter Horses and there were 1,281,177 registered horses. Applications for registration come in today at an average rate of about 100,000 a year. The active membership in the organization in 1977 was 91,344—in 1940 it was 40. Today it costs about $7 million to operate the association. In 1940 it cost just a little less than $1,250, and the office

Johnny Dial, World's Champion Quarter Horse, 1952.

Go Man Go, World's Champion Quarter Horse, 1955–57.

was the back bedroom of the apartment I rented in Bryan, Texas, during the college year.

Quarter Horse racing had an equally large and rapid expansion. All the activities that surround the running quarter horse, increased as rapidly as the association grew. There were more races, faster times, and fatter purses. In 1940 match racing was still the backbone of the sport. In 1977 most racing states not only recognize the quarter running horse but allow organized pari-mutuel races to be written for him. It used to be impossible for a quarter running horse to make a dollar on a recognized track, unless it was registered as a Thoroughbred. Recently Easy Date, the bay daughter of Easy Jet, won $849,709 in purse races. Five other quarter running horses have won over half a million dollars. In 1977 purses for quarter running horses totaled $28,328,661, and 11,986 races were run at 440 yards or less.

The gigantic two-year-old race officially called the All-American Futurity, was

261

Mr. Bar None, World's Champion Quarter Horse, 1958.

started at Ruidoso, New Mexico, in 1959. The track officials thought it might be worth trying. The basic idea was simple. Any breeder could enter a colt by making a series of payments, culminating on the day of the race with a final post fee. Today a million dollars in purses waits for the completion of this one futurity. The winner gets one third of the total. At this writing the *least* a finalist can win is $27,000. Even the winner of the consolation purse gets $21,000. Forty horses in all win back their nomination fees! The Ruidoso futurity, first run on Labor Day in 1959 for an estimated total purse of $50,000, has come a long way—as has quarter racing.

No Butt, World's Champion Quarter Horse, 1962.

When Melville Haskell raced in Arizona in the early 1940s, a $100 purse was a good one, and $50 closer to the average. The first big step came when the state of California legalized pari-mutuel betting, and Frank Vessel built the Los Alamitos Racetrack. This track is the largest and the most influential of the many short tracks now in existence. The Champion of Champions Race held at Los Alamitos has as much prestige as the All-American Futurity. It is open only to those who have won the most important races.

It comes as no surprise to the quarter horse historian to learn that the faster horses

Goetta, World's Champion Quarter Horse, 1964.

Mr. Jet Moore, World's Champion Quarter Horse, 1972.

Tiny's Gay, World's Champion Quarter Horse, 1974.

Dash for Cash, World's Champion Quarter Horse, 1976–77.

carry considerable Thoroughbred blood. A point often overlooked is that the Quarter Horse that does not race can also have close-up Thoroughbred blood. It has always been so since the Thoroughbred became an American breed in 1868. Before then the breeder just crossed fast horses, sprinting or staying as he desired. One interesting modern development has been the importation of foreign (other than English) Thoroughbreds that are producing short speed. *Noholme II is such a stallion. Imported by Verna Lea and Gene Geoff, this stallion and his offspring are responsible for a whole string of current speedy horses, such as Pass Over, Shecky Greene, Pass 'Em Up, and Nodouble. Other stallions have come from Mexico and France to influence the quarter running horses.

Running fast, setting records, and winning large purses have also increased the monetary value of the horses. Dash for Cash won the prestigious Champion of Champions Race at Los Alamitos two years in a row. He is jointly owned by the King Ranch and by Anne and B. E. Phillips. Dash for Cash was sired by Rocket Wrangler, by Rocket Bar. Rocket Wrangler was out of a daughter of Go Man Go. Dash for Cash syndicated for $2.5 million.

CHAMPION QUARTER RUNNING HORSES, 1940–77

1940	Clabber	1959	(No award)
1941	Shue Fly	1960	Vandy's Flash
1942	Shue Fly	1961	Pap
1943	Shue Fly	1962	No Butt
1944	(No award)	1963	Jet Deck
1945	Queenie	1964	Goetta
1946	Miss Princess	1965	Go Josie Go
1947	Miss Princess	1966	(No award)
1948	Miss Princess	1967	Laico Bird
1949	Bright Eyes	1968	Kaweah Bar
1950	Blob Jr.	1969	Easy Jet
1951	Monita	1970	Kaweah Bar
1952	Johnny Dial	1971	Charger Bar
1953	Miss Meyers	1972	Mr. Jet Moore
1954	Josie's Bar	1973	Truckle Feature
1955	Go Man Go	1974	Tiny's Gay
1956	Go Man Go	1975	Easy Date
1957	Go Man Go	1976	Dash for Cash
1958	Mr Bar None	1977	Dash for Cash

Speed is also increasing, with better times recorded each year. Miss Princess ran a 440-yard race in the 1940s against Barbra B in Del Rio in 22.2 seconds. It was a new world's record. Various horses before the 1940s were supposed to have run faster. Bob Wade held the world's record of 21¼ seconds, undoubtedly set with a scored (running) start. Peter McCue was said to have run a 21-flat quarter mile, also with a scored start. Melville Haskell experimented and found that a scored start gave right at a one-second advantage over a race run by quarter horses who have their noses on the starting line. Clocks start when the gate is open, not 60 feet afterward. So Miss Princess' time of 22.2 was equal to 21.2. Now times are faster. Dash for Cash ran 440 yards in 1977 in 21.17.

Some great individuals have appeared since 1940. Some stand out even among the tremendously improved quarter running horses of today. During the late 1940s, Miss Princess dominated the tracks. She was sired by Bold Venture and foaled in 1943, bred by the King Ranch. Her dam was Bruja, by Livery and out of Chicaro's Hallie. She beat the best while she was running.

The next horse to dominate his period was Go Man Go. He too could look back to the King Ranch, because his sire, Top Deck, was foaled there. Go Man Go was truly a super sprinter, as well as a super sire. He was the first two-year-old to run 400 yards in 20.6 seconds. He was also the first two-year-old to be named a World's Champion. To show those who questioned whether a two-year-old had proven much at that age, he won the title again as a three-year-old. Then he was named World's Champion for a third consecutive year. When retired to the stud, he was equally brilliant. Go Man Go sired two All-American Futurity winners, Goetta in 1960 and Hustling Man in 1962. His daughters foaled two others, Rocket Wrangler in 1970 and Mr. Kid Charge in 1971. He is also the leading sire of All-American finalists, with twenty-three. He was the leading sire of Register of Merit horses between 1955 and 1972. He has sired 190 AAA and AAAT horses. He could run, he could reproduce speed, and at this writing he is still actively breeding.

The other outstanding stallion during the years after the 1940s was Three Bars, a Thoroughbred. While running on Thoroughbred tracks he won nineteen races, including eight handicaps. He was not the racehorse Go Man Go was, but as a sire he was equal. He sired 542 foals, and 430 of them started on the short tracks. Of that total 315 were good enough to make the Register of Merit, and 209 were AAA or AAAT. He sired two winners of the All-American Futurity: Galobar in 1959 and Pokey Bar in 1961. He also sired the dam of Easy Jet, who won in 1969.

Any way you look at the quarter running horse—the association, the racing, or the horse—the growth has been stunning. It has been a development without parallel in the industry. It is reminiscent of that nineteenth-century quarter horse tout who explained the success of his favorite sprinter by saying, "He came off the mark like a hoop rolling." The rolling hoop that is the quarter running horse industry today is difficult to explain, although some factors causing the surge can be seen. The American people have more free time and more money than ever before. The quarter horse (in the beginning at least) is owner-bred, trained, and raced. It is something anyone can do without being a retired millionaire. Another factor that undoubtedly helped was the acceptance of artificial insemination by the association. Good blood became readily available. Finally, more people found that the outside of a horse was good for the inside of a man. Whatever the reasons, the modern quarter running horse is a pleasure to own, to watch, and to race.

Notes

CHAPTER 1

1. Henry William Herbert, *Frank Forester's Horse and Horsemanship of the United States*, 2:11. Hereafter cited as *Frank Forester's Horse and Horsemanship*.
2. Quoted by John L. O'Connor in Robert Moorman Denhardt, *The Quarter Horse*, 2:36.
3. J. F. D. Smyth, *A Tour in the United States of America* . . ., 1:361.
4. David Ramsey, *The History of South Carolina*, 2:403.
5. *Horse Lover Magazine*, August–September, 1949, p. 23.
6. Clark Wissler, "The Influence of the Horse in the Development of Plains Culture," *American Anthropologist* 16 (January–March, 1914): 7.
7. Ramsey, *History of South Carolina*, 2:403; Francis Culver, *Blooded Horses of Colonial Days*, p. 131.
8. For more on Chickasaw horses see Fairfax Harrison, *The Johns Island Stud;* and Thorton Chard, "The Chickasaw Horse," *Horse Lover Magazine*, April–May, 1949.
9. P. R. Saward, "Eighteenth Century Quarter Racing in England" (manuscript).
10. Herbert, *Frank Forester's Horse and Horsemanship*, 1:128.
11. Patrick Nisbett Edgar, *The American Race-Turf Register, Sportsman's Herald, and General Stud Book*, Introduction, p. ix. Hereafter cited as *The American Race-Turf Register*. This same theme was repeated in later years by Skinner, Herbert, Wallace, Culver, and Anderson (see Bibliography). It may have been true for the East Coast gentlemen breeders.

CHAPTER 2

1. Daniel Denton, *Description of New York*, p. 6.
2. John H. Wallace, *The Horse of America*, pp. 90–91.
3. Smyth, *A Tour in the United States*, 1:22–23.
4. Wallace, in *The Horse of America*, said that Morton's *Traveler was the only race horse advertised in 1751–52 in the Virginia newspapers. Edgar, in *American Race-Turf Register*, called this horse Moreton's *Traveler, while Sanders De Weese Bruce, in *The American Stud Book*, correctly listed him as Morton's *Traveler.
5. Culver, *Blooded Horses of Colonial Days*, p. 131.
6. John B. Irving, *History of the Turf in South Carolina*, p. 26.
7. Hugh Jones, *The Present State of Virginia*, p. 84.
8. Wallace, *The Horse of America*, p. 92.

9. W. G. Stanard, "Racing in Colonial Virginia," *Virginia Magazine of History and Biography* 2 (1895): 293.

10. Harrison, *Johns Island Stud*, pp. 68-69; and *American Turf Register and Sporting Magazine* 3 (April, 1932), hereafter cited as *American Turf Register*.

11. Wallace, *The Horse of America,* p. 114.

12. James Goodwin Hall, "The Quarter Horse and Quarter Racing," *Cattleman*, September, 1941, p. 25.

13. A full citation of their works can be found in the Bibliography. None of them agree on all details, although for the most part their descriptions are similar.

14. For the best critical evaluation of the source materials see Fairfax Harrison, *The Background of the American Stud Book*.

15. Edgar, *American Race-Turf Register*, p. 23.

16. John H. Wallace, *Wallace's American Stud-Book; Being a Compilation of the Pedigrees of American and Imported Horses*, p. 27. Hereafter cited as *American Stud-Book*.

17. Edgar, *American Race-Turf Register*, p. 47.

18. Ibid., p. 40.

19. Ibid., p. 23.

20. Bruce, *The American Stud Book*, 1:28.

21. Wallace, *American Stud-Book*, p. 206.

22. Herbert, *Frank Forester's Horse and Horsemanship*, 1:462. Many horses carried the name Celer. Edgar does not list any as being imported but shows two native Celers. Herbert lists only one, and Wallace lists five. Bruce has two under stallions and lists one more, Meade's Celer, under his dam, Brandon. Five distinct Celers can be identified, but only Meade's Celer is of importance to the quarter running horse.

23. John S. Skinner, *The Gentleman's New Pocket Farrier*, p. 352.

24. Edgar, *American Race-Turf Register*, pp. 39–40.

25. *American Turf Register* 3 (1836): 445.

26. Ibid., 1 (1829): 462.

27. Bruce, *The American Stud Book*, 1:257.

28. Ibid., 2:566.

29. Ibid., p. 325.

30. Ibid.

31. *American Turf Register* 3 (1836): 272.

32. Ibid., 1 (1829): 462.

33. Harrison, *The Roanoke Stud*, p. 194.

34. Herbert, *Frank Forester's Horse and Horsemanship*, 1:140.

35. *AmericanTurf Register* 1 (1829): 4.

36. Ibid., 3 (1832): 505–509.

37. John Hervey, *Racing in America, 1665–1865*, 1:76.

38. Edgar, *American Race-Turf Register*, p. 33.

39. Herbert, *Frank Forester's Horse and Horsemanship*, 1:128.

40. Bruce, *The American Stud Book*, 1:96.

41. William Robinson Brown, *The Horse of the Desert*, p. 176.

42. Edgar, *American Race-Turf Register*, pp. 66–72.

43. Bruce, *The American Stud Book*, 1:145–46; Wallace, *The Horse of America*, pp. 93–95, 132–33; Skinner, *The Gentleman's New Pocket Farrier*, p. 318.

44. *American Farmer* 9 (1827): 223.

45. Wallace, *The Horse of America*, p. 132.

46. Ibid., p. 94.

47. Edgar, *American Race-Turf Register*, p. 389.

48. Bruce, *The American Stud Book*, 1:694.

49. *American Turf Register* 2 (1830): 27.

50. Joseph Battell, *American Stallion Registry*.

51. Herbert, *Frank Forester's Horse and Horsemanship*, 1:144.

52. Edgar, *American Race-Turf Register*, p. 156.

53. Herbert, *Frank Forester's Horse and Horsemanship*, 1:145.

54. Bruce, *The American Stud Book*, 2:499.

55. Edgar, *American Race-Turf Register*, p. 478.

CHAPTER 3

1. Wallace, *The Horse of America*, p. 91.

2. John Thomas Scharf, *History of Maryland*, 2:73.

3. Culver, *Blooded Horses of Colonial Days*, p. 113.

4. Both Hervey, in *Racing in America, 1665–1865*, and Jane Carson, in *Colonial Virginians at Play*, have good descriptions of colonial quarter racing.

5. Edgar, *American Race-Turf Register*, p. 537.

6. This race is described in Harrison, *The Roanoke Stud*, p. 70.

7. *American Turf Register* 3 (1832): 419–20.

8. Ibid., p. 420.

9. The account of this race appears in several places: first in *American Turf Register* 3 (1832): 450–52; then in *Spirit of the Times* 1 (1832): 4; and, almost one hundred years later, in Harrison, *The Roanoke Stud* (1932).

10. *American Turf Register* 3 (1832): 452.

11. Ibid.

12. Edgar, *American Race-Turf Register*, pp. 381–82.

13. Ibid., p. 509.

14. Bruce, *The American Stud Book*, 3:209.

15. Much of this story can be found in Edgar, *American Race-Turf Register*.

16. Ibid., p. 436.

17. Ibid., pp. 217, 308.

18. Ibid., p. 486.

19. Ibid., p. 114.

20. Bruce, *The American Stud Book*, 1:701.

CHAPTER 4

1. Edgar, *American Race-Turf Register*, p. 52.

2. Considerably more information can be found about John Goode in *American Turf Register* 4 (1832): 115.

3. Allen Jones Davie, *American Turf Register* 3 (18)2): 420, 452.

4. *California Freemason* 22:159.

5. Herbert, *Frank Forester's Horses and Horsemanship*, 1:127.

6. Bruce, *The American Stud Book*, 1:37.

7. Herbert, *Frank Forester's Horse and Horsemanship*, 1:150.

CHAPTER 5

1. Herbert, *Frank Forester's Horse and Horsemanship*, 1:140.

CHAPTER 6

1. Snelling, like Peter Stewart, is an example of the American Negro's participation in early quarter racing. Both Stewart's horse, Moggy, and Snelling's Black Snake were mighty hard to outrun.

2. William H. Robertson, *The History of Thoroughbred Racing in America*, p. 41.

3. A letter from Will Williams, quoted in Herbert, *Frank Forester's Horse and Horsemanship*, 1:141.

4. Robertson, *The History of Thoroughbred Racing in America*, p. 41.

5. James Douglas Anderson, *Making of the American Thoroughbred*, p. 258.

6. Bruce, *The American Stud Book*, 2:24, calls him Hanie.

7. Herbert, *Frank Forester's Horse and Horsemanship*, 1:141.

CHAPTER 7

1. Bruce, *The American Stud Book*, 2:566.

2. Herbert, *Frank Forester's Horse and Horsemanship*, 2:78.

3. Battell, *The American Stallion Register*, 4:192.

4. *American Turf Register* 1 (1829): 172.

5. John Lawrence O'Connor, *Notes on the Thoroughbred from Kentucky Newspapers*, n.p. Hereafter cited as *Notes on the Kentucky Thoroughbred*.

6. Ibid.

7. Ibid.

8. *American Turf Register* 4 (1833): 323.

9. Bruce, *The American Stud Book*, 2:61.

10. *American Turf Register* 1 (1829): 171.

11. Herbert, *Frank Forester's Horse and Horsemanship*, 2:79.

12. *American Turf Register* 1 (1829): 171.

13. O'Connor, *Notes on the Kentucky Thoroughbred*.

14. Ibid.

15. Bruce, *The American Stud Book*, 2:507.

16. Herbert, *Frank Forester's Horse and Horsemanship*, 1:171–72.

17. *American Turf Register* 1 (1830): 165.
18. O'Cononr, *Notes on the Kentucky Thoroughbred*.
19. Ibid.
20. Wallace, *The Horse of America*, p. 484.
21. Ibid., p. 451.
20. Wallace, *The Horse of America*, p. 484.
21. Ibid., p. 451.
22. Herbert, *Frank Forester's Horse and Horsemanship*, 2:17.
23. Ibid., 1:146.
24. Anderson, *Making of the American Thoroughbred*, p. 59.
25. O'Connor, *Notes on the Kentucky Thoroughbred*.
26. Ibid.
27. Bruce, *The American Stud Book*, 2:262.
28. O'Connor, *Notes on the Kentucky Thoroughbred*.
29. Ibid.
30. Bruce, *The American Stud Book*, 2:563.
31. O'Connor, *Notes on the Kentucky Thoroughbred*.
32. Ibid.
33. Ibid.

CHAPTER 8

1. William E. Railey, *History of Woodford County*, p. 33.
2. *Kentucky Livestock Record* 1 (1875): 153.
3. *American Turf Register* 4 (1832): 653.
4. O'Connor, *Notes on the Kentucky Thoroughbred*.

CHAPTER 9

1. Herbert, *Frank Forester's Horse and Horsemanship*, 2:84.
2. Ibid., pp. 89–90.
3. *Clarksville* (Texas) *Northern Standard*, March 20, 1844; April 24, 1844; May 13, 1845.

CHAPTER 10

1. Denhardt, *The Quarter Horse*, 3:104–105.
2. *American Turf Register* 5 (1833): 48.
3. Ibid., 4 (1832): 15.
4. *Spirit of the Times* 22 (1852): 186.
5. Ibid., 23 (1853): 475.
6. *Wilke's Spirit of the Times* 9 (1864): 290.
7. *Spirit of the Times* 23 (1853): 186.

8. *Turf, Field, and Farm* 13 (1871): 47.

9. *Spirit of the Times* 24 (1872): 47.

10. Ibid., 23 (1853): 462.

11. *Wichita* (Kansas) *Eagle*, July 12, 1872.

12. Wayne Gard, *The Fabulous Quarter Horse Steel Dust*, p. 31.

13. Bruce, *The American Stud Book*, 1:248.

14. Much of the information here about Alfred Bailes came from my sister-in-law, Mrs. Marion Dildy, of Sulphur Springs, Texas, a member of a pioneer Texas family.

15. Denhardt, *The Quarter Horse*, 1:78–79. The letter mentioned is in the Denhardt Files, Steel Dust Folder.

16. *Spirit of the Times* 22 (1852): 186.

17. Ibid., 37 (1857): 265.

18. Samuel C. Hildreth, *The Spell of the Turf*, p. 27.

19. Tom Gregory, *History of Yolo County*, p. 182.

20. *Spirit of the Times* 21 (1851): 174.

21. *Alta California*, October 11, 1857.

22. *Spirit of the Times* 27 (1857): 330.

23. *Turf, Field, and Farm* 12 (1871): 296.

24. *Spirit of the Times* 26 (1872): 164.

CHAPTER 11

1. Denhardt, *The Quarter Horse*, 2:101.

2. Ibid., 1:13.

3. *Life and Adventures of Sam Bass*, p. 4. My wife's family is descended from the Egans, for whom Sam Bass worked while he lived in Denton, and many stories have been handed down about this outlaw.

4. Gard, *The Fabulous Quarter Horse Steel Dust*, p. 33.

5. See Robert Moorman Denhardt, *Quarter Horses: A Story of Two Centuries*, p. 32, for a discussion of Barney Owens' breeding.

6. Bruce, *The American Stud Book*, 1:1106.

CHAPTER 12

1. Denhardt Files, Steel Dust Folder.

2. Ibid., Jim Brown Folder.

3. Hildreth, *The Spell of the Turf*, pp. 71–72.

4. Ibid.

5. Denhardt Files, Fleming Folder.

6. See T. T. Ewell's good book, *A History of Hood County, Texas*.

7. Marriage Records, Dade County, Book A, 1871–81.

8. *Breeder and Sportsman*, January 24, 1885.

CHAPTER 14

1. Salvator, "Sprinters Old and New," *Thoroughbred Record* 3 (1930): 327.
2. For more on Della Moore and Boyd Simar see Denhardt, *Quarter Horses: A Story of Two Centuries*, pp. 56–57.
3. In a letter to me dated December 20, 1939, Walter Trammell wrote, "Regards Callise and Panzaretta—they show to be mothered by a mare called Caddie Griffith, but their mother was Minyon by Rancocas, 1st dam Heely by Blue Dick, 2nd dam Mittie Stephens by Shiloh Jr. They go back to the quarter horse." Denhardt Files, Walter Trammell Folder.
4. John Hendrix, "Panzarita," *Cattleman*, September, 1945.
5. See Denhardt, *The Quarter Horse*, 3:160.
6. For more on milk races see Denhardt, *Quarter Horses: A Story of Two Centuries*.

CHAPTER 15

1. Denhardt, *Quarter Horses: A Story of Two Centuries*, pp. 35–36.
2. Agnes Wright Spring, *Western Horseman*, March, 1949, p. 18.
3. For those interested in Traveler, some of the stories about this great sire can be found in Lewis Nordyke, "Traveler Country," *Quarter Horse Journal*, December, 1954; and in Nelson C. Nye, *The Complete Book of the Quarter Horse*, pp. 215–16.
4. Nye, *The Complete Book of the Quarter Horse*, p. 216.
5. Melville H. Haskell, *Racing Quarter Horses*, p. 13.
6. Denhardt Files, Rocky Mountain Tom Folder.
7. Bruce, *The American Stud Book*, 10:871.
8. Denhardt Files, Anson Folder #3.
9. A. D. Reed was registered by the Jockey Club as Dr. B. H. See Bruce, *The American Stud Book*, 12:594.
10. For an interesting description of how Zantanon was trained and treated in Mexico, read Volpe's letter in Denhardt, *Quarter Horses: A Story of Two Centuries*, pp. 68–69.

CHAPTER 16

1. *History of Hancock County* has several notices of the Wade family.
2. Denhardt Files, Breeder File, Tape #2, 0-50.
3. See especially William Welch, "Peter McCue's Family Tree," *Quarter Horse Journal*, February, 1949.
4. See *They Left Their Mark in Oakford*, 1872, pp. 64–67. This pamphlet was issued by the citizens of Oakford to celebrate the town's centennial.
5. These horses are found in the Appendix of Bruce, *The American Stud Book*, vol. 6.
6. Deeds, bk. 57, p. 237, Court House, Wellington, Kans.
7. Denhardt Files, Peter McCue Folder.
8. For more information on this event see Robert Moorman Denhardt, *The King Ranch Quarter Horses: And Something of the Ranch and the Men That Bred Them*, pp. 76–77.

9. Franklin Reynolds, ''Cradle of the Modern Day Quarter Horse,'' *Quarter Horse Journal*, March, 1957, p. 31.

10. Denhardt, *The Quarter Horse*, 1:25–26.

11. Denhardt Files, Casement Folder.

12. Ibid., Shely and Almond Tapes.

13. Ibid., Ott Adams Folder.

14. Ibid., Anson Folder #2.

15. This information was published in detail in *Western Horseman*, December, 1941, and January, 1942.

16. Denhardt Files, Anson Folder #3.

Essay on Source Materials

AMONG the most useful source materials for the Quarter Horse historian are those produced by various attempts to establish a satisfactory studbook for the American racehorse. Obviously many of the early racehorse stallions and mares produced both sprinters and stayers, so the early records contain information about both.

Not too much need be said here about the English *General Stud Book*. It was originally compiled by Thomas Weatherby and then carried on by others of his family. Twenty-seven volumes were published in London between 1808 and 1929. The first volume, which covers the eighteenth century and so is the historical foundation of the modern horse, has been revised several times. It started out in 1791 as "an Introduction to a General Stud Book." Then came two so-called supplements and a few "editions," until finally nine in all had appeared by 1891. There was also one American issue, published by J. S. Skinner in Baltimore in 1834. Its title said in part—*The General Stud Book. . . with an Appendix Giving Extended Pedigrees of Stallions Imported into the United States and Their Most Noted Progeny*. The first part was taken from the second London edition of the *General Stud Book* (Vols. 1–3), and the Appendix was an incomplete list of imported American Thoroughbreds.

The first person to start an thorough American studbook was George W. Jeffreys, of Person County, North Carolina. He was encouraged in the effort by many horse-breeding friends. Beginning in 1828, the various pedigrees he gathered were collected and published as an appendix in Peter Cottom's fourth edition of *Mason's Farrier and Stud Book*. In 1830, Cottom combined other sources and ran this section of *Mason's Farrier* under the title *American Stud Book*. This was the first published book to bear that name.

The title of the fifth edition was: *The Gentleman's New Pocket Farrier; Comprising a General Description of the Noble and Useful Animal the Horse, by Richard Mason, Formerely of Surrey County, Virginia. Fifth edition . . . .* The book was printed by Peter Cottom in Richmond in 1830. It proved very popular and went through many editions. On page 286 is an addendum, "Annals of the Turf and American Stud Book, Rules of Training, Racing, etc." After a ten-page historical essay on the horse in America, the studbook starts on page 315 and continues to page 403. It also has a forty-page appendix listing the pedigrees of winning horses since 1839.

John Stuart Skinner, who exerted tremendous influence on the racing world with his publications, especially with *The Gentleman's New Pocket Farrier*, which contained racing and pedigree information. From Harrison, *Background of the American Stud Book*.

After printing six editions, Cottom sold the copyright to Gregg, Elliott, and Company of Philadelphia. This company borrowed Skinner's name as editor for a seventh edition, published in 1848. Five other editions appeared, the last being the twelfth, dated 1883.

Later, Jeffreys, J. J. Harrison, of Brunswick County, Virginia, and Theophilus Field, of the same county, worked together to make a registry. After much labor they were forced to stop, but they turned their papers over to Patrick Nisbett Edgar, who in 1833 published his famous work, entitled *American Race Turf Register*, *Sportsman's Herald*, and *General Stud Book*. It is in Edgar's studbook that the Quarter Horse people find the records of many of their foundation animals. Fortunately for the reader, Edgar liked Quarter Horses, and his anecdotes about them are as fascinating as any that can be found. Incidentally, it is also in Edgar that the part played by horses in the Revolutionary War can be studied. His description of the famous horse Black and All Black is a case in point.

Edgar became interested in compiling a studbook for the American blood horse through his contacts with Captain J. J. Harrison, who lived on a famed horse farm on the Meherrin River in Brunswick County, Virginia. Edgar showed his regard for Harrison in the introduction to his studbook, calling him the "Father of the American Turf." A little later Edgar really let himself go, writing Harrison that "in private life you may also be styled a dignified link in the chain of polite society: for I am at loss which to admire most, your noble virtues, your inoffensive life, or the suavity of your manners." How much of this Harrison deserved is impossible to tell, but the fact

278

The first four studbooks of the Thoroughbred. Top to bottom: Skinner, Edgar, Wallace, and Bruce. Much of the early history of the quarter running horse is found in these books. Books in author's collection.

remains that he did start to create an American studbook. Harrison first obtained the services of Theophilus Field, who had been collecting and organizing pedigrees. When Field became ill and eventually died, Harrison turned to the blarney-coated Irishman Patrick Nisbett Edgar and talked him into finishing the book.

Edgar had been working for Harrison, after a fashion, since 1822, when he had been sent "riding through the Southside from end to end" in search of old pedigrees. Upon Field's death, Harrison entrusted Edgar with all of the accumulated papers.

279

AMERICAN STUD BOOK.

A.

ABELINO, g. c. by Dragon, dam Celerrima.
1804. John Hoomes.
ACQUITTAL, by Timoleon, dam (dam of Bolivar) by Sir Hal, &c.
William Wynne.
ACTEON, ch. h. by Dandridge's Fearnought, dam [by imp'd] Fearnought,
gr. dam by imp'd Jolly Roger, out of an imp'd mare, &c.
Chesterfield, Va. 1712. Thos. Woolridge
————————ch. c. by Kosciusko, dam Artless.
1829. S. Carolina. Harrison
ACTIVE, by Chatam, dam Shepherdess, [by imp'd] Slim.
ADAMANT, b. h. by Boxer, dam by Lindsay's Arabian, g. dam by Oscar,
out of Kitty Fisher.
1799. Nicholas Wynne.
ADELINE, b. f. by Henry, dam by Old Oscar, g. dam the Maid of Nor-
thumberland, &c. New Jersey. J. Vandike.
————————br. m. by Spread Eagle—Whistle Jacket—Rockingham—
Old Cub, &c.
1806. John Tayloe.
————————Young, by Topgallant, dam Adeline by Spread Eagle.
1809. John Tayloe.
ADELA, b. f. by Ratler, dam young Adeline.
Dr. Irvine.
ADELAIDE, b. f. by Thornton's Ratler, dam Desdemona by Miner Es-
cape, &c.
ADRIA, b. f. by Pacific, dam Oceana.
1831. J. Southall.
ADMIRAL NELSON, [imp'd] b. h. by John Bull, dam Olivia, by Justice
—Cypher, &c.
Foaled 1795. William Lightfoot.
AFRICAN, bl. h. by Careless, dam by Lloyd's Traveller, gr. dam by
Othello.
Flatbush, 1788. A. Giles.
AGNES, or the Thrift mare, by Bellair, dam by Wildair, gr. dam by
Fearnought, &c. William Thrift.
————————b. m. by Sir Solomon, (by Tickle Toby,) her dam Young
Romp, by Duroc, g. dam Romp, by [imp'd] Messenger.
1822. Gen Coles
28

Page from the earliest stud-book, which appeared in *Mason's Farrier*. The book contained much general horse information and went through many editions.

There is no way of knowing exactly how much was accomplished by Field, although quite a number of the horses listed carry Field's name at the end, suggesting that his notes supplied the pedigree for that horse. On the other hand, there is a certain uniformity to the somewhat careless method of listing the animals in the studbook that suggests that one author, Edgar, was primarily responsible for the work. Edgar has been criticized for not always being critical of the evidence supplied him. He is also

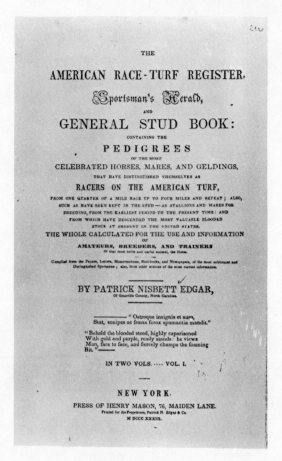

THE

AMERICAN RACE-TURF REGISTER,

Sportsman's Herald,

AND

GENERAL STUD BOOK:

CONTAINING THE

PEDIGREES

OF THE MOST

CELEBRATED HORSES, MARES, AND GELDINGS,

THAT HAVE DISTINGUISHED THEMSELVES AS

RACERS ON THE AMERICAN TURF,

FROM ONE QUARTER OF A MILE RACE UP TO FOUR MILES AND REPEAT; ALSO, SUCH AS HAVE BEEN KEPT IN THE STUD — AS STALLIONS AND MARES FOR BREEDING, FROM THE EARLIEST PERIOD TO THE PRESENT TIME; AND FROM WHICH HAVE DESCENDED THE MOST VALUABLE BLOODED STOCK AT PRESENT IN THE UNITED STATES.

THE WHOLE CALCULATED FOR THE USE AND INFORMATION OF

AMATEURS, BREEDERS, AND TRAINERS

Of that most noble and useful animal, the Horse.

Compiled from the Papers, Letters, Memorandums, Stud-books, and Newspapers, of the most celebrated and Distinguished Sportsmen; also, from other sources of the most correct information.

BY PATRICK NISBETT EDGAR,

Of Granville County, North Carolina.

———— "Ostroque insignis et auro,
Stat, sonipes ac fræna ferox spumantia mandit."

"Behold the blooded steed, highly caparisoned
With gold and purple, ready stands: he views
Man, face to face, and fiercely champs the foaming
Bit."————

IN TWO VOLS..... VOL. I.

NEW YORK.

PRESS OF HENRY MASON, 76, MAIDEN LANE.

Printed for the Proprietors, Patrick N. Edgar & Co.

M DCCC XXXIII.

Title page of *Edgar's American Race Turf Register, Sportsman's Herald, and General Stud Book*, 1833. It was the first studbook that carried quarter horse information. Only one volume was published.

criticized for changing some of the pedigrees given to him. It would seem that one or the other of the criticisms would be wrong. In any case, the value of his work is not questioned. Only one volume was published, but it had great influence on the next two studbooks to be published, Wallace's and Bruce's. Much of Bruce's book is taken almost intact from Edgar, especially the records of those horses both men considered Thoroughbreds. On the other hand, few of the quarter horses listed by Bruce carry the quarter horse tag given them by Edgar.

Many people, especially William T. Porter, tried unsuccessfully to get Edgar to complete volume two of his studbook. Porter was very influential in racehorse circles as editor of the most popular sporting journal *Spirit of the Times: A Chronicle of the Turf.''* In 1837, Edgar ran a notice in the January 13 issue of *Spirit of the Times*, saying that he would publish all the materials he had accumulated since he issued Volume 1

Title page of *Wallace's American Stud-Book*, 1867, the first and only volume published.

(1833), on the condition that 1,300 persons subscribed to Volume 2 and that all copies of Volume 1 were sold. One thing after another intervened, and Edgar died without ever publishing Volume 2. His papers were never found, so no one knows how much more he actually had gathered.

Patrick Nisbett Edgar was born in Dublin, Ireland, about 1785, and was named for his father. He arrived in Virginia in the early 1800s. Fairfax Harrison tells of the

THE

AMERICAN STUD BOOK:

CONTAINING FULL PEDIGREES OF ALL THE IMPORTED

THOROUGH-BRED STALLIONS AND MARES,

WITH THEIR PRODUCE, INCLUDING THE

ARABS, BARBS, AND SPANISH HORSES,

FROM THE

EARLIEST ACCOUNTS OF RACING IN AMERICA, TO THE END OF THE YEAR
1872; ALSO, ALL THE NATIVE MARES AND THEIR PRODUCE.

ALPHABETICALLY ARRANGED.

WITH AN APPENDIX,

*GIVING PEDIGREES OF ALL THE NATIVE STALLIONS WHOSE DAMS HAVE
NO NAMES, WITH FULL AND COPIOUS INDEX TO
PRODUCE OF THE MARES.*

BY

S. D. BRUCE,

Editor of the "Turf, Field and Farm."

L. C. BRUCE, CO-EDITOR.

IN TWO VOLUMES.—VOL. I.

A to L.

REVISED IN 1884. WITH SUPPLEMENTARY INDEX.

NEW YORK:

SANDERS D. BRUCE

"TURF, FIELD AND FARM."

Title page of Bruce's *American Stud Book*, Volume 1, 1868. Bruce published six volumes in all and then turned it over to the Jockey Club.

tradition in Virginia that Edgar had left Ireland in a hurry after accidentally killing his father's gardener. Whatever the truth was, he lived in Virginia and North Carolina from 1808, on a remittance he received from Ireland. He never established a residence but roamed the Southside, a welcome guest at the many plantation homes. He was called Sir Patrick and welcomed by master, mistress, and servants. He always found ways to show his gratitude and never overstayed his welcome. It was during one of his moves, from one plantation home to another, that he died during a snowstorm on the south bank of the Roanoke in 1857. His saddlebags, once stuffed with pedigrees, are now in the possession of the Virginia Historical Society.

With Edgar's death a great deal of the early history of the Quarter Horse was lost, as was much of the part played by the horse in the Revolutionary War. Luckily his interests came through his studbook, and as a result there are many stories and other interesting data to be found in this book. It was evident to anyone reading the title page of Edgar's studbook that he was going to include information about Quarter Horses as well as Thoroughbreds. Right after the words "General Stud Book" appeared "Pedigrees of the Most Celebrated Horses, Mares and Geldings That Have Distinguished Themselves as Racers on the American Turf From One Quarter of a Mile Race up to Four Miles and Repeat. . . ."

Edgar divided his book into five parts. First he listed all of the blooded English imports. Then he had a section of the Arabian imports, followed by a list of the Barbs brought into America. The fourth section contained the pedigrees of the Spanish horses imported. The last and largest section (and the one that contains the most about Quarter Horses) listed the American-born horses that distinguished themselves on the turf. He himself stated, on page xii of the Introduction, that the last section "includes also the pedigrees of the Quarter racing stock." It is interesting to find that both Edgar and Bruce distinguished between the Thoroughbreds and quarter horses. In both one comes across statements saying that the second dam of such and such a quarter horse was a Thoroughbred mare, or vice versa.

Following Skinner's and Edgar's early studbooks the next attempt was made by John H. Wallace, secretary of the Iowa State Board of Agriculture, who while in that position saw the need for an adequate American registry for the running horse. He went to work and soon produced a 1,017-page volume, handsomely bound in green and gold, called *Wallace's American Stud-Book*, published in New York by W. A. Townsend and Adams in 1867. It contained a supplement on trotting horses.

As soon as the first volume was published, Wallace turned to the second. He traveled extensively looking for pedigrees. In 1870 the book was completed, but then he made the discovery that not all printed information was automatically correct. He found errors in hundreds of pedigrees, made through ignorance or dishonesty or both. He decided that the section volume should not be published.

Wallace's Stud-Book failed for three reasons: first, because there were many inaccuracies; second, because he used a system of listing the entries that was not familiar to American horsemen; and third, because Bruce came out with a better book at just the same time. Wallace, discouraged, turned to the records of trotters, a task for which he was well suited and to which he made a lasting contribution.

284

Sanders De Weese Bruce, the real father of the American studbook for the Thoroughbred. He also published the magazine *Turf, Field, and Farm*. From Harrison, *Background of the American Stud Book*.

Sanders DeWeese Bruce, who followed Wallace, was the real father of the present American studbook. He was the publisher of *Turf, Field, and Farm* and was well acquainted with historical methods of evaluation and research. He was born in Lexington, Kentucky, on August 16, 1825, and was attracted to horses and racing as a boy. Perhaps his lifework with racehorses was set when he witnessed, as a boy of fourteen, the historic match race between Wagner and Gray Eagle. He began collecting pedigrees from all available sources. For years he owned the Phoenix Hotel in Lexington, and because it was a headquarters for the racing crowd, he presided over a group of turfmen and breeders from all over the country. He bought, sold, and bred Thoroughbreds and also became interested in politics. When the Civil War came, he joined the North and served with distinction, becoming a colonel in the Union Army. His brother fought for the South.

After the war Bruce and his brother started *Turf, Field, and Farm*, and in it they published regular installments of the studbook. After about three years they had collected enough to publish the first volume, and Bruce realized a lifelong dream.

The publication of the book itself presented a problem to Bruce. He did not have the money to publish it himself. Finally, he interested enough people, and the first

285

copies were printed by a law firm in Chicago. It was beautifully done, tooled and bound with leather and containing many steel engravings. In 1873, when Volume 2 was ready to be published, Bruce was no longer on friendly terms with his Chicago publishers. The first edition had contained the record of pedigrees from A to K, inclusive. In the new edition he included L, so that A to L was covered. He started Volume 2 with M. With that simple expedient the remainder of the original edition of volume 1 became useless as soon as Volume 2 appeared, while both volumes of the new edition were necessary. Today, for this reason, only a few copies of the first edition of Volume 1 are in existence.

Because of the expense of printing such a book, and because of the relatively limited sale, *The American Stud Book* was never a financial success. Bruce also became involved with the Jockey Club in a long and bitterly fought lawsuit over the studbook. The expenses were ruinous. He won in the lower court but the Jockey Club appealed to a higher court. By then Bruce was over seventy and broke, but fortunately he had the public on his side. The Jockey Club finally listened to good advice and settled out of court. They bought the studbook outright in 1896 for a price that has been quoted as $35,000. From that date on, all volumes have been published by the Jockey Club.

Bruce's work provides the quarter horse historian with one of the best references for quarter horses during the last quarter of the nineteenth century. While the main body of the studbook is not as good as Edgar's, the appendix that Bruce added is invaluable. Bruce's Appendix lists horses bred and running who were not clean-bred—that is, whose ancestry could not be traced back to the *General Stud Book*. Since quarter horses were allowed to compete with Thoroughbreds on the tracks at that time, we find such quarter horses as Steel Dust, Copperbottom, Billy and others. Through this we can trace many of their pedigrees, offspring, and owners.

Bruce's studbook, now carrying the imprint of the Jockey Club, has become America's official Thoroughbred studbook and a valuable tool of the quarter horse breeder. No book was of greater value until the *Official Stud Book and Registry* of the American Quarter Horse appeared in 1940.

Probably the first book to contain references about the quarter running horse in the American colonies was J. F. D. Smyth's *A Tour of the United States of America; Containing an Account of the Present Situation of That Country. . .etc*. Smyth wrote a two-volume travelogue about his adventures in America. He also described the life of the colonists and of the natives in the area he traveled. The books were beautifully bound in brown and red leather with gold lettering and trim, and were published right after the war, in 1784, when interest in the lost colonies was at its highest. On the title page it is noted that the work was printed for G. Robinson of Pater-Noster Row, J. Robinson of New Bond Street, and J. Sewell of Cornhill. One must suspect that the three gentlemen, all having offices in business districts, put up some money to help finance the venture.

Another valuable work for the Quarter Horse historian is the two volume *Frank Forester's Horse and Horsemanship of the United States and British Provinces of North America*, written by Henry William Herbert and published in New York by Stringer and Townsend in 1857. While not as good a source for colonial days as it is for the 1800s, it is nevertheless one of the best resource books. In it are found letters from horsemen like Will Williams of Tennessee, which are invaluable for historians. In the late 1700s Williams had personally seen and known sons of *Janus. In fact, his grandfather had owned Mead's Celer. Herbert also quoted from other letters and sources and gave his own impressions. He had arrived in America from England in 1831, and he made several interesting observations comparing American and English horses.

Besides books, there were also many magazines and newspapers that covered the turf history of the nineteenth century and, to a certain extent, the colonial period. Some of them were farm journals that carried small sections on horses and racing. There were also others that specialized in the sporting field. In these magazines and newspapers are records of match races, pedigrees of stallions at stud, and historical articles on the horses of earlier days that are helpful to the quarter horse historian. Examples include the *American Turf Register and Sporting Magazine*. On the front page of this magazine for December, 1844, was, besides the title, a picture showing a race of several horses, all types of sporting weapons and game, two horsemen, fishnets, spears, and just about everything else of a sporting nature the artist could think of. Under the date at the foot of the picture the words appear ''New York: Edited by Wm. T. Porter, and Published by J. Richards, Proprietor, at the office of the 'Spirit of the Times,' newspaper. Price $5 per annum, in advance.'' The magazine was founded and edited by J. S. Skinner from 1829 to 1835. Allen J. Davie was editor in 1836, Gideon S. Smith from 1837 to 1839, and William Trotter Porter from 1840 to 1844.

One of the best newspapers was the *Spirit of the Times*, in whose office the magazine was published. This newspaper was founded by William T. Porter, who was not himself a horseman. His first love was fishing. However, as a journalist he soon replaced Skinner in the sporting field, and he had no peer in his day. The *Spirit of the Times* had a varied career from 1831 until 1861. Porter remained editor until 1850. The last editor was E. E. Jones. Curiously enough, there was another newspaper called *Porter's Spirit of the Times*. It was started in 1856 by George Wilkes, a one-time editorial assistant to Porter. Seven volumes of the paper were published in New York between 1856 and 1860.

John Stuart Skinner published the *American Farmer* in Baltimore from 1819 until

William Trotter Porter, the influential and popular editor of two basic sporting magazines, *Spirit of the Times* and the *American Turf Register*, both important reading for the quarter running horse historian.

1829. It started out as a farm journal, but before long it included a section called "Sporting Olio," which carried racehorse information, most of which appeared later in Cottom's *Mason's Farrier and Stud Book*.

There were also several annual publications worth mentioning that appeared about the time of the Civil War. There were *Whitney's Crickmore*, 1861–69; *Bruce's Turf Register*, 1870–76; *Crickmore's Guide to the Turf*, 1877–84; and *Goodwin's Turf Guide*, 1883–1908. From 1897 on, the *American Racing Manual* has been published by the *Daily Racing Form*.

Occasional references can also be found in books devoted to pioneer life and to life during the heyday of the cattle industry on the Great Plains. Examples are works like Everett Dick's *The Sod House Frontier*, published in New York in 1937 by D. Appleton-Century Company; and *A Ranchman's Recollections*, by Frank S. Hastings, printed in Chicago by the *Breeder's Gazette* in 1921.

In the late nineteenth and early twentieth centuries most references to quarter running horses are found in local newspaper reports of quarter racing or in livestock journals. The historian who is interested in a special horse race generally needs to know the date and place where the race was held. By reading the newspaper from that town, he can usually find coverage of the race. For example, in running down information on Steel Dust and Shiloh, Wayne Gard utilized the old files of the *Dallas Daily Herald*, especially the issues of June 9 and 13, 1875.

One magazine deserves special mention, since it was the first devoted entirely to Quarter Horses. That is the *Quarter Horse*, the official publication of the now-extinct National Quarter Horse Breeders Association. The magazine first appeared in 1946. It was entered as second-class matter at Knox City, Texas, the home of its first editor, Ed Bateman, Sr. The first edition, which appeared in April, was printed on 7½ by 10 newsprint. Ed Bateman was editor through the December, 1947, issue, and in January, 1948, two editors were listed on the masthead, C. H. Moss and Dale Graham. Beginning with Volume 3, Number 8, in November, 1948, the magazine was somewhat redesigned, and the name of David J. Woodlock appeared as editor. The last editor was E. E. Kingsbury, and the last issue was Volume 4, Number 7, October, 1949.

Two modern scholars of Thoroughbred pedigrees have also been a boon to the quarter horse historian, Fairfax Harrison and the "Sage of Schuylerville," John O'Connor. Harrison first attracted attention with his book *The Equine F. F. V.'s*, published in Richmond, Virginia, in 1928. Harrison was born in New York City in 1869 and died in 1938. He received an A.B. from Yale and an M.A. from Columbia. After studying law, he joined the staff of the Southern Railway as a solicitor. By 1933 he was assistant to the president, and ten years later he became president of the affiliated Chicago, Indianapolis, and Louisville Railroads. Later he became president of the Southern Railway system and remained so until he retired in 1937.

Harrison's interest in things southern came naturally. His father, Burton Harrison, was private secretary to Jefferson Davis during the Civil War. His mother was a well-known novelist and famous for her social events and personal charm. Fairfax Harrison spent much of his younger life playing polo and fox hunting. He owned an estate south of Middleburg, Virginia, on a spur of the Southern Railway. Charles II had granted his family the lands lying between the Potomac and the Rappahannock rivers. The land had not been well explored when the grant was made, and the mouths of the two rivers were close together. When the true course of the rivers was discovered, the grand included some five million acres.

Harrison was always interested in blood horses and in Virginia history. The Virginia Historical Society asked him to do a paper on early Virginia horses. The result was the now famous *Equine F.F.V.'s*. It was through this work that he got to know John O'Connor, and they eventually became good friends and acknowledged authorities.

When Harrison had his *Equine F.F.V.'s* pretty well along, he sent a copy to Henry Worchester Smith. Smith was an important scholar of southern history, being the outstanding authority on fox hunting. He also spent years working on the horse paintings of Edward Troye, the greatest horse painter of the nineteenth century—and perhaps of any other as far as the blood horse goes. Smith, in turn, submitted Harrison's paper to O'Connor.

John O'Connor was an Irishman who started out working for some butchers. He did well, and from his employers he picked up an interest in racing. That led him to pedigrees. About the same time electricity came into use, he started a school for electricians. O'Connor knew little about electricity or the newfangled incandescent lamp, but he hired men who did know electricity and made a modest fortune from his New York Electrical School. O'Connor invested much of his money in old sporting magazines, newspapers, and books. He also hired people to go through newspapers in the South looking for early stallion advertisements. Soon they had accumulated a great fund of knowledge on early American horse pedigrees.

When O'Connor received the manuscript from Smith, he had no idea who Fairfax Harrison was. He took a red pencil and scribbled across the first page, "All wrong, kid, all wrong," and mailed it back. When Harrison got the manuscript, he telegraphed O'Connor asking "What's wrong?" O'Connor telegraphed back "You are merely repeating the errors of your predecessors."

To make a long story short, Harrison went to New York and visited O'Connor. After that Harrison went to work, and he even uncovered some newspapers and pedigrees that O'Connor had missed.

No scholar can do basic pedigree work on American racehorses without being familiar with the works of these two men. O'Connor produced one book, an extremely limited edition of five known copies that Louis Lee Hagin had printed in the 1920s. The book has no publication date, and the pages are not numbered. It was printed in Lexington, Kentucky, by the Transylvania Printing Company. I was fortunate enough to have access to the copy owned by my friend Alexander McKay Smith. It covers all the stallion advertisements in the Kentucky newspaper from February 16, 1788, to November 21, 1833. Harrison's books are listed in the Bibliography that follows.

Bibliography

The following is a selected list that includes those books to which a direct reference is made in the text. Also included are a few of the earlier periodicals that contain a significant amount of quarter running horse information.

Alta California. San Francisco, 1849–91. Irregularly published; title changed to *Daily Alta California*, 1850.

American Farmer. Baltimore, 1819–29.

American Turf, The: An Historical Account of Racing in the United States. Ed. Lyman Horace Weeks. New York, 1898.

American Turf Register and Sporting Magazine. Baltimore and New York, 1829–44.

Anbury, Thomas. *Travels Through the Interior Parts of North America*. London, 1789.

Anderson, James Douglas. *Making of the American Thoroughbred; Including Reminiscences of the Turf by Balie Peyton*. Nashville, 1946.

Anson, William. *Breeding a Rough Country Horse*. Chicago, 1910. Pamphlet printed for Anson by the *Breeders Gazette*.

Appalachian Indian Froniter. Ed. Wilbur Jacobs. Lincoln: University of Nebraska Press, 1959.

Battel, Joseph. *The American Stallion Register*. 4 vols. Middleburg, V., 1909.

Bayliss, M. F. *The Matriarchy of the American Turf, 1875–1930*. New York: printed by Robert L. Gerry, 1931.

Bernard, John. *Retrospections of America, 1791–1811*. New York, 1887.

Biographical Encyclopedia of Kentucky. Cincinnati, Ohio, 1878.

Blake, Coke. *The Pride of Mayes County*. Pryor, Okla.: privately printed. Pamphlet.

Blanchard, Elizabeth Amis Cameron. *The Life and Times of Sir Archy*. Chapel Hill: University of North Carolina Press, 1958.

Breeder and Sportsman. San Francisco, 1882–1919.

Breeders Gazette. Chicago, 1881–.

Brown, William Robinson. *The Horse of the Desert*. New York, 1947.

Bruce, Philip Alexander. *Economic History of Virginia in the Seventeenth Century*. 2 vol. New York, 1896.

———. *Social Life of Virginia in the Seventeenth Century*. Rev. ed. Lynchburg, Va., 1927.

Bruce, Sanders De Weese. *The American Stud Book*. 6 vol. New York, 1868–94. Continued by the Jockey Club.

———. *Bruce's Turf Register*. New York, 1870–75. Yearly racing report.

Burnaby, Andrew. *Travels Through the Middle Settlements of North America in 1759 and 1760*. London, 1775.

Californian. San Francisco, 1864–68.

Carson, Jane. *Colonial Virginians at Play*. Williamsburg, Va., 1965.

Cattleman. Fort Worth, 1914–.

Cottom, Peter, ed. *Mason's Farrier and Stud Book, New Edition; The Gentleman's New Pocket Farrier*. 6th ed. Richmond, Va., 1833.

Culver, Francis Barnum. *Blooded Horses of Colonial Days*. Baltimore, 1922.

Denhardt, Robert Moorman. *The King Ranch Quarter Horses: And Something of the Ranch and the Men That Bred Them*. Norman: University of Oklahoma Press, 1970.

——. *The Quarter Horse*. 3 vols. Fort Worth, Texas, 1941; Eagle Pass, Texas, 1945; Amarillo, Texas, 1950.

——. *Quarter Horses: A Story of Two Centuries*. Norman: University of Oklahoma Press, 1967.

Denhardt Files. American Quarter Horse Association, Amarillo, Texas. Letters, interviews, pictures, tear sheets, tapes, notes, pamphlets, and other records accumulated by Robert Moorman Denhardt and Helen Michaelis.

Denton, Daniel. *Description of New York*. N.p., 1845.

Edgar, Patrick Nisbett. *The American Race Turf Register, Sportsman's Herald, and General Stud Book*. New York, 1833.

Ewell, Thomas T. *A History of Hood County, Texas*. Granbury, Texas, 1895.

Fairfield, Asa M. *Pioneer History of Lassen County*. San Francisco, 1916.

Field, Turf, and Farm; Sportsman's Oracle and County Gentleman's Newspaper. New York, 1865–1902.

Franklin Farmer. Frankfort, Ky., 1837–40. Then issued as *Kentucky Farmer*, 1840–42.

Gard, Wayne. *The Fabulous Quarter Horse Steel Dust*. New York, 1958.

——. *Sam Bass*. New York, 1936.

Gee, Ernest R. *Cherished Portraits of Thoroughbred Horses*. Privately printed, 1929.

Goodwin's Annual Turf Guide. New York, 1883–1919.

Gordon, Adam. "Journal of an Officer Who Traveled in America. . . ." In *Travels of the American Colonies*. Edited by Newton D. Mereness. New York, 1916.

Gregory, Tom. *History of Yolo County, California*. Los Angeles, 1913.

The Half Breed Stud Book. 2 vol. New York, 1925–30.

Harrison, Fairfax. *The Background of the American Stud Book*. Richmond, Va., 1933.

——. *The Bellair Stud, 1747–1761*. Richmond, Va.: privately printed, 1929.

——. *Early American Turf Stock*. 2 vol. Richmond, Va.: privately printed, 1934–35.

——. *The Equine F.F.V.'s*. Richmond, Va.: privately printed, 1928.

——. *The Johns Island Stud, 1750–1788*. Richmond, Va.: privately printed, 1931.

——. *The Roanoke Stud, 1795–1833*. Richmond, Va.: privately printed, 1930.

Haskell, Melville H. *The Quarter Running Horse*. Tucson, Ariz., printed for the American Quarter Racing Association, 1945–50. Five pamphlets.

——. *Racing Quarter Horses*. Tucson, Ariz., printed for the Southern Arizona Horse Breeders Association, 1943–44.

Herbert, Henry William. *Frank Forester's Horse and Horsemanship of the United States*. 2 vol. New York, 1857.

Hervey, John. *Racing in America, 1665–1865*. New York: privately printed, 1944.

Hildreth, Samuel C. *The Spell of the Turf*. Philadelphia, 1926.

History of Hancock County. Carthage, Ill., 1968.

History of the Turf of South Carolina. Charleston: South Carolina Jockey Club, 1857.

History of Yolo County. Edited by William O. Russell. Woodland, Calif., 1940.

Illustrated Atlas and History of Yolo County, California. San Francisco, 1879.

Irving, John B. *History of the Turf in South Carolina*. Charleston, 1857.

Jones, Hugh. *The Present State of Virginia*. Edited by Richard L. Morton. Chapel Hill: University of North Carolina Press, 1956.

Kentucky Livestock Record. See *Thoroughbred Record*.

Laune, Paul. *American Quarter Horses*. New York, 1973.

Life and Adventures of Sam Bass . . . . Dallas, 1878.

Mackay-Smith, Alexander. *The Thoroughbred in the Lower Shenandoah Valley, 1785–1842*. Winchester, Va., 1948. Pamphlet.

McGrady, Edward. *History of South Carolina under the Royal Government, 1719–1776*. New York, 1889.

McLean, Malcolm D. *Fine Texas Horses*. Fort Worth: Texas Christian University Press, 1966.

Michaelis, Helen, and Robert M. Denhardt. *The Quarter Horse: Why He Is What He Is*. Eagle Pass, Texas: printed for the American Quarter Horse Association, 1945.

National Quarter Horse Breeders Association Permanent Stud Book. Edited by J. M. Huffington. 2 vol. Houston, 1947–48.

Newman, Niel. *Famous Horses of the American Turf*. 8 vol. New York, 1931–33.

Nye, Nelson C. *Champions of the Quarter Tracks*. New York, 1950.

———. *The Complete Book of the Quarter Horse*. New York, 1964.

———. *Outstanding Modern Quarter Horse Sires*. New York, 1948.

O'Connor, John Lawrence. *Notes on the Thoroughbred from Kentucky Newspapers*. Lexington: privately printed, n.d.

Official Stud Book and Registry of the American Quarter Horse Association. Fort Worth, Eagle Pass, Amarillo, Texas 1941–.

Porter's Spirit of the Times. New York, 1856–60.

Quarter Horse. Knox City, Texas, 1946–49.

The Quarter Horse Breeder. Edited by M. H. Linderman, Wichita Falls, Texas, 1959.

Quarter Horse Journal. Amarillo, Texas, 1947–.

Quarter Horse News, Colorado Springs, Colo., 1950–51.

Quarter Racing in Kentucky and Other Sketches. Edited by W. T. Porter. Philadelphia, 1846.

Railey, William E. *History of Woodford County*. Versailles, Ky., 1968.

Ramsey, David. *The History of South Carolina*. 2 vol. Charleston, 1809.

Ridgeway, William. *Origin and Influence of the Thoroughbred Horse*. Cambridge: at the University Press, 1905.

Robertson, William H. *The History of Thoroughbred Racing in America*. Englewood Cliffs, N. J., 1964.

Scharf, John Thomas. *History of Maryland*. Baltimore, 1879.

Skinner, John S. *The Gentleman's New Pocket Farrier*. Philadelphia, 1854.

Smelker, Van A., Jr. *The Quarter Running Horse*. Tucson: Racing Division, American Quarter Horse Association, 1949. Pamphlet.

Smyth, John Ferdinand Dalziel. *A Tour in the United States of America; Containing an Account of the Present Situation of That Country* . . . . 2 vol. London, 1784.

Spirit of the Times: A Chronicle of the Turf . . . . New York, 1831–61.

Spirit of the Times and New York Sportsman. New York, 1859–1902.

They Left Their Mark in Oakford, 1872. Edited by Hallie M. Hamblin. N.p. [Oakford, Ill.] n.d. Centenniel pamphlet.

Thoroughbred Record. Lexington, Ky., 1875–. Vols. 1–22 issued as *Kentucky Livestock Record*; vols. 23–41 as *Livestock Record*; vols. 42– as *Thoroughbred Record*.

Trevathan, Charles E. *The American Thoroughbred*. New York, 1905.

Turf, Field, and Farm. New York, 1865–1903. Vol. 1 issued as *Field, Turf, and Farm*.

Virginia Magazine of History and Biography (Virginia Historical Society). 1893–.

Vosburg, W. S. *Racing in America, 1866–1921*. New York: privately printed, 1922.

Wallace, John H. *The Horse of America*. New York, 1897.

———. *Wallace's American Stud-Book; Being a Compilation of the Pedigrees of American and Imported Horses*. New York, 1867.

Western Horseman. Colorado Springs, Colo., 1936–.

Wilke's Spirit of the Times. New York, 1859–1915.

Youatt, William. *The Horse*. London, 1855.

Index

INDEX